"An essential read for anyone committed to truly understanding and implementing effective, child-centred education methods."

Hyejeong Ahn, *Senior Lecturer in Language and Literacy Education, Melbourne Graduate School of Education, Australia.*

"Wyse and Hacking's insightful guidance about how to build different aspects of reading tuition around picture books is probably unique and should ensure widespread impact."

Usha Goswami, *Professor of Cognitive Developmental Neuroscience, University of Cambridge, UK.*

"The Double Helix as a new model for conceptualizing literacy development and how it can be achieved through balanced instruction is a substantive theoretical contribution to the field."

David Reinking, *Emeritus Distinguished Professor of Education, Clemson University, USA.*

"Offer(s) a valuable perspective for enhancing children's engagement as learners, readers, and writers."

Rebecca Jesson, *Associate Professor in Literacy Education, University of Auckland, New Zealand.*

The Balancing Act

Dominic Wyse and Charlotte Hacking present a ground-breaking account of teaching phonics, reading, and writing. Created from a landmark study, new research, new theory, and cutting-edge teacher professional development, this *balanced approach* to teaching seeks to improve all children's learning and therefore life chances.

The book dismantles polarised debates about the teaching of phonics and analyses the latest scientific evidence of what really works. It shows, in vivid detail, how phonics, reading, *and* writing should be taught through the creativity of some of the best authors of books for children. By describing lessons inspired by 'real books', it showcases why the new approach is more effective than narrow phonics approaches.

The authors call for a paradigm shift in literacy education. The chapters show how and why education policies should be improved on the basis of unique analyses of research evidence from experimental trials and the new theory and model the Double Helix of Reading and Writing. It is a book of hope for the future in the context of powerful elites influencing narrow curricula, narrow pedagogy, and high-stakes assessments.

The Balancing Act will be of interest to anyone who is invested in young children's development. It is essential reading for teachers, trainee teachers, lecturers, researchers, and policy makers world-wide who want to improve the teaching of reading and writing in the English language.

Dominic Wyse is Professor of Early Childhood and Primary Education at the Institute of Education, University College London, UK.

Charlotte Hacking is Director of Learning and Programmes at the Centre for Literacy in Primary Education (CLPE), UK.

The Balancing Act
An Evidence-Based Approach to Teaching Phonics, Reading and Writing

Dominic Wyse and Charlotte Hacking

LONDON AND NEW YORK

Designed cover image: credit for front cover image goes to Caroline Tye, and Dominic Wyse, and Charlotte Hacking as the originators of the double helix image.

First published 2024
by Routledge
4 Park Square, Milton Park, Abingdon, Oxon OX14 4RN

and by Routledge
605 Third Avenue, New York, NY 10158

Routledge is an imprint of the Taylor & Francis Group, an informa business

© 2024 Dominic Wyse and Charlotte Hacking

The right of Dominic Wyse and Charlotte Hacking to be identified as authors of this work has been asserted in accordance with sections 77 and 78 of the Copyright, Designs and Patents Act 1988.

All rights reserved. No part of this book may be reprinted or reproduced or utilised in any form or by any electronic, mechanical, or other means, now known or hereafter invented, including photocopying and recording, or in any information storage or retrieval system, without permission in writing from the publishers.

Trademark notice: Product or corporate names may be trademarks or registered trademarks, and are used only for identification and explanation without intent to infringe.

British Library Cataloguing-in-Publication Data
A catalogue record for this book is available from the British Library

Library of Congress Cataloging-in-Publication Data
Names: Wyse, Dominic, 1964– author. | Hacking, Charlotte, 1979– author.
Title: The balancing act : an evidence-based approach to teaching phonics, reading and writing / Dominic Wyse and Charlotte Hacking.
Description: Abingdon, Oxon ; New York, NY : Routledge, 2024. | Includes bibliographical references and index.
Identifiers: LCCN 2024001548 (print) | LCCN 2024001549 (ebook) | ISBN 9781032565934 (hardback) | ISBN 9781032580234 (paperback) | ISBN 9781003442134 (ebook)
Subjects: LCSH: Reading—Phonetic method. | Reading—Phonetic method—Research. | English language—Composition and exercises—Study and teaching. | Educational change. | Education and state.
Classification: LCC LB1573.3 .W97 2024 (print) | LCC LB1573.3 (ebook) | DDC 372.46/5—dc23/eng/20240327
LC record available at https://lccn.loc.gov/2024001548
LC ebook record available at https://lccn.loc.gov/2024001549

ISBN: 978-1-032-56593-4 (hbk)
ISBN: 978-1-032-58023-4 (pbk)
ISBN: 978-1-003-44213-4 (ebk)

DOI: 10.4324/9781003442134

Typeset in ITC Galliard Pro
by Apex CoVantage, LLC

Access the Support Material: www.routledge.com/9781032580234

Dominic Wyse:
This book is dedicated to my niece, Robin Wyse, who started primary school in England in 2021. Robin's creativity was already plain to see in her natural explorations of writing, drawing, dancing, and music from a very early age. In addition to supporting this creativity, Robin's mother Helen experienced shock when she encountered England's synthetic phonics due to her work as a teaching assistant, a role that had been changed from supporting individual children with special educational needs to one supporting children in a phonics ability group.

Robin's father, Pascal, my brother, has helped us all learn about music composition and sound design because of his awe-inspiring work such as on *Cautionary Tales* (also the famous Berger and Wyse cartoons). And we both owe this creativity to our father Barrie Wyse and our mother Vera Wyse. Barrie trained at Trinity Music College in London, then ultimately taught music, drama, and English in inner-city Hull. He also worked as a teacher educator and was central to the RSA's Opening Minds curriculum. Vera Wyse inspired hundreds of early years and primary trainee teachers in her very long career in early years teaching, then teacher education. Her thinking was driven by her passions that included writing poetry and her wide engagement with English literature and music.

This book brings a range of sources of knowledge to the questions it raises. An additional source is people's knowledge and professional experience that for some stretches over many decades and includes the accumulated wisdom of multiple generations. This is wisdom that needs to be listened to, and acted on, as part of the debates about education which are all too prone to the whims of short-term political cycles.

Charlotte Hacking:

Just as it takes a village to raise a child, it takes a number of people to raise lifelong readers and writers. This book is dedicated to those in my life who have done this for me. First, to my Dad and his determination that one of his children would be the first in the family to go to university.

To Pat Hutchins and Brian Patten, whose picturebooks and poetry introduced me to the joy of reading. To Elizabeth Forai and Bob Jope, both inspirational reading teachers. To Margaret Meek and Myra Barrs, who influenced the teacher I am and whose work still lies at the heart of all we do at CLPE. To every single child I've taught and every teacher I've taught alongside, all of whom have taught me so much.

To Ed Vere, Matt Goodfellow, Joe Todd-Stanton, Sarah Crossan, and Dominic Wyse, who have lifted me to greater things and whose trust and faith in me as a creative is valued more than words can ever say. To my family at home and my work family at CLPE, whose support and patience have helped me to build the practice that has culminated in this book and given me the time to write it and to Steve and Ed at Beckenham Library for providing a writing haven.

And finally, to my daughter Lily, who is living proof of the approach in action over the last 18 years and whose creativity and brilliance inspire me every single day.

Contents

About the authors — xiv
Permissions, figures, and tables — xv
Acknowledgements — xviii

Introduction — 1

PART I
The politics and science of reading and writing — 5

1 **The reading wars** — 7
   Snapshots of policy and practice in different countries 8
     England 8
     Australia and New Zealand 8
     Ireland 9
     The USA 9
     Canada 10
   True stories? 11
     Centralising synthetic phonics in England 11
     Screening phonics in Australia 14
     Advocating synthetic phonics in the USA 15
     Children's rights to read in Ontario, Canada 21
     Whole language in New Zealand 23
   Why does the politics of reading matter? 24

2 **The development of reading and writing** — 29
   The three cues of reading 29
   Marie Clay's Reading Recovery 32
   The Simple View of Reading 33
   The interpretation of the simple view in England's Rose Report 35
   The Reading Rope 36
   Models of writing 38
   The Double Helix of Reading and Writing 42

3 How texts teach what children learn — 49
Real books and whole language 49
Scheme books and real books 51
   Sit In! 51
   Cat on the Mat 53
   Peck Peck Peck 54
Selecting texts for three- to eight-year-olds 55
Time to read 59

4 The science of teaching reading and writing — 63
Which research and why? 63
   A note about 'science' 64
   Selecting research studies 65
General findings from systematic and tertiary reviews 67
   Teaching phonics and reading 67
   Teaching writing 69
   Teaching reading for writing and writing for reading 71
Classroom practices for teaching reading 73
   Studies of typically developing readers 75
   Studies of struggling readers 78
   Summarising the evidence from systematic reviews and longitudinal research studies 80

PART II
The art of teaching — 85

5 The balanced approach to teaching phonics, reading, and writing — 87
The child and their language(s) 89
Reading and writing 90
The child and their environment, including texts 90
Motivation and meaning 92
Comprehension 92
Composition 92
Phonological awareness and the alphabetic code 93
Knowledge of morphemes and other word structures 93
Planning lessons and activities 94
The programme of lessons 94
Planning teaching based on children's development 95

6 Building the foundations — 103
Creating the conditions for learning 104
The importance of reading for pleasure 104
Developing reader identity 105

Developing understanding of the purpose of writing 109
Early phonological development 110
Rhythm and rhyme 111
Tuning into sounds in words 112
The vital role of rhyme and poetry 112
Linking the spoken word with the written 115

7 **Cracking the alphabetic code** 118
Using real books to teach phonics 118
The links between phonics, reading, and writing 119
A contextualised approach to teaching the basic code 120
Words that do not conform to letter-phoneme correspondences taught 123
A lesson introducing initial grapheme-phoneme correspondences 123
Lesson 1: Introducing the book 124
Lesson 2: Building engagement with the text and understanding of ideas within it 126
Lesson 3: Using letter-phoneme correspondences to blend and segment words 133
Lesson 4: Developing deeper connections with a text 135
Lesson 5: Reading the whole book and extending comprehension 138

8 **Gaining control** 142
Phonemes represented by more than one letter 145
Introducing consonant digraphs and developing blending and segmenting skills 148
Lesson 1: Introducing the book and a new consonant digraph 148
Lesson 2: Responding to the book and developing segmenting skills to write sentences 153
Lesson 3: Introducing a new digraph for reading and writing 154

9 **The complexities of English** 161
Developing children's understanding of alternative letter-phoneme representations 165
Lesson 1: using and applying phonic knowledge at the point of reading and writing 166
Lesson 2: Encouraging the development of fluent reading and engaging in creative acts 168
Lesson 3: shared reading to demonstrate and develop reading fluency 170
Lesson 4: Developing understanding of language and vocabulary 170
Lesson 5: Extending sentences from simple sentences to compound sentences 174
Lesson 6: Extending knowledge of letter-phoneme correspondences and developing empathy through reading 176
Lesson 7: Reading and reflecting on the text as a whole 177

10 Spelling — 180
Introducing children to visual patterns in words 182
Recognising word families 182
Introducing compound words 182
Segmenting words into larger chunks – syllables and parts of words 182
Using The Way Home for Wolf *to teach concepts* 183
Exploring morphology 187
Using Unfortunately *to teach concepts* 187
Exploring etymology 193
Exploring homophones, homographs, and homonyms 193
Emphasising investigation 197

11 Developing fluency and comprehension — 201
Reading aloud 204
The importance of re-reading 208
Providing opportunities for discussion about texts 208
Dramatising reading 209
Reading and performing poetry 210
Using picture books with children of all ages 212
Presenting informational writing 213
Opportunities for children to read independently 214

12 Meeting the needs of all pupils — 217
Children for whom English is an additional language 218
Ensuring access to texts 219
Recognising and responding to children's needs 219
   Lack of motivation as a reader and/or writer 220
   Composing writing 221
   Developing fluency 223
   Developing comprehension 224
   Letter formation and handwriting 224
   One-to-one correspondence 225
   Knowledge of letter-phoneme correspondences 226
   Ability to blend and segment 226
   Developing automaticity 227
   Children who can already read 228

13 The reader in the writer — 230
Developing writer identity 230
The complexities of writing 231
Reading as a model for writing 232
Example of a writing lesson 234

Following an authentic writing process 236
Impact on teachers and pupils 242
Voice, choice, and agency (G) 244

14 A better future for children's education   247
The balanced act 249

Glossary   252
References   254
Index   265

About the authors

Dominic Wyse is Professor of Early Childhood and Primary Education at the Institute of Education (IOE), University College London (UCL). He is the Founding Director of the Helen Hamlyn Centre for Pedagogy (0 to 11 Years) (HHCP), a research centre which specialises in improving pedagogy for children and teachers. Dominic has researched the teaching of reading and writing, and primary curriculum and pedagogy, for more than 30 years. His publications include leading research papers and best-selling books for teachers. Prior to working in universities, he was a primary school teacher.

Charlotte Hacking is Director of Learning and Programmes at the Centre for Literacy in Primary Education (CLPE). As well as overseeing the development of CLPE's CPD programmes and resources, she developed and leads the CLPE's Power of Pictures and poetry research programmes. In 2022, Charlotte was awarded the Anna Craft Creativities in Education Prize by the British Educational Research Association (BERA). Before joining CLPE, she held several leadership posts, including assistant headteacher, literacy, early years foundation stage, more able pupils, and KS2. She was a literacy consultant within a local authority, focusing on early years, phonics, and primary literacy.

Permissions, figures, and tables

Figures

2.1	Three sources of information used in reading, from Pearson (1976)	32
2.2	Marie Clay's "Four Types of Cue" visual model	33
2.3	Diagram from the Rose Report interpreting the Simple View of Reading	35
2.4	The Reading Rope	37
2.5	Model of a simple view of writing	40
2.6	Cognitive perspective on writing processes	41
2.7	The Double Helix of Reading and Writing	44
5.1	The CLPE reading scale	97
5.2	The CLPE writing scale	99
6.1	Interior page spread from *Lenny Has Lunch* by Ken Wilson-Max	107
6.2	Interior page spread from *Lulu's Nana Visits* by Anna McQuinn, illustrated by Rosalind Beardshaw	108
6.3	Page spread of sharing the poem "Wibble Wobble Clown" from the book *Big Green Crocodile*	114
7.1	Front cover of the book *Stanley's Stick*	124
7.2	Example of a letter-card for the taught letter-phoneme correspondence	125
7.3	Opening page spread from the book *Stanley's Stick*	127
7.4	Teacher's scribing of children's responses to the initial page spread from *Stanley's Stick*	128
7.5	Second page spread from *Stanley's Stick*	130
7.6	Sentences with focus high-frequency word underlined	131
7.7	Example of a word-card, handwritten by the adult	131
7.8	Photograph of children watching a fire created from sticks as part of their stick activity related to *Stanley's Stick*	132
7.9	Photo of child aged four to five engaged in weaving sticks with wool and string as a stick activity	134
7.10	Examples of observational drawings of sticks produced by children aged four to five	135
7.11	Group poem by children aged four to five years	137
7.12	Photo of display of a variety of children's work inspired by *Stanley's Stick*	140
8.1	Front cover of *Peck Peck Peck* by Lucy Cousins	149
8.2	A letter-card showing the consonant digraph /ck/	150
8.3	Internal page spread from *Peck Peck Peck* by Lucy Cousins (pp. 16–17)	152
8.4	Final page spread from *Peck Peck Peck* by Lucy Cousins (p. 32–33)	156

8.5	Writing sample from a child age five: "Toilet rools"	158
9.1	Front endpapers from *The Great Paint* by Alex Willmore (p. 2–3)	167
9.2	Internal page spread from *The Great Paint*	171
9.3	Internal page spread from *The Great Paint*	173
10.1	The front cover of the book *The Way Home for Wolf*	184
10.2	First double page spread of *The Way Home for Wolf*	185
10.3	Word card for the compound word 'rainbow', showing fold in middle	186
10.4	Front cover of *Unfortunately*	188
10.5	Opening page spread from *Unfortunately*	190
10.6	Second page spread from *Unfortunately*	191
10.7	Front cover of *Astro Girl*	194
10.8	Opening page spread from *Astro Girl*	195
10.9	Internal page spread from *Astro Girl*, containing the focus words astronaut, Astrid, and asteroid	196
10.10	Opening page spread from *Fruits*	199
11.1	Opening page spread from *Barbara Throws a Wobbler*	206
11.2	Second page spread from *Barbara Throws a Wobbler*	207
11.3	The poem "My Shell", from *Caterpillar Cake*	211
12.1	Inside page spread from *Yucky Worms*	222
12.2	Letter/phoneme ping-pong balls and pebbles to support knowledge of letter-phoneme correspondences	227
13.1	Internal page spread from *Growing Frogs*	235
13.2	Writing sample by a child aged five: "Frog eggs are surrounded by jelly and they eat seaweed"	236
13.3	Writing sample by a child aged five: "The frogs suddenly grow strong back legs so they can jump"	236
13.4	CLPE's model demonstrating the core components of an authentic writing process	237
13.5	Preparatory sketches for the novel *Moon Bear*, sharing the development of Gill Lewis' initial story ideas	239
13.6	Preparatory work from Ed Vere for *How to Be a Lion*	240
13.7	Example of a page from a published picture book by a seven-year-old pupil on CLPE's The Power of Pictures programme	243

Tables

2.1	Frank Smith's depiction of the processes of writing	39
4.1	Systematic reviews of the teaching of phonics and reading	68
4.2	Systematic reviews of the teaching of writing	70
5.1	The balanced approach to teaching reading compared to synthetic phonics	88
5.2	An outline of the content covered in the chapters of this book	100
7.1	Suggested order to teach letter-phoneme correspondences	121
8.1	Letter-to-phoneme representations	145
8.2	Consonant clusters	146
8.3	Disyllabic words	147
9.1	Phonemes and their representations by multiple letter combinations	163
9.2	The '-ed' suffix	174
9.3	Alternative representations of the /ai/ phoneme	175

10.1	Base words and morphological changes	188
11.1	Comprehension skills and strategies to be taught across planned reading experiences	203
12.1	Key indicators for assessing children's reading and writing	220

Acknowledgements

We are very grateful to the following people for their help in various ways as we wrote the book. Many colleagues have provided peer-review of a version of the complete manuscript, comments, and suggestions, in addition to those people we work with who engaged with our ideas. These conversations no doubt resulted in adjustments to the chapters as they emerged. The responsibility for all the content remains with us.

Hyejeong Ahn, University of Melbourne, for reading the manuscript, providing comments, and her passionate engagement with the subject. Thanks also for agreeing to present at the seminar and book launch. We are also grateful to University College London (UCL) colleague and linguist John O'Regan for introducing us to Hyejeong.

Barbara Bleiman, English Consultant and former Co-Director at the English and Media Centre, for reading the manuscript and providing such thoughtful comments.

Alice Bradbury, Co-Director of the Helen Hamlyn Centre for Pedagogy (HHCP), for her work on the Wyse and Bradbury (2022) paper on assessing and teaching reading, and for many other collaborations, including our work together on the Independent Commission on Assessment in Primary Education (ICAPE).

Ghassan Essalehi, HHCP, for his expertise, very skilled communications, and extensive preparations for the HHCP annual conference, where The Double Helix was first introduced, and for the launch of this book.

Alison Foyle, Routledge, who commissioned this book. Alison's support during the writing of the manuscript and during production has been unfailing. Her insights about the text were an important part of our final revisions.

Usha Goswami, University of Cambridge, for reading the manuscript and providing her comment. I was very fortunate to be supported by Usha when I was at the University of Cambridge and Churchill College Cambridge and will always be grateful for that time.

Rhea Gupta, editorial assistant at Routledge, who helped us put the book into production and has been our contact throughout the process. It was also a pleasure to work with Rhea during production of the Routledge book *Teaching English, Language and Literacy (5th Edition)*.

Sinead Harmey, Institute of Education (IOE), UCL, for her insightful peer review. Sinead's expertise about Marie Clay, Reading Recovery, and many other areas is second to none, not least because of her time spent working in the USA and in Ireland.

Dominic wants to thank Charlotte (Hacking) for her superb contribution to this book. Her profound knowledge of children's literature and her inspirational work supporting teachers, children, and authors is exceptional. Before this book project I had not written with Charlotte. During the writing journey, points of difference were discussed, worked on, and transformed to select and synchronise relevant research and theories with what we felt could be best practice. Little could I have known that the collaboration would be so dynamic, productive, and truly generative. In our many meetings, emails, and multiple drafts of writing, something new emerged, drawing in multiple ways from our knowledge, our expertise, and our passion for primary education.

Louise Hayward, University of Glasgow, for her comments about the manuscript, and for our many years of work together seeking to improve curriculum, pedagogy, and assessment.

Gorana Henry, IOE, UCL, for reading a draft of the manuscript and providing such memorable comments.

Rachel Heydon, Western University, Ontario, Canada, for reading a draft of the manuscript, providing comments, and her generous response to our contact with her. Thanks also for agreeing to present at the seminar and launch of this book.

Rebecca Jesson, University of Auckland, for reading a draft of the manuscript and providing her comments insightfully focused on theory, research, and practice. Thanks also for agreeing to present at the seminar and launch of this book.

Young (Young-Suk) Grace Kim, University of California, Irvine, for our work together on the International Literacy Association (ILA) Dyslexia Task force, and for agreeing to talk at the launch of this book.

Gill Lewis and Ed Vere, for their permissions to include their creative work in process.

Roger McDonald, University of Greenwich, for peer review of the manuscript and for his support when president of the United Kingdom Literacy Association (UKLA). Thanks also for agreeing to present at the seminar and launch of this book.

Pooja Nakamura and Adria Molotsky, American Institutes for Research, Washington DC, for their observations about the ReadWrite Inc evaluation that they carried out with colleagues.

Monika Ożdżyńska, HHCP, for all her support in relation to the book but also our work at the HHCP.

Publishers' support, through our treasured contacts, for allowing us to include page spreads from books: Alanna-Max Books, Hachette Children's Group, Macmillan Children's Books, Otter-Barry Books, Penguin Random House, Tate Publishing, and Walker Books.

David P Reinking, Clemson University, USA, for reading the manuscript. David's profound knowledge of teaching reading and writing in the USA and beyond enabled his powerful insights into the book.

Schools, children, and teachers who have brought our practices to life through their examples featured in the book: Easterside Academy, Middlesbrough; St Stephen's School, Richmond; Staplehurst Primary School, Kent; Summercroft Primary School, Bishop's Stortford; Virginia Primary, Tower Hamlets; Ysgol Maes Y Mynydd, Wrexham.

Farrah Serroukh, Anjali Patel, and the teaching team and the staff at CLPE past and present, and the teachers and schools who have worked on our programmes – for the legacy of work that lies at the heart of the approach and for putting it into practice in classrooms.

Patrick Sullivan, National Council for Curriculum and Assessment (NCCA) Ireland, for reading the manuscript and offering his comments. Patrick's leadership and work with colleagues on curriculum development in Ireland are exemplary.

Jackie Wyse, outstanding editor and proofreader, and my partner for more than 40 years. Jackie has lived and breathed this book with me.

Many other colleagues have helped us in so many ways, we can only apologise for any omissions from this list of acknowledgements.

Introduction

This book offers a new approach to one of the most important and contentious topics in education: how best to help young children learn to read and write. Our main argument is that in any country where the English language is taught as a main language in schools, a *balanced approach* to teaching phonics, reading, and writing should be used in preference to discrete *synthetic phonics* (G)[1].

In January 2022 a research paper presented evidence showing that a balanced approach to teaching reading was the most effective. The research was described on the front page of the *Guardian* newspaper as "a landmark study"[2] and attracted attention from media internationally.[3] Although the research paper provided some clear recommendations about changes to policy and practice, a research paper is not the place for a more detailed account of a new approach to teaching. Hence the proposal for a book was developed in collaboration with co-author of this book, Charlotte Hacking from the Centre for Literacy in Primary Education (CLPE) in London, which for decades has developed and led professional development work, and research, with teachers.

The Balancing Act is what teachers do day-in day-out as part of their professional lives: they use teaching methods which balance competing influences. One influence comes from the evidence of pupils' learning that teachers observe and assess in their classrooms. If pupils seem to be motivated, and if they are making good progress in their learning, then teachers reasonably make positive assumptions about the merits of the approaches to teaching that they are using. If pupils are demotivated and aren't learning as well as they should then teachers will adjust their approach. At least they will adjust their approach if they are *allowed* to within the statutory constraints of their work.

Another influence that varies in intensity is the demand that education policies make on teachers' work. Perhaps the hardest balance of all is when teachers know that their job is being unduly controlled by politicians, with policies not derived primarily from the needs of children, nor from democratic collaboration with teachers, researchers, and other education experts, but instead a product of political ideology and political control. For example, teachers may know that they are legally required to test all the six-year-old children in their class for a national phonics test in spite of misgivings about the effects that that test has on their children, on their teaching methods, and on the school curriculum. Even though they are able to mitigate some of the worst effects of this kind of 'high-stakes' testing, such as a narrowed curriculum and stress for children and their families, mitigating the effects on teachers themselves is much less easy. This is particularly acute when the high stakes of the test are reinforced by a system of political levers that includes punitive inspections of schools and teaching, all of which are designed to forcefully hold teachers to account.

DOI: 10.4324/9781003442134-1

2 Introduction

There are other influences that are part of The Balancing Act, for example, research evidence about teaching methods. Teachers come into contact with research in a variety of ways. Many teachers undertake formal research as part of their study for master's degrees and doctorates. Schools in partnership with universities, for example, supporting teacher education and training, will also encounter university research. Some schools have a formal role as part of a network of schools designated as research schools. Various organisations, such as 'think tanks' and inspectorates, refer to education research in their reports. Education policies sometimes include references to research as part of the texts that communicate the policies to schools and teachers. And teachers will encounter research through various forms of media, including social media. Teachers work in collaboration with a range of professional colleagues to weigh up and balance a range of research to determine the extent to which their approaches to teaching, and their classroom practice, might change.

Balance is also a prime attribute of the best research and of the work of researchers. An evidence-based approach to teaching phonics, reading, and writing needs to be based on multiple sources of evidence. Weighing-up research requires knowledge of research methods and the contributions that different kinds of research make in relation to the debate. When the research evidence points strongly in a direction that differs from the direction of national or regional education policies about teaching reading and writing, researchers may have to challenge political orthodoxies. Occasionally the work of researchers and their collaborators produces a 'paradigm shift': a time when prevailing orthodoxies are overturned and a new paradigm of thinking becomes established.

This book makes an original evidence-based contribution to teaching phonics, reading, and writing in these main ways:

- the presentation of a new approach to teaching built on a new model called the Double Helix of Reading and Writing;
- new analyses of the most robust research studies undertaken to determine the most effective ways to teach phonics, reading, and writing;
- new analyses of studies focused on the connections between reading and writing for all children and about effective teaching of children with reading difficulties;
- a case made for using 'real books' as part of teaching phonics, reading, and writing;
- guidance on the selection and use of a unique selection of picture books for children that are outstanding quality, inclusive, and diverse in their representations of people and places;
- a detailed picture of how the balanced approach to teaching phonics, reading, and writing can be implemented by teachers;
- the articulation of many principles for practice that can be adapted for teaching in any primary classroom;
- the identification of an international trend towards narrow forms of synthetic phonics teaching (G) and analysis of why this is not appropriate.

Part I of the book addresses the politics of 'the reading wars', influential theories of teaching reading and writing, and the research that underpins the balanced approach. The Double Helix of Reading and Writing is presented in Chapter 2, "The Development of Reading and Writing". This chapter includes reviews of theories and visual models of reading, including those that have been popular with teachers such as the Reading Rope and the Three Cues Model. Chapter 3, "How Texts Teach What Children Learn", makes the case for the vital place of 'real books' as part of teaching. The most robust research evidence on effective teaching of phonics, reading, and writing, what some describe as 'the science of reading', is thoroughly reviewed in Chapter 4.

Part II of the book shows in vivid, memorable, and engaging examples what our theory of teaching phonics, reading, and writing can look like in the real world of primary schools, teachers' classrooms, offering the potential of different futures for millions of children.

We begin the book by engaging with the new frontier of 'the reading wars', fought in the context of teaching in England, Australia, Canada, New Zealand, the USA, and Ireland.

Notes

1 The '(G)' for Glossary notification only appears on first use of a technical term.
2 Weale, S. (2022). *Focus on Phonics to Teach Reading Is 'Failing Children', Says Landmark Study*. Retrieved January 19, 2022, from https://www.theguardian.com/education/2022/jan/19/focus-on-phonics-to-teach-reading-is-failing-children-says-landmark-study

   Wyse, D., & Bradbury, A. (2022). Reading Wars or Reading Reconciliation? A Critical Examination of Robust Research Evidence, Curriculum Policy, and Teachers' Practices for Teaching Phonics and Reading. *Review of Education*. Retrieved December 1, 2023, from https://doi.org/10.1002/rev3.3314
3 An example of the international media attention includes this: Barras, C. (2023). As Tricky as ABC. *The New Scientist*, 42–45. Retrieved December 1, 2023, from https://www.newscientist.com/article/mg25834350-200-we-know-how-kids-learn-to-read-so-why-are-we-failing-to-teach-them/

Part I
The politics and science of reading and writing

1 The reading wars

The English language is the most-used language in the world,[1] and hence there is great interest in understanding how young children can best be taught to read and write in English. Many children 'crack the alphabetic code' successfully and go on to experience reading and writing as rewarding and vital aspects of their lives. However, there are also millions of children worldwide who are not learning to read and write as well as they should. The United Nations recognises the urgency of improving literacy in its Sustainable Development Goals that include targets for all children to have access to education and for teaching to be high quality. The challenges in low-income countries and regions are particularly acute. However, the urgent need to improve the teaching of reading and writing is not unique to low-income countries. In countries such as the USA, New Zealand, Canada, Australia, Ireland, and the countries of the UK, there are significant numbers of pupils who do not learn to read and write as well as they should.

If we take a wealthy country like England, we can see from national tests that for pupils age 10 to 11 (Year 6), at the end of primary education, approximately one quarter of these pupils have over many years not met the expected standards for their age. This trend continued in national statutory tests in 2023, with 27% of children not meeting the standard in reading and 29% not meeting the standard for writing.[2]

When children in England are about age six (Year 1), they must all sit a test that is called a Phonics Screening Check (PSC) (G).[3] If they fail this test, they must sit it again when they are about seven (Year 2). This phonics test requires children to decode a list of individual words and nonsense words (pseudo words). In 2023, 21% of children did not achieve the expected standard in the PSC in Year 1, in spite of more than a decade of the PSC.[4] What's more, statutory teacher assessments at the end of Key Stage 1 (children aged six to seven) in 2023 that assess reading more holistically than the PSC showed that 32% of children had not met the expected standard for reading, and 40% had not met the expected standard for writing.[5] The PSC is part of an extensive set of policies in England designed to prescribe one teaching method, synthetic phonics[6] (G), and to hold teachers and schools to account: therefore the PSC can also be seen as a key political lever.[7]

The potential consequences for children not progressing sufficiently well in reading and writing are profound and include being less able to access vital services in society; missing out on the pleasures of reading and writing; missing out on learning across the whole curriculum in lessons in primary and secondary education; and higher probability of poorer mental health, lower wages in life, and even ending up in prison.[8] Therefore it is vital that teaching practices and education policies are informed by the most robust evidence of what works in the teaching of reading and writing. This book puts forward the case for a new approach to teaching phonics, reading, and writing based on the most robust evidence.

DOI: 10.4324/9781003442134-3

8 *The politics and science of reading and writing*

Snapshots of policy and practice in different countries

The phrase 'the reading wars' has been used to characterise some of the intense debates about the best ways to teach young children to read in the English language. To introduce you to these debates, and important aspects that are also themes in the rest of the book, we begin with five snapshots from different countries where English is a main language taught in schools. After these snapshots we provide evidence of the ways in which one view of phonics teaching (G) is being promoted in some of these regions. The tactics and lines of argument that have been used are critiqued so that readers will be able to evaluate similar developments in future.

England

At 8:55 am five-year-old Alfie arrives in good time for registration in his Reception[9] class. He hangs up his coat and puts his Paw Patrol lunch bag with the other children's lunch bags and boxes. When the teacher calls his name he says, "Yes, miss. Packed lunch." Once the register is done the teacher says, "OK, children, it is time for your phonics lesson. Line up please." For this first lesson of every day the four- and five-year-old children walk to one of three different classrooms depending on their phonics ability. Alfie is in what he knows is the 'bottom group' even though it is called Ladybird Phonics Group by his teachers.

A different teacher from Alfie's normal class teacher starts the lesson: "Right, children, who can tell me what sound we learned about yesterday?" Alfie has a sudden exciting thought: he remembers that it's his Dad's turn to look after him, and they are going to play football in Sefton Park, his favourite activity. The teacher says, "Well done, Zenab, it was the /ah/[10] sound yesterday. Who can remember a word that uses that /ah/ sound?"

Alfie doesn't like being separated from his friends for his phonics lessons, but this will happen every day for two years. There are lots of other school activities he would prefer to be doing, but often there doesn't seem to be much time for other things, like music, art, or even science.

Although the previous scene is fictional, it is based on a range of real practices that were happening to the vast majority of four- and five-year-old children in England every day from the start of their primary (kindergarten and elementary)[11] education until they were at least seven years old. There were also requirements and increasing pressures to teach phonics in nursery classes (pre-kindergarten, children aged three to four). Alfie's lesson is a synthetic phonics lesson, which means teaching children first and foremost about the ways that the sounds (more accurately the *phonemes* [G]) of spoken English are represented by letters. Synthetic phonics was the approach mandated by government in England.

The phrase *systematic synthetic phonics* (G) (sometimes abbreviated to SSP) had been used by governments in England for 17 years, but the term is tautologous. The approach in England was *synthetic phonics*, which is by definition systematic. Other systematic approaches to teaching phonics and reading were to varying degrees not permitted, in spite of the fact that research evidence clearly shows that a range of approaches to phonics teaching are effective, as you will see in Chapter Four, "The Science of Reading and Writing". In England, for more than a decade, children had been taught first and foremost about phonemes and the ways that phonemes are represented by letters. For children who failed to learn to read, phonics teaching simply continued.

Australia and New Zealand

For many years the state in Australia where a university-based teacher trainer worked had a balanced approach to teaching reading, but then the ideas of a Member of Parliament from England influenced first that state then other states to radically change curriculum policy. The changes included the introduction of a phonics screening test and synthetic phonics teaching.

The lecturer had been a primary teacher in New Zealand, and had taught reading in a holistic way. Children's enjoyment of reading was central to the approach, as was a focus on meaning and whole texts, printed and digital. The national curriculum that had been in place in New Zealand since 2007 was diverse and inclusive, including the parallel national curriculum, Te Marautanga o Aotearoa. Teaching about the alphabetic code was done less systematically than in synthetic phonics. The lecturer was struck by how New Zealand had continued to perform well in PISA and PIRLS[12] tests, in spite of having a whole-language approach.

Following some media articles in New Zealand about the reading war, the lecturer was concerned that plans for a 'refreshed' national curriculum to be implemented from 2025 might move the whole-language orientation of the curriculum towards narrow synthetic phonics.

The national curriculum in New Zealand had been a whole-language curriculum for many years and could be seen as a polar opposite to the national curriculum in England that was dominated by synthetic phonics, particularly the version established from 2014. And yet New Zealand had consistently performed well in the international comparisons.

Ireland

After more than 20 years of an unchanged national curriculum in Ireland a senior civil servant was informed by the government that the moment had come to start development of a revised national curriculum. A research-informed, long-term, collaborative process was started to develop a new national curriculum. Teachers' autonomy and children's agency (G) were to be central to the new curriculum. Phonics was to be put in its rightful place – as only one important part of learning to read and write.

Because of their knowledge of research, including the history of curriculum development, the civil servants leading the changes were able to reflect on the moment after the 2009 PISA results when the government in Ireland had experienced 'PISA shock'. Ireland's test outcomes on this international comparative study had shown a one-off fall. A national literacy strategy was introduced to address the perceived fall in standards of reading. However, a knee-jerk reaction towards synthetic phonics was not part of this plan, in spite of media pressure to do so. A balanced approach to language, reading, and writing was maintained.

Ireland, like New Zealand, had had a long period without major change to its national curriculum and had been one of the highly ranked regions in the international comparative studies. Ireland's approach had been a balanced approach to teaching reading. The development of a new framework for the national curriculum, from 2020 onwards, maintained this balance but also introduced some important progressive changes, including a focus on teachers' and children's autonomy (or *agency*) over elements of the curriculum, particularly teachers' control over the methods of teaching that they used.[13]

The USA

In the USA a journalist uncovers what they portray as a shocking conspiracy in education. Children are being failed by elementary teachers because they are not being taught to read in the correct way. The correct, and only, way is based on 'science', and it is called synthetic

> phonics. The reasons that teachers are not teaching correctly is because they have not been trained properly.
>
> According to the journalist the problems began not in the USA but in New Zealand where an influential teacher then theorist called Marie Clay developed Reading Recovery, an approach to teaching children who were struggling with reading. Clay's ideas, and particularly the idea of "three cueing", spread to teachers in the USA (and other countries). The journalist alleged that one of the reasons these ideas spread was because teachers were particularly influenced by three university lecturers, and one in particular, "The Superstar",[14] Lucy Calkins. These lecturers trained teachers with ideas about the teaching of reading that had been known to be wrong for more than 20 years. What's worse, the publisher of the lecturers' books "made a lot of money" from these erroneous ideas.

Later in this chapter you will learn about the work of Emily Hanford, a journalist in the USA who in 2022 created an influential series of podcasts called *Sold a Story*: the previous example draws heavily on some of the main ideas that Hanford conveys through the podcasts. The debates in the USA, and other regions where the English language is a main language in schools, are an important part of understanding why truly evidence-based teaching of reading is frequently not implemented. Understanding 'what works' in the teaching of reading is a story of teachers' practices and research but also politics and journalism.

Canada

> A senior official in the Ministry of Education in Ontario, Canada, is worried. Ever since the start of international comparisons such as PISA, Ontario in Canada had performed better than any other region where English is a main language in education. For many years Ontario's language curriculum had been a holistic one with social practices at the heart of its programmes of study. Phonics had been a small part of the text of Ontario's curriculum. But then a new report was published by a human rights organisation with legal powers. The main thrust of the report was that because children had not been getting "scientifically based reading instruction", their rights to a good education were being denied. Ontario's holistic curriculum was rewritten with a heavy emphasis on synthetic phonics.

The provinces in Canada that have been included in PISA and PIRLS comparative studies have a history of being towards the top of these league tables, including the state of Ontario. In 2022 the use of children's rights as a way to criticise teaching methods in Ontario, and to strongly advocate for synthetic phonics, was a new variant of the reading wars. Children's rights are a pressing and important concern for many people. These rights involve the need to protect the most vulnerable children, including trying to bring families out of poverty in all regions of the world, and with particularly serious implications in economically poorer regions and those affected by wars. So to see children's rights used as the basis for advocating synthetic phonics was surprising to say the least.

The criticisms were published in a report by the Ontario Human Rights Commission (OHRC), which has the power to hold inquiries in the public interest. The outcome of its inquiry into "students with reading disabilities"[15] was to challenge the Ministry of Education in Ontario on why children were not being taught using systematic phonics first and foremost. The report strongly recommended that pre-service teacher education and school boards should change their practices. The report claimed that the reason that teaching of reading had failed was because it had been informed by the "three cueing system",[16] by "balanced literacy", *and* by "whole language" approaches, which it alleged were not "scientifically based reading instruction". Before long the OHRC influence had spread to other Canadian provinces. In Chapter 2, "The Development of Reading and Writing", we review the rigour of some of the most popular models of reading, including what is called by some the "Three Cues Model". We also present our new model, the Double Helix of Reading and Writing.

True stories?

The previous examples, from different regions where English is a main language in schools, reflect composites of real events combined with some dramatised aspects. The countries and regions featured in the examples had all been performing above the average total score in PISA,[17] and in most cases towards the highest scores, yet these regions' approaches to teaching reading and writing differed in important ways, particularly the way that phonics was part of their curricula. However, from about 2017 onwards there was a resurgence of synthetic phonics, particularly in Australia; Ontario, Canada; and the USA, in some cases inspired by what had been happening in England since 2010. In the next section we go into more detail about the real events linked to the examples from some of these regions, but we begin in England where the dominance of synthetic phonics began.

Centralising synthetic phonics in England

In 1997 British Member of Parliament Nick Gibb MP was first elected to parliament, where, like his fellow politicians in 'the opposition', he joined 'the back benches' of the House of Commons in London. From at least 2007 he regarded the requirement for primary school teachers to use one form of teaching reading, synthetic phonics, as one of his most important goals in education.[18] In time he secured the political power to have far reaching consequences for policies on curriculum and teaching reading because he served terms as the minister of state for schools in the government's Department for Education (DfE; including being reappointed in October 2022).

In 2023 Nick Gibb announced that after a long period as an MP he would step down at the next general election. In his message to the people of his political constituency of Bognor Regis in England, he said this:

> I am proud that over my 10 years as a minister standards in schools have risen. England is 4th in the world in reading as a result of the phonics reforms and we are rising internationally for maths and English. We have transformed the curriculum so that it is knowledge rich.[19]

The bold claim about England being fourth in the world in reading was based on his very selective interpretation of one research study, the PIRLS 2021 study released in 2023. The unique circumstances of PIRLS 2021 data collection in England related to the Covid-19 pandemic was clearly identified as a factor in England's performance in a series of three *UCL Institute of Education* blogposts,[20] and the fact that England was 42nd out of 57 countries when measured on how much pupils enjoyed reading, which Gibb omitted to mention, was also pointed out. The National Education Union's (NEU) response to Gibb's decision to stand down was a damming indictment that included this view from Daniel Kebede, then general secretary of the NEU:

> Gibb has been a centraliser. He has sought to micro-manage the teacher education curriculum,. He has imposed on schools his preferred method for the teaching of reading. Through establishing the Oak National Academy as a government agency, he has worked towards a degree of control over the curriculum whose educational consequences will be disastrous. In the name of 'standards', these policies are actually reducing the quality of education, worsening the conditions of teachers and lessening pupils' motivation and enjoyment.[21]

By 2023 the centralisation and micro-management of education policies on the teaching of reading and writing in England had become a stark outlier compared to Australia, Canada, New Zealand, the USA, Ireland, and the other countries of the UK. The following list of key features illustrate what made England an outlier internationally.

1. England's national curriculum, implemented since 2014, had more content on synthetic phonics than any other national curriculum worldwide. The national curriculum has to be followed by all government funded schools.[22]
2. The government DfE validated and approved commercial synthetic phonics schemes. Although legally schools could choose to teach phonics without using an approved scheme, in reality schools used the commercial synthetic phonics packages that had been officially approved by government because of the pressures associated with the Office for Standards in Education, Children's Services and Skills (Ofsted) inspections of schools that would expect to see use of approved schemes.
3. The required synthetic phonics teaching was dominant and separate from other aspects of reading, such as reading comprehension. The detail of the DfE selection criteria for approval of phonics schemes illustrates this:

   > A programme should promote the use of phonics as the route to reading unknown words, before any subsequent comprehension strategies are applied. It should not encourage children to guess unknown words from clues such as pictures or context, rather than first applying phonic knowledge and skills. It should not include lists of high-frequency words or any other words for children to learn as whole shapes 'by sight'. The focus should be on phonemes, and not on 'consonant clusters' (/s/+/p/+/l/ not /spl/) or 'onset (G) and rime (G)' (/c/+/a/ +/t/ not c-at, m-at, b-at).[23]

   The involvement of the DfE in such minutiae of primary education, signalled by the language of "should" and "should not", marked an extreme level of control of primary teaching.
4. A national phonics test, called the PSC, had been mandated by the DfE since 2012. This test was taken by all six-year-old children at a set time in the year. In addition to some real words, children were required to read a list of words known as *pseudowords,* strings of letters which conform to some rules of orthography (G) but are not real words and so have no meaning (also known as 'nonsense words' by many people). This test was

one of many national assessments that children sat which are known as *high-stakes tests*[24] because the consequences for teachers and schools if the children don't perform well are serious or, in other words, 'high stakes'. These kinds of tests also distort the curriculum that children experience.[25] Test outcomes were entered into a national pupil database and used to track progress and to hold teachers and schools to account.

5. A system of inspecting schools, carried out by Ofsted, had over the years increased its power to influence how teachers should teach. In 2023 a school would be judged as Grade 1 Outstanding, Grade 2 Good, Grade 3 Requires Improvement, or Grade 4 Inadequate.[26] The consequences of failing an inspection were serious for individual teachers and for school communities. Ofsted had used statutory test results, particularly the PSC, as a main way to hold schools to account for many years. Evidence of strong emphasis on synthetic phonics was also seen in the concept of 'deep dives' that were used to inspect the work of schools and teachers. The following quote is taken from an Ofsted blog post:

To prevent myths being created, I've set out here what inspectors will be looking at during deep dives into early reading. They will consider the extent to which:

- direct, focused phonics is taught every day in Reception and key stage 1
- children read from books with the sounds they know, while they are learning to read
- teachers and teaching assistants provide extra practice through the day for the children who make the slowest progress (the lowest 20%)
- all children in Year 3 and above can read age-appropriate books
- teachers instil in children a love of literature: the best stories and poems[27]

In 2023, concerns about Ofsted not being fit for purpose were growing very strongly.[28]

6. In 2019 government incursions into the roles of professionals was extended to include university teaching staff. A mandated DfE curriculum for university programmes called the ITT Core Content Framework of Initial Teacher Training[29] was developed which included strong emphasis on synthetic phonics as the only way to teach early reading. A very small number of research studies about teaching phonics and reading were cherry picked to support the government's preferred narrative in the document. The Education Endowment Foundation (EEF), funded by the DfE, 'approved' the Core Content Framework in a way that was not typical of the EEF's more normal role in relation to evaluations. This incursion into the academic freedom of university departments to determine curriculum and teaching methods was unprecedented and raised wider questions about academic freedom in universities.[30]

7. Government extended its grip on the work of professionals by publishing an extensive document effectively mandating how reading should be taught. First published in January 2022, The Reading Framework[31] meant that ministers were even more forcefully directing teaching methods, an area that historically had always been seen as the responsibility of teachers as professionals. The very selective use of research studies, seen in the citations in the framework, was once again a problem.

To some readers it may be that each separate element of the previous list of seven political control mechanisms is not particularly unreasonable. After all, the education system in any country should be accountable to the taxpayers whose money supports it. On the other hand, it may appear extraordinary to you that the work of professionals and of university education departments could be so rigidly and powerfully controlled by any government.

This unique combination of control mechanisms in England listed previously only states the formal position. In the daily lives of children, teachers, schools, and teacher trainers there were a range of related consequences. If the pressures caused by a PSC caused the curriculum to be unacceptably narrowed because of the understandable response of teachers to 'teach to the test', if children felt as though they were failures because of their allocation to phonics low ability groups,[32] if the inspectorate Ofsted applied undue pressure on schools to use government approved synthetic phonics schemes, if teachers were not allowed to determine the teaching methods that they use, if teacher educators in universities were not allowed to determine the teaching methods they recommend to their students, if teacher educators in universities faced pressure not to cite research that did not reflect the evidence 'allowed' by the government department, then there really was a problem with government policy! And if other countries and regions adopt some of the same policies, this would reflect a worrying international trend.

The example of Alfie at the start of this chapter was derived from various sources. In addition to the policy documents we have already cited, there was evidence from surveys of teachers, and other research studies, revealing the details of what was happening in primary schools. Some well-informed specialist education media accounts also provided useful information. We can add to this our own anecdotal evidence from our professional knowledge which, in addition to our research carried out with schools, includes several decades of direct engagement with teachers in schools, with colleagues in teacher education/training, and with teachers doing professional development courses. Teachers in primary schools and colleagues in university teacher education told us about the nature of the pressures that were at play in England's education system. 'Fear' of not carrying out government mandates was a word we heard too often. New teachers described by experienced teachers as 'deskilled' because they were not being made aware of alternative evidence-based approaches to the government's line was also regularly commented on.

Screening phonics in Australia

In 2017, Nick Gibb MP visited Australia to recommend the approach taken to synthetic phonics in England, including the introduction of a phonics screening test. The politics of Gibb's Australia trip was evident from the start, as it was hosted by the conservative think tank, the Centre for Independent Studies, which wanted Australia to follow the UK example of more explicit instruction in schools.[33] The Australian government subsequently committed $10.8 billion to a "phonics health check" and literacy hub. The wording "health check" is interesting. The wording is used to suggest that testing children on pseudowords and real words is akin to a routine health check, perhaps like going to the dentist for a check-up. But, of course, the test is nothing like a health test. For example, the results of the test are not confidential to the child and their parents. Rather like the phrase "The Phonics Screening Check", the wording "health check" obfuscates the real meaning, which is a high-stakes test that all children are required to sit and which is designed to hold schools and teachers to account.

The politics that led to the introduction of the phonics test in Australia is common to most of the regions we cover in this chapter. In 2019, the media covered the story that Australia's overall score for reading in the international comparative tests of the PISA had declined.[34] Media reporting of these international comparative reports such as PISA often neglect important details from the full reports, including those about trends in performance over time. When responding to the outcomes of these reports, politicians and groups with vested interests in the politics of reading can try to twist the outcomes to suit their perspectives. By 2022, the phonics test had been made compulsory in the states of New South Wales and South Australia, and in other states the pressure to adopt synthetic phonics was growing. The influence of a single politician from England had spread. Prior to these developments Australia's curriculum, represented in a national curriculum at federal level, represented what we regard as a balanced approach to teaching reading. Phonics teaching was always part of the curriculum but not unduly emphasised compared to the other important aspects of teaching reading.

Advocating synthetic phonics in the USA

"The Great Debate" about teaching reading was originally described in the 1980s by US academic Jean Chall[35] as a disagreement about the merits of two main approaches: the 'top-down approach' for example, 'whole-language teaching' (G), which focused first and foremost on whole texts and used these to teach the small parts of language, including words and letters, versus the 'bottom-up approach' that advocated beginning with teaching of letters and sounds (phonemes), for example, systematic phonics. The phrase 'the reading wars' was also first used in the USA at this time. As we outline in Chapter 5, "The Balanced Approach to Teaching Phonics, Reading, and Writing", there are now three main orientations to teaching early reading: whole language, synthetic phonics, and the balanced approach.

This section about the USA is longer than others because the issues that we address are common in various ways to other nations. The US was also the originator of the influential National Reading Panel, which continues to be cited in different countries, and debates in the USA have continued in relation to research evidence, the media, and politics.

A new twist on the old story of the reading wars in the USA was communications technology: in this case the podcast format. Emily Hanford, a journalist in the USA, had been investigating the teaching of reading for some years. Her six-episode podcast series launched in 2022 was titled *Sold a Story*.[36] According to the *Sold a Story* website[37] and related media accounts, as a result of the podcasts, a significant number of states in the USA abandoned their previous approach to teaching reading and adopted what they called an approach based on 'the science of reading'. What they actually adopted was synthetic phonics. There are a number of engaging features about the podcasts, not least the stories about individual readers, which are concerning when they have failed to learn to read and uplifting when they succeed. And while we agree with the argument that phonics teaching is an important part of the teaching of reading, the main problem with the podcasts is that they did not portray the research evidence, and other important aspects of education, in a balanced or sufficiently accurate way; hence their conclusions and their apparent influence are dubious, as we will show.

The meaning of the title *Sold a Story* alludes to Hanford's main allegation that the US-based academics Irene Fountas, Gay Su Pinnell, Lucy Calkins and their publisher had become rich selling an idea about how to teach reading, but the idea was seriously wrong because 'the science of reading' showed it was wrong. Hanford argued that phonics teaching is *the* essential element in learning to read and that teachers in the USA were not using the approach to phonics teaching that the podcasts assert is the best way to teach. This quote from the first episode revealed Hanford's view:

> Schools think they're teaching kids to read. Of course they do. But it turns out there's a big body of scientific research about reading and how kids learn to do it. This research shows there are important skills that all kids need to learn to become good readers. And in lots of schools, they aren't being taught these skills.[38]

The argument of *Sold a Story* continues with the claim that from 2001 onwards the ideas of a famous educator and researcher from New Zealand called Marie Clay were responsible for a lack of phonics teaching in primary schools. Hanford says this: "I'm gonna tell you about that study [Clay's] in a minute – because in time, Marie Clay and her research would influence the way millions of children around the world are taught."[39] In particular, a model of teaching reading that Hanford called "three cueing" was to blame. The theory of children using different *cues* to work out words when they are reading was not created by Marie Clay; it came from the reading researcher Ken Goodman, as we show in Chapter 2, "The Development of Reading and Writing". The *Sold a Story* podcasts assert that Clay's theory led to a very widespread lack of phonics teaching in US primary schools and that the Reading Recovery intervention that Clay developed to help children with reading difficulties was a big part of the problem.

Section 5 of the Reading Recovery teaching procedures in Clay's most famous and seminal book, *The Early Detection of Reading Difficulties (3rd Edition)*,[40] is called "Hearing the Sounds in Words".[41] Section 10 is called "Linking Sound Sequences with Letter Sequences", which addresses helping children to analyse spoken sounds into phonemes and to understand the links with letters and written words. Clay says this:

> In many classrooms around the world while teachers have been teaching phonics competently children have probably been learning something much more useful, they have been constructing the complex associations between sound sequences and letter sequences that enable us to become fluent readers.[42]

So it is not accurate to suggest that Clay's approach had *no* phonics teaching. In relation to arguing the merits or otherwise of Clay's work, *Sold a Story* also did not address powerful evidence of the effectiveness of Marie Clay's Reading Recovery approach, for example, from a robust randomised controlled trial,[43] which was just one of several robust studies showing the effectiveness of Reading Recovery. Nor did the podcast series acknowledge that Clay's original ideas that: 1. children with reading difficulties needed early identification (by the time they were age six), 2. this early identification should be followed by regular one-to-one support, and 3. this support should be based on a systematic teaching programme are overall *the* most effective ways of improving the reading skills of children with reading difficulties.[44]

Sold a Story also alleges that Marie Clay's ideas about reading inspired influential US education researcher Lucy Calkins, and that Calkins' ideas were also a main cause of teachers in the USA failing to teach children to read. Apparently, according to *Sold a Story*, Calkins was overcome by romanticism because she had seen progressive education in 1970s Britain.[45] And in what we regard as an unnecessarily personal line of argument, it is suggested that Calkins' ideas were based on the privileged life she had led, which Hanford compared unfavourably to the circumstances that disadvantaged pupils in the USA face.

In our view, speculations of this kind about someone's childhood and background are very dubious, not based on research evidence, and lack sufficient relevance to what really matters in relation to effective teaching of reading and writing. When social and other media has featured personal attacks and responses using patronising or offensive language rather than respectful critique, this is always a sign of weakness in any argument.[46]

Apart from mentions of Calkins' resources for teachers, which are extensive, published by Heinemann, the only citation of Calkins' work in *Sold a Story* appears to be one about writing: *The Art of Teaching Writing*.[47] *Sold a Story* tries to suggest that Calkins' ideas about how children learn to write were the source of her ideas about teaching reading. A more balanced reading of Calkins' research as a whole shows that even though Calkins later conceded that she should have paid more attention to experimental research on phonics, her approach to teaching writing can now be positively linked to recent robust research, as you will see in Chapter 4, "The Science of Teaching Reading and Writing".

While *Sold a Story* deals harshly with education researchers, the portrayal of some other researchers is different. For example, Hanford says that according to the US neuroscience researcher Reid Lyon, who was head of part of the National Institute of Child Health and Human Development, 60% of children need direct and explicit instruction in learning to read. Explicit instruction is not the same as narrow synthetic phonics; it means that children need well-planned teaching of reading that includes phonics *and* other vital elements (as you will see from the robust research evidence presented in Chapter 4, "The Science of Teaching Reading and Writing"). Lyon's statistic could also be interpreted as 40% of children do *not* need direct explicit phonics instruction. The importance of considering the needs of significant numbers of typically developing readers can be linked with the view of another researcher Hanford quotes, the US neuroscientist Bruce McCandliss:

> McCandliss: So some children really just have this knack. . . . [They are] really great at like, hearing all of the individual sounds within words, they play around with them a lot, and when they are exposed to reading, they start to make all of these connections sort of beautifully.[48]

If reliable (G), the 40% figure is certainly important context for the balanced approach to teaching reading that allows for teaching that is adapted for different kinds of readers, including those with reading difficulties and those who are more typically developing readers. And for the avoidance of doubt that children can learn to read *without* systematic phonics, there is research on children who were able to read prior to starting primary school.[49] For some children, a minimum of teaching, and sufficient exposure to print supported by interaction with more advanced readers including family members, is enough to learn to read. For these children, the use of whole language–approach teaching strategies could be sufficient (see Chapter 3, "How Texts Teach What Children Learn"), but effective use of a balanced approach should be ideal for all children.

Neuroscience and education research

Some of the main arguments in the *Sold a Story* podcast series are the same ones that US neuroscientist Mark Seidenberg laid out in his book published five years before *Sold a Story*.[50] To some degree Seidenberg's book builds on his theory known as Parallel Distributed Processing, published with colleague James McClelland.[51] One aspect of this theory is a diagram that features three circles, connected with lines and arrowheads pointing both ways which show paths between the circles. Inside the circles are the words "Meaning", "Orthography", and "Phonology". A fourth circle is called "Context". The useful Seidenberg and McClelland interactive model, which deals with processing of mono-syllabic words, is further described as follows:

> We also assume, in keeping with this inherently interactive view, that word processing [decoding] can be influenced by contextual factors arising from syntactic, semantic, and pragmatic constraints, although the scope and locus of these effects is a matter of current debate (see McClelland, 1987; Rumelhart, 1977; Tanenhaus et al., 1987, for discussion). We assume that at least some of these types of information constrain the construction of the representation at the semantic level and, thus, indirectly influence construction of representations at the other levels, and conversely, that the construction of a representation of the context is influenced by activation at the semantic level.

This interactive model seems to us a better fit with a balanced approach to teaching reading, not a narrow synthetic phonics approach. We leave readers to weigh up this conjecture and also whether the three circles of David Pearson's Three Cues Model that we show in Chapter 2, "The Development of Reading and Writing", are similar to the Seidenberg and McClelland theory.

Seidenberg's subsequent research with colleagues on computational models of reading processes showed that learning to read requires, and develops, the connections between the meaning of written language and texts (semantics) and understanding of the way that letters represent phonemes in words. These connections can be seen in studies of the brain but also in behavioural studies of cognition.

The argument that in general phonics teaching is important is well made in Seidenberg's book, but the basis for the criticisms of the work of teachers, teacher educators, and some education research, admittedly from the USA context, does not take sufficient account of relevant research, particularly from the discipline of education. Let's take an example from the book:

> If the whole-language/balanced-literacy approach is as flawed as described, many children will struggle to learn. What happens to them? In thousands of schools in America and other English-speaking countries, those children participate in Reading Recovery (RR), a remedial program devised by Marie Clay, a New Zealand educator. Reading Recovery is a short-term program focused on first graders who have made little progress. Clay, a whole-language popularizer, focused on the guessing idea and the use of many types of information – semantics, grammar, background knowledge, and so on – to identify words and understand texts. Children who have not learned to do this fall behind. Reading Recovery provides tutoring in the use of these strategies.[52]

In this short paragraph there are several points which we think are not sufficiently supported by research evidence:

1. the evidence base for a balanced approach is different from and much stronger than that for whole language, as we show in this book;
2. the quote overgeneralises about an intervention with struggling readers (those who receive the Reading Recovery intervention) into an argument about typical readers (whole-language populariser);

3. if the idea that Clay was a "whole-language popularizer" means that she actively promoted "whole language", no evidence is presented to support this;
4. "the guessing idea" is not a reasonable depiction of what Clay portrayed and has become a trope in the reading wars. In Chapter 2, "The Development of Reading and Writing", we address the precise nature of what "guessing" means, and does not mean, in the context of teaching;
5. the book focuses on the US with very little evidence from or about "other English-speaking countries", for example, England whose policies have been very much synthetic phonics first and foremost for more than a decade.

A more unexpected source of difference between Seidenberg's views and the evidence from education research was the doubts expressed about the value of randomised controlled trials (RCTs) in education,[53] nicknamed "the gold standard of evidence". In a curious paradox, the criticism that randomised controlled trials in education are "even more complicated than a drug trial" because they face the multiple influences of classroom, school, community and home factors is very similar to the criticisms made by some education researchers who favour qualitative research methods. But once again there is solid peer-reviewed (G) education research evidence about the value, complexities, and pros and cons of RCTs in education which could have been cited.[54]

What's more, the EEF in England has used rigorous standards based mainly on RCTs and systematic reviews to evaluate teaching methods to arrive at its guidance for teachers. EEF guidance about teaching reading, for teachers of children aged five to seven, includes this: "Use a balanced and engaging approach to developing reading, teaching both decoding and comprehension skills".[55] Once you have finished reading our book, we hope you will see this could also be its strapline, although only if writing was added to the balance. It is certainly true that carrying out RCTs in education is demanding and complex. Our example of an EEF RCT evaluation, of ReadWrite Inc., which was of the most popular synthetic phonics schemes in England, demonstrates this (see Chapter 4, "The Science of Teaching Reading and Writing"). Presumably for reasons of independence from the political context in England, this RCT was carried out by a team of researchers from the US and Northern Ireland. Our perspective on RCTs in education is also informed by our own research in which we have been team members on some of the most complex RCTs undertaken in education.[56]

Neuroscience, like any academic discipline, has a diversity of views, but this diversity is not sufficiently represented in the *Sold a Story* podcasts. For example, a UK-based neuroscientist said this: "every science base that you address shows how important it is to use child-centred play-based learning if you want to optimise children's cognitive potential and also their emotional well-being".[57] This is the view of the neuroscientist Usha Goswami, who won the Yidan Prize, perhaps the equivalent of a Nobel prize for education. Goswami did ground-breaking research on the teaching of reading,[58] and her neuroscientific work with Jo Zeigler on the *psycholinguistic (G) grain size theory* importantly shows how consideration of larger units, including words and syllables, is a vital part of understanding how children learn to read.[59] Practical links relevant to teaching have been made with this work, for example, the importance of nursery rhymes for young children and the importance of learning by analogies (G). Goswami's view about the teaching of reading is far closer to ours than the *Sold a Story* interpretation of neuroscience in advocacy for a particular view of phonics teaching.[60]

Because the lines of argument in the podcasts of *Sold a Story* and the book *Language at the Speed of Sight* are in some aspects so close, the limitations are the same. Perhaps in the development of *Sold a Story*, the allure of tales from one form of science, a small selection of US-based 'neuro-science', was strong; consequently research evidence from other forms of science such as 'social science' was not accounted for.

Criticising teachers and teacher educators

In common with some other commentators, the podcasts include assertions about what teachers or teacher educators are *not* doing right, but with a lack of robust research evidence to back these assertions up. This is actually a weakness in the research field: there is a lack of recurrent robust research with data relevant to what teachers do in practice. The only recent example we could find which was relevant to primary schools in the USA was a survey of 674 kindergarten to Grade 2 teachers and special education teachers.[61] When asked what their philosophy of teaching reading was, 22% of survey respondents said that their approach was explicit systematic phonics with language comprehension as a separate focus. In other words, discrete phonics teaching that is separate from the other aspects of reading. 68% said that balanced literacy was their philosophy: balanced literacy includes phonics teaching. However, when asked to define what they meant by balanced literacy, 52% ($n = 238$) of these respondents said that phonics was a defining feature of their balanced approach, which indicates a strong phonics orientation by teachers overall, including as part of a balanced approach.

Further evidence of what teachers actually do came from a very large-scale initiative in the USA. In 2001 President George Bush launched Reading First (RF), an initiative based on the same view of 'the science of reading' advocated in *Sold a Story*. This was a seriously high-profile political initiative launched at the very start of the presidency, helped with more than $5 billion of funding. *Sold a Story* claims that RF was defeated by advocates of the 'Three Cues Model' and by politics. More objective evidence comes from the formal evaluation of RF, which surveyed a nationally representative sample of RF schools ($n = 1,092$) and non-RF schools ($n = 541$). This study found that schools that received RF funding did indeed change their practice and were more likely to use reading material aligned with "scientifically based reading research".[62]

Unfortunately the study also "found no evidence that Reading First had a statistically significant impact on student reading comprehension test scores in grades 1, 2 or 3 across the three years of the study" (p. 12). It is vital that any approach to reading has a positive effect on reading comprehension, because comprehension is the essence of reading. The RF study did find a positive impact on students' decoding skills, something that is expected if teaching changes to more emphasis on decoding through phonics teaching. It really isn't 'rocket science': if you teach children more phonics, they will usually improve their understanding of the alphabetic code. But the science of *teaching* reading and writing is much more complex: how do you balance the different important parts of reading and writing, at different stages of children's development, with different groups of children, for optimal progress?

Synthetic phonics devotees almost never acknowledge that there are risks inherent in their advocacy. One of the most serious risks with an unduly heavy emphasis on phonics in any country is that the children who have already learned to decode words may find that they have to continue doing synthetic phonics lessons when their time could be better spent on all the other aspects of engaging with books and texts, including in other areas of the primary school curriculum. It is surprising that the risks of this impact on the experiences in school of perhaps up to 40% of pupils has not been brought to the fore in the latest debates in the USA.

Evidence over long periods of history shows that phonics has nearly always been an important part of primary school teaching, evidence which contrasts with claims that most teachers do not use phonics. The lack of attention to the history of teaching reading, and shaky claims about what teachers do, are tropes in the reading wars that need to be challenged. The more recent claim that balanced teaching of reading is the 'whole-language approach' or the Three Cues Model in disguise is a suggestion that is not backed by evidence, as US education researchers David Reinking, George Hruby, and Victoria Risko clearly argue.[63] They also provide evidence of a "phonics first ideology" arising from a combination of new legislation, politics, and the media, which they show has amounted to a direct and dramatic impact on the state of Tennessee in the USA.

The selection of researchers and research that is cited in any account needs to represent *a balanced approach*. Even if we restrict our attention to journalism only, there are more balanced accounts of the debates about phonics and reading, for example, Helen Amass' piece in the *Times Educational Supplement* (TES),[64] Colin Barras' piece in *The New Scientist*,[65] or Valerie Strauss in the *Washington Post*.[66] And for an interesting perspective on how to detect four types of bias errors in media and other accounts about the 'science of reading', Maren Aukerman's piece on the US Literacy Research Association web page is helpful.[67]

Children's rights to read in Ontario, Canada

Some aspects of the debates about phonics and reading in different countries and regions that we have outlined so far have been seen recurrently in the course of the history of the reading wars. However, examples such as the introduction of a national statutory PSC in England, combined with the other factors we mentioned earlier in this chapter, were an intensification of control over the work of teachers and teacher educators. In 2022 a development in Ontario, Canada, was a wholly new development in relation to the history of debates. The OHRC made a challenge against Ontario's education system on the basis that children's rights to an adequate education had been breached because they were not getting scientifically based reading teaching. We are completely in support of children's rights, for example, in relation to the requirements of the UN Convention on the Rights of the Child, but to use a children's rights argument as a lever to force governments to adopt synthetic phonics is quite a different matter. At the very least any recommendations about teaching reading would have to be completely rigorous and balanced; otherwise there are risks of children not receiving optimal teaching approaches.

The OHRC report called *Right to Read* alleged that systematic phonics teaching was not taking place in schools. The report began with reference to a legal case where the Supreme Court of Canada ruled that the school boards had discriminated against a student's right to intensive support and interventions to address his dyslexia (G). The report then said this: "The right to read applies to ALL students, not just students with reading disabilities. This inquiry found that Ontario is not fulfilling its obligations to meet students' right to read."[68] By this same logic, if a trend of too much emphasis on synthetic phonics was found, contrary to what research suggests is optimal, then this would also breach students' rights. For example, students have a right to a broad and balanced curriculum, one that ensures that they have sufficient time to engage with texts that motivate them to read and that important aspects such as reading comprehension are not unduly marginalised.

On reading the report we were struck by some trends that were part of *Sold a Story* in the USA and in other parts of the world. The report was authoritarian, almost impatient in style, for example, saying that the debates on reading have been "settled" because of 'the science of reading'. The report identified the main problem in Ontario's reading curriculum to be the "cueing systems" model which it called "discovery and inquiry-based learning" *and* a "whole language philosophy". In a somewhat eclectic range of causes that were identified, the report added that balanced literacy was the problem because apparently it was practised in Ontario school boards.[69] The report said that balanced literacy was equivalent to the whole-language approach. The following quote from the executive summary shows these features of the report:

> Unfortunately, the current Ontario Curriculum, Language, Grades 1–8, 2006 (Ontario Language curriculum) and teacher education in Ontario's faculties does not promote these highly effective approaches to early word-reading instruction [explicit instruction in phonemic awareness (G), and phonics]. Instead, with few exceptions, the main approaches in Ontario are teaching word-solving skills with the three-cueing system and balanced literacy. The three cueing system encourages students to guess or predict words using cues or clues from the context and their prior knowledge. In balanced literacy (or comprehensive balanced literacy), teachers "gradually release responsibility" by first modelling text reading, sharing text reading, then guiding students' text reading, with the eventual goal of the student reading texts independently. These approaches for word reading are rooted in a whole language philosophy which suggests that by immersing children in spoken and written language, they will discover how to read. Given this philosophy, many of the other important literacy outcomes beyond word-reading skills may also not receive adequate explicit, evidence-based instruction.[70]

The description of balanced literacy in the report is not accurate, for example, the claim that a balanced approach is rooted in whole-language philosophy.

The main research evidence relevant to teaching is presented in the report's Chapter 8, "Curriculum and Instruction". The report includes the diagram of the Reading Rope, based on the Simple View of Reading, both of which we address in Chapter 2, "The Development of Reading and Writing". A selection of previously published reports that had reviewed research on the teaching of reading was summarised. No differentiation appeared to be made between the quality of the reports that were cited. So, for example, there is a very substantial difference between the reports of the USA's National Reading Panel published in 2000 and Sir Jim Rose's report *The Independent Review of the Teaching of Early Reading*, published in 2006 in England, that influenced the move to 'discrete synthetic phonics', yet in the OHRC report, they are treated as equivalent in their status as research evidence.

The US National Reading Panel did not advocate one approach to teaching phonics, and it underlined the importance of the combination of phonics teaching with four other key elements. The Rose report did advocate one approach: discrete systematic phonics, which became narrow synthetic phonics. In addition to the citation of some reports, some single research studies are cited in the Human Rights report, but not a robust longitudinal randomised controlled trial carried out in Ontario itself that showed the effectiveness of a balanced approach.[71] As you will see in Chapter 4, "The Science of Teaching Reading and

Writing", there are an increasing number of relevant systematic reviews of research, covering hundreds of relevant research studies published in peer-reviewed research journals: these are not mentioned in the OHRC report. Therefore, like so many reports before it, the evidence featured in the OHRC report appeared to be cherry picked to support the main argument for more phonics teaching rather than be a balanced exploration of the relationships between research and effective teaching of reading.

In September 2023 the longstanding Ontario curriculum was replaced with a new curriculum that included extensive expectations in the following separate sections of the curriculum: Phonemic Awareness, Alphabetic Knowledge, Phonics: Grapheme-Phoneme Correspondence [sic], Word-Level Reading and Spelling: Using Phonics Knowledge, and so on.[72]

Whole language in New Zealand

The national curriculum in New Zealand was remarkable for at least two things: 1. It had a whole-language orientation to the teaching of reading, and 2. at the time of writing, it had remained largely unchanged since 2007. The reading wars have produced many extreme reactions about the teaching of reading. The whole-language approach has been one target of such reactions and, on occasion, unreasonably subject to ridicule. Reading these debates, you can get the impression that a whole-language approach is as bad as thinking that the earth is flat, yet in New Zealand they have for many years had a successful national curriculum which we regard as based on a whole-language orientation. New Zealand has continued to perform well compared with other regions where English is a medium of instruction in schools, for example, in the PISA tests.

First and foremost the New Zealand curriculum takes a holistic view of children and young people as learners. Its vision puts developing creativity in learners as its first statement. One of the "key competences" in the curriculum is "Using language, symbols and text" (p. 12). "Making meaning" is prioritised, hence its inclusion in the first sentence of this section.

New Zealand's national curriculum text had only two occurrences of the word stem 'phon'.[73] In a section on the achievement objectives for the subject of English, the following quote shows the emphasis on what is called "grapho-phonic" information:

Listening, reading, and viewing speaking, writing, and presenting processes and strategies

Students will:

- Select and use sources of information, processes, and strategies with some confidence to identify, form, and express ideas.

INDICATORS:

- selects and reads texts for enjoyment and personal fulfilment;
- recognises connections between oral, written, and visual language;
- selects and uses sources of information (meaning, structure, visual and grapho-phonic information) and prior knowledge with growing confidence to make sense of increasingly varied and complex texts.[74]

The emphasis on "grapho-phonic information" was appropriately preceded by emphasis on students making selections of texts for enjoyment. You can see that, even for this occurrence of the word 'phonic', it is also appropriately preceded by the emphasis on students forming and expressing ideas. It would appear that Marie Clay's emphasis on cues for reading words, or what was later also known as "sources of information",[75] are represented in the clarification about which sources of information students should use to make sense of texts: "meaning, structure, visual and grapho-phonic information"; meaning is, again, first and foremost.

The curriculum in New Zealand, which is the final example in this section of the chapter, not only shows that the whole-language approach is viable at national scale but also reveals the wide differences in the nature of curricula in the different regions we have covered. The national curricula in New Zealand and England represented two extremes. England was an outlier, particularly because of its curriculum developments from 2012 onwards which put such an unusually heavy emphasis on synthetic phonics. As England's approach is not sufficiently aligned with robust research evidence, the recent developments in Australia and Ontario, Canada, which to varying degrees are influenced by England's approach,[76] are a concern.

Why does the politics of reading matter?

One of the things that we have illustrated through the examples in this chapter is the ways in which politicians, politics, and the media have been an inseparable part of the reading wars. We have identified a new international trend that is resulting in inappropriate pressure to adopt narrow forms of phonics teaching. The politics of reading matters because some politicians, some organisations, and even some journalists appear to have an increasingly strong influence on the daily lives of children and teachers in schools. If their policies are inappropriate, then children will not learn as well as they should. Whatever the policies are, they should not be unduly influenced by political ideology or by individual people or organisations. Our argument in this book is that a rigorous combination of the most appropriate research realised in practice and policy, through genuinely collaborative curriculum development, is one of the best ways of ensuring that children's learning is optimal.

There appears to be agreement from people coming from many different perspectives, including some powerful political leaders, that research evidence is an important part of the debate about how to teach children to read. The problem is that research is too often being interpreted in ways that do not match the evidence from multiple studies. We think there is broad agreement on some aspects of the research. For example, it is generally accepted that systematic phonics teaching is *one* important part of learning to read. However, the very large gap between those who advocate a heavy emphasis on *discrete* phonics teaching, which is separate from other aspects of teaching reading (in daily lessons and the total duration of phonics teaching in a child's life at school), and those who advocate less emphasis on phonics according to children's individual differences and the need to carefully connect the different elements of learning to read in every reading lesson represents an area of strong disagreement.

If we fail to ensure that teaching children to read in schools genuinely reflects research evidence on 'what works', then some, potentially all, children's lives will be negatively affected, something that people on all sides of the debates want to avoid. The main disagreements in the debates lie in these questions:

- What kinds of phonics teaching are most effective?
- How much phonics teaching do you need for typically developing children compared with those children with reading difficulties?

- Should phonics teaching be directly connected with other important aspects of reading, such as reading comprehension, in all lessons?
- What kinds of texts are most likely to support children learning to read, and why?
- What are the most appropriate ways to select and interpret research to ensure that practices in schools and early years settings are as effective as they possibly can be?
- What are the most appropriate theories and models to inform the *teaching* of reading?

This book addresses these questions, and we present our interpretation of what the research says in relation to effective teaching of reading in Chapter 4, "The Science of Teaching Reading and Writing".

In the next chapter we turn to influential and relevant theories of reading and writing, some represented in visual images, some of which have been seen as useful by teachers. We also present our own new theory and visual image of teaching based on our interpretation of robust research, appropriate theory, and exemplary practice.

Notes

1. In some measures English is the most used language; for other measures it is one of the most used. Crystal, D. (2010). *The Cambridge Encyclopedia of Language* (3rd ed.). Cambridge University Press.
2. GOV.UK. (2023). *Academic Year 2022/23. Key Stage 2 Attainment: National Headlines*. Retrieved November 24, 2023, from https://explore-education-statistics.service.gov.uk/find-statistics/key-stage-2-attainment-national-headlines/2022-23
3. (G) indicates that the definition of a word can be found in the glossary at the end of this book.
4. GOV.UK. (2023). *Academic Year 2022/23. Key Stage 1 and Phonics Screening Check Attainment*. Retrieved November 24, 2023, from https://explore-education-statistics.service.gov.uk/find-statistics/key-stage-1-and-phonics-screening-check-attainment#
5. GOV.UK, *Academic Year 2022/23*.
6. Wyse, D. (2023, 20th October). *Teaching Synthetic Phonics and Reading: PIRLS of Wisdom?* Retrieved December 1, 2023, from https://blogs.ucl.ac.uk/ioe/2023/10/10/teaching-synthetic-phonics-and-reading-pirls-of-wisdom/
7. Wyse, D., & Bradbury, A. (2022). The Passion, Pedagogy and Politics of Reading. *English in Education*. Retrieved December 1, 2023, from https://doi.org/10.1080/04250494.2022.2091987
8. The Government Office for Science. (2008). *Foresight Mental Capital and Wellbeing Project (2008). Final Project Report*. The Government Office for Science.
9. Reception class in England is for children aged four to five, so it is equivalent to pre-kindergarten in some other countries.
10. Forward slashes / are used in this book to indicate as closely as possible a phoneme (sound) using letters that approximate that sound.
11. In this book we particularly focus on education for children from age 4 to age 11. We use the term primary education because it is the one used in England where we work, but we intend this to be equivalent to what is called kindergarten and elementary education in other regions (with some variation in children's ages in these phases).
12. PISA is the international comparative assessment of 15-year-old pupils' reading, mathematics, and science, called the Program for International Student Assessment.
    PIRLS, the Programme in International Reading Literacy Study, is another international comparative study. It assesses the reading of pupils aged nine to ten.
13. From 2020 Dominic Wyse became one of four academic advisors for developments in Ireland's national curriculum.
14. Text in double quotation marks in this snapshot is taken from the transcripts of the podcasts called *Sold a Story*, which we have analysed in full: Hanford, E. (2022). *Sold a Story*. Retrieved December 1, 2023, from https://features.apmreports.org/sold-a-story/. There are no page numbers in the transcripts.

15 Ontario Human Rights Commission. (2022). *Right to Read. Public Inquiry into Human Rights Issues Affecting Students with Reading Disabilities.* Government of Ontario. Retrieved December 1, 2023, from www.ohrc.on.ca
16 Ontario Human Rights Commission. (2022). *Executive Summary. Right To Reading. Public Inquiry into Human Rights Issues Affecting Students with Reading Disabilities* (p. 21). Government of Ontario.
17 Students are tested in reading, and other aspects, when they are about age 15 for the PISA study. Students are about aged 10 when they are tested for the PIRLS study. PISA is the more demanding measure because its outcomes reflect what is the end of school education for many students.
18 Gibb, N. (2021). *My Advice to My Successors at the Department for Education.* Retrieved September 29, 2023, from https://www.nickgibb.org.uk/news/my-advice-my-successors-department-education
19 Gibb, N. (2023). *Nick Gibb MP to Step Down at Next General Election.* Retrieved November 18, 2023, from https://www.nickgibb.org.uk/news/nick-gibb-mp-step-down-next-general-election
20 Wyse, *PIRLS of Wisdom?*
21 National Education Union. (2023, 13th November). *Nick Gibb Departure. All the Problems Facing the Educational System Have Deepened during the Period in Which Gibb Has Presided over Schools.* Retrieved November 23, 2023, from https://neu.org.uk/latest/press-releases/nick-gibb-departure
22 There are some schools in England that are not legally required to follow the national curriculum. These include private/independent schools and schools that are 'academies'. In reality, though, academy schools tend to follow the national curriculum, not least because they have to take part in the national statutory assessments, and they are inspected by the inspectorate Ofsted, who enforced key features of education policy such as synthetic phonics.
23 From "Note 1": Department for Education (DfE). (2022). *Validation of Systematic Synthetic Phonics Programmes: Supporting Documentation.* Updated 18th January 2022. Retrieved March 2, 2022, from https://www.gov.uk/government/publications/phonics-teaching-materials-core-criteria-and-self-assessment/validation-of-systematic-synthetic-phonics-programmes-supporting-documentation#essential-core-criteria
24 Madhaus, G., & Russell, M. (2009/2010). Paradoxes of High-Stakes Testing. *The Journal of Education, 190*, 21–30.
25 Wyse, D., Bradbury, A., & Trollope, R. (2022). *The Independent Commission on Assessment in Primary Education. Final Report.* Retrieved December 1, 2023, from https://www.icape.org.uk
26 Retrieved December 1, 2023, from https://www.gov.uk/government/publications/school-inspection-handbook-eif/school-inspection-handbook, pages 241 to 245 of the School Inspection Handbook of the time.
27 Jones, G. (2019, 12th November). *Early Reading and the Education Inspection Framework.* Retrieved December 1, 2023, from https://educationinspection.blog.gov.uk/2019/11/04/early-reading-and-the-education-inspection-framework/
28 Perryman, J., Bradbury, A., Calvert, G., & Kilian, K. (2023). *Beyond Ofsted: An Inquiry into the Future of School Inspection. Final Report of the Inquiry.* National Education Union (NEU).
29 The Department for Education (DfE). (2019). *The ITT Core Content Framework.* Department for Education.
30 Ellis, V. (2023). *England's ITE Crisis Is a Wake-Up Call on Academic Autonomy.* Times Higher Education. Retrieved November 22, 2023, from https://www.timeshighereducation.com/opinion/englands-ite-crisis-wake-call-academic-autonomy
31 Department for Education (DfE). (2023). *The Reading Framework.* Department for Education.
32 Bradbury, A. (2018). The Impact of the Phonics Screening Check on Grouping by Ability: A 'Necessary Evil' Amid the Policy Storm. *British Educational Research Journal, 44*(4), 539–556.
33 Robinson, N., & Armitage, R. (2017). *Australia Urged to Use Phonics in Reading Strategy as British Schools Minister Tours Country.* Retrieved September 29, 2023, from https://www.abc.net.au/news/2017-04-11/could-introducing-phonics-help-children-learn-to-read/8435562
34 Robinson, N. (2019). Reading Wars Rage Again as Australian Government Pushes to Introduce Phonics Test. *ABC News.* Retrieved December 1, 2023, from https://www.abc.net.au/news/2019-06-30/australian-phonics-war-on-how-to-teach-kids-to-read-rages-on/11258944
35 Chall, J. (1983). *Learning to Read: The Great Debate* (Updated ed.). McGraw Hill.

36 Hanford, E. (2022). *Sold a Story*. Retrieved December 1, 2023, from https://features.apmreports.org/sold-a-story/
37 Hanford, *Sold a Story*.
38 Hanford, *Sold a Story*, Episode one. No page number.
39 Hanford, *Sold a Story*, no page number.
40 Clay, M. (1979). *The Early Detection of Reading Difficulties* (3rd ed.). Heinemann.
41 Clay, *Early Detection*, p. 64.
42 Clay, *Early Detection*, p. 75.
43 What Works Clearinghouse. (2013). *Beginning Reading: Reading Recovery*. US Department of Education. Institute of Education Sciences. Retrieved December 1, 2023, from https://ies.ed.gov/ncee/wwc/InterventionReport/420#:~:text=Reading%20Recovery®%20was%20found,1%20with%20low%20literacy%20achievement
44 For example, this tertiary review clearly shows the importance of one-to-one support: Neitzel, A., Lake, C., Pellegrini, M., & Slavin, R. (2021). A Synthesis of Quantitative Research on Programs for Struggling Readers in Elementary Schools. *Reading Research Quarterly*, 57(1), 149–179.
45 We cite evidence of the positive benefits of progressive education in Britain in the last chapter of this book.
46 There is a particularly unacceptable example on Twitter shown in this blog post: Wyse, D., & Bradbury, A. (2023). *The Politics of 'Scientifically-Based' Teaching: Phonics for Reading and Grammar for Writing*. Retrieved November 25, 2023, from https://www.bera.ac.uk/blog/the-politics-of-scientifically-based-teaching-phonics-for-reading-and-grammar-for-writing
47 Calkins, L. M. (1986). *The Art of Teaching Writing*. Heinemann.
48 Hanford, *Sold a Story*. Episode 2.
49 Durkin, D. (1974). A Six Year Study of Children Who Learned to Read in School at the Age of Four. *Reading Research Quarterly*, 10(1), 9–61.
    Clarke, M. M. (1976). *Young Fluent Readers: What Can They Teach Us?* Heinemann Educational.
    Wyse, D. (2007). *How to Help Your Child Read and Write*. Pearson Education Limited.
50 Seidenberg, M. (2017). *Language at the Speed of Sight: How We Read, Why So Many Can't, and What Can Be Done About It*. Basic Books.
51 Seidenberg, M., & McClelland, J. (1989). A Distributed, Developmental Model of Word Recognition and Naming. *Psychological Review*, 96(4), 523–568.
52 Seidenberg, *Language at the Speed of Sight*, p. 336. Underline added.
53 Seidenberg, *Language at the Speed of Sight*. See page 335. For an alternative view from researchers who have experience researching both in health settings and education settings, see this: Torgerson, C., & Torgerson, D. (2017). 'True' Experimental Designs. In D. Wyse, N. Selwyn, E. Smith, & L. Suter (Eds.), *The BERA/SAGE Handbook of Educational Research* (pp. 416–435). SAGE.
54 Connolly, P. (2018). The Trials of Evidence-Based Practice in Education: A Systematic Review of Randomised Controlled TRIALS in Education Research 1980–2016. *Educational Research*, 60, 276–291.
55 Education Endowment Foundation (EEF). (No date). *Improving Literacy in Key Stage 1: Guidance Report* (p. 16). Education Endowment Foundation (EEF). Retrieved November 23, 2023, from https://d2tic4wvo1iusb.cloudfront.net/production/eef-guidance-reports/literacy-ks-1/Literacy_KS1_Guidance_Report_2020.pdf?v=1700712326
56 For example, this is the report summarising five randomised controlled trials, or five different interventions, each with about 100 schools randomly assigned to intervention or control groups: Anders, J., Shure, N., Wyse, D., Sutherland, A., Barnard, M., & Frerichs, J. (2021). *Learning About Culture Overarching Evaluators' Report*. Education Endowment Foundation (EEF).
57 Retrieved December 1, 2023, from https://www.bera.ac.uk/media/in-conversations-with-professor-usha-goswami. Access to the recording of this interview with Usha Goswami is for members of the British Educational Research Association.
58 Goswami, U., & Bryant, P. (1991). *Phonological Skills and Learning to Read*. Lawrence Erlbaum Associates.
59 Ziegler, J., & Goswami, U. (2005). Reading Acquisition, Developmental Dyslexia and Skilled Reading Across Languages: A Psycholinguistic Grain Size Theory. *Psychological Bulletin*, 131(1), 3–29.

60 Wyse, D., & Goswami, U. (2008). Synthetic Phonics and the Teaching of Reading. *British Educational Research Journal, 34*(6), 691–710.
61 EdWeek Research Centre. (2020). *Early Reading Instruction: Results of a National Survey.* Retrieved December 1, 2023, from https://epe.brightspotcdn.com/1b/80/706eba6246599174b0199ac1f3b5/ed-week-reading-instruction-survey-report-final-1.24.20.pdf
62 US Department of Education. (2011). *Reading First Implementation Study 2008–09: Final Report* (p. x). Abt Associates Inc.
63 Reinking, D., Hruby, G., & Risko, V. (2023). Legislating Phonics: Settled Science or Political Polemics? *Teachers College Record, 125*(1), 104–131.
64 Amass, H. (2022, 22nd April). How Phonics Became an Education Culture War. *Tes Magazine.* Retrieved December 1, 2023, from https://www.tes.com/magazine/teaching-learning/primary/how-phonics-became-education-culture-war
65 Barras, C. (2023). As Tricky as ABC. *The New Scientist*, 42–45.
66 Strauss, V. (2023). *ANSWER SHEET: On the Latest Obsession with Phonics.* Retrieved November 25, 2023, from https://www.washingtonpost.com/education/2023/05/23/phonics-reading-analysis/
67 Aukerman, M. (2023). *The Science of Reading and the Media: Is Reporting Biased?* Retrieved November 25, 2023, from https://literacyresearchassociation.org/stories/the-science-of-reading-and-the-media-is-reporting-biased/?s=09
68 Ontario Human Rights Commission, *Right to Read.*
69 School boards are elected bodies in Canada who set the vision for publicly funded schools including their programmes of education.
70 Ontario Human Rights Commission, *Executive Summary.*
71 Phillips, L., Norris, S., & Mason, M. (1996). Longitudinal Effects of Early Literacy Concepts on Reading Achievement: A Kindergarten Intervention and Five-Year Follow-up. *Journal of Literacy Research, 28*, 173–195.
72 Government of Ontario. (2023). *Curriculum and Resources: B2. Language Foundations for Reading and Writing.* Retrieved November 27, 2023, from https://www.dcp.edu.gov.on.ca/en/curriculum/elementary-language/grades/grade-1/b/b2
73 We use the stem 'phon' as a search term to locate text about phonological, phonemes, or phonics in a curriculum.
74 Ministry of Education. (2007). *The New Zealand Curriculum for English-Medium Teaching and Learning in Years 1–13* (p. 54). Learning Media Limited. Underline added.
75 Clay, M. (2016). *Literacy Lessons Designed for Individuals* (p. 129). The Marie Clay Trust.
76 For example, the human rights report from Ontario cites the Rose Review from England.

2 The development of reading and writing

In the last chapter we introduced some different countries and contexts that show how research about the teaching of reading and writing can be used and misused in relation to education practice and policy. We now turn to the first fundamental source of evidence that informs the balanced approach to teaching reading and writing that is the focus of this book: theories of the development of reading and writing. Some theories have been illustrated in visual images and diagrams which, when effective, sum up complex ideas in authentic and memorable ways. If these theories and images are informed by robust research they can helpfully contribute to teaching and learning. But theories and their visual images must not only be evidence based, they must also be strongly logical, and, crucially when applied by teachers in classrooms, they should support more effective teaching. We review some theories and visual models that have been influential, including some that have become popular with teachers. We also show how these models all have limitations, and hence at the end of the chapter we present a new theory and visual representation of teaching reading and writing.

The three cues of reading

The three cues of reading is an important place to begin because, as we showed in Chapter 1, the idea of cues has been influential, controversial, and also misinterpreted. Ken Goodman published his theory about the errors that children made when reading aloud in his paper from 1967 called "Reading: A Psycholinguistic Guessing Game", published in *The Journal of the Reading Specialist*, now called *Literacy Research and Instruction*. Towards the end of the paper Goodman presented what he called a series of 11 non-sequential "steps". The following quote from step number five of the model is key to the origins of what some people imprecisely call the 'three cueing' system. Goodman argued that when a pupil is faced with a word that they are unsure of, the pupil "searches his memory for related <u>syntactic, semantic and phonological cues</u>. This may lead to selection of more graphic cues and to reforming the perceptual image".[1]

Rather than see children's oral reading deviations from a printed text as errors, Goodman said these should be analysed and called "miscues" (see Chapter 3, "How Texts Teach What Children Learn", for more about Goodman's ideas). A key aspect of the Three Cues system was the hypothesis that when readers see a word that they are unsure about how to read, they use three 'cues' to try to work out the word: 1. semantic cues: the potential meaning of the target word based on what has been read so far and in the context of the sentence; 2. syntactic cues: what kind of word the target word might be in relation to the

DOI: 10.4324/9781003442134-4

syntax (G), or grammar, of the word in the sentence; and 3. graphophonic cues: the way that the letters represent phonemes (G) in the target word.

Imagine a child is reading aloud the following sentence: 'When Tim fell into the hole his feet got wet through.' Instead of reading the sentence completely accurately, the child reads this: 'When Tom fell into the hole his feet got wet through'. The substitution of Tom for Tim may show that the child was using semantic and syntactic cueing. Tom is syntactically similar to Tim; that is, it is a noun representing a person's name. The word 'Tom' makes complete sense in the sentence, so the miscue also shows use of semantic cueing.

Even if the child had been using semantic and syntactic cueing successfully, they were not using graphophonic cueing accurately enough because they failed to identify that the letter O in Tom makes the /o/ phoneme, whereas the letter I in Tim makes the /i/ phoneme. If the child had read 'When time fell into the hole his feet got wet through', this may show that the child had used some graphophonic cueing; it does not show semantic cueing because it does not make complete sense (putting aside the creative possibility that 'time' could be a character in a work of fiction!).

Let's take another example to illustrate the three cues. Imagine a child is trying to read the following word: 'read'. In relation to graphophonic cueing, if the child knows that the letter R nearly always makes the /r/ phoneme, then they will have one clue to the word. The next letter, the letter E, is more of a challenge. E can in its own right, or in combination with other letters, represent numerous different phonemes: for example, in the word 'remember', the letter e represents three different phonemes. If the child has been taught that when the letter E is combined with A, it can represent several different phonemes, for example, /ee/ as in seal, /e/ as in dread, or /ea-r/ as in near, then the chid has a somewhat uncertain second graphophonic clue to the word 'read'.

The main problem is that the word 'read' literally cannot be decoded and understood without taking account of the whole sentence, more specifically the semantic and syntactic aspects of the word in the sentence. The phoneme that the letters E and A represent in the word 'read' can *only* be known if the meaning and syntax of the sentence is known. The sentence 'I read a book' makes some sense semantically, but without other words and/or another sentence, it does not make full sense. However, in the sentence 'Tomorrow I will read a book', the meaning of the word 'read' makes full sense, as it does in 'Yesterday I read a book'.

The key point in terms of using knowledge about phonemes to work out this word 'read' is that the middle phoneme of the word 'read' cannot be known without the semantic and syntactic context. And so in this case to preclude children from using semantic and syntactic cues, or what some people call 'guessing', would be completely inappropriate, and indeed nonsense!

The example of the word 'read' is not an isolated example; there are many words that require the semantic and syntactic context to be known in order to know what the phonemes are and hence how a word in text matches words in the child's oral vocabulary. What's more, the process of a child checking any sounding out of letters against known words in their oral vocabulary is a *semantic* check. Most important of all, if a child does not check that the word that they have read makes sense in the context of the sentence and text, then they are not reading at all because reading is about comprehending text, which cannot be done without hypothesising and confirming meaning. While it is appropriate to encourage children to try to sound out words using their knowledge of phonemes and letters, it is also essential that they be encouraged to use semantics and syntactics at the same time to check the accuracy of their attempts to decode.

Many teachers have encountered children who can sound words out but still do not understand the word and sentence, because they fail to link the sounding out of letters successfully with the semantic and syntactic function of the word and confirming the word by linking with their oral vocabulary. Hearing a child decode without sufficient understanding of meaning is an uncomfortable experience, for the child and for the listener, something that has been called 'barking at print' due to the very stilted sound of the reading. A poem by the famous author of children's books Alan Ahlberg called "I-am-in-the-slow-readers-group"[2] is a vivid example of the effects of barking at print, including the emotional impact on children placed in low-ability groups which is a feature of much synthetic phonics teaching (G).

If we return to Goodman's original ideas that became known as the Three Cues System, to say that Goodman rejected the importance of understanding the role of phonemes and letters in words completely is a misreading. Indeed his attention to graphophonic cueing includes this statement in the seminal paper: "Certainly without graphic input there would be no reading. But, the reader uses syntactic and semantic information as well."[3] And this: "Though the beginning reader obviously needs more graphic information in decoding and, therefore, needs to be more precise than skilled readers."[4] It is, however, true to say that Goodman did not emphasise systematic phonics teaching in his publications, and this is a weakness in the contribution. Another limitation of the Three Cues System is that its main focus was on assessment and analysis of children's word-reading, which is one important part of the reading process, rather than a more comprehensive model of *teaching* reading that accommodates all necessary processes of reading.

One of Goodman's main contributions was to say that children's mistakes when reading aloud should not be viewed only as careless errors but of potential evidence of their active thinking and problem solving as they tried to work out what a word was. This is surely an appropriate way to think about children's misconceptions generally and in the specific case of reading. The idea of theorising children's 'errors' as evidence of productive thinking, rather than negative features, that motivated Ken Goodman has had wider application including in children's writing, as Gunther Kress' early work showed.[5] And in the USA this was seen in the work of Jerome Harste and colleagues' work in recognising the logical thinking about the writing of three-year-old children in a deprived area.[6] And if we return briefly to neuroscience research, its findings have emphasised more and more the incredible capacity of the child's brain and mind for curiosity and problem-solving in all aspects of their lives. You would have hoped that we had left deficit models of children's thinking behind many years ago. Unfortunately since that time, the alternative of regarding children's errors as a deficit has been on the rise.

Goodman's idea of semantic, syntactic, and graphophonic cues represented in a diagram with three elements was as far as we are aware first published in a paper by David Pearson in 1976, as Marilyn Jager Adams' exploration discovered.[7] Figure 2.1 shows Pearson's diagram. Interestingly, one of the uses that Pearson saw for the model was to evaluate different teaching activities and resources by considering if the main emphasis of a given activity was on one of the cues or a combination of two or three of the cues. Pearson emphasised the importance of "phonics in context".[9]

32 *The politics and science of reading and writing*

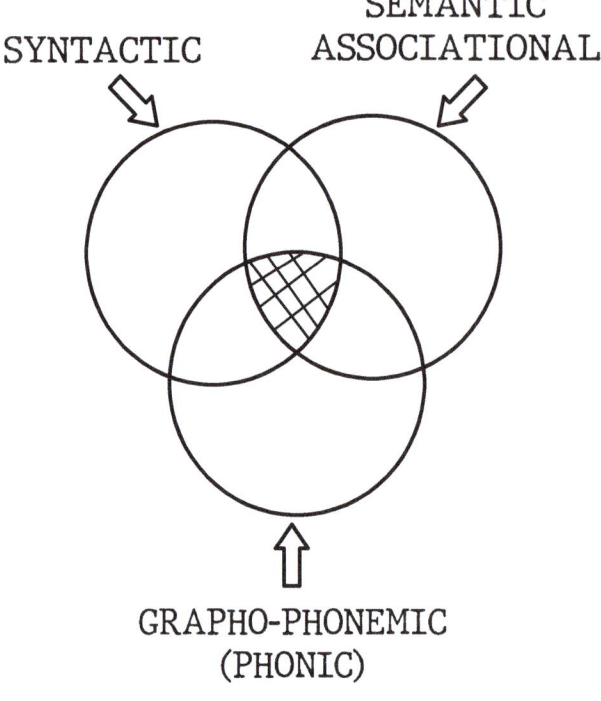

SOURCES OF INFORMATION USED IN READING

Mature reading occurs when all three sources of information are used in concert.

Figure 2.1 Three sources of information used in reading, from Pearson (1976)[8]

Marie Clay's Reading Recovery

Marie Clay also used the idea of cues in her early work. Clay's diagram from her seminal book showed "four types of cue", as can be seen in Figure 2.2.

Clay said this about the diagram:

> **"Four types of cue** From the theory of reading behind these recovery procedures there are four types of cue any two of which may be cross-checked to confirm a response. They can be represented by a square."[11]

Although there are some similarities between Goodman's and Clay's ideas, as we explained in Chapter 1, it is inaccurate to say they are the same. Importantly, in later work cues were renamed in Clay's work as "sources of information in texts",[12] making a further clear distinction between Goodman's ideas and Clay's ideas. What's more, an important part of Clay's work that we do not address in this book was her contribution of "Running Records" that my colleague Sinead Harmey and Bobbie Kabuto addressed in detail,[13]

The development of reading and writing 33

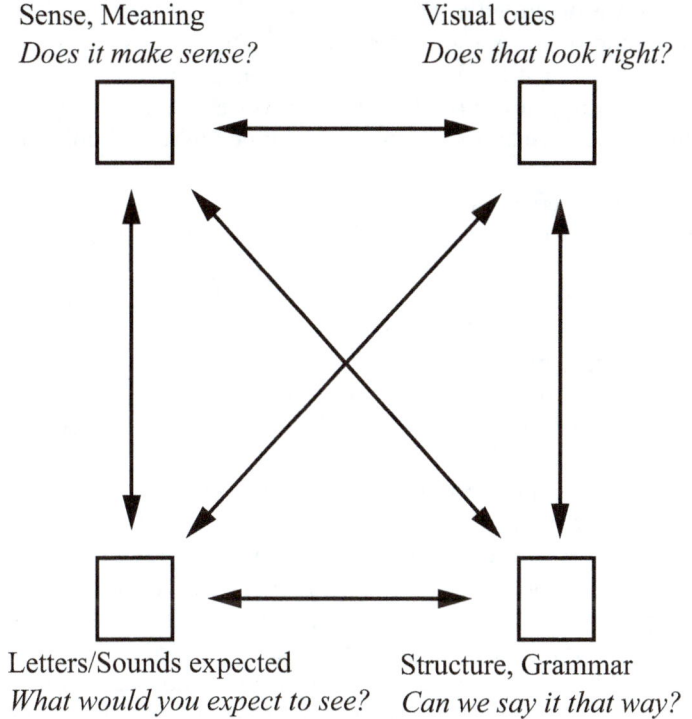

Figure 2.2 Marie Clay's "Four Types of Cue" visual model[10]

along with a more complete review of the theoretical underpinnings of Clay's work than we have space for in this book.

In summary, Clay's Four Types of Cue Model was published in her seminal book about how to help children with reading difficulties. Clay herself said that her Reading Recovery Teaching Procedures were aimed at children who had been at school for one year but were not making satisfactory progress. She clearly stated that her detailed procedures were not necessary for most children. The update of Clay's ideas published in 2016 continued the focus on how to help individual children not making satisfactory progress. Our focus in this chapter is to develop a new model of teaching that might better apply to all children, and in doing so redress the lack of attention to the teaching that is most appropriate for typical readers.

The Simple View of Reading

One of the simplest visual representations of the reading process is not pictographic like the Three Cues Model; it was represented as a form of equation. The 'Simple View of Reading' (SVR) was first published by Philip Gough and William Tunmer. Like the inspiration for Marie Clay's theory, Gough and Tunmer's interest was "reading disability", hence the publication of their paper in the journal *Remedial and Special Education*.[14]

The SVR states that Reading is the product of Decoding and Comprehension, represented in the equation R = D × C. C is not completely synonymous with reading comprehension: it was described as "the process by which, given lexical (i.e. word) information, sentences and discourses are interpreted."[15] The 'interpretation of discourse' is a very broad idea, and one that fits with our emphasis on meaning as the essence of reading. Reading comprehension is a narrower idea that involves understanding of the words of a given text: literal comprehension at first, and in time inferential understanding of texts develops.

Gough and Tunmer were clear that their paper was not theorising teaching: "We begin by noting that the issue we wish to discuss is not that of the place of decoding in reading instruction."[16] The paper outlining their SVR has a strong focus on what they called reading disability. They apply the model in relation to research on readers with dyslexia (G) but also to what they call "hyperlexia", which they explain as the condition of a child who has superior skill in decoding but accompanied by average or even inferior comprehension. If any model is to be used to support an approach to teaching reading, then it needs to be appropriate for typically developing readers, who are the majority in schools, and also for non-typically developing readers.

The SVR is a seminal and important research contribution to understanding reading; however, in addition to its main focus being studies of children with reading difficulties, and that the SVR was never intended to be a model of teaching, we see some other limitations in relation to theorising the *teaching* of reading. Prior to learning to decode, children's development of reading is a gradual process with key milestones. One of these developmental milestones is the ability to recognise some words, such as the child's name, and other words which they are familiar with, for example, shop signs or text on packaging. A child at this stage is comprehending the meaning of such words, because they are able to see the word then say it orally, but they are not likely to be decoding the correspondences between phonemes and letters. Gough and Tunmer correctly argued that "if there is no comprehension, then reading is not taking place" and therefore the converse must be part of their logic: "if there is no decoding, then reading is not taking place",[17] yet the child who recognises their name, or the shop sign, *is* in our view reading yet cannot decode. The child understands that print carries meaning, and they ascribe the correct meaning to the word. They have not, however, fully developed as a reader: they are at a particular stage in their development, and they are yet to develop the ability to decode in the way that they need to. Recognition of stages of development in children's reading is a vital part of teachers' knowledge because it allows them to pitch their teaching at an appropriate level for any child based on their understanding of children's development (see Chapter 5, "The Balanced Approach to Teaching Phonics, Reading, and Writing", for scales of development of reading and writing). For a model to inform the teaching of reading, we think it has to reflect both emergent literacy and also later stages of development in reading and writing.

Because the SVR was not intended as a basis for 'reading instruction', it necessarily does not include some other components relevant to how to teach children to read, for example, the need to stimulate the child's motivation to read in the first place; the nature of texts and how these impact children's reading; and the importance of visual images as an integrated part of the meaning of the text, not least the interweaved story-telling that is a feature of the combination of pictures and words in the best books for children (and increasingly common in digital texts such as social media and communications applications), nor does the simple view include reference to the prior knowledge that readers bring to the text which is essential to their interpretation of texts including as a part of literal and ultimately inferential reading comprehension. Robert Savage and colleagues' thoughtful contribution to understanding the application of the SVR noted the importance of factors

The development of reading and writing 35

outside of the SVR, which they called "shared contextual ecological factors", for example, "shared contexts across countries and schools".[18] The SVR is a well-regarded depiction of an important aspect of reading development, but it is not an adequate model for *teaching* reading.

The interpretation of the simple view in England's Rose Report

In an appendix to England's Rose Report, researchers Morag Stuart and Rhona Stainthorp provided a different description and interpretation of Gough and Tunmer's SVR. The appendix to the Rose Report included a four-quadrant diagram summarising some patterns of children's reading (Figure 2.3).

Figure 2.3 usefully depicts some types of reading difficulties. For example, the idea that children can have good word recognition but also poor comprehension: this is important because these children would need support that enabled their comprehension to develop. The figure was intended to make "explicit to teachers that different kinds of teaching are needed to develop word recognition skills from those that are needed to foster the comprehension of written and spoken language"[20] However, as we have said, Gough and Tunmer's SVR was never intended to be a model for teaching.

The narrative that accompanied the diagram made a case for the *separation* of language comprehension and word recognition as part of teaching. But there appeared to be some uncertainty in this because it was also argued that "these four patterns of performance reflect *relative* differences in the *balance* of word recognition and language comprehension abilities: as both dimensions are continuous, children can vary continuously on each."[21] The implications of this point about children's continuous development on both, and the need to balance them, suggest to us that teaching should connect these elements, not

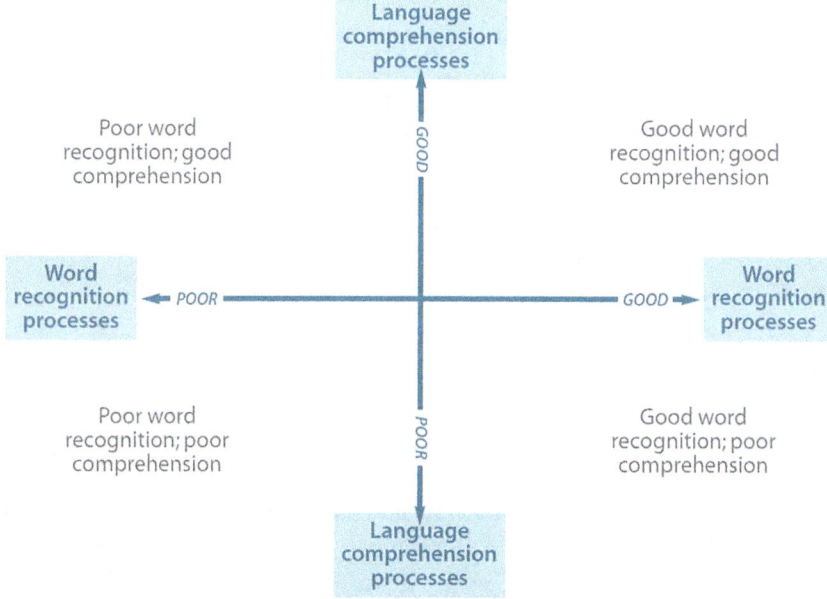

Figure 2.3 Diagram from the Rose Report interpreting the SVR[19]

separate them. This implication also seems justified by a paper that Morag Stuart published with Yvonne Griffiths some years later in which it was concluded that

> The largest gains in word-level reading can be observed for 'at-risk' children when structured phonics instruction is *embedded* within a broader literacy curriculum (Swanson, 2000), *with* word-level and *text reading and writing* exercises, to put their new phonic knowledge and strategies to use when reading or writing new words. (Ehri et al., 2001; Hatcher et al., 1994; Wanzek & Vaughn, 2007)[22]

We review the study by Peter Hatcher et al. in Chapter 4, "The Science of Teaching Reading and Writing".

Somewhat at odds even with its appendix, the Rose Report concluded that phonics should be taught *discretely* from other aspects of reading, and this recommendation has influenced the policies on the teaching of reading in England (and recently some other regions) ever since.

Although for the purposes of analysis in research we might choose to separate word recognition from comprehension, that is not the same as providing evidence that teaching is more effective if these elements are taught more separately. For all these reasons, and because there was undue emphasis on one research study carried out in Scotland,[23] the Rose Report, including its revision of the SVR, did not provide a compelling case for the move to discrete synthetic phonics (G). What's more, an over-emphasis on one element, such as decoding, can result in insufficient emphasis on other elements, such as comprehension.

The main implication that we draw from considering the four quadrants diagram is that individual children may require different emphases in teaching on word recognition *and* comprehension depending on their development but also dependent on the particular text they are reading at any given moment. These developmental differences, in relation to comprehension and word recognition, are not well served by a heavy 'one-approach-fits-all', such as synthetic phonics first and foremost, not least because comprehension is neglected.

The appendix in the Rose Report could not make a definitive argument about how to *teach* reading, as it is a descriptive account based on an interpretation of Gough and Tunmer's SVR; in fact the argument appeared to be unfinished because there was no conclusions section in the appendix. Nor does the version in the Rose Report fit well enough with what we now know, from multiple robust longitudinal experimental research studies, about how to teach children to read, as we show in Chapter 4, "The Science of Teaching Reading and Writing".

The Reading Rope

Another diagram that became well known was the Reading Rope, as can be seen in Figure 2.4. You will recall, for example, that this image appears in the Ontario Human Rights Commission report.

The Reading Rope includes some of the important elements that are required in order to learn to read. Building on the SVR, the unravelled part of the rope on the left-hand side categorises the elements into 'language comprehension' and 'word recognition'. The elements are integrated on the right-hand side of the diagram, as 'skilled reading'; however, the diagram has been used to advocate separate teaching of key elements rather

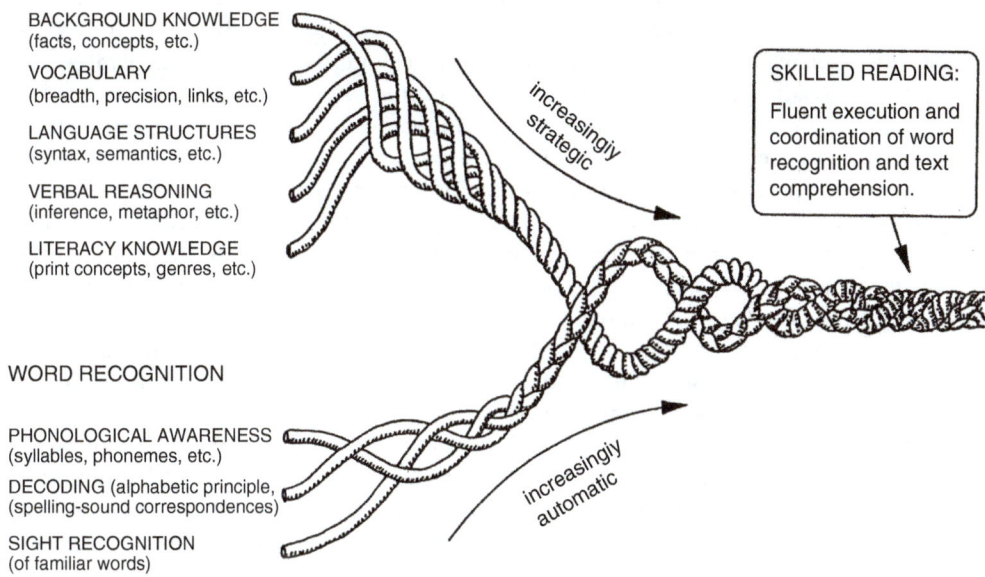

Figure 2.4 The Reading Rope[24]

than contextualised teaching. The originator of the Reading Rope, Hollis Scarborough, said that,

> It is customary to consider separately the strands involved in recognizing individual printed words from those involved in comprehending the meaning of the string of words that have been identified, even though <u>those two processes operate (and develop) interactively</u> rather than independently.[25]

The interactive nature of the components of reading is an important aspect that has not to date been well captured in models of teaching reading, although there are important interactive models of reading development, such as the distributed model of Mark Seidenberg and James McClelland,[26] that have received less attention. The important points made by Hollis Scarborough about the interactions between comprehension and word recognition based on the SVR differ from the basis of the conclusions of England's Rose Report.

The main limitation with the Reading Rope as a possible model for teaching reading is that although a systematic review of research studies informed the chapter in which the Reading Rope image was published, the focus of the systematic review was on children with reading difficulties. This means that the image is not mainly informed by a review of studies of typically developing readers. In addition, the Reading Rope does not include some of the same components of reading that are absent from other models, such as readers' motivation, what readers bring to a text as they comprehend and interpret it, and the importance of the texts that are selected by teachers to support the teaching of reading. The Reading Rope does not account for wider aspects of learning to read such as the social contexts for children's language use and development that are also a vital part of understanding and teaching reading. And in common with nearly all the theories, models, and diagrams reviewed so far, there is no mention of writing, which is a vital underappreciated part of learning to read. Also, in terms of the visual and aesthetic features of the image, which relate at some level to how effectively the logic and meanings are expressed,[27] although the Reading Rope image communicates some important aspects of the reading process, the visual depiction of a rope as an inanimate object doesn't represent well the organic nature of the human mind which learns to read.

One feature of the influential models of reading presented so far in this chapter is how long ago it was when they were first published. It appears that for a model to become influential, it requires a test of time before it gains popular appeal. There have been some more recent visual models. For example, in one of its guidance reports for teachers published in 2019, England's Education Endowment Foundation (EEF)[28] used the visual image of a house to represent the components that lead to reading comprehension, but this is again based on the SVR so has some limitations already outlined in this chapter. It also draws heavily on an image first published in 2011.[29]

Another visual model drawing on the SVR, also based on the metaphor of a building, is Young-Suk Grace Kim's Direct and Indirect Effects Model of Reading (DIER), published in 2023.[30] In addition to its roots in robust research the DIER has three key features: 1. its review of the SVR results in adding identifying important elements of reading that are not present in the simple view, 2. it provides greater recognition of the connections between the different elements of the DIER Model, and 3. it includes vital features such as social-emotional development and discourse knowledge that have been absent from all the other models so far described in this chapter.

Models of writing

In discussion of the selection of models of reading in this chapter, writing has been a feature only in so far as the orthography (G) of text is so closely connected to reading. A novel part of our contribution in this book is to systematically consider the development of reading and writing as both influencing development in each. For that reason we argue that the teaching of reading should systematically include the teaching of writing, and vice versa. Visual models representing the development and teaching of writing are less common than for reading. This reflects the relative neglect of writing as a focus of research and of policy and practice.

The work of Frank Smith became well known at about the same time as those of Ken Goodman. Smith's book *Reading*, first published in 1978, was probably successful because it is very readable! However, too many of its main arguments were unsubstantiated: in fact for a serious attempt to explore reading, it has only six references, four of which are to Smith's own work. Smith's other popular book, *Writing and the Writer*, first published in 1982, has a similar readable journalistic style, including Smith's analysis of his own writing of the book itself, but also a more typical list of research references and chapter notes at the end of the book.

Early on in the book Smith summed up the processes of writing (see Table 2.1). The establishment of the concepts of the two sides of writing as composition versus transcription was one of Smith's important contributions. Smith's main point, and main categorisation in the table, was that when someone is writing, the author role can be in conflict with the secretary role, both of which are needed ultimately to create an effective piece

Table 2.1 Frank Smith's depiction of the processes of writing[31]

Composition (Author)	Transcription (Secretary)
Getting ideas	Physical effort of writing
Selecting words	Spelling
Grammar	Capitalisation
	Punctuation
	Paragraphs
	Legibility

of writing. Recognition that composition and transcription components are necessary but sometimes in competition became linked with the idea that teaching writing needed to accommodate time for different drafts of writing to be produced, as opposed to the one-off writing exercises that historically had been common in lessons. In early drafts of writing the writer could pay less attention to the transcription components which could be addressed more in later drafts, something which Smith and others have recognised as akin to the process that experienced writers go through.[32]

Although Smith's distinction between composition and transcription had merit his work on writing was not quite as popular with teachers as two other researchers in the USA, Donald Graves, and Lucy Calkins who we introduced in Chapter 1. As far as teaching writing in primary education was concerned, it was Donald Graves who had the most popularity. We return to Graves' work and what research says about writing in Chapter 4.

The teaching of writing has not attracted popular visual models that have become influential with teachers in the way that the teaching of reading has. For that reason we now turn to two interesting academic models. Although less well known than the SVR, a simple view of *writing* was, as far as we know, first proposed by the US-based researchers Connie Juel and colleagues as part of their 'path analysis' of longitudinal data.[33] Subsequently Virginia Berninger, Steve Graham, and colleagues, also working from a cognitive perspective, developed a simpler visual model[34] which emerged from work they did around 1998 on handwriting. It has long been recognised that fluent handwriting is important to enable fluent composition of writing. We have constructed a visual image of the simple view of writing (Figure 2.5) from the description in the paper written in 2002. The simple view of writing reported in the paper from 2002 is important because it makes clear that effective teaching requires a focus on multiple components of writing, including a range of transcription and composition components.

Also working from a cognitive perspective, John Hayes' model (Figure 2.6) proposed that the two key components of writing are the environment for writing and the individual writer. The environment for writing activities, or *task environment* in the diagram, is subdivided into the *social environment* and the *physical environment*. A key component of the social environment is the actual *audience* for the writing (rather than simply knowledge about audience in more general terms). This will be a known audience if, for example, writing a letter to a particular person, or unknown/anticipated audience if, for example, writing a story. *Collaborators* may be a part of the social environment for writing. *The physical environment* includes the composing medium, for example, pen and paper or word processor. Any text, notes, or stimuli for writing are part of *the text so far*.

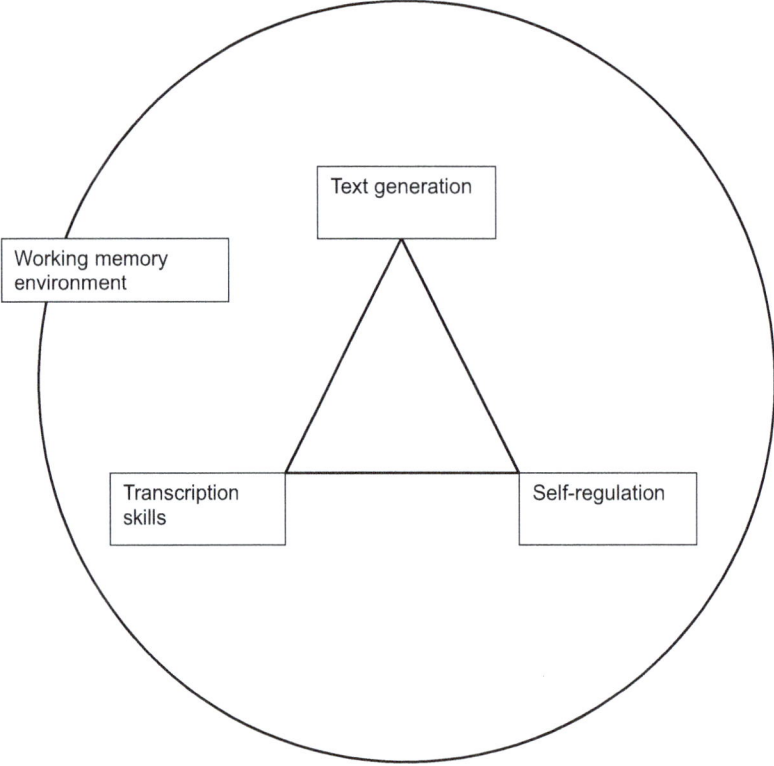

Figure 2.5 Model of a simple view of writing

The individual and their writing are characterised by the writer's *cognitive processes, motivation, working memory* (G), and *long-term memory*. The writer's motivation is subdivided into *goals* for writing, their *predispositions, beliefs and attitudes*, and *cost/benefit estimates* where writers will weigh up what the benefits are for them doing the writing in the first place.

The writing process, it was argued by Hayes, like all mental processes, is driven by working memory. *Phonological memory* allows the writer to convert spoken language into written language, and vice versa. The *visuospatial sketchpad* deals with information that is visual or spatial in character. For example, when children engage with images in texts, this requires processing. Semantics, and *semantic memory*, is a vital part of the writing process and the process of reading, as we have already shown. Semantics, or meaning, exists at many levels, from the overall intention that underlies a text, to the inferences that readers make, to the smaller details of the literal meanings created through the cohesion of sentences, phrases, and words.

Cognitive processes, in Hayes' model, include *text interpretation*. The writing process requires *reflection* and continual interpretation and re-interpretation of what the writer has already written in order to know how to continue writing, which is the *text production*.

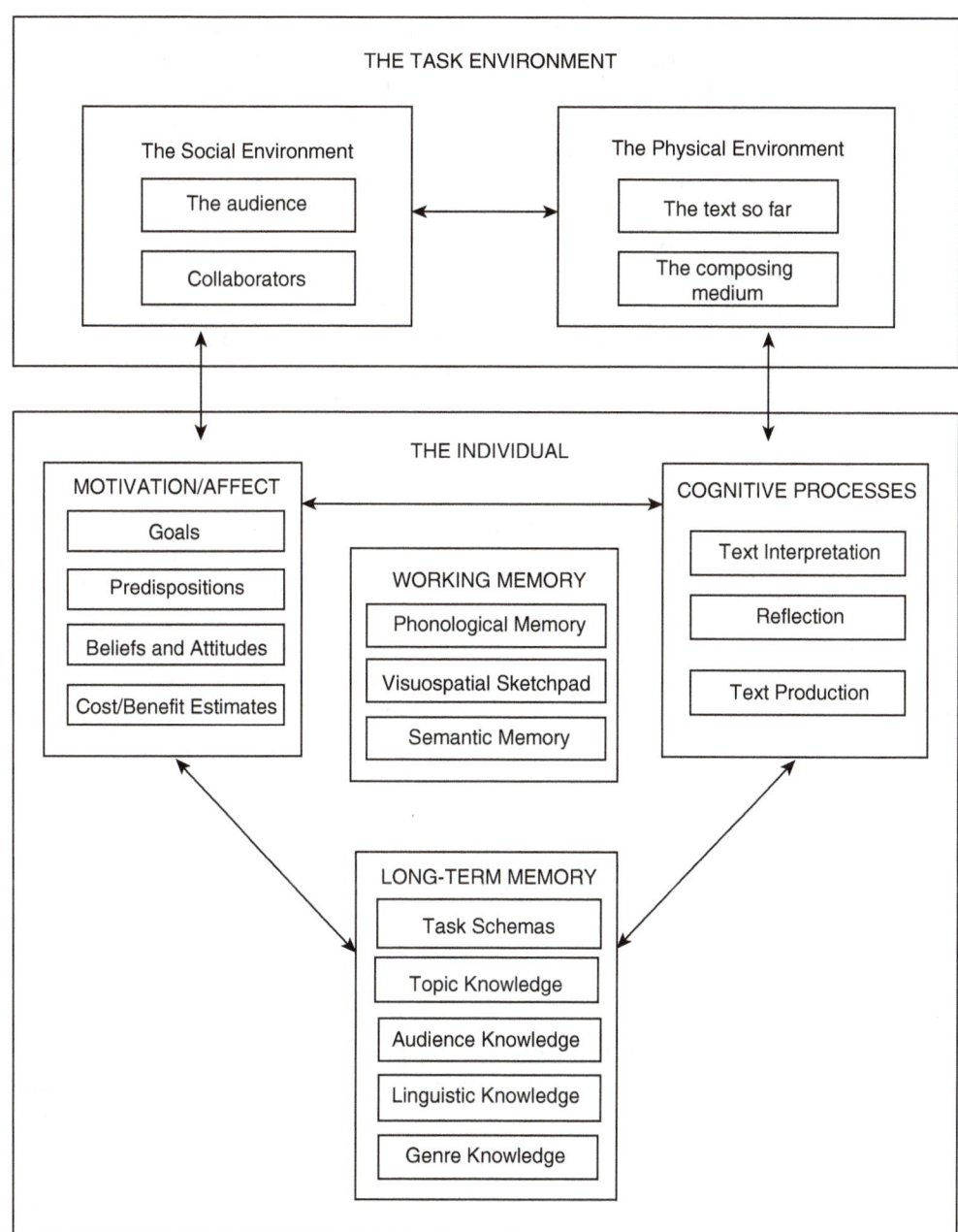

Figure 2.6 Cognitive perspective on writing processes[35]

Writing also requires use of the *long term memory*. *Task schemas* are established ways of thinking about a task. Within the task schema of writing, the writer has to be cognizant of what the audience for the writing might expect. For any writing there is a need to express thoughts in relation to a particular topic, something that requires *topic knowledge*. For non-fiction writing, the particular use of material collected through research is part of this, but also the knowledge the writer has more generally about the topic. For the fiction writer the topic is bound to the overall concept of the story and its realisation through the characters in the story. *Linguistic knowledge* requires a precise understanding of how language is used, including grammar. Genre *knowledge*[36] is knowledge of the particular conventions that are required for an effective piece of writing in the particular genre, a concept we prefer to call knowledge about 'text structures'.

These models of writing suggest to us that decontextualised and narrow teaching of aspects such as phonemes, letters, handwriting, spelling, and grammar is unlikely to be effective. For example, our own research has shown that a range of types of grammar teaching have either been ineffective or at best only had minor influences on pupils' writing and that there are better multi-component strategies for improving children's writing.[37]

The Double Helix of Reading and Writing

All the models we have featured in this chapter so far shed light on important aspects of *learning* to read and write. However, in different ways they all have some limitations in relation to representing and informing *teaching*. One limitation is that they were all designed to illustrate reading *or* writing without systematically connecting both forms at all levels. In a number of cases the models are more appropriate as a way to represent selected parts of reading development but less useful as a comprehensive model of the processes of teaching reading and writing. A number of the models arose from research about struggling readers rather than typically developing readers. It is important that a theory and model of teaching reading and writing be able to accommodate both typically developing readers and writers *and* those who are less typical. Finally, aesthetically and logically, the metaphors that images represent should represent appropriately what are human processes of language use. In our view inanimate objects as metaphors fail to capture the essence of reading and writing: that they are unique characteristics of the human species.

Figure 2.7 is a new model that builds on our analysis of the range of models presented in this chapter to represent a new theory of effective teaching of reading and writing. The box shows the definitions of the key words that are part of Figure 2.7. The new model was created by first reviewing robust empirical research studies on effective teaching of reading (see Chapter 4, "The Science of Teaching Reading and Writing." See also the Wyse and Hacking 2024 paper in the peer-reviewed journal *Literacy*.[38]). Influential theories and models of reading and writing that had sufficient links with teaching were also reviewed, as you have seen in this chapter. Our aim was to create a theory and visual model that would be a good fit with what primary teachers have to do in their practice, based on the most up-to-date analysis of our selections of existing theories and empirical research studies but also our knowledge of teachers' practices derived from our work with teachers. The decision to base the model on the shape of the double helix emerged while we attempted to represent our theory in a visual model that would have some relevance to the organic nature of the human child as a reader. Finally, the process of writing about the model resulted in further checking of and adjustments to the representations of concepts, their wording, and their emphases in the lines, shapes, and shading of the figure.

One of the most important concepts underpinning the Double Helix of Reading and Writing is that the individual components are systematically connected, during the teaching of phonics, reading, and writing. Two seminal studies demonstrated the importance of the connections between phonics and other elements of reading. Anne Cunningham's study[39] of typically developing readers established that teaching key elements such as awareness of phonemes in a contextualised way was more effective than decontextualised or discrete teaching. And in relation to children with reading difficulties, on the basis of their experimental trial, Peter Hatcher, Charles Hulme, and Andrew Ellis[40] established that emphasis on phonological skills needs to be integrated with the teaching of reading: they called this "the phonological linkage hypothesis". We give some more information about these studies in Chapter 4, "The Science of Teaching Reading and Writing", which provides the research' evidence that also informs our theory and model.

Key for Figure 2.7, the Double Helix of Reading and Writing

The child and their language(s): reading and writing originates from the human capacity for oral language.

The child and their environment including texts: the child, their learning, and the home and education environment are at the heart of the model. Texts, including books, are part of the environment that a child encounters, whether at school, at home, or in other contexts.

Motivation and meaning: a child has to be motivated to engage with any text. This motivation is driven by human curiosity and the drive for communicating and understanding meaning.

Babies first become aware of **sound** in general. In time this develops as understanding of spoken sounds and ultimately understanding of the concept of the phoneme.

Babies encounter **objects** in their environment. In time, implements and materials that enable the **making of marks** are used.

Comprehension begins as oral language comprehension, then develops as reading comprehension.

The **composition** of writing is part of the meaning-making processes of reading and writing.

Text structures: aspects of text above the level of words and sentences – form, genre, titles, sections, layout, paragraphs.

Sentences: organisation of **words** as the building blocks of written language, supported by punctuation.

Phonological awareness: awareness of the sound structures of words, such as syllables.

Phonemes (the smallest unit of sound in a spoken word) are represented in written language by **letters**.

Knowledge of **morphemes** (the smallest meaningful units of written language) is particularly useful for spelling development.

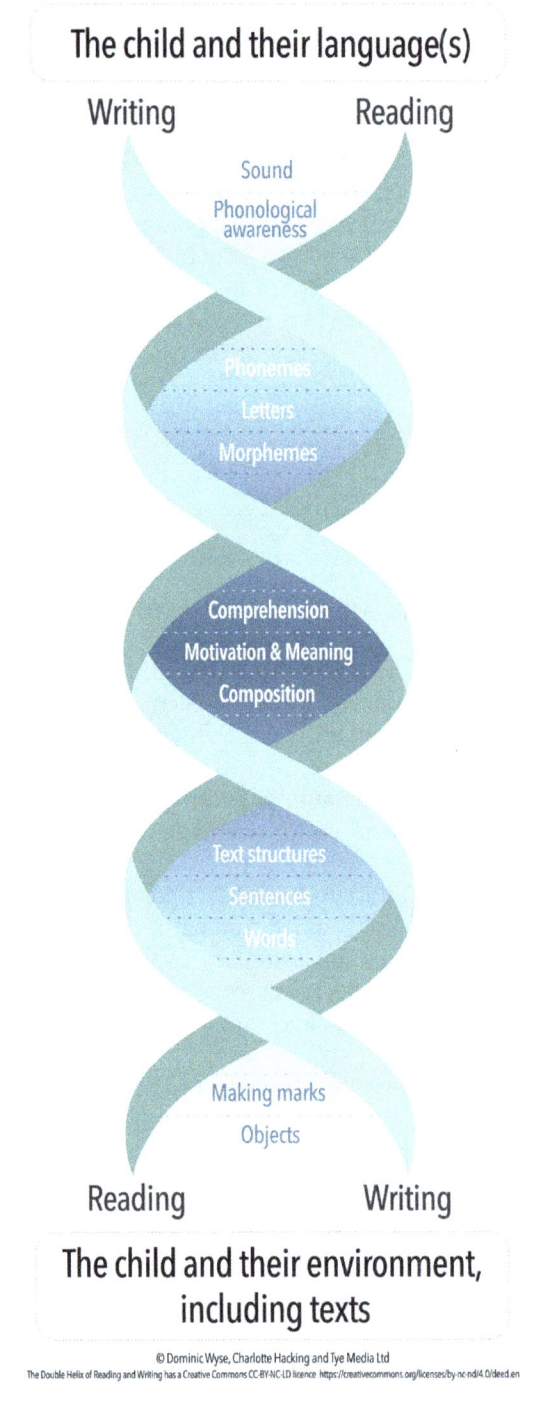

Figure 2.7 The Double Helix of Reading and Writing[41]

Unlike other models that are based on inanimate objects or are abstract diagrams, our model is based on a living phenomenon and the essence of life, the double helix shape that is part of human DNA. The use of this inspiration for our visual image is an important reminder that learning to read is very much a phenomenon unique to the human animal: a combination of the brain, mind, and body. The link with the organic nature of the human brain is also why the child, and the literacy environment they find themselves in, are the starting points for teaching, represented as surrounding the top and bottom of the model. And strongly connected to the child's language and their environment is children's motivation and curiosity to find meanings, represented at the centre of the model. Children bring their experiences to any teaching context, including their prior knowledge of a range of texts.

The diagram represents the idea that all processes of oral and written language start to develop in embryonic and emergent forms as soon as children are born, based on the development of the brain, eyes, and ears during the time prior to birth. Children's development of reading and writing is not a simple linear progression; hence the model allows for different emphases on the different elements, depending on children's development. These developmental aspects are a vital part of teachers' knowledge which links with teaching through their decisions on the most relevant interaction and activities for children.

The elements at the outer edges of the model represent the fundamental contexts for literacy. The two curled ribbons or strands, which pass up and down the model, illustrate that reading and writing are closely connected and influence development in each other. If one looks at the end of a ribbon labelled 'reading', then proceeds to follow the strand up or down, it arrives at writing, and vice versa.

The sections at the top and bottom of the diagram represent the first months of a human life, which are focused on basic survival and in time become more focused on development of language and literacy. The outer edges of the model begin with people and their use of language(s), which are the human baby's first encounter with the world of language as part of the senses of sight, hearing, and touch. Quite soon the baby will also engage with objects, for example, grasping toys, which will in time become opportunities to make marks with fingers then with implements. The child's environment is to varying degrees full of texts, by which we mean any types of written language in the child's environment, including signs, books, and digital sources. Support from the people in the child's family and immediate community is augmented in time by more formal structures of education.

There are five main sections in the model, represented by the five spaces bounded by the curves of the strands. The five spaces are each divided into two or three components essential to learning to read and write. The teaching emphases necessary for any of these sections and their components will vary according to the age of children and the needs of individual children.

The central space of the five, which features motivation and meaning, comprehension, and composition, should orient and drive development in all other sections; hence it has the darkest-colour background. Effective teaching is rooted in the recognition that if children are to learn to read and write most effectively then they need to be motivated because motivation and reading achievement influence each other. It is hoped that children will be intrinsically motivated to read and write for a range of purposes. Teachers play an important part in encouraging reading motivation, including carefully selecting activities and resources to engage children's interests. In the teaching of reading, this motivation happens, for example, through the careful selection of texts by the teacher, another hallmark of this book and our approach.

Communication of meaning is the organising force of all human language; therefore the teaching of reading and writing should be driven by composing and comprehending meaning. All the constituent knowledge and skills of reading and writing, represented in the other spaces, contribute to comprehending written language in reading and composing through writing. Comprehension begins with noticing and thinking about images and text in the child's environments. Composition begins with the intention to communicate meaning through marks.

The spaces directly above and below the central space represent the smaller parts of language that are the building blocks of comprehension and composition. Their subservience to the central space is depicted with lighter grey backgrounds. Early awareness of sound in the environment, including the organised sounds of music, is supported in time by phonological awareness, which is awareness of the sound structures of words in oral language such as syllables.

When children are about age five, teaching in early years settings and schools will prioritise learning about how phonemes (G) are represented by letters[42] in words. Getting the balance right between this phonics teaching and other elements in the Double Helix of Reading and Writing is fundamental. This teaching about phonemes and letters will always be rooted in meaning as the driving force of language, and so each lesson will start with whole texts in order that children always make strong connections between learning about the smaller parts of language and their functions as part of whole texts. The teaching will also be built on positive assessments of children's learning prior to this point, for example, recognition that children will be aware of some written words, such as their name and signs and texts that are part of home and their community. These prior experiences will include multiple languages for many children. Assessments of children's reading will efficiently and accurately determine when they no longer need phonics teaching for reading, and as a result their teaching will focus more on a wide range of engagements with texts.

Teaching about phonemes and letters is integrated with other aspects of reading and writing. In addition to the whole texts which are the starting point for all lessons, words, and sentences as part of the meanings of texts are constant referents to contextualise understanding about the links between phonemes, letters, and words and to ensure accurate knowledge about language underpins teaching. The integration of reading and writing in all lessons includes attention to the ways in which words are structured in sentences as part of the grammar of language.

Some structural aspects of texts are referred to early on in the child's development in school, for example, the concepts that are part of books, such as author, front cover, and physical orientation of conventional written English – such as moving from left to right on the page. Other aspects of text structures, for example, the particular features that are part of different text forms, will be addressed as children develop including through wider attention to reading and writing across the whole curriculum.

The Double Helix of Reading and Writing is a new model to represent what is most important in the effective teaching of reading and writing. It has connections with other models of reading and writing outlined in this chapter, but it aims to take the field forward by addressing some limitations in previous models. All the chapters in this book are informed by or inform the Double Helix of Reading and Writing. In Chapter 4, "The Science of Teaching Reading and Writing", we address the empirical research base for the model and the balanced approach, particularly evidence on effective teaching of reading and writing. The chapters in the second half of the book give detailed examples of teaching, all of which are informed by the model: Chapter 5 goes into more detail about the knowledge that teachers need in order to implement the balanced approach informed by the Double Helix. But first we turn to the nature of texts that can be used to teach reading and writing.

Notes

1. Goodman, K. (1967). Reading: A Psycholinguistic Guessing Game. *Literacy Research and Instruction*, 6(4), 126–135. Retrieved December 1, 2023, from https://doi.org/10.1080/19388076709556976. Underline added.
2. Ahlberg, A., & Ahlberg, J. (1984). *Please Mrs Butler*. Puffin.
3. Goodman, Reading: A Psycholinguistic Guessing Game.
4. Goodman, Reading: A Psycholinguistic Guessing Game.
5. Kress, G. (1982). *Learning to Write*. Routledge & Kegan Paul.
6. Harste, J. C., Woodward, V. A., & Burke, C. L. (1984). *Language Stories & Literacy Lessons*. Heinemann Educational Books.
7. Adams, M. J. (2000). *The Three-Cueing System*. Retrieved July 30, 2023, from http://www.ednews.org/articles/6017/1/The-Three-Cueing-System/Page1.html
8. Pearson, D. (1976). A Psycholinguistic Model of Reading. *Language Arts*, 53(3), 309–314. NCTE has granted permission to reproduce this figure.
9. Pearson, Psycholinguistic Model of Reading.
10. Clay, M. (1979). *The Early Detection of Reading Difficulties* (p. 74, 3rd ed.). Heinemann Education. All reasonable attempts have been made to locate and contact copyright holders of this image.
11. Clay, *Early Detection*.
12. Clay, M. (2016). *Literacy Lessons Designed for Individuals* (p. 129). The Marie Clay Trust.
13. Harmey, S., & Kabuto, B. (2018). Metatheoretical Differences between Running Records and Miscue Analysis: Implications for Analysis of Oral Reading Behaviors. *Research in the Teaching of English*, 53(1), 11–33.
14. Gough, P. B., & Tunmer, W. E. (1986). Decoding, Reading and Reading Disability. *Remedial and Special Education*, 7(1), 6–10. Retrieved December 1, 2023, from https://doi.org/10.1177/074193258600700104
15. Gough & Tunmer, Decoding.
16. Gough & Tunmer, Decoding.
17. The Gough and Tunmer 1986 paper argues this but does not use this precise wording.
18. Savage, R., Burgos, G., Wood, E., & Piquette, N. (2015). The Simple View of Reading as a Framework for National Literacy Initiatives: A Hierarchical Model of Pupil-Level and Classroom-Level Factors. *British Educational Research Journal*, 41(5), 820–844.
19. Rose, J. (2006). *Independent Review of the Teaching of Early Reading: Final Report*. DfES Publications.
20. Rose, *Independent Review*. Italic in original. Underline added.
21. Rose, *Independent Review*. Italic in original. Underline added, p. 80.
22. Griffiths, Y., & Stuart, M. (2013). Reviewing Evidence-Based Practice for Pupils with Dyslexia and Literacy Difficulties. *Journal of Research in Reading*, 36(1), 96–116. Italic font added.
23. See Wyse, D., & Goswami, U. (2008). Synthetic Phonics and the Teaching of Reading. *British Educational Research Journal*, 34(6), 691–710.
24. Scarborough, H. (2001). Connecting Early Language and Literacy to Later Reading (Dis)abilities: Evidence, Theory, and Practice. In S. Neuman & D. Dickinson (Eds.), *Handbook for Research in Early Literacy*. Guilford Press. Permission to use this figure was paid for via the CCC Marketplace.
25. Scarborough, Connecting Early Language. Underline added.
26. Seidenberg, M., & McClelland, J. (1989). A Distributed, Developmental Model of Word Recognition and Naming. *Psychological Review*, 96(4), 523–568.
27. Tufte, E. R. (1983). *The Visual Display of Quantitative Information*. Graphics Press USA.
28. Higgins, S., Martell, T., Waugh, D., Henderson, P., & Sharples, J. (n/d published 2021). *Improving Literacy in Key Stage 2: Guidance Report*. Education Endowment Foundation (EEF).
29. Hogan, T., Bridges, M. S., Justice, L., & Cain, K. (2011). Increasing Higher Level Language Skills to Improve Reading Comprehension. *University of Nebraska – Lincoln Special Education and Communication Disorders Faculty Publications*, 79, 1–20.
30. Kim, Y.-S. G. (2023). Simplicity Meets Complexity: Expanding the Simple View of Reading with the Direct and Indirect Effects Model of Reading (DIER). In S. Cabell, S. Neuman, & N. Patton-Terry (Eds.), *Handbook on the Science of Early Literacy* (pp. 9–22). Guilford Press.
31. Smith, F. (1995). *Writing and the Write* (2nd ed.). Routledge. Table reproduced with permission from Routledge.
32. Wyse, D. (2017). *How Writing Works: From the Invention of the Alphabet to the Rise of Social Media*. Cambridge University Press.

33 Juel, C., Griffith, P., & Gough, P. (1986). Acquisition of Literacy: A Longitudinal Study of Children in First and Second Grade. *Journal of Educational Psychology, 78*(4), 243–255.
34 Berninger, V. W., Vaughan, K., Abbott, R., Begay, K., Coleman, K., Curtin, G., Hawkins, J., & Graham, S. (2002). Teaching Spelling and Composition Alone and Together: Implications for the Simple View of Writing. *Journal of Educational Psychology, 94*(2), 291–304.
35 Hayes, J. R. (2006). New Directions in Writing Theory. In C. MacArthur, S. Graham, & J. Fitzgerald (Eds.), *Handbook of Writing Research* (pp. 28–40). The Guilford Press. Permission to use this figure was paid for via the CCC Marketplace.
36 Genre in this case does not only refer to the genres of novels, such as science fiction, historical fiction, and so on, but refers to different forms of writing such as newspaper front pages, dictionary entries, shopping lists, poems, and other elements.
37 Wyse, *How Writing Works*.
  Wyse, D., Aarts, B., Anders, J., de Gennaro, A., Dockrell, J., Manyukhina, Y., Sing, S., & Torgerson, C. (2022). *Grammar and Writing in England's National Curriculum. A Randomised Controlled Trial and Implementation and Process Evaluation of Englicious*. Retrieved December 1, 2023, from https://discovery.ucl.ac.uk/id/eprint/10144257/
  Wyse, D., & Torgerson, C. (2017). Experimental Trials and 'What Works?' in Education: The Case of Grammar for Writing. *British Educational Research Journal, 43*(6), 1019–1047. Retrieved December 1, 2023, from https://doi.org/10.1002/berj.3315(30)
38 Wyse, D. and Hacking, C. (2024). Decoding, Reading and Writing: The Double Helix Theory of Teaching. *Literacy*.
39 Cunningham, A. (1990). Explicit Versus Implicit Instruction in Phonemic Awareness. *Journal of Experimental Child Psychology, 50*, 429–444.
40 Hatcher, P., Hulme, C., & Ellis, A. (1994). Ameliorating Early Reading Failure by Integrating the Teaching of Reading and Phonological Skills: The Phonological Linkage Hypothesis. *Child Development, 60*, 41–57.
41 Reproduction of 'The Double Helix' image is permitted under the CC license provided the following reference is cited in full: Dominic Wyse & Charlotte Hacking (2024). *The Balancing Act: An evidence-based approach to teaching phonics, reading and writing*. Routledge.
42 We use the term 'letters' because this aspect of our model refers to alphabetic languages.

3 How texts teach what children learn

Books created by authors for young readers, in the normal ways that fiction and other books are created and published (known as the *trade press*), are first and foremost written as part of a creative process to engage, excite, motivate, and stimulate children's curiosity and emotions. These 'real books' also enable children to experience and learn a wide range of important things beyond only learning to decode text. The title of this chapter is almost the same as the title of a short text about teaching reading that became influential in the late 1980s: Margaret Meek Spencer's book *How Texts Teach What Readers Learn* (Meek, 1988).[1] Books for children specially developed for reading schemes were at the time rather unimaginative. Their texts had vocabulary that was controlled to ensure that children only encountered words that would be straightforward for them to read, according to their level on a reading scheme. These words were repeated in texts so that children would learn them. The modern equivalent is 'decodable books' (G) whose vocabularies are controlled to match the sequences of synthetic phonics teaching (G).

To give an example of how Meek saw texts, she illustrated the ways in which a seemingly simple picture book for young children, the still popular *Rosie's Walk* by Pat Hutchins (1968),[2] can help children learn many things: for example, the concepts of author, title, dedicatees, front cover; the importance of well-drawn characters that Meek reminded us is a feature of all good story writing; the careful orientation of single and double pages, drawing the reader in to certain features; and, in particular, the interplay between texts and pictures that goes way beyond simple literal interpretation of words only. Most important of all are the layers of meaning that the reader can comprehend in the text. For example, understanding the intrigue of the fox, a main character in *Rosie's Walk*, who appears only in the pictures and not in the words of the text. The legacy and contemporary relevance of Meek Spencer's work was memorably captured in 2022 in a special issue of the journal *English in Education* published by the UK-based National Association for the Teaching of English (NATE) edited by Judith Graham and Colin Mills.[3]

Real books and whole language

Three years before Margaret Meek Spencer produced her book, another short book had offered an approach to teaching reading that became known as *The Real Book Approach*, particularly in England. Liz Waterland's experience as a teacher delivering systematic phonics teaching led her to be dissatisfied with her children's response to this teaching and as she saw it their lack of reading development: her book was called *Read With Me. An Apprenticeship Approach to Reading*.[4] The real book approach focused first and foremost on teachers' selections of texts that would engage children's attention and hopefully motivate them to learn to read. Elements of reading such as phonics were still taught but in a more incidental way than current versions of systematic phonics.

Theories and practical approaches similar to the real book approach were also being tried in the USA and other countries; in particular the work of Ken and Yetta Goodman was influential and became known as the *whole-language approach*. In Chapter 2, we described how Ken Goodman's influential paper of 1967 is regarded as central to the debate.[5] Given the repeated calls for attention to 'the science of reading', perhaps surprisingly to some people, Goodman built his argument on an appeal to science: the motivation for his paper was to replace "pre-existing, naïve, common-sense notions" to "offer a more viable scientific alternative".[6]

A vital characteristic of Goodman's work was his prior experience as a teacher: his theory of reading drew from his experience of teaching then researching how children read in schools. Goodman's idea of analysing children's word reading errors when reading aloud to gain insight into their mental processing, which he called "miscue analysis", provided teachers with a tool to think more deeply about children's reading.

Partly in response to Goodman's ideas, the seminal paper about the Simple View of Reading[7] (which we addressed in Chapter 2) critically addressed Goodman's theory. One of the components of Goodman's theory was that learning to read was almost the same as learning to talk, so reading was seen as a natural process. This aspect of Goodman's theory was overplayed because we now have further research evidence showing that learning to read and write require systematic teaching, which is not the same as oral language that develops more naturally for nearly all children.

In other research papers claims were made in support of or in opposition to Goodman's theory on the basis of whether studies of people's eye movements while reading proved that people attend to every letter when reading words or whether they only attend to some letters in a word in order to read it.[8] Irrespective of these arguments about 'precise perception', the lack of attention to systematic phonics teaching in Goodman's theories can, with hindsight, be seen as a weakness. Since Goodman published his theory, multiple research studies have confirmed the beneficial effect of teaching children in the early stages of learning to read about letters and the speech sounds that they represent.

In 2023 the researcher Catherine Compton-Lilly published a paper that re-examined the legacy of the work of Ken Goodman.[9] Goodman's early experiences in schools had led him to focus particularly on the language differences that pupils in different cultural groups brought to their processes of reading. In a rebuttal of another researcher's criticisms of his work, Goodman had this to say:

> There is abundant evidence black children wherever they are and whatever the status of their dialects are not linguistically deprived. Rystrom is a diligent researcher. It seems predictable that if he pursues this direction, he will also find it a dead end. He certainly will not find the evidence to support the flamboyant, baseless assertions of pseudo-authorities such as Carl Bereiter and Siegfried Engelmann (1966). The myth of linguistic deprivation which produces cognitive deficits is another example of assuming that children who can't talk like whites have nothing worth talking about (1970, p. 603).[10]

At about the same time as Goodman's early work researchers in other fields were also challenging deficit views of the language of people of colour, for example, the work of the linguist William Labov, who persuasively showed how culturally sensitive linguistic analysis of African American language revealed perceptive, logical, and effective ideas on the part of the people involved in his research study.[11] More recent scholarship on language and standards is, for example, seen in the work of Ian Cushing, who has focused on aspects such as conceptions of Standard English in England, including in policies such as the national curriculum and inspection practices of the inspectorate Ofsted.[12]

Goodman's view that teachers should regard children's 'errors', or what he called "miscues", as children's positive attempts to understand written language is surely still vitally important in today's classrooms. The opposite way of thinking, to simply regard their mistakes as errors without thought, is quite rightly described as a 'deficit view' of children's thinking.

Scheme books and real books

The nature of the texts to be used for teaching reading were central to the debates about the real book approach and the whole-language approach. However, part of our argument in this book is not only that teachers' selection of specific texts is still highly relevant to effective teaching but also that we have seen a strong trend towards only using synthetic phonics scheme books for teaching reading.

To further illustrate the nature and role of whole texts as part of teaching, we now turn to some examples. To illustrate some key differences between real books and phonics scheme books, known as 'decodable books', we selected the book called *Sit In!* from a popular relatively recently developed synthetic phonics scheme called Little Wandle, which was quickly becoming one of the most-used schemes in England. We chose a book from the Little Wandle scheme that included an author who also publishes books for children in the trade press in order to try to make the comparison with a real book as close as possible. We selected a real book that has important similarities with the scheme book, for example, its use of very few words and a simple repetitive structure: *Cat on the Mat*, written and illustrated by Brian Wildsmith (1986).[13]

Sit In!

The Little Wandle synthetic phonics scheme book *Sit In!* is written by Clare Helen Welsh and illustrated by Julia Seal (2021).[14] It is clear from the front and back covers of the book that this is a scheme book rather than a 'real book' because it includes six small boxes of text, and some logos, describing that it is book number two from the Little Wandle Letters and Sounds Revised collection. This is not how real books are presented, so straight away there is a difference. The inside covers of the book include two pages of instructions for teachers and parents about how they should use the book to teach "decoding, prosody and comprehension" across three lessons. The copyright of this book is to the publisher HarperCollins. The following people are listed on the copyright page:

Author: Clare Helen Welsh
Reading ideas author: Liz Miles
Phonics consultant: Jacqueline Harris
Phonics reviewer: Rachel Russ
Illustrator: Julia Seal (Advocate)

Commissioning editor: Sarah Thomas
In-house editor: Alexandra Wells
Project manager: Emily Hooton
Proof-reader: Gaynor Spry
Designer: 2Hoots Publishing Services Ltd
Production controller: Katharine Willard
Developed in collaboration with Little Wandle Letters and Sounds revised
Reviewed and aligned to the Little Wandle Letters and Sounds Revised framework by Catherine Baker.

(Welsh, 2021, back cover)

By comparison, the real book only has the author, Brian Wildsmith, named on the copyright page. These two different listings express a fundamental difference between the two books. The synthetic phonics scheme book is devised by a group of people who carefully check the book to ensure it is delivering the government required synthetic phonics approach. In comparison, the real book is *created* to engage children in its meanings.

The title of the synthetic phonics book sounds like an authoritarian request to 'sit in' something, due to the use of an exclamation mark, but this does not reflect the much more friendly invitations for children to sit in a play car that is the focus of the book. Apart from the character's names, the book has only two words: 'sit' and 'in'. All the character names are three letters: Sam, Sid, Nad, Pam, Tam. The restricted length of the names and the restriction to consonant vowel (G) consonant words means the names are very unlike real names – this means that the characters lack authenticity.

Children will probably be curious about the main event of the story, which is when the main character Sam has to get out of the car because there are too many children in the car. The final two pages of the book are what is called an "I spy sounds" activity. Children are to be encouraged to spot items in the picture that begin with the /n/ phoneme (G), which is described as the "/n/ sound". Once again, this use of a teaching activity within the book shows the book as different from a real narrative fiction book.

The text of the first four pages of the book features the words "Sit in", followed by a three-letter character name:

Sit in Sam.
Sam sits in.
Sit in Sid.
Sid sits in.

The context for the words and pictures is this:

Page two, first page of double spread: Sit in Sam. (Picture of adult with arms wide)
Page three, second page of double spread: Sam sits in. (Picture of girl getting into the play car).
Page four, spread across pages four and five: Sit in Sid. (Picture of Sam and Sid sitting in the car).
Page five: Sid sits in.

The text, "Sit in Sam", does not for some reason include speech marks, yet it appears from the picture that an adult male is encouraging Sam to sit in the play car. Historically, the lack of speech marks has been a feature of reading schemes. In the context of teaching, this would be called a punctuation error. What's more, the use of a comma, as in 'Sit in, Sam', might be preferred by some people to avoid a fanciful ambiguity, although the more realistic dialogue might be something like this: 'Hi Sam, would you like to sit in the car?' The pictures are simple, somewhat stereotypical, and provide very little additional meaning apart from linking literally with the actions of the characters.

Although this book ensures that children encounter words that feature phonemes that they have learned, and there are some benefits in this, it is hard to believe that this book would motivate children to read, and it certainly provides very little in the text and pictures to provoke curiosity or to stimulate much more interesting conversations. Most concerning of all is the very limited and unnatural text. This is not a criticism of the Little Wandle phonics scheme per se; it is simply a reflection of the criteria for 'decodable books' in most synthetic phonics schemes that are validated by the Department for Education in England. In some other countries and regions there is still more flexibility for provision in reading schemes that include phonics. For example the American Reading Company includes real books as part of its teaching resources.[15]

Cat on the Mat

The front cover of Brian Wildsmith's book *Cat on the Mat* features a large, imaginatively drawn tabby cat, sitting on a red rug, with green eyes looking directly at the reader with a smile on its face. The absence of the word 'the' in the title is curious.

The text and illustrations for the first four unnumbered pages of the book are these:

Page 1 of double-page spread: Part of the red rug: no words on this page.
Page 2 of double-page spread: Picture of the cat sitting on the red rug. "The cat sat on the mat."
Page 3: Picture of a sleepy-looking dog on the left side of the rug. The cat is now standing. "The dog sat on the mat."
Page 4: The cat arching its back and looking a little apprehensively at the dog, and a goat: no words on this page.

The text is appropriate for a developing reader of about age five and importantly begins with the rhyming sentence that is a familiar childhood trope (The cat sat on the mat), which adds layers of additional meaning to its simplicity. Although the words are important, the story is also developed through Wildsmith's imaginative illustrations, and particularly through the facial expressions of the cat. The names of the characters are all real names of animals, so children learn some new vocabulary. These names are all three- or four-letter words, until the elephant sits on the mat.

The cat reacts very angrily to this intrusion on the mat by all these animals, with the wonderful word (and minor sentence) "Sssppstt!" which captures the hissing noise that cats make when frightened. All the other animals flee from the cat and the mat, and the story finishes as it began, with the cat sitting contentedly on its mat.

The combinations of words and pictures on each double-page spread of the text provide multiple opportunities for discussions about the text which would support children's reading comprehension and their interpretation of the text (in the chapters in the second half of the book, we give many examples of the kinds of questions that teachers use when using the balanced approach). The word "Sssppstt!" provides a natural and meaningful opportunity for sounding out each letter if the teacher wanted to draw the children's attention to this, and the rhyme between cat, sat, and mat provides opportunities to explore syllables, phonemes, and letters.

Both the books we have described are written for young children, but only the real book carries the depths of meaning that are essential for children's motivation and learning. The real book provides ample opportunity to focus on systematic phonics, if this is a focus decided on by a teacher, and offers more possibilities to accommodate the needs of a wide range of learners. The phonics scheme book may not motivate those children who can already read, whereas in the hands of a skilled teacher, the real book offers opportunities to extend the learning of all children commensurate with their stage of development. The lack of authenticity in the synthetic phonics scheme book means that children are not being introduced to an accurate portrayal of books and book language. Overall, the problem is not any particular synthetic phonics scheme; the problem is the criteria laid down by government that are used to validate these schemes, which forces the developers to conform.

In all published synthetic phonics programmes teachers are required to use decodable books, so children will, during the synthetic phonics lessons, be denied the reading of real books. The justification for this is that the children should not be introduced to books that contain words with phonemes that are beyond what they have learned about in the phonics lessons. For example the handbook of another of the most popular phonics schemes in England, Read Write Inc, gave this guidance:

> once children have learnt the Set 1 Speed Sounds and can blend words made up of these sounds, they can start on the Sound Blending Books, then the Red Ditty Books and the Get Writing! Red Ditty Books. When they move onto the Green Storybooks and the Get Writing! Green Books, they are taught the Set 2 Speed Sounds and continue to review Set 1 Speed Sounds and blending.[16]

In the first phase of the Read Write Inc approach, the separation between phonics teaching and whole texts was explicit. Children were to be taught some sounds and blends separately, and only then could they try these with books, and only decodable books. Also, if children had not been assessed as knowing the 'Set 1 phonemes', they could not move onto 'Set 2', which includes reading of whole texts. Although there are opportunities to engage with real books outside of synthetic phonics lessons, the balance is very strongly towards decodable books based on the phonemes that have been learned. In Chapter 4, "The Science of Teaching Reading and Writing", we review a robust large-scale experimental research study that compared the methods of Read Write Inc with a control group.

One of the key features of the balanced approach described in this book is the use of real books in reading and writing lessons. As a first example of how we think about books in use in teaching, here is an analysis of the book *Peck Peck Peck* that features in more detail in Chapter 8, "Gaining Control".

Peck Peck Peck

Peck Peck Peck, written and illustrated by Lucy Cousins (2014),[17] engages the reader with authentic language and storytelling. The high-quality artistic illustrations support the humour of the story, which features the unintended consequences of a baby bird doing just what its father told it to, and will delight young readers, who will be keen to see what the young woodpecker will peck next. The text and illustrations are excellent for building vocabulary, listing and illustrating common and less familiar items that the woodpecker pecks its way through. The rhyming text introduces children to patterned language, supporting young readers to take over the reading for themselves whilst also providing a multitude of opportunities to use and apply their developing phonic knowledge in practice.[18] One of the book's engaging features is the holes through the front cover and throughout the book, denoting the action of the main protagonist: a young woodpecker keen to be able to practise and show off its pecking skills.

The decision to feature animals as characters reflects children's interest in the natural world. The adult and child relationship shown in the characters of the two woodpeckers is of course one that children would be living through. And the focus on learning a new skill also is the essence of why children are at school. Hence, like all books written for children, it seeks to both engage children with familiar ideas but also challenge them with new ideas.

The text rhymes, something which supports an early reader's awareness of syllables and phonemes. There are many words that children will be able to read for themselves as they master the basic letter-to-sound relationships by learning a common letter representation for each of the phonemes. The opening page spread reads, "Today my daddy said to me, 'It's time you learnt to peck a tree.'"

A vibrant illustration accompanies the text, depicting a large and a small woodpecker perched on a branch, the smaller one looking up to the larger one, their gaze held. The text continues on the next spread: "'Now hold on tight, that's very good. Then peck peck peck peck peck the wood.' PECK PECK PECK 'Oh look, yippee! I've pecked a hole right through this tree.'" The accompanying illustration shows the larger and smaller woodpecker positioned on the trunk of the tree, with the larger one looking on as the smaller one pecks the tree. The pecking is demarcated by a punched hole in the trunk.

The rest of the book takes us on the little woodpecker's pecking adventures, with many opportunities for the children to use their developing knowledge and skills to read parts of the text independently whilst being motivated by the storyline and accompanying illustrations.

The simple, rhyming text also gives ample opportunity for children to use and apply their phonic knowledge through the phonemes represented by digraphs (G) in words like n<u>ow</u>, <u>th</u>en, g<u>oo</u>d, p<u>e</u>ck, w<u>oo</u>d, l<u>oo</u>k, <u>th</u>is, and tr<u>ee</u>; trigraphs (G) in t<u>igh</u>t and r<u>igh</u>t; and consonant clusters at the end and beginning of words in words like ho<u>ld</u> and <u>tr</u>ee. The text can be used to teach children about segmenting and blending words in order to read, as well as opportunities to practise reading common words like 'very', 'the', and 'oh'.

We now turn to further aspects of teaching related to texts, in particular how teachers can think about selecting texts for use in the classroom.

Selecting texts for three- to eight-year-olds

In his seminal work *The Reading Environment*,[19] Aidan Chambers outlined what he saw as three categories of essential classroom activities that would be facilitated by "a trusted, experienced adult reader":

- Selection: The book stock available in the classroom and school and its accessibility and presentation.
- Reading: Having time to read, hearing it done, and doing it for yourself.
- Response: The enjoyment of reading, formal talk about books, and book gossip.

Reading begins with selection, choosing what is to be read. Children need a varied selection of texts on offer to support their development as independent readers. Selecting what these texts should be for each individual class will require knowledge of the children's characteristics and backgrounds, the languages they speak and read, and their interests and preferences, as well as knowledge about their progress and attainment. In any well-stocked selection of texts in classroom and school there should be a wide and varied range of text types to ensure that there is something that will appeal to each and every reader as well as offering alternative genres and text types to broaden the range of reading material that children encounter. For children aged three to eight, whose experiences we are primarily focused on, the selection will include but is not limited to:

- Alphabet books
- Rhymes and songs
- Poetry
- Picture books
- Traditional and folk tales
- Illustrated fiction
- Short stories
- Non-fiction titles on themes and topics of interest
- Comics
- Graphic novels
- Magazines
- Newspapers and other news sources
- Technology to access digital texts, including audiobooks

Poetry is an ideal form for focusing children's attention on the patterns of words and language and for improving children's understanding of the flow of language through its musicality and rhythmic patterns, something that can also support increasing reading fluency (G). Listening to poets perform poetry, live or through video or audio recordings, reading poems, finding word patterns, and discussing their meanings before giving time to groups, pairs, and individual children to practice and perform helps to build understanding about word structures, consolidate meaning, recognise how punctuation affects reading, and develop fluency.[20]

Collections that are particularly tuned into the needs and experiences of three- to five-year-olds include *Big Green Crocodile: Rhymes to Say and Play*, written by Jane Newberry and illustrated by Carolina Rabei; *A Great Big Cuddle*, written by Michael Rosen and illustrated by Chris Riddell; *Blow a Kiss, Catch a Kiss*, written by Joseph Coelho and illustrated by Nicola Killen; and *Caterpillar Cake*, written by Matt Goodfellow and illustrated by Krina Patel-Sage.

As children progress in their reading, the following collections offer much to engage readers from five to eight years old: *A Ticket to Kalamazoo*, written by James Carter and illustrated by Neal Layton; *A First Book of Dinosaurs*, written by Simon Mole and illustrated by Matt Hunt; *Marshmallow Clouds*, written by Ted Kooser and Connie Wanek and illustrated by Richard Jones; *Cherry Moon*, written by Zaro Weil and illustrated by Junli Song; *Poems to Perform*, edited by Julia Donaldson; and *A Dinosaur at the Bus Stop*, written by Kate Wakeling and illustrated by Eilidh Muldoon.

Picture books are often children's first step into reading, their short text form and illustrations providing the ideal motivation for readers at the earliest stages as well as an opportunity to engage in beginning reading skills. It is important to remember, however, that picture books are essential and engaging reading for children of all ages, not just younger readers. In the 21st century, the skill of analysing and interpreting images is even more essential for children, allowing them to navigate their way successfully in an increasingly visual world, for example, in understanding and interpreting films or in understanding the ways in which words and pictures are used in news stories and social media and how these can be biased or misleading.

For readers aged three to five, the works of Ken Wilson-Max, Anna McQuinn with Ruth Hearson and Rosalind Beardshaw, Chris Haughton, Daisy Hirst, Gaia Cornwall, Atinuke and Lauren Tobia, and Petr Horáček are ideal. All these authors and illustrators craft stories which are excellent examples for young readers, tuning into their needs, interests, fascinations, and personal experiences as they learn about themselves and the world around them.

At the earliest stages, board book formats allow children to develop essential book handling skills and provide durability in settings that incorporate learning in the indoor and outdoor environments. As readers progress, picture books offer sophistication in styles of illustration and the themes and topics covered in the texts. Works by Nathan Bryon and Dapo Adeola, Ed Vere, Benji Davies, Mini Grey, Jon Klassen, Bethan Woolvin, Tom Percival, Viviane Schwarz, Lauren Child, and Joe Todd-Stanton provide examples of a range of satisfying story types; engaging themes; high-quality illustrations that take the reader far beyond the text on the page; and rich, judiciously chosen vocabulary that extends children's repertoire of language as well as giving children opportunities to personally connect with texts.

In poetry and picture books, the brevity of the text is a strength, supporting children to be able to read ahead and keep their pace, improving flow. Children listening to audiobooks and performances and recording themselves reading favourite picture books or poems aloud encourage them to select personal favourites, building their identities as readers; to monitor and reflect on their own reading; and to present reading with a focus on meaning in a way that is engaging for others to listen to.

Traditional tales provide children with strong narrative structures, engaging storylines, and characters and settings which often form a bridge between fantasy and reality. Traditional tales include a wide range of narratives – folk tales, fairy tales, and fables, as well as myths and legends. Their strong story shapes and patterned language support children's language, reading, and ultimately writing. Such texts can also be used to introduce children to a diverse range of cultures as well as helping them understand that many similar stories appear across the world.

Traditional tales and twists on them like *Hungry Hen* by Richard Waring, illustrated by Caroline Jayne Church; *No Dinner!* and *Please Mr Magic Fish*, by Jessica Souhami; *The Gigantic Turnip* by Aleksei Tolstoy, illustrated by Niamh Sharkey; Nick Sharratt and Steven Tucker's *Lift the Flap Fairy Tales* series; and *Little Red and the Very Hungry Lion* by Alex T. Smith offer a perfect introduction for children aged three to five.

For developing readers of five to eight years old, the following texts offer increased sophistication in storytelling, language, and structures: *Pattan's Pumpkin*, written by Chitra Soundar and illustrated by Frané Lessac; *Little Red, Rapunzel* and *Hansel and Gretel* by Bethan Woolvin; *The Robot and the Bluebird* by David Lucas; and the stories in Axel Scheffler's Fairy Tales series.

As young readers develop in their stamina to listen and read for longer periods, illustrated fiction becomes an important addition to book selections on offer. These may encompass short stories bound up in a collection and short novels. Humour is an important element for many children, who will frequently ask for funny stories. Books in series can draw children into the world of reading and maintain their interest.

At the earliest stages, texts such as *The Big Alfie and Annie Rose Storybook* and *The Big Alfie Out of Doors Storybook* by Shirley Hughes, *The Elephant and Piggie* books by Mo Willems, *Frog and Toad Are Friends* by Arnold Lobel, and the *Bear and Bird* series by Jarvis are perfect introductions to longer texts.

As young readers progress, the *Nikhil and Jay* series, written by Chitra Soundar and illustrated by Soofiya; Ann Cameron's *Julian* books; the *Anna Hibiscus* books written by Atinuke and illustrated by Lauren Tobia; the *Claude* series by Alex T. Smith; and the *Rabbit and Bear* books, written by Julian Gough and illustrated by Jim Field, develop children's interest and engagement. Between seven and eight years old, they may also enjoy highly illustrated longer texts such as those by Philip Reeve and Sarah McIntyre and the Tola series by Atinuke and Onyinye Iwu.

Comics and graphic novels engage young readers directly: they are vivid and action-filled and offer a multi-modal reading experience. They require different reading skills and stamina to navigate and follow the narrative and are often complex reading, which is sometimes not appreciated by adult readers. As Neil Gaiman outlined in his 2013 Reading Agency lecture,[21] "Comics have been decried as fostering illiteracy. It's tosh. It's snobbery and it's foolishness." The work of Mo Willems introduces a graphic style to the youngest readers, first in his series of *Pigeon* books and then in the *Elephant and Piggie* stories. Authors/illustrators Viviane Schwarz and Nadia Shireen often deploy comic and graphic novel techniques in their picture books. Mika Song's Norma and Belly series, which begins with *Donut Feed the Squirrels*, is a perfect introduction to the genre for readers from five to seven.

For developing readers aged seven and older, *The Phoenix Has Taken Off* is a popular comic, with a series of published titles of its most popular stories alongside a weekly comic. Jamie Smart's *Bunny vs Monkey*, Neil Cameron's *Mega Robo Bros*, and Joe Brady's *Claire: Justice Ninja* have all been popular titles. Joe Todd-Stanton's Brownstone Series of books offers readers lessons in history as well as being incredibly engaging adventures.

There is much evidence of the power of reading fiction, in particular, to develop awareness of ourselves, our emotions, and the world we live in.[22] However, a rich reading diet will include a range of texts, including non-fiction. Access to good non-fiction is an important part of the wider curriculum, as well as being significant in children's reading experience. Discussions about reading for pleasure focus too often solely on fiction, but high-quality books which present knowledge in new and informative ways are an engaging and enjoyable reading experience for many children and therefore form a crucial part of classroom collections. In *Information and Book Learning*, Margaret Meek-Spencer turned her attention from texts supporting children in learning to read, to texts supporting children in 'reading to learn'. Books of note drawn out by her in this publication were at the time a newer form of narrative non-fiction crossover texts. In her view The *Read and Wonder* series from Walker Books made learning far more attractive and approachable than "other formulaic productions of topic material" (p. 102) such as the standard photographic reference books with paragraphs delivering packages of facts prevalent at the time.

Non-fiction titles now are published in ways that delight in stimulating children's awe and wonder of the world around them, often giving readers greater empathy with the subject matter and knowledge than an information book with a more traditionally conventional layout. To provoke intrigue in the earliest readers, teachers can try titles such as the How It Works series from publisher Little Tiger; *My Pet Goldfish* by Catherine Rayner; *Hey, Water!* by Antoinette Portis; *Our Very Own Dog* by Amanda McCardie, illustrated by Salvatore Rubbino; and *10 Things I Can Do to Help My World* by Melanie Walsh.

For developing readers, books such as *My Big Book of Outdoors* by Tim Hopgood; *A Planet Full of Plastic* by Neal Layton; *Winter Sleep, Busy Spring*, and *Wild Summer* written by Sean Taylor and Alex Morss and illustrated by Cinyee Chiu; and *White Owl, Barn Owl*, written by Nicola Davies and illustrated by Michael Foreman, engage children with the natural world and their place within it. *The Great Big Book of Families*, written by Mary Hoffmann and illustrated by Ros Asquith, and *Grow: Secrets of Our DNA*, written by Nicola Davies and illustrated by Emily Sutton, focus on human life and *A Walk in London* by Salvatore Rubinno on learning about specific places.

Text selections are just as important in the home environment. As teachers build a picture of the children in their class, it is important to know which children have a greater access to texts in their home environment, either through book ownership or through being a member of a public library. Book gifting programmes are available which provide children with a collection of books at home which they can call their own. One of the most well known is Dolly Parton's Imagination Library, which is dedicated to inspiring a love of reading by gifting books free of charge to children from birth to age five through funding shared by Dolly Parton and local community partners in the United States, Canada, United Kingdom, Australia, and the Republic of Ireland. In 2020–23 the Centre for Literacy in Primary Education ran a joint research programme with the Dolly Parton Imagination Library UK, evaluated by the Institute for Employment Studies (IES),[23] which showed evidence of the positive impact of this book gifting on children's engagement and motivation as readers. The evaluation noted that the monthly delivery of a real book, chosen by the Imagination Library Book Selection Panel, to each child at their home and to each child's teacher:

- was particularly beneficial for children from less advantaged backgrounds in their class who did not have their own collection of books at home and were not being read to;
- was valuable for the parents of children who were non-native English speakers, who may not have a good understanding of UK children's authors and appropriate English-language texts to buy;
- created excitement in the physical delivery of the book to the child's home, which the child identified as their book;
- created visible excitement whenever teachers chose to read aloud these texts at school during a carpet session, as children recognised the text and would always comment that they had the same book at home;
- created a bonding experience for the children by providing them with shared access to a book they enjoyed and knew well;
- was successful in getting children more interested in books.

Time to read

In a busy curriculum, providing adequate time to read can be a challenge for teachers. Data from a survey conducted in England by children's publisher Farshore suggested that nationally only 24% of children aged seven to ten years old were read to daily at school and that only 46% of five- to seven-year-olds were read to daily/nearly every day at home. Of more concern is that by the time children are eight to ten years old, this had reduced to 25%.[24]

As well as providing adequate selections of books, teachers need to dedicate time to reading in the classroom. This includes teachers reading to children, both as uninterrupted story time to simply engage in the pleasure of hearing a text read aloud, and to teach reading skills and strategies as part of the curriculum. It is also important that teachers make time to read with children individually and in small groups to teach reading skills and strategies and target specific development needs.

Time for children to read independently and uninterrupted for the pleasure of reading is important, just as reading aloud is so that teachers can observe reading and record and monitor children's progress. The classroom reading environment can also have a bearing on children's willingness to engage in reading – comfortable surroundings where children can read on a bean bag or cushion, cuddled up with a toy or a blanket, might be more appealing than being sat at a table.

As children engage in reading with the selection of texts on offer, it is important to allow space for children to respond to what they have read. This provides valuable insights for the teacher on the tastes and preferences of children; how children are engaging with what has been read and what teachers might need to do to develop the book stock or provision. This might be informally listening to children talk together about reading experiences, through providing a medium for children to review books that they have read, or as part of more structured discussions during or after reading or listening to a text being read. The sessions and lessons outlined in the second half of the book show examples of activities that arise out of engaging with texts and learning about phonics and other aspects of reading and writing.

Teachers need to continually build their knowledge of texts for children. They need to be able to select texts for lessons, offering the right levels of support and challenge for children to develop their knowledge, skills, and attitudes to reading, as they progress on their journey towards independence. Teachers need to know what will engage children to read on an individual basis so that they are able to provide the right books for the right children at the right times to foster their enthusiasm and motivation for reading and to broaden their reading range, This involves a great deal of knowledge about the children, their needs, interests, tastes, and preferences; their prior experiences of reading; and the support they have for reading outside of school so that teachers are able to provide the right texts and opportunities for reading to encourage children to read for pleasure. It also requires teachers who approach the teaching of reading first and foremost through motivating children to comprehend and compose meaningful texts, adopting a balanced approach to teaching phonics and other aspects of reading and writing.

In recent years the number of synthetic phonics schemes has proliferated. In England this proliferation has been helped by the government 'validating' schemes and strongly encouraging schools to adopt a government approved scheme. This is similar to other countries and regions which to varying degrees use validation, promotion, and selection applied by politicians as part of their contacts with commercial companies who market phonics schemes and as a result profit from education. The criteria for approval of phonics schemes do not typically include any attention to the literary merits of books in the schemes. Some schemes do have scheme book authors who publish books for children in the trade press as well, but they have to work under such difficult controls, for example, a vocabulary controlled to meet the demands of the sequence of phonemes taught as part of the scheme, that it is not possible to create a book that has the benefits of a real book.

In this chapter we have explored a fundamental starting point for teaching reading and writing, the rationales for selecting texts to support teaching and children's learning. Having also introduced readers in previous chapters to some key aspects of the debates about teaching reading, and to theories of teaching reading, we now turn to look at the evidence from some of the most robust research studies about how phonics, reading, and writing can be taught effectively.

Notes

1. Meek, M., & Spencer, M. M. (1988). *How Texts Teach What Readers Learn*. Thimble Press.
2. Hutchins, P. (1968). *Rosie's Walk*. Macmillan.
3. Graham, J., & Mills, C. (2022). Margaret Meek Spencer: Taking Her Work On. *English in Education, 56*(3), 205–208.
4. Waterland, L. (1985). *Read with Me: An Apprenticeship Approach to Reading*. Thimble Press.
5. Goodman, K. (1967). Reading: A Psycholinguistic Guessing Game. *Literacy Research and Instruction, 6*(4), 126–135. Retrieved December 1, 2023, from https://doi.org/10.1080/19388076709556976
6. Goodman, Reading: A Psycholinguistic Guessing Game.
7. Gough, P. B., & Tunmer, W. E. (1986). Decoding, Reading and Reading Disability. *Remedial and Special Education, 7*(1), 6–10. Retrieved December 1, 2023, from https://doi.org/10.1177/074193258600700104
8. For example, Perfetti, C. (1995). Cognitive Research Can Inform Reading Education. *Journal of Research in Reading, 18*(2), 106–115.
9. Compton-Lilly, C. (2023). Into the Fray: Black English, Reading Politics, and the Legacy of Dr. Ken Goodman. *Journal of Adolescent Adult Literacy, 67*, 111–121.
10. Compton-Lilly, Into the Fray, p. 113.
11. Labov, W. (1972). The Logic of Nonstandard English. In A. Cashdan & E. Grugeon (Eds.), *Language in Education: A Source Book*. Routledge and Kegan Paul.
12. Cushing, I., & Snell, J. (2022). The (White) Ears of Ofsted: A Raciolinguistic Perspective on the Listening Practices of the Schools Inspectorate. *Language in Society, 52*, 363–386.
13. Wildsmith, B. (1986). *Cat on the Mat*. Harper Collins.
14. Welsh, C. H., & Seal, J. (2020). *Sit I!: Phase 2 Set 2 (Big Cat Phonics for Little Wandle Letters and Sounds Revised)*. HarperCollins Publishers Limited.
15. Retrieved December 1, 2023, from https://americanreading.com/about-us/. There may also be future benefits to be gained from using real books directly as part of the systematic phonics programme in this scheme to ensure integration of phonics teaching with other vital aspects of reading, as we argue in this book.
16. Miskin, R. (2021). *Read Write Inc. Phonics Handbook 1* (p. 11). Oxford University Press. Retrieved December 1, 2023, from https://global.oup.com/education/content/primary/series/rwi/phonics/?region=uk
17. Cousins, L. (2014). *Peck Peck Peck*. Walker Books Limited.
18. You can see the front cover and some of the illustrations of *Peck Peck Peck* in Chapter 8.
19. Chambers, A. (2011). *Tell Me: Children, Reading and Talk with the Reading Environment*. Thimble Press.
20. A project about memorising poems can be found here: Retrieved December 1, 2023, from https://www.cam.ac.uk/research/features/they-sailed-away-for-a-year-and-a-day-why-learning-poetry-by-heart-is-good-for-you
21. Gaiman, N. (2013). *The Reading Agency Annual Lecture: Why Our Future Depends on Libraries, Reading and Daydreaming*. Retrieved October 26, 2023, from https://www.theguardian.com/books/2013/oct/15/neil-gaiman-future-libraries-reading-daydreaming
22. Rosenblatt, L. (1978). *The Reader, the Text, the Poem: The Transactional Theory of the Literary Work*. Southern Illinois University Press.

O'Sullivan, O., & McGonigle, S. (2010). Transforming Readers: Teachers and Children in the Centre for Literacy in Primary Education Power of Reading project. *Literacy, 44*(2), 51–59.

Chiaet, J. (2013). *Novel Finding: Reading Literary Fiction Improves Empathy.* Retrieved November 13, 2023, from https://www.scientificamerican.com/article/novel-finding-reading-literary-fiction-improves-empathy/

Hammond, C. (2019). *Reading Fiction Has Been Said to Increase People's Empathy and Compassion. But Does the Research Really Bear That Out?* Retrieved November 13, 2023, from https://www.bbc.com/future/article/20190523-does-reading-fiction-make-us-better-people

23 Buzzeo, J., Muir, D., & Patel, R. (2023). *Closing the Vocabulary Gap: Project Evaluation Report.* Retrieved December 1, 2023, from https://www.employment-studies.co.uk/system/files/resources/files/CVG%20evaluation_final%20report%20%28003%29.pdf

24 Mackinlay, M., & Coles, R. (2023). *Farshore Storytime Trial Research Report.* Retrieved December 1, 2023, from https://www.farshore.co.uk/wp-content/uploads/sites/46/2023/09/Farshore_Storytime-in-Schools_Whitepaper_FINAL.pdf

4 The science of teaching reading and writing

The main argument of this book is that we think there is strong evidence for teaching reading and writing using a balanced approach based on the theory of the Double Helix of Reading and Writing. A crucial part of this balance is the emphasis that phonics teaching (G) should have and how this relates to the teaching of other elements. In this chapter we review research studies that underpin our approach and model for teaching reading and writing.

The purpose of the chapter is to present an account of what research evidence tells us about the most effective ways to teach reading and writing, particularly taking into account the role of phonics teaching. The problem, though, for this book and for many other topics in education, is not so much identifying research studies; it is more a problem of how to *select* research studies given that the teaching of reading and writing have attracted a very large amount of research.

Which research and why?

The teaching of reading and writing has attracted thousands of research studies from hundreds of researchers in a range of disciplines including education, history, neuroscience, philosophy, and psychology. Many of these studies feature very good research: in other words, they are robust in their research methods and execution and therefore need to be considered carefully to see if they could be the basis for more effective teaching. For example, perspectives from philosophy have included critique of synthetic phonics (G), such as the book by Andrew Davis.[1] We can find much in histories of education and other relevant areas, for example, Alberto Manguel's autobiographical history of reading.[2] Expertise in children's literature, including its histories, influenced Morag Styles'[3] sense of how to approach the politics of phonics and teaching reading at a time when the reading wars had erupted again in England caused by Martin Turner's pamphlet called "Sponsored Reading Failure". Linguistics also has much to offer not only in the technicalities of language but also in understanding language and identity in education which hinge on attitudes to 'standard English'.[4] And we have already cited some neuroscientific work in Chapter 1. It is not just in single academic disciplines of knowledge where we find research; interdisciplinary work is also important: a way of thinking that has been used productively, for example, in the exploration of writing across the life course.[5] However, for this chapter, we focus on a particular method of research, the 'experimental trial', that has been used in natural sciences, including in medicine but also social sciences such as education, psychology, and sociology.

DOI: 10.4324/9781003442134-6

If the main question driving a research study is how effective a teaching approach is compared to another teaching approach, then an experimental trial is an appropriate research design. In brief, the classic example of an experimental trial is where an approach, often called 'the intervention', is compared with a 'control' condition, which might be typical teaching, known as 'business as usual', or a different teaching approach. Ideally the trial should include random allocation of pupils to the intervention or the control group. Random allocation is important because natural imbalances, for example, in pupils' prior reading attainment, are usually equally distributed across the intervention and control groups due to the random allocation: part of the design of what are known as randomised controlled trials (RCTs). In trials of teaching interventions in education, the random allocation is often of schools or classes, known as 'clusters', hence the description 'cluster randomised controlled trial'. However, it is only a *probability* that the distribution of imbalances will be equal: sometimes an unequal distribution occurs from the random allocation, which is why tests carried out before a research intervention starts are checked and, if necessary, adjustments made in the subsequent analyses of the data used to determine if the intervention was effective or not.[6]

It is important to state here that no research method is perfectly suited to address any given research questions: all methods have limitations, including experimental trials. Even for those people with expertise in the methods of experimental trials, there is debate about which experimental trial design should be used, and there are multiple decisions to be made within a given trial.

Critiques of experimental trial methods have come from those who use other research methods, such as qualitative research: for example, the idea that because human social contexts, like the teaching of reading, are so variable an experimental trial cannot be reliable (G) because every time an intervention is tried its outcomes will differ due to the constantly changing nature of the social context. Those who advocate for experimental trials counter this argument on the basis that sufficient scale of research, for example, numbers of schools/pupils, random allocation, and rigorous approach, more generally should be enough to detect genuine effects of an intervention. Whether that intervention might be appropriate at a larger scale than an early trial, and particularly at the scale of a whole country or other large region, is another very challenging issue which requires evidence from multiple studies.

It is not that we don't think that research methods other than experimental trials have anything to offer the debates about teaching reading and writing; it is just that our particular focus in this book, which is the effectiveness of approaches to phonics, reading, and writing, is well served by experimental trials, particularly RCTs. The other reason that we are having to address experimental trials is that the debates in many countries worldwide have featured claims that what some people call 'the science of reading' proves their point, for example, that synthetic phonics first and foremost is the best way to teach early reading. The basis for these claims is experimental trials. However, some of these claims are erroneous, and some represent poor understanding of research in education and therefore need to be challenged, a task which requires us to address any evidence base that it is claimed supports a view of teaching reading. Some advocates of phonics refer mainly to single experimental trials, but the evidence from multiple research studies, which we will come to later in this chapter, is vital.

A note about 'science'

Before we turn to our interpretation of what the research studies tell us about effective teaching, a quick note about the term 'science' in 'the science of reading'. Some commentators imply that there is a simple truth about teaching reading to be gleaned from what they call science. In other words, you do the science, for which it is often implied that RCTs are the only method, sometimes even called 'the gold standard', then this proves the one method of teaching reading that is effective. This is of course a misreading even of how research in natural sciences works. Putting aside the fact that work in, say, the study of the universe differs from medical science or from chemistry, even within one area of science, the norm is for debate: the ongoing reporting of original findings, contestation, then gradual accumulation of knowledge to inform our perceptions of the world we live in.

As an example of the processes of natural science, let's choose a topic that has attracted high-quality scientific research, including in the medical sciences – the effects of smoking cigarettes on human health. The seminal study that established a link, or what is called a correlation, between smoking and lung cancer was done by Ernest Wynder and Evarts Graham and was published in 1950. They used a survey of people with and without lung cancer to determine what their smoking habits had been, using a research design called a case-control study. They found that the more people smoked, the more likely they were to get lung cancer. A causal link, where given a particular context there is a very high probability that something will cause something else to happen, was only deemed to have been established four years later, though.[7]

In spite of robust scientific evidence of this causal link between smoking and cancer, the findings were resisted at first, probably because so many people were smokers at that time, and smoking was advertised in persuasive ways by tobacco companies.[8] The first country to ban smoking in enclosed workplaces was Ireland in 2004,[9] which was of course 54 years after the seminal study of Wynder and Graham! The 'science' was robust, but the topic proved controversial, and the route from science to changing behaviour, for example, through new laws, was complicated and took a long time.

When it comes to teaching approaches, unlike the science of smoking and lung cancer, which relied on establishing a link between the human behaviour of smoking and a physical reaction, that is, cancer, there are many variables which have to be considered when researching teaching and learning. Teaching is a social process that aims to change children's mental processes. Although incredible progress continues to be made, we still only have partial understandings about how the human brain works in relation to learning and teaching, and very little which maps directly from neuroscience to educational practices, in spite of regular exaggerated claims to the contrary.

It is one thing for a researcher to carry out a very effective research project about reading or writing, and quite another thing to interpret, or 'translate', that research in order to change teaching so that young children learn better. Recommendations for changes to teaching practices and education policies not only have to be based on rigorous research and rigorous syntheses of research, but they also have to make sense and be effective when implemented by teachers in the particular country and region where the new practices are to be implemented. In order for this translation from research to practice to happen, the research and work of education researchers is often a vital contribution that has sometimes been neglected by policy makers.

Selecting research studies

There are hundreds if not thousands of experimental trials relevant to our focus on teaching and learning reading and writing. One way to manage the selection of research, and to avoid the risks of 'cherry picking' single research studies, is to select and review multiple research studies systematically. There are now increasing numbers of research studies that use the methods of *systematic reviews* that can help us in our understanding of what is likely to work best. Systematic reviews have transparent procedures for comprehensively selecting research studies on a given topic.

The first stage of any systematic review is to establish suitably focused research questions. This is followed by identifying established libraries of research, which are databases sometimes known as indexes, of which there are many. Even these databases have their own characteristics, so, for example, APA PsychInfo is owned by the American Psychological Association and focuses on journals in psychology, whereas the British Educational Research Index is currently owned by Ebsco. There is also the Australian Education Index now produced by the Cunningham Library as part of the Australian Council for Educational Research.

Robust systematic reviews involve key word and key phrase searches of relevant databases and other sources. One common limitation with specialist databases is that they don't typically index books and book chapters because the indexes are set up to work with journal articles and other research reports. Research papers are as a matter of course thoroughly peer-reviewed (G), whereas for academic books and book chapters the nature of peer review is more variable. There are also very good academic books in the trade press that have to satisfy different criteria to be accepted for publication, for example, the perception by an agent and/or a publisher that the book will be sufficiently distinct to be successful in competitive markets. These academic books often arise from the peer-reviewed research of the authors but are presented in a more accessible way.

One of the criteria for selection of any research paper to inform whether a teaching approach is effective is the scale of the research being reported. Studies with, for example, appropriately large numbers of teachers and pupils who are part of intervention and control groups allow for generalisation of the findings. The other advantage of selecting studies that include particular kinds of quantitative data and analyses is that quantitative findings can be further analysed through *meta-analysis*. Meta analyses combine the quantitative findings, for example, the pupil tests in multiple studies, in order to establish more generalisable findings. These analyses often combine the *effect sizes* of individual studies, which are a measure of the extent of an effect, for example, the extent to which children's reading improved when tested on a standardised measure of reading before and after an intervention.

Effect sizes go beyond simply establishing whether an approach has worked; they give an indication of how well it worked through their measure of the *extent of difference* between comparison groups in experimental studies. An effect size from 0.01 to 0.1 has been considered a low effect and roughly equivalent to between zero and two months of education progress as measured by standardised tests appropriate to the nature of learning measured. An effect size from 0.26 to 0.44, equivalent to a range of three to six months of progress, has been considered moderate. An effect size of 0.5 to 1.0 has been described as high effect to very high effect, within the range of six months' to one year's progress.[10] But because it is so complicated to determine what has affected learning, and in particular how to quantify the amount of learning, newer thinking has started to question what kind of effect sizes are reasonable to expect in an education intervention and what the magnitude of those effects are likely to be.[11] Another of the challenges with meta-analysis is to be sure that individual studies are sufficiently comparable to each other so that generalisation across different studies can be made. Systematic approaches have now even been developed to combine the outcomes of multiple systematic reviews, a form that is sometimes called a *tertiary review*. And in our work we have established the method of the systematic qualitative meta-synthesis (SQMS) that also informs the new reviews in this chapter.[12]

The teaching of reading and writing has attracted multiple systematic reviews that are relevant to our focus. One of the aspects of the debates that we explore in this book is whether typically developing readers require the same or different approaches to struggling readers, so the following account of our selection of systematic reviews of reading, then writing, includes some consideration of these two broad groups separately.

Our search for systematic reviews about the teaching of reading to feature in this chapter limited its search to 2008 onwards because a research paper was published that reviewed relevant research prior to 2008, including the influential large-scale systematic review work of the National Reading Panel (NRP) in the USA.[13] The paper in 2008 by education researcher Dominic Wyse and neuroscientist Usha Goswami[14] highlighted the problems with the approach to research taken by the Rose Report,[15] including the limitations of overemphasising one study, carried out in Clackmannanshire in Scotland, which was singled out as a major influence on its findings. The Wyse and Goswami paper was framed by research on reading across different languages, and it included an analysis of the teaching methods of all of the phonics teaching studies included in the NRP systematic review called *Alphabetics* and of the systematic review by Carole Torgerson et al.[16] One of the main findings of Wyse and Goswami was that more of the effective teaching interventions included in the NRP and Torgerson systematic reviews used phonics teaching that was contextualised for pupils within sentence-level and text-level work as opposed to those studies that had discrete phonics teaching. And the main point of the paper was that the Rose Report recommendation that phonics should be taught discretely as the prime approach to teaching reading was not supported by the research because a range of approaches to teaching phonics and reading had been shown to be effective.

General findings from systematic and tertiary reviews

Teaching phonics and reading

Table 4.1 summarises the main findings of relevant systematic reviews published since 2008 in relation to our focus on effective teaching of phonics and reading. It is worth remembering that each systematic review will have started with thousands of titles and abstracts, then whittled down to hundreds of relevant research studies until finally selecting a smaller number that were appropriate to the research questions of the systematic review.

It is important to highlight that the conclusions of these systematic reviews show that discrete, or isolated, phonics teaching is *not* the most effective way to teach reading. Combining phonics with other aspects of learning to read is particularly important, not least combining phonics with reading comprehension. We reiterate that these conclusions are formed on the basis of multiple robust individual research studies, not claims based on a single study.

There is another important criterion for selecting research: studies with longitudinal research designs. Longitudinal research designs include ways to measure changes in pupils' reading and writing over longer periods of time. We want to know which approaches improve reading and writing over the long term, not only immediately after the intervention

Table 4.1 Systematic reviews of the teaching of phonics and reading

Author and year of publication	Type of study	Age of pupils	Main findings
Typically developing readers			
Olusola Adesope et al. (2010)[17]	SR*	5 to 12	Peer interaction <u>focused on shared meaning</u> was more beneficial than systematic phonics instruction. This review focused on pupils who had English as a second language.
Carole Torgerson et al. (2018)[18]	TR	Multiple SRs, hence multiple ages	The evidence does not support a 'phonics only' teaching policy; because "many studies have added phonics to whole-language approaches, <u>balanced instruction is indicated</u>."
Geoffrey Bowers (2020)[19]	TR	Multiple SRs, hence multiple ages	There is no evidence that systematic phonics is better than other methods of teaching reading, including whole-language approaches. Although learning about the alphabetic code is important there are a range of teaching methods that can be used to do this.
Dominic Wyse and Alice Bradbury (2022)[20]	SQMS	5 to 14	The research evidence does not support a narrow synthetic phonics orientation to the teaching of reading: the evidence shows that a balanced instruction approach is most likely to be successful.
Struggling readers			
Sebastian Suggate (2010)[21]	SR	4 to 13	Phonics interventions (including practice in reading) are more successful early in a child's development, before they are about age 7. Comprehension interventions or mixed interventions have an advantage later in a child's development.
Robert Slavin et al. (2011)[22]	SR	5 to 10	One-to-one teaching implemented by teachers was most effective. Reading Recovery was effective, but the inclusion of systematic phonics was important in all interventions.
Katharina Galuschka et al. (2014)[23]	SR	6 to 13	Teaching letter-sound correspondences and decoding strategies, and the application of these skills in reading and writing activities to enhance reading fluency, is the most effective method for improving literacy skills of children and adolescents with reading disabilities.
Genevieve McArthur et al. (2018)[24]	SR	5 to 16	Update of an SR from 2012. Phonics training may have helped at-risk readers' decoding of pseudowords and phonetically regular words, but quality of research evidence was low. Review only focused on " 'pure' phonics programmes that train phonics-based reading skills alone" (p. 6).

(Continued)

Table 4.1 (Continued)

Author and year of publication	Type of study	Age of pupils	Main findings
Amanda Neitzel et al. (2021)[25]	SR	5 to 12	One-to-one tutoring for struggling readers produced large positive effects. One-to-small group tutoring also produced positive effects. There are insufficient numbers of longitudinal studies.
Russell Gersten et al. (2020)[26]	SR		The interventions in the review included attention to comprehension, passage reading fluency, and sometimes writing. Interventions that included writing resulted in higher effect sizes.
Stephanie Otaiba et al. (2022)[27]	TR	5 to 12	Systematic interventions that focus on the alphabetic code *and* meaning dimensions of reading and writing are most effective. Improvements in phonics-based reading skills were stronger than in improvements in comprehension.
Colby Hall et al. (2022)[28]	SR	5 to 11	The focus of this review of studies relevant to pupils with dyslexia was on foundational skills. Effects on reading comprehension were smaller than word reading or spelling. Multi-component interventions that included attention to spelling in addition to reading components were beneficial.
Combined typically developing readers and struggling readers			
Sebastian Suggate (2016)[29]	SR	5 to 12	Phonics interventions that included a comprehension component were more effective. Phonemic awareness (G) training was more effective than phonics interventions.

* Key: SR = Systematic Review. TR = Tertiary Review. SQMS = Systematic Qualitative Meta Synthesis.

has finished. In other words, do the effects of an intervention result in sustained positive changes to children's reading and writing? We regard the systematic review by Sebastian Suggate (2016) as particularly important because *all* the studies that were included in this review were longitudinal, which was not the case in any of the other systematic reviews. More specifically, this meant that a study would be excluded from the Suggate review if it did not include tests carried out at least 11 months after the end of the intervention. We look at the details of individual studies from the Suggate (2016) systematic review later in this chapter.

Teaching writing

The teaching of writing has also attracted multiple systematic reviews, meta-analyses, and tertiary reviews focused on which approaches to teaching writing are effective. Table 4.2 summarises the findings from systematic reviews focused on teaching writing published from 2004 onwards.

Table 4.2 Systematic reviews of the teaching of writing

Author and year of publication	Type of study	Age of pupils	Main findings
Typically developing writers			
Richard Andrews et al. (2004)[30]	SR	5 to 16	Grammar teaching has virtually no impact on pupils' writing. Teaching of syntax (G) in English should cease to be part of the curriculum.
Steve Graham and Dolores Perin (2007)[31]	SR	9 to 17	Effective interventions for teaching writing, in order of effectiveness: strategy instruction, summarisation, peer assistance, setting writing product goals, word processing, sentence combining, process writing.
Steve Graham and Dolores Perin (2007)[32]	SR including qualitative studies	9 to 17	Effective interventions for teaching writing, in order: strategy instruction, summarisation instruction, collaborative writing, setting goals for writing, word processing, sentence-combining, prewriting activities, inquiry activities, process-writing.
Leslie Ann Rogers and Steve Graham (2008)[33]	SR	7 to 18	Effective interventions for teaching writing: strategy instruction for planning/drafting, teaching grammar and usage, goal setting for productivity, strategy instruction for editing, writing with a word processor, reinforcing specific writing outcomes, use of prewriting activities, teaching sentence construction skills, and strategy instruction for paragraph writing.
Steve Graham and Michael Hebert (2011)[34]	SR	6 to 18	**Writing** instruction can improve **reading**. Writing about material that has been read enhances reading comprehension. Teaching writing skills improves reading. Increasing the amount of writing that pupils do improves reading.
Steve Graham et al. (2012)[35]	SR		Effective intervention types: 1. Teaching processes, skills or knowledge: strategy instruction; strategy instruction with self-regulation; text structure; creativity/imagery instruction. 2. Scaffolding or supporting pupils' writing. 3. Other interventions – word processing, extra writing, comprehensive writing programmes.
Tanya Santangelo and Steve Graham (2015)[36]	SR	5 to 15	Individualised handwriting instruction and handwriting instruction via digital technology improved legibility.
Steve Graham et al. (2016)[37]	TR	5 to 18	Presents six general evidence-based practices for teaching writing. Includes evidence that the process approach was effective.
Steve Graham et al. (2018)[38]	SR	5 to 18	Teaching **reading** strengthened **writing** overall and improved writing quality, words written, and spelling. The impact on writing was maintained over time.

(*Continued*)

Table 4.2 (Continued)

Author and year of publication	Type of study	Age of pupils	Main findings
Struggling writers			
Russell Gerston and Scott Baker (2001)[39]	SR	6 to 15	Found that three components were effective: 1. Explicit teaching of the steps of the writing process, 2. dimension of different writing genres, and 3. extensive feedback from teachers or peers.
Typically developing writers and struggling writers			
Steve Graham and Karin Sandmel (2011)[40]	SR	Elementary school to high school	Process approach improved writing for typically developing writers but not for struggling or at-risk writers.

We next highlight two main aspects of the research covered in the systematic reviews on the teaching of writing:

1. The evidence on teaching writing to help reading, and vice versa. This is important in relation to the main strands of our Double Helix of Reading and Writing model that we presented in Chapter 2, "The Development of Reading and Writing".
2. The evidence for the process approach to teaching writing. This is important because the debates about the process approach to writing have in the past shared some similarities with the reading debates.

In view of our caution about individual studies or people dominating the debates, you will have noticed that Steve Graham features repeatedly as an author in the systematic reviews for writing. This is because he has made an extraordinary contribution to research on writing, particularly his work on systematic reviews, so the inclusion of his work simply represents the field of systematic reviews as it was.

Teaching reading for writing and writing for reading

One of the unique features of our Double Helix of Reading and Writing is the direct links made at all levels of the model between the teaching of writing and reading. Key sources of research to support this link are the two systematic reviews that addressed teaching reading to improve writing, and vice versa. Steve Graham and Michael Hebert's[41] paper introduces its topic by noting that two of the largest initiatives to improve the teaching of reading in the USA, No Child Left Behind and Reading First, had not been as successful as hoped. You will recall that we referred to Reading First in the *Sold a Story* account in Chapter 1. These large-scale US federal initiatives included strong emphasis on phonics teaching and the other main components of reading addressed in the five reports of the USA's NRP.[42] Graham and Herbert say that a possible explanation was that the approaches to teaching reading in the two national initiatives were too narrow and not comprehensive enough.

The Graham and Hebert study found that *teaching writing to improve reading* had positive effects in all 21 studies selected for the meta-analysis. The types of effective writing interventions included process writing, teaching focused on text structure, and teaching focused on paragraphs/sentences, which all resulted in improved reading comprehension. If pupils wrote about material that they had read, this also enhanced their reading comprehension. In addition to a positive effect on reading comprehension, the positive effects included improved word reading. The impact on reading fluency (G) was for pupils aged 6 to 13, and the impact on reading comprehension was seen in pupils aged 9 to 18.

The systematic review by Steve Graham et al.[43] concluded that 19 out of 20 studies found a positive effect for *teaching reading to improve writing performance* overall but also on specific measures of writing quality, spelling, and writing output. Phonological awareness, phonics, and comprehension teaching also resulted in improvements in pupils' writing. In the 20% of studies that were longitudinal, the performances in writing were maintained, although at slightly lower levels. The review found that increasing pupils' interactions with texts, such as reading individual words, increasing the amount of reading, analysing text produced by others, or observing readers interact with text enhanced pupils' writing performance. These positive effects were seen in pupils aged from 5 to 18.

In Chapter 1 we described how the *Sold a Story* podcasts alleged that the work of the US academic Lucy Calkins was one of the main reasons children were not accessing scientifically based reading teaching, and more particularly synthetic phonics. Curiously, the only direct citation Hanford made of Calkins' work was to one of her books on writing. At the heart of Calkins' approach to teaching writing was 'the process approach to writing', which was made popular in primary schools by Donald Graves, another US academic with a background in school teaching. In essence the process approach to writing seeks to emulate in the classroom some of the aspects of authentic writing in the real world. Pupils are encouraged to make choices over their writing and to work towards some kind of publication, often a book made in class, to be shared with peers and sometimes communities beyond the school. The process approach stresses that writing is not usually a one-off event, such as underlining the verbs in sentences on a worksheet activity; it is a *process* that often requires stages of drafting and redrafting.

Many years after Calkins and Graves theorised the process approach to writing, based on their practical experiences and research, subsequent evidence in experimental trials proved that some of their ideas about how to teach writing were in fact correct. Steve Graham, Karen Harris, and Amber Chambers[44] examined the evidence for process writing and found that on average the approach resulted in a positive *effect size* of 0.48 for pupils aged 6 to 11. The process approach may not be as effective with struggling writers, as Steve Graham and Karin Sandmel[45] found.

The process approach to teaching writing has been studied in its own right as an approach but also in research studies focusing on the processes of writing more generally. For example, Steve Graham and Delores Perrin[46] found that *strategy instruction* was one of the most effective approaches to teaching writing. This involves explicitly teaching pupils about planning, revising, and editing their writing, something which is also used in the process approach, although less systematically. The other most effective strategy was *summarisation*, which involves pupils concisely and accurately representing information that they have read in their writing. Once again this underlines the importance of teaching reading and writing together. One of the very few RCTs on writing carried out in England concluded that the combination of memorable experiences plus strategy instruction was effective for the writing of pupils aged 11 and 12 who had writing difficulties.[47] Another RCT carried out in England on writing and grammar found a lack of impact for the approach to grammar teaching overall but a positive effect that may have been similar to the kind of positive effect seen in research on 'sentence-combining'.[48]

The systematic reviews addressed in this chapter provide powerful evidence that the teaching of phonics needs to be carefully balanced with other vital aspects of teaching reading but also the likelihood that writing needs to be taught at the same time. The evidence does not support a narrow approach to synthetic phonics. There is some evidence that struggling readers may particularly benefit from phonics teaching, but not at the expense of other elements, for example, reading comprehension, which is a vital part of all teaching of reading.

Systematic reviews of effective teaching of writing show that a range of components of writing need to be taught together. These components range across transcription elements and composition elements. Crucially, teaching writing helps reading, and teaching reading helps writing; therefore undue separation of reading and writing should be avoided. Emphasis on teaching writing as a process is strong, and the process approach to writing has a good evidence base, although less so with struggling writers.

Classroom practices for teaching reading

Although systematic reviews provide powerful evidence in general, related to a range of features of effective teaching of phonics, reading, and writing, it is important to examine the details of the teaching practices that were used in the most relevant single studies, selected on the basis of transparent and relevant criteria. For the purpose of this chapter we focused once again on studies about the teaching of reading, and selected the systematic review by Sebastian Suggate (2016) because it is the only one to only include research studies that were longitudinal: more specifically, these studies all included tests of reading at least 11 months after the end of the intervention. Longitudinal measures are the toughest test of an intervention and provide an indication of whether an intervention's effectiveness is sustained over time. Most importantly we want to be reassured that an intervention undertaken when children are, say, five years old will benefit their reading and writing later, in other words, will be a sustained positive impact.

The method we used for selecting and analysing individual studies was a systematic qualitative meta synthesis.[49] The criteria for selection of individual studies to feature in this part of the chapter were as follows:

- the research included a measure of reading comprehension, because this is the essence of reading;
- the language used for teaching the intervention and control was English, because the focus of this book is the English language;
- the sample of children was from age five to age eight because we are particularly interested in helping young children's reading and writing;
- the study focused mainly on typically developing readers <u>or</u> on struggling readers (consistent with the focus of our two main reviews of studies);
- the teaching intervention was delivered by teachers because regular class teachers have to help all children learn to read and write.

With regard to typically developing readers, eight of the 55 research papers from the Suggate systematic review met nearly all of these criteria. None of these studies with a main focus on typically developing readers had been done in England. However, prior to focusing on the details of these eight robust longitudinal experimental studies to see what we can learn about teaching approaches used in the effective interventions, there is one large-scale RCT study carried out in England, published in 2022, that directly focused on synthetic phonics that we need to mention.

One of the commercial synthetic phonics programmes validated by the Department for Education (DfE) in England (see Chapter 1, "The Reading Wars") was Read Write Inc

(RWI). The originator of RWI is Ruth Miskin, who had long campaigned to have synthetic phonics on the curriculum in England. In 2007 her work was featured in an article in the Sunday *Times* titled "Read My Lips, I Can Fix Our Schools."[50] Nick Gibb MP, who ultimately became government minister for schools, was aware of Miskin's work in 2007 and had maintained an "obsession"[51] with synthetic phonics since then. RWI was one of the most-used synthetic phonics programmes in primary schools in England.[52] In 2022 the Education Endowment Foundation (EEF), which is funded by the DfE, published a report on a large-scale robust RCT that had evaluated RWI (aimed at children aged four to nine) and a related RWI catch-up programme called Fresh Start (FS – aimed at children aged 9 to 13).[53]

The outcomes of many RCTs in education are small positive effect sizes which do not reach statistical significance. Some RCTs result in large positive effect sizes that are significant. Only rarely do RCTs report negative effects – in other words, pupils in the intervention group make less progress than pupils in the control group. This means that their learning has been impeded by the intervention, something that everyone wants to avoid.

The outcomes of the EEF RCT of RWI and FS reported five out of eight measures where the effects were <u>negative</u> for the pupils. The FS intervention showed minus three months or minus two months estimated progress for pupils' reading. The effect size for RWI was 0.05, a small positive effect, which was estimated as one month of additional progress compared to the control group, but this did not reach statistical significance. The confidence interval for the effect size was estimated to be between –0.02 and 0.12.

There were some issues with the implementation of research methods as part of the RCT. For example, there was a relatively high number of participant pupils not included in the final data analysis because, for example, they had moved school or a school had withdrawn from the study, a problem for RCT studies called 'attrition'. Also some schools in the intervention groups did not deliver the programme. One of the reasons given for intervention schools not delivering RWI was the physical space requirements in the schools. Putting pupils into phonics ability groups required more space than mixed ability teaching would have.

As a result of these challenges for the implementation of the research methods in the study, the EEF regarded the RCT for RWI to have a low to moderate 'security rating' (two out of five EEF 'padlocks'), as opposed to the findings for FS, which were regarded as having a moderate security rating (three out of five padlocks). This means that although in general terms the study is robust, hence it was published by the EEF, there are some limitations that mean it was not awarded four or five EEF padlocks, which are used to indicate the highest quality of implementation of appropriate research methods in a study.

The other reason for caution about the findings of the study is that the control groups in primary schools were receiving some kind of synthetic phonics teaching, because this was required by the DfE, so the experimental comparison was between carefully controlled intensive interventions with significant professional development support from the programme developers (RWI and FS) versus less consistent and more variable phonics teaching ('business as usual'; BAU).

One of the many consequences of England's government strategies to mandate synthetic phonics is that it would be very difficult to carry out a large-scale RCT to test alternatives to current practice, because schools in an experimental group would be reluctant to take on non–DfE-approved approaches for fear of criticism if their school is inspected. The list of DfE-validated synthetic phonics schemes means that in effect, schools are required to choose one, even though the technical legal position is that they do not have to. This is not a healthy state of affairs for so many reasons, not least the lack of opportunity to learn from new robust research studies undertaken in England. For this reason the EEF study is important because it was the only one of its kind, a large-scale RCT, carried out in England to evaluate synthetic phonics. Taken as a whole the EEF study should at least have caused the DfE and others to reflect on its outcomes, but we could find no public response from the DfE. This is of course only one research study, and we have argued the importance of considering multiple studies, but due to the lack of studies undertaken in England and the popularity of RWI at the time, it is an important study to consider. At the very least the negative impacts of FS and the modest impact of RWI should have given pause for thought given that this is one of the most long-standing, influential, and profitable synthetic phonics schemes. Our analysis of many other RCTs, which informs this chapter, shows that different approaches to phonics teaching have been more effective.

Studies of typically developing readers

A key point of disagreement about the teaching of phonics for reading has been whether it is more effective to focus on synthetic phonics separately from other aspects of reading or to integrate the teaching of phonics with whole texts in all phonics lessons. Six of the eight effective interventions finally selected through our SQMS included phonics lessons that included both the teaching of phonics *and* teaching with whole texts. The type of phonics teaching varied considerably and had multiple components. Narrow synthetic phonics of the kind mandated in England was not the kind of phonics teaching that was used in the interventions in the studies.[54]

All the selected studies included the use of texts specially created to enable reading; however, these appeared to vary considerably. A direct comparison of the effectiveness of reading scheme texts, such as 'decodable texts', versus the effectiveness of using 'real' books and texts has not been researched using an RCT with longitudinal design. However, a systematic review of research studies was carried out to examine the question of whether decodable or non-decodable texts were more effective.[55] Unfortunately in most of the studies that were included in this systematic review, the researchers had not provided enough specific information about the texts used as part of the teaching intervention, so we have to be cautious interpreting the findings.

The conclusions of the systematic review included the hypothesis that the use of both decodable (phonics programme books) (G) *and* non-decodable books (real books) together in lessons was likely to produce the greatest improvements in pupils' reading, but we stress again that RCT research is needed to test this hypothesis. As you saw in Chapter 3, "How Texts Teach What Children Learn", we strongly advocate more use of real books as part of our Double Helix Model. The lessons featured in the second half of this book all use real books to teach phonics and other aspects of reading and writing, not least because these books offer a much wider range of learning and are much more likely to engage children.

In four of the eight studies of typically developing readers that we selected in our SQMS, the interventions were not delivered by teachers, for example, delivered by what are known as *paraeducators* or volunteer tutors. The positive aspect of this is the evidence that people other than teachers can effectively contribute to children's reading development. The limitation is the relative lack of research about effective interventions that primary school teachers deliver in the course of their normal teaching.

Another important consideration for effective teaching of reading is how much time should be devoted to any particular intervention. The first thing to note is that the successful interventions typically included daily lessons/activities up to four times per week lasting about 30 minutes duration per lesson. The minimum amount of hours total duration for an intervention was approximately 9.1 hours, and the maximum was approximately 60 hours. The interventions carried out in Norway reported in Solveig-Alma Lyster's (2002) paper were notable for the lowest number of hours for delivery of the effective interventions: approximately 9.1 hours delivered in about 35 minutes per week in one or two lessons.[56] If 60 hours were divided into 30-minute lessons, they could be completed within 24 weeks. If we also remember the idea that not all children need systematic phonics to learn to read, then it is even more important that children not be subjected to too much phonics teaching at the expense of all the other important aspects of reading and writing that they should be engaging with. Strong politically driven moves to impose synthetic phonics teaching typically distort these important balances and result in children not receiving optimal teaching.

One of our key messages learned from studying these studies is that the maximum duration of phonics teaching lessons probably should be one year for typically developing readers. For some readers the duration of phonics teaching needed will be much less than a year; therefore it is important that as soon as children can decode appropriate texts independently, they be removed from systematic phonics programmes. Rather than a phonics screening check (G), a more useful assessment would be an initial assessment of children's reading of continuous text soon after they start primary school (perhaps at about age five). Those who could read when they enter school should not be put on a phonics programme to teach reading.

The reality at the moment is that *all* children are often required to stay on synthetic phonics programmes for as long as three years in England. The importance of not holding children back, that is, removing them early from systematic phonics teaching programmes, is given added weight when taking account of children's capacity to learn to read themselves, something that has been called the *self-teaching hypothesis*.[57] The complexity of the spelling-to-sound relationships in the English language means that teachers can only provide at best simplified models of phoneme-to-letter(s) correspondences, and hence teachers should enable children to teach themselves rather than over-teaching the complexities of the alphabetic code. Overcomplicating teaching, including the introduction of unnecessary technical terms, is another problem in many synthetic phonics policies and has the impact of undermining the natural expertise that well-educated teachers and parents bring to the task of helping their children, in part by virtue of their own successes in reading and writing.

Only two of the studies selected in our review carried out in the English language were taught by classroom teachers rather than paraeducators/other assistants. The study undertaken in Canada by Linda Phillips, Stephen Norris, and Jana Mason[58] included groups in the experimental trial where parents delivered the intervention. However, only the group that did not involve parents delivering the intervention showed positive gains for reading when students were retested in Grade 4, four years after the intervention was first introduced. One possible explanation for the impact of teachers and not parents is that the groups that included parents *and* teachers were a more complicated teaching context. Parents would not have the skills of trained teachers, in particular the knowledge that develops as a result of teaching reading to multiple classes of children over many years. There is a significant separate field of studies focused on the most appropriate ways that parents can help their children with reading, but less so for writing.

The successful intervention in the Phillips, Norris, and Mason study included materials clearly built on a rationale of the importance of texts to *contextualise* the teaching of the alphabetic code, for example:

> The reading intervention materials (McCormick & Mason, 1990) consisted of a series of booklets with the following features and rationale: (a) They were thematic

and contained familiar topics to increase the child's expectation that text should make sense. . . . c) There was a strong fit between illustrations and text to develop the concept that both text and picture frame the meaning.[59]

Apart from its use of specially designed texts rather than real books, this intervention could be described as a whole-language approach; however, both intervention groups and control groups also had separate teaching from the Language Development Reading Series (McInnes, 1988), the purpose of which is "to cultivate familiarity with print (McInnes, 1988, p. ix)."[60] Overall, the materials were designed "to fit closely the early literacy needs of children entering school at risk of failure",[61] so once again, even with this study, we have to be cautious about the extent to which the findings are generalisable to children with typical reading development. And although this study meets more of the inclusion criteria than any other studies, it was still was not undertaken in England. Another English-language intervention delivered by classroom teachers was carried out in the USA[62] but the final longitudinal outcomes were not statistically significant – another important reminder that systematic phonics is not a panacea for helping all children.

Other studies that were carried out using the English language were those undertaken by Patricia Vadasy and colleagues in the USA, although the interventions were implemented by paraeducators, not by teachers. The lessons in the effective interventions, published across three papers,[63] addressed both teaching in the alphabetic code and teaching with whole text, although it is not clear to what extent connections were made between these two aspects:

> Students assigned to treatment received individual systematic and explicit phonics tutoring instruction in English, which included letter-sound correspondences, phonemic decoding, spelling, and <u>assisted oral reading practice in decodable texts</u>. . . . In a typical tutoring session, paraeducators spent 20 min on phonics activities and 10 min <u>scaffolding students' oral reading practice in decodable texts</u>.[64]

Nearly all of the most effective approaches to teaching phonics and reading in our selection of longitudinal studies connected the phonics learning with whole texts, and whole sentences and whole words, in all phonics lessons, for example, by applying the alphabetic knowledge learned by practising reading, with support from adults. The most basic whole text contextualisation, but nevertheless important, involved the pupils practising reading whole texts after their phonics input. While there is evidence of this simple contextualisation being effective if we take the general evidence from systematic reviews *and* the teaching approaches in the individual research studies, then a balanced approach where phonics teaching is contextualised in whole texts, including a focus on comprehension and including the teaching of writing within reading lessons is, we argue, more likely to be effective for typical readers.

Our hypothesis that the *contextualised phonics teaching* that is part of our Double Helix of Reading and Writing Model is more effective than discrete synthetic phonics teaching is also supported by a seminal study that directly addressed the question of discrete verses contextualised phonics teaching. Robust proof of the concept of contextualisation was established in an experimental trial as early as 1990. Anne Cunningham's study directly compared a decontextualised phonics teaching (oral segmentation of phonemes [G] and blending phonemes in relation to single words) group with a contextualised phonics teaching group and also compared with a control group who listened to a story and answered questions about it. For precision, it is worth quoting the contextualised phonics intervention in full from the paper:

> The second instructional program provided students with a metalevel knowledge of phonemic awareness. In this program, the children were directed to reflect upon their own thinking regarding phonemic awareness and explicit discussion of the goals and purposes of learning phonemic awareness to improve overall reading ability were emphasized. For example, children may be told that when they came upon a word they did not know . . . to think about the story they were reading and decide if /b/a/t/ <u>fits into their story of a baseball player</u>. Thus, <u>a more contextualized approach</u> was provided whereby the skill was taught and linked explicitly to earlier lessons and the activity of reading. The value and utility of this skill for future reading was explicitly emphasized by providing readers with an appreciation of task requirements and an awareness of the utility of their actions.[65]

The results of the research showed that the contextualised phonics intervention was more effective than decontextualised phonics because it bridged the learning about phonemes, with input on reading more generally, in order to promote broader transfer of skills.

Given that this finding has been known for more than 30 years, it is particularly worrying that decontextualised narrow teaching of phonics continues to be advocated and increasingly appears to be influencing education policies. We are grateful to journalist Colin Barras for reminding us of the Cunningham study as part of meetings to discuss research on reading, including Dominic and Alice Bradbury's contribution to Barras' excellent piece about the teaching of reading in The New Scientist.[66]

Studies of struggling readers

The systematic reviews summarised in Table 4.1 show that effective teaching of children with reading difficulties should have multiple components including systematic phonics *combined* with an emphasis on meaning and comprehension, and teaching writing to help reading. There was also evidence that one-to-one tuition, including Marie Clay's Reading Recovery, is effective in supporting struggling readers. The systematic review by Katharina Galuschka et al.[67] found that phonics teaching was effective for struggling readers but only when *applied* in the context of reading and writing activities to enhance reading fluency. Indeed it was found that training in reading fluency alone was less effective than the combination of reading fluency and phonemic awareness. What's more, there was evidence that using the same approach repeatedly is unlikely to be effective:

> Ever since the meta-analyses of the NRP in the year 2000, it has been apparent that interventions are not equally effective for different age groups or grade levels. Providing children of a wide age span with the same interventions is therefore not a recommended option for research settings and clinical practice.[68]

The 55 papers of the Suggate (2016) systematic review featured 17 teaching interventions for struggling readers shown to be effective at a minimum 11 months after the intervention end. Sixteen of these interventions integrated phonics teaching with other aspects of reading teaching. None of the interventions were delivered by regular classroom teachers; typically they were delivered by trained teachers hired to do the research intervention.

As far as struggling readers are concerned, there were two studies carried out in England that met all bar one of our criteria (i.e. apart from the criterion about inclusion of typically developing readers, which is not relevant to this section of the chapter): the studies by Paula Clarke, Margaret Snowling, Emma Truelove, and Charles Hulme[69] and by Peter Hatcher, Charles Hulme, and Andrew Ellis.[70] The study by Hatcher et al. is important not only because it is one of only two robust experimental longitudinal studies that met our criteria, including being carried out in England, but also because it explicitly addressed the issue of whether discrete phonics teaching was more effective than contextualised phonics teaching. Children with reading difficulties across the county of Cumbria in England were selected on the basis of screening tests. Through a process of matching based on test outcomes, 128 children were allocated to one of four groups: 1. Reading with Phonology (R + P), 2. Reading Alone (R), 3. Phonology Alone (P), and 4. a Control group. The *phonological linkage hypothesis* is the idea that teaching phonics in isolation, or discretely such as synthetic phonics, will be less effective than teaching that explicitly links phonics teaching with other aspects of learning to read. The intervention involved children being taught individually for forty 30-minute sessions over 20 weeks. It is worth quoting their main conclusion in full:

> In line with the phonological linkage hypothesis, we have shown that an effective way of improving reading skills involves a joint approach that integrates the training of phonological skills with the teaching of reading. Spending an equivalent amount of time concentrating on either component in isolation (reading or phonology) is less effective. Although the individual teaching of reading received by the Reading Alone group did produce some gains, they were not as large as in the group given both reading and phonological training. This is an important, and not at all obvious, result. Generally the most effective way to teach a given skill is to teach it directly. Our children given the reading and phonology package actually received less time being directly taught reading skills than did the Reading Alone group. The fact that they nevertheless made significantly more progress in reading is quite surprising and impressive.[71]

One of limitations with this study is that although it had random allocation to groups, it used a pupil matching design with relatively small samples of children in each group. Random allocation of children with reading difficulties is challenging due to them being a smaller population of children, and they are distributed across many schools in a given region.

The other study carried out in England, by Paula Clarke et al.,[72] was a RCT focused on ameliorating children's reading comprehension difficulties and did not include a focus on phonics because the criteria for the sample of eight- to nine-year-old children included having sufficient decoding skills to access the teaching materials of the intervention. The intervention consisted of three 30-minute sessions per week (two session in pairs and one session for an individual) for 20 weeks. The authors concluded that specific reading comprehension problems were relatively common, and their intervention was effective in ameliorating these problems.

A study carried out in Canada by Robin Morris et al.[73] was the RCT with the largest sample size in our selection of studies with children with reading difficulties. It is also an important example because the study sought to explicitly investigate teaching components of reading in combination. The pupils in the study were on average age seven years nine months at the start of the intervention. The intervention consisted of 70 sessions of 60 minutes per day five days a week over one school year. The study found that incorporating multiple components within interventions was more effective than the control conditions that predominantly emphasised phonologically based reading teaching. The four intervention programmes spanned two types of groups: 1. experimental groups: a. phonics and word identification and b. phonics and word work, including engagement with language, and 2. control groups: c. maths plus classroom skills and d. phonics plus classroom skills. These intervention programmes evolved so that multiple combinations could be measured. In what was a complex set of interventions, the authors concluded that the multiple language component interventions were more effective than predominantly phonologically based reading interventions.

A study carried out by Janice Ryder, William Tunmer, and Keith Greaney[74] in New Zealand was unusual in that it adopted an isolated phonics approach, at least at the beginning of the programme. The sample size was much smaller that the Morris et al.[75] study. Twenty-four children with a mean age of seven years and eight months were matched in pairs, then allocated at random to two groups of 12 children. The programme did not introduce reading of 'decodable texts' until lesson 28 of the 56 lessons, which took place over a period of 24 weeks. The lack of statistically significant gain in reading comprehension compared to the gains in phonemic awareness and pseudoword decoding perhaps could be attributed to the fact that half of the programme delivered the phonics in isolation from whole texts and other aspects of reading. This attribution is supported by the findings from nearly all the other studies that we have reviewed in this section that showed that combining components was more effective than isolating phonics.

Summarising the evidence from systematic reviews and longitudinal research studies

The most robust research appropriate to answering the question 'what works best in the teaching of phonics, reading, and writing?', called by some people 'the science of reading', clearly shows that a balanced approach to teaching reading is the most effective. A balanced approach to teaching reading includes, in all phonics lessons, phonics teaching systematically combined with other elements that are vital to teaching children to read and write.

The elements which need to be systematically combined in phonics and reading lessons are portrayed in the Double Helix of Reading and Writing (Chapter 2), which includes human language and literacy as the background for understanding teaching and learning; the child and their motivation to read as central to any teaching approach; the importance of the general environment for literacy at home and at school; real texts chosen by teachers; teaching making connections between reading and writing; constant reference to meaning driving all teaching of reading and writing, including emphasising comprehension and composition; teaching about words, sentences, and larger text structures; and learning about the alphabetic code as a fundamental part of the teaching, particularly when children are about age five. The research does *not* show that discrete synthetic phonics of the kind practised in England and some other countries and regions should be first and foremost because this reflects an undue influence on one part of the balance of elements that make up successful reading.

Part I of this book has situated the debates about how best to teach phonics, reading, and writing in the international context of countries where the English language is a main language taught in primary schools. The Double Helix of Reading and Writing has been presented as a new model to inform teaching. This model is informed by many robust research studies that have addressed the effective teaching of reading and writing that were summarised in this chapter. The fundamental importance of the texts selected by teachers to use in their phonics, reading, and writing lessons has also been portrayed. In Part II of the book we turn to how teaching is undertaken when informed by our model and the research underpinning it. So the structure of the book moves from its new account of theory and research to an account of the new approach in practice. The first chapter in Part II provides an overview of the main practical elements that teachers will need to implement in all lessons that are part of the balanced approach to reading and writing that are described in vivid detail in the subsequent chapters.

Notes

1 Davis, A. (2017). *A Critique of Pure Teaching Methods and the Case of Synthetic Phonics*. Bloomsbury.
2 Manguel, A. (1996). *A History of Reading*. Flamingo.
3 Styles, M., & Drummond, M. J. (1993). Editorial: The Politics of Reading. *Cambridge Journal of Education, 23*(1), 3–13.
4 For example, Kerswill, P. (2007). Standard and Non-Standard English. In D. Britain (Ed.), *Language in the British Isles*. Cambridge University Press.
5 Wyse, D. (2017). *How Writing Works: From the Invention of the Alphabet to the Rise of Social Media*. Cambridge University Press.
6 Readers interested in more of the details of experimental trials could read Torgerson, C., & Torgerson, D. (2017). 'True' Experimental Designs. In D. Wyse, N. Selwyn, E. Smith, & L. Suter (Eds.), *The BERA/SAGE Handbook of Educational Research* (pp. 416–435). SAGE.
7 Wynder, E. (1988). Tobacco and Health: A Review of the History and Suggestions for Public Health Policy. *Public Health Reports, 103*(1), 8–18.
8 For evidence of the undermining of the evidence about smoking, and later the undermining of evidence about the human contribution to climate change, see this powerful account: Oreskes, N., & Conway, E. (2011). *The Merchants of Doubt*. Bloomsbury.
9 Retrieved December 1, 2023, from https://www.bbc.co.uk/news/newsbeat-32958975
10 Higgins, S., Kokotsaki, D., & Coe, R. (2012). *The Teaching and Learning Toolkit: Technical Appendices*. Education Endowment Foundation & The Sutton Trust. There is some debate about how accurate bands of effect sizes are in relation to child development when combining these in meta analyses.
11 Kraft, M. (2020). Interpreting Effect Sizes of Education Interventions. *Educational Researcher, 49*(4), 241–253.
12 Wyse, D., & Bradbury, A. (2022). Reading Wars or Reading Reconciliation? A Critical Examination of Robust Research Evidence, Curriculum Policy, and Teachers' Practices for Teaching Phonics and Reading. *Review of Education*. Retrieved December 1, 2023, from https://doi.org/10.1002/rev3.3314
13 National Reading Panel. (2000). *National Reading Panel. Teaching Children to Read. An Evidence-Based Assessment of the Scientific Research Literature on Reading and Its Implications for Reading Instruction. Reports of the Subgroups*.
14 Wyse, D., & Goswami, U. (2008). Synthetic Phonics and the Teaching of Reading. *British Educational Research Journal, 34*(6), 691–710.
15 Rose, J. (2006). *Independent Review of the Teaching of Early Reading: Final Report*. DfES Publications.
16 Torgerson, C. J., Brooks, G., & Hall, J. (2006). *A Systematic Review of the Research Literature on the Use of Phonics in the Teaching of Reading and Spelling*. Department for Education and Skills (DfES).
17 Adesope, O., Lavin, T., Thompson, T., & Ungerleider, C. (2010). Pedagogical Strategies for Teaching Literacy to ESL Immigrant Students: A Meta-Analysis. *British Journal of Educational Psychology, 81*, 629–653.
18 Torgerson, C., Brooks, G., Gascoine, G., & Higgins, S. (2018). Phonics: Reading Policy and the Evidence of Effectiveness from a Systematic 'Tertiary' Review. *Research Papers in Education*. Retrieved December 1, 2023, from https://doi.org/10.1080/02671522.2017.1420816

19 Bowers, J. (2020). Reconsidering the Evidence that Systematic Phonics Is More Effective Than Alternative Methods of Reading Instruction. *Educational Psychology Review*. Retrieved December 1, 2023, from https://doi.org/10.1007/s10648-019-09515-y
20 Wyse & Bradbury, Reading Wars or Reading Reconciliation?
21 Suggate, S. (2010). Why What We Teach Depends on When: Grade and Reading Intervention Modality Moderate Effect Size. *Developmental Psychology, 46*, 1556–1579.
22 Slavin, R., Lake, C., Davis, S., & Madden, N. (2011). Effective Programs for Struggling Readers: A Best-Evidence Synthesis. *Educational Research Review, 6*, 1–26.
23 Galuschka, K., Ise, E., Krick, K., & Schulte-Korne, G. (2014). Effectiveness of Treatment Approaches for Children and Adolescents with Reading Disabilities: A Meta-Analysis of Randomized Controlled Trials. *PLoS One, 9*, 1–12. Retrieved December 1, 2023, from https://doi.org/10.1371/journal.pone.0089900
24 McArthur, G., Sheehan, Y., Badcock, N. A., Francis, D. A., Wang, H. C., Kohnen, S., Banales, E., Anandakumar, T., Marinus, E., & Castles, A. (2018). *Phonics Training for English-Speaking Poor Readers. Cochrane Database of Systematic Reviews 2018, Issue 11. Art. No.: CD009115*. John Wiley and Sons.
25 Neitzel, A., Lake, C., Pellegrini, M., & Slavin, R. (2021). A Synthesis of Quantitative Research on Programs for Struggling Readers in Elementary Schools. *Reading Research Quarterly, 57*(1), 149–179.
26 Gersten, R., Haymond, K., Newman-Gonchar, R., Dimino, J., & Jayanthi, M. (2020). Meta-Analysis of the Impact of Reading Interventions for Students in the Primary Grades. *Journal of Research on Educational Effectiveness, 13*(2), 401–427.
27 Otaiba, S., McMaster, K., Wanzek, J., & Zaru, M. (2022). What We Know and Need to Know about Literacy Interventions for Elementary Students with Reading Difficulties and Disabilities, Including Dyslexia. *Reading Research Quarterly, 58*(2), 313–332.
28 Hall, C., Dahl-Leonard, K., Cho, E., Solari, E., Capin, P., Conner, C., Henry, A., Cook, L., Hayes, L., Vargas, I., Richmond, C., & Kehoe, K. (2022). Forty Years of Reading Intervention Research for Elementary Students with or at Risk for Dyslexia: A Systematic Review and Meta-Analysis. *Reading Research Quarterly*, 1–28. Retrieved December 1, 2023, from https://doi.org/10.1002/rrq.477
29 Suggate, S. (2016). A Meta-Analysis of the Long-Term Effects of Phonemic Awareness, Phonics, Fluency, and Reading Comprehension Interventions. *Journal of Learning Disabilities, 49*, 77–96.
30 Andrews, R., Torgerson, C., Beverton, S., Freeman, A., Locke, T., Low, G., Robinson, A., & Zhu, D. (2004). *The Effect of Grammar Teaching (Sentence Combining) in English on 5 to 16 Year Olds' Accuracy and Quality in Written Composition*. Retrieved December 1, 2023, from http://eppi.ioe.ac.uk/cms/
31 Graham, S., & Perin, D. (2007). A Meta-Analysis of Writing Instruction for Adolescent Students. *Journal of Educational Psychology, 99*(3), 445–476.
32 Graham, S., & Perin, D. (2007). What We Know, What We Still Need to Know: Teaching Adolescents to Write. *Scientific Studies of Reading, 11*, 313–335. Retrieved December 1, 2023, from https://doi.org/10.1080/10888430701530664
33 Rogers, L. A., & Graham, S. (2008). A Meta-Analysis of Single Subject Design Writing Intervention Research. *Journal of Educational Psychology, 100*, 879–906.
34 Graham, S., & Hebert, M. (2011). Writing to Read: A Meta-Analysis of the Impact of Writing and Writing Instruction on Reading. *Harvard Educational Review, 81*, 710–745.
35 Graham, S., McKeown, D., Kiuhara, S., & Harris, K. (2012). A Meta-Analysis of Writing Instruction for Students in the Elementary Grades. *Journal of Educational Psychology, 104*(4), 879–896.
36 Santangelo, T., & Graham, S. (2015). A Comprehensive Meta-Analysis of Handwriting Instruction. *Educational Psychology Review, 28*, 225–265.
37 Graham, S., Harris, K., & Chambers, A. (2016). Evidence-Based Practice and Writing Instruction: A Review of Reviews. In C. MacArthur, S. Graham, & A. Chambers (Eds.), *Handbook of Writing Research* (2nd ed.). Guilford.
38 Graham, S., Xinghua, L., Bartlett, B., Ng, C., Harris, K., Aitken, A., Barkel, A., & Kavanaugh, C. (2018). Reading for Writing: A Meta-Analysis of the Impact of Reading Interventions on Writing. *Review of Educational Research, 88*, 243–284.

39 Gersten, R., Darch, C., & Gleason, M. (1988). Effectiveness of a Direct Instruction Academic Kindergarten for Low-Income Students. *The Elementary School Journal*, 89, 227–240.
40 Graham, S., & Sandmel, K. (2011). The Process Writing Approach: A Meta-Analysis. *The Journal of Educational Research*, 104, 396–407.
41 Graham & Hebert, Writing to Read.
42 National Reading Panel, *Teaching Children to Read*.
43 Graham, Xinghua, Bartlett, Ng, Harris, Aitken, Barkel, & Kavanaugh, Reading for Writing.
44 Graham, Harris, & Chambers, Evidence-Based Practice.
45 Graham & Sandmel, The Process Writing Approach.
46 Graham & Perin, What We Know.
47 Torgerson, D., Torgerson, C., Ainsworth, H., Buckley, H., Heaps, C., Hewitt, C., & Mitchell, N. (2014). *Improving Writing Quality: Evaluation Report and Executive Summary*. Education Endowment Foundation.
48 Wyse, D., Aarts, B., Anders, J., de Gennaro, A., Dockrell, J., Manyukhina, Y., Sing, S., & Torgerson, C. (2022). *Grammar and Writing in England's National Curriculum. A Randomised Controlled Trial and Implementation and Process Evaluation of Englicious*. Retrieved December 1, 2023, from https://discovery.ucl.ac.uk/id/eprint/10144257/
49 See the following for an account of the method of SQMS: Wyse & Bradbury, Reading Wars or Reading Reconciliation?
50 Marrin, M. (2007, 21st October). Read My Lips, I Can Fix Our Schools. Interview with Ruth Miskin. *The Sunday Times*, p. 5.
51 Wyse, D. (2023, 9th October). *Teaching Phonics and Reading: PIRLS of Wisdom?* Retrieved December 1, 2023, from https://neu.org.uk/latest/blogs/teaching-phonics-and-reading-pirls-wisdom
52 Wyse & Bradbury, Reading Wars or Reading Reconciliation?
53 Molotsky, A., Dias, P., & Nakamura, P. (2022). *Read Write Inc. Phonics and Fresh Start: Evaluation Report*. Retrieved December 1, 2023, from https://educationendowmentfoundation.org.uk/projects-and-evaluation/projects/read-write-inc-and-fresh-start
54 Of the eight papers, two published by Vadasy and colleagues featured the same intervention.
55 Pugh, A., & Kearns, D. (2023). Text Types and Their Relation to Efficacy in Beginning Reading Interventions. *Reading Research Quarterly*, 1–23. Retrieved December 1, 2023, from https://doi.org/10.1002/rrq.513
56 Lyster, S.-A. (2002). The Effects of Morphological Versus Phonological Awareness Training in Kindergarten on Reading Development. *Reading and Writing: An Interdisciplinary Journal*, 15, 261–294.
57 Share, D. (1995). Phonological Recoding and Self-Teaching: Sine Qua Non of Reading Acquisition. *COGNITION*, 55(2), 151–218.
58 Phillips, L., Norris, S., & Mason, M. (1996). Longitudinal Effects of Early Literacy Concepts on Reading Achievement: A Kindergarten Intervention and Five-Year Follow-up. *Journal of Literacy Research*, 28, 173–195.
59 Phillips, Norris, & Mason, Longitudinal Effects.
60 Phillips, Norris, & Mason, Longitudinal Effects.
61 Phillips, Norris, & Mason, Longitudinal Effects, p. 180.
62 Gunn, B., Smolkowski, K., & Vadasy, P. (2011). Evaluating the Effectiveness of Read Well Kindergarten. *Journal of Research on Educational Effectiveness*, 4(1), 53–86.
63 For example, Vadasy, P., & Sanders, E. (2012). Two-Year Follow-Up of a Kindergarten Phonics Intervention for English Learners and Native English Speakers: Contextualizing Treatment Impacts by Classroom Literacy Instruction. *Journal of Educational Psychology*, 104, 987–1005.
64 Vadasy & Sanders, Two-Year Follow-Up. Underline added.
65 Cunningham, A. (1990). Explicit versus Implicit Instruction in Phonemic Awareness. *Journal of Experimental Child Psychology*, 50, 429–444. Underline added.
66 Barras, C. (2023). As Tricky as ABC. *The New Scientist*, 42–45. Retrieved December 1, 2023, from https://www.newscientist.com/article/mg25834350-200-we-know-how-kids-learn-to-read-so-why-are-we-failing-to-teach-them/
67 Galuschka, Ise, Krick, & Schulte-Korne, Effectiveness of Treatment Approaches.
68 Galuschka, Ise, Krick, & Schulte-Korne, Effectiveness of Treatment Approaches.

69 Clarke, P., Snowling, M., Truelove, E., & Hulme, C. (2010). Ameliorating Children's Reading-Comprehension Difficulties: A Randomized Controlled Trial. *Psychological Science*, *21*(8), 1106–1116.
70 Hatcher, P., Hulme, C., & Ellis, A. (1994). Ameliorating Early Reading Failure by Integrating the Teaching of Reading and Phonological Skills: The Phonological Linkage Hypothesis. *Child Development*, *60*, 41–57.
71 Hatcher, Hulme, & Ellis, Ameliorating Early Reading Failure. Underline added.
72 Clarke, Snowling, Truelove, & Hulme, Ameliorating Children's Reading-Comprehension Difficulties.
73 Morris, R., Lovett, M., Wolf, M., Sevcik, R., Steinbach, K., Frijters, J. C., & Shapiro, M. (2012). Multiple-Component Remediation for Developmental Reading Disabilities: IQ, Socioeconomic Status, and Race as Factors in Remedial Outcome. *Journal of Learning Disabilities*, *45*(2), 99–127.
74 Ryder, J., Tunmer, W., & Greaney, K. (2008). Explicit Instruction in Phonemic Awareness and Phonemically Based Decoding Skills as an Intervention Strategy for Struggling Readers in Whole Language Classrooms. *Reading and Writing: An Interdisciplinary Journal*, *21*, 349–369.
75 Morris, Lovett, Wolf, Sevcik, Steinbach, Frijters, & Shapiro, Multiple-Component Remediation.

Part II
The art of teaching

5 The balanced approach to teaching phonics, reading, and writing

Historically the reading wars have been portrayed as two main approaches in opposition to each other: the top-down approach to teaching reading versus the bottom-up approach. But more recently three main orientations to teaching reading have been described:[1]

1. Synthetic Phonics (G): a focus <u>first and foremost</u> on teaching children about *phonemes (G) and letters*. As part of this approach, at key moments in the teaching programme, phonics teaching (G) is separate from practising reading with whole texts. In the early stages of the approach in particular, whole text reading is required to be done with 'decodable' books (G), which are reading scheme/basal books with vocabularies controlled to enable repetition of key words learned during the phonics programme;
2. Whole Language: a focus first and foremost on *whole texts*, 'real' books (trade books created by authors as part of standard publication practices), that it is theorised children will enjoy more and will be motivated by. The whole-language approach is driven by reading for meaning. Phonics teaching, and other aspects of reading, are taught in a relatively non-systematic way and carried out through examples related to the real books being read;
3. The Balanced Approach: a focus first and foremost on the *balance* between teaching based on use of whole texts and systematic teaching about the alphabetic code *and* also other linguistic features. With this approach, the importance of comprehending the meaning of written language is carefully balanced with the acquisition of a range of skills and knowledge. Lessons make explicit links between phonics teaching and other linguistic aspects with whole texts, which are often a combination of real books and reading scheme books with controlled vocabularies.

Table 5.1 summarises the main ways in which a synthetic phonics approach differs from phonics taught as part of the balanced approach to teaching reading.

The balanced approach includes the use of a range of approaches to systematic phonics teaching commensurate with the research evidence. This also allows teachers flexibility to be responsive to the particular children that they are working with and their different levels of development. Teachers are assumed to have the professional knowledge to teach reading and writing using methods that they select on the basis of this knowledge.

DOI: 10.4324/9781003442134-8

Table 5.1 The balanced approach to teaching reading compared to synthetic phonics

Balanced approach	Synthetic phonics approach
The main aim of the balanced approach is to motivate children to read by sharing authentic texts as the stimulus and material for reading. Systematic phonics teaching is closely linked with these texts whenever it is taught.	The main aim of synthetic phonics is to teach children about phonemes, and their representations in letters and words, to aid reading.
Teachers use their professional knowledge to plan lessons.	Teachers follow a commercially published synthetic phonics scheme of lessons.
Built on the rationale that decoding and reading comprehension develop together.	Built on the rationale that decoding is taught first in sequence, separately from comprehension, in separate synthetic phonics lessons.
Whole texts are always the basis of phonics lessons.	In some stages of the phonics programme the reading of whole texts may not be allowed to ensure a focus on decoding.
Phonics lessons emphasise books written for children published in the trade press. Decodable books may be used on some occasions.	Phonics lessons use 'decodable books', books written as part of phonics schemes that have vocabulary of words selected for their use of particular phonemes.
A main emphasis is placed on comprehending and enjoying whole texts. Phonics is seen as one important strategy to support learning to read.	The main emphasis is on learning the sequence of phonemes and their corresponding letters in order to decode words.
Usually taught as mixed-ability whole class lessons.	Nearly always taught in ability groups: as class 'sets' or in-class ability groups.
Lessons begin with reading from real whole texts.	Lessons begin with emphasis on the phoneme(s) to be learned.
Lessons include reading of the word and the sentence in a whole text that contains the phoneme being focused on.	Lessons emphasise reading single words that contain the phoneme(s) that are the focus of the lesson.
Using 'cues' such as the meaning of the sentence, its syntax (G), and pictures to help with decoding words is encouraged.	Using cues other than phoneme-grapheme correspondences is discouraged. Using other cues is dismissed as 'guessing'.
Lesson ends with reading of, and discussion about, aspects of the text.	Lesson ends with plenary to consolidate learning about the chosen phoneme(s).

The approach advanced in this book differs from other accounts of a balanced approach in four main ways:

1. It is based on and explicitly details a new theoretical model.
2. It is based on new analyses of rigorous research studies.
3. It includes reading *and* writing as a necessary combination to help both develop in the most effective ways.
4. It features new teaching practices arising from the theory and research which are explored in detail in the second part of this book.

The Double Helix of Reading and Writing that we introduced in Chapter 2 is the model for our balanced approach to teaching reading and writing. Chapter 4, "The Science of Teaching Reading and Writing", showed the research evidence that underpins our model and approach. This chapter addresses practices relevant to each of the elements of the Double Helix Model, which in combination are required for effective teaching of phonics, reading, and writing.

The child and their language(s)

The starting point for implementing the balanced approach to teaching reading and writing is understanding that it begins with, and arises out of, the nature of human language. Humans in nearly all cases learn to speak naturally and without the need for systematic teaching due to human genetics combined with the natural facilitation that parents and other important people in children's lives bring to support children's development of oral language. Learning to read and write are much less natural processes that require systematic teaching.

Oral language is at the root of learning to read and write in a range of ways but most importantly in the complex ways that written language links with and represents oral language. A key area of knowledge for teachers is their understanding not only of the ways that written language represents oral language but also the ways that written language differs from oral language.

A key practical aspect of the distinction between oral language and written language is how teachers should respond to pupils' use of both. Effective teachers make a distinction between feedback to their pupils about written language, which follows more established language conventions, compared to engaging with pupils' oral language contributions, which are less formal. Oral language is more personal to the speaker and closely linked with their identity, so if teachers 'correct' oral language, this is risky and nearly always linguistically inappropriate. Written language is not so closely connected to personal identity, and all writers are using the same conventions of writing to express meaning, so it is more pertinent to teachers working with pupils to help them learn the conventions of written language. Teachers recognise and build on children's early unconventional use of written language, a characteristic known as 'emergent literacy'.

Oral language communication is driven by the intent to communicate meaning to a person or people who are present in real time. This may be communication at a distance using digital communications technology. As part of conversations, people will interject to check meanings, and the person speaking may re-phrase things if they think they are not being clear enough. Written communication is driven by the same intent – to communicate meaning. However, composition of writing happens at a distance from the reader, so in-the-moment clarification of meanings is not possible in the way that it is in oral conversations. This is one of the reasons written language is bound by conventions, to aid clarity of meaning and to try to minimise ambiguity.

To take another example of the similarities and differences between oral and written language, we can think about phonemes and their representation by letters. A phoneme is a unit of oral language. In the English language, letters only rather loosely represent phonemes: unlike some other languages, the English language is an extreme example of this loose representation. Teaching some of the correspondences between phonemes and letters results in children making some general assumptions about the representation of oral language in writing. Once armed with a little knowledge, the human brain continues to seek patterns that in due course enable children to learn to read words fluently. It is not possible, necessary, or desirable to try to teach all of the links between phonemes and their representation in written language. For this reason teachers' decisions about whether children need phonics teaching, for example, if they can already decode, and when to stop teaching phonics are vital in order to ensure that children's time is not wasted and so they experience a broad and balanced curriculum.

The languages that people speak are another component of the links between oral language and learning to read and write. In 2022, 29.1% of children in state-funded nursery classes in England (children aged three to four) used a first language other than English at home.[2] This means that any approach to the teaching of reading and writing has to take account of multiple languages. Key aspects of this include 1. multilingual pupils' greater understanding of how languages work as a result of their thinking about and use of more than one language; 2. the understanding that for multilingual children, their development of reading and writing in English can be slower at first but then accelerate quickly at key developmental points; and 3. the need for understanding of strategies to support learners who are new to English.

Accents and dialects are also an important feature of the distinctions between oral and written language, for example, in relation to how teachers might articulate separate phonemes to exemplify blending and how they explain the ways in which letters represent phonemes. The middle phoneme of the word 'bath' is pronounced differently in the South of England compared to the North of England: /b/ /ar/ /th/ in the south and /b/ /a/ /th/ in the North. Variation in pronunciation resulting from children's cultural backgrounds and variation in pronunciation of words evident through television programmes, films, and digital games that children will engage with is part of the context that teachers work within when explaining how phonemes and letters work.

Understanding linguistic similarities and differences between oral language and written language, and using this understanding to inform teaching programmes, is an important aspect of teacher knowledge.

Reading *and* writing

One of the unique aspects of our approach is the way that the teaching of reading and writing are systematically connected at all levels, from text level down to phonemes and letters. Learning about writing is an essential part of learning to read. Approaches to teaching reading have rarely included the teaching of writing as a systematically planned element of reading lessons, particularly when this planning includes children's composition of whole texts. At the level of phonemes and letters, a child's understanding of both requires them to decode to read and encode to write. Subtly different mental processes are then engaged in solving the same core problem, which is knowing how letters represent phonemes in words and how words function in sentences and texts. By encouraging use of a wider range of mental processes during lessons, the child's understanding of the specifics of learning to read and write is improved.

The child and their environment, including texts

Effective teaching requires understanding of learners' perspectives, prior experiences, and motivations. Children's experiences with reading and writing in their homes are an important reference point for teaching, for example, the kinds of texts that are present in homes and the ways in which different people in the home environment interact with children. Stereotypes of groups of children are too common, for example, summed up in the expression 'these kids have no language', so it is important that teaching is based on valid information about individual children's experiences at home. Well-organised approaches that schools use for sending books home are one important element in supporting children's reading, although these rarely connect writing with reading, and there is some evidence that parents are less confident to engage with children's writing.[3] Libraries in communities and schools are vital, as are well-organised selections of texts in every classroom. The resources of the classroom, including use of displays, are designed to give maximum access to print and texts and to stimulate children's curiosity.

Teachers have to develop knowledge of texts that will engage children and be most appropriate for their learning at different stages. The best real books, books created by authors to engage children, offer creative ways to think about many things relevant to children's learning. The unique ways in which meanings are created through the interplay of pictures and text are a vital part of the sophistication of real books. Sometimes the underlying messages of such books are profound and touch on serious issues that are part of growing up in an uncertain world. Often real books are also just great fun. While books created for teaching programmes specially to support the skills of reading may have a place in teaching reading, particularly in children's early stages of learning about phonemes and letters, they do not offer the experiences and sophisticated meanings that are an essential facet of real books (see Chapter 3, "How Texts Teach What Children Learn"). Given that the balanced approach includes attention to comprehension in many varied ways, the lack of variety in phonics scheme decodable books is a significant limitation.

A classroom and school environment rich in texts and real-life experiences, where children are encouraged to learn and grow through play, will support the development of children's imagination and their use of language for writing. Teachers need to interact purposefully with children's play, alongside children, supporting reading comprehension through discussions and supporting writing to communicate and share ideas.

Phonics lessons are most effective when contextualised in whole texts and when these are real texts. This is essential for children to have full understanding of each of the constituent parts of written language, from the level of phonemes and letters, to words and sentences, to whole texts. A focus on the constituent parts of the reading process requires teachers and children to keep in mind at all times the real purposes of reading and writing, which are to understand and communicate meanings. Children have to 'make sense' of reading and writing at all times in phonics, reading, and writing lessons.

A literacy-rich environment where adults and children talk, read, and write together and where children have opportunities to be read to and read with their peers and adults is an important part of a balanced approach. In this environment, activities that are part of 'continuous provision' (G), which extends out of the work done in phonics lessons, are designed to meet the needs and interests of children. The literacy environment of the classroom is well stocked with a wide range of high-quality texts. In the early stages of learning to read, these texts should support children in three main ways:

Learning to decode
A wide range of straightforward texts, fiction, non-fiction, and poetry, suited to children's stage of development. In the early stages of learning to read, from about age four, these texts will include features such as natural repetition of words, and some will include rhyming structures. Some texts will be selected to enable children to use and apply their developing phonic knowledge at the point of reading.

Fiction and poetry for engaging children and extending reading
These texts will be at a reading level that children may not be able to read independently. They will be read aloud by teachers and other adults and may be used as a focus for other lessons.

Non-fiction for engaging children and extending reading
These texts will be high-quality information texts and may be print based and/or digital. They will be targeted towards common interests of children in the class, to extend children's knowledge across the wider curriculum and to support the interests of individual children.

For children in nurseries/pre-kindergarten, texts can also be chosen to support learning in the outdoor environment, for example, posters and signs and opportunities to make marks as precursors to conventional writing. The literacy environment should also provide a wide variety of invitations for children to write, with a range of resources to do so.

Motivation and meaning

A child who is motivated will learn more than one who is not motivated. One aspect of motivation is the natural curiosity that children are born with. This drives them to engage with texts which are a feature of their environment, just as they are naturally curious about most things that they encounter. Teaching reading and writing has to engage children's interests.[4] One part of this is planning lessons and activities that are engaging. Our approach shows how teaching reading and writing can motivate and engage children. It is sometimes said that synthetic phonics does not have to be boring. However, discrete synthetic phonics teaching is less likely to motivate children than phonics teaching that is contextualised in outstanding books and other texts written for children as part of a balanced approach.

The central place of meaning in teaching reading and writing includes teachers situating lessons in authentic purposes for reading and writing. Children have to understand why learning to read and write will be important in their lives. Reading and writing are not just lessons in schools decontextualised from purpose and meaning, they are vital to human development, including a source of great pleasure for many people. This attention to authentic purposes does not shy away from the fact that learning to read and write is challenging for many children. And, in the case of writing particularly, there is a life-time of work to acquire 'the ear of the writer'.[5]

Meaning drives the balanced approach to teaching reading and writing. It is the essence of human language; hence it should be the essence of teaching. It is an anchor and common referent for every lesson. Teaching about phonemes and letters is meaningless unless contextualised in words, sentences, and whole texts. So any teaching about phonemes locates the lesson in the meanings of whole texts, sentences, and words.

Comprehension

From birth onwards children are naturally disposed to try to understand the environment they find themselves in. With regard to language this curiosity results in their earliest attempts at understanding spoken language, then their experimentation with speaking themselves. And it is in comprehension where the similarity between oral language and written language is strong because some of the same mental processes are used to comprehend oral and written language. Support for comprehension of written texts does not have to wait until children have fully learned how to decode independently. When teachers share texts with children, for example, reading text aloud to children as part of phonics lesson, there are so many opportunities to engage children with the meanings of texts. Children's own queries about texts also provide an important way for teachers to engage children with comprehension, and literal comprehension of texts can very quickly become more inferential, for example, in fruitful contestation about interpretations of the meanings of texts.

Composition

There is much that young children can learn about the voice (G), style, language and form of different kinds of writing from what they hear read aloud, and from what they read themselves. Texts represent ideas. Ideas are formed from the original concepts that preceded the author's composition of texts, but also in the details of narrative flow and other structural means to create meaning. Ideas are also part of each sentence that combine to create a cohesive text. Ideas are at the heart of the meaning-making process that is the composition of writing.

Children's attempts to compose meanings in writing link with the way that they approach the comprehension of texts in reading. The letter-by-letter, word-by-word, sentence-by-sentence composition of ideas in writing represents the building blocks for comprehending texts when reading. The composition of writing also requires understanding of how the larger blocks of language, for example, text forms, text sections, paragraphs, and layout features, work together to create meanings. Even the relatively simple concept of the title of a book belies the sophisticated ways that titles sum up whole texts.

Phonological awareness and the alphabetic code

Phonological awareness is a child's awareness of the sounds that make up spoken words. As text is a representation of speech, children have to learn to make links between the ways that letters represent spoken sounds. Phonological awareness begins with children's growing awareness of sounds, then when children are about age three they gradually become more aware of salient units of words such as syllables, for example, through enjoying nursery rhymes. Systematic phonics teaching, which should start from when children are about age five, focuses on phonemes by helping children to understand the most common representations of phonemes by the letters of the alphabet. The teaching of these representations is always set in the context of words and texts. Once children have sufficient understanding of some of the many correspondences between phonemes and letters, they self-generate that learning and in time develop fluent visual recognition of words as a result of teaching to support this. As children use and apply their knowledge about phonemes and letters in their writing, they are also practising and consolidating their skills and knowledge about how to decode words in reading. The core knowledge about phonemes, letters, and words they are taught supports them in their journey to read whatever they want to read and write whatever they want to write.

Knowledge of morphemes and other word structures

If children are to learn to read and write fluently they need to acquire knowledge about morphemes (G). Morphological (G) knowledge is particularly useful for learning the spelling system of the English language. Children soon reach a point where their emergent knowledge of the alphabetic code is not sufficient for their reading and writing to continue to develop. For writing there are many visual patterns in English spelling that can be learned in order to help spelling. Patterns such as 'ough', for example, in the words 'tough' and 'ought', challenge children's expectations about the phonemes that the letters O U G and H more usually represent in a range of commonly used words. There are also many other aspects of word structures that can help children remember spellings and to attempt to spell words for the first time in their writing; these aspects include prefixes, suffixes, changing words from singular to plural, rhymes, and mnemonics.

Because of the way English has developed historically, it has a complex orthography (G). There are multiple ways that letters can represent phonemes, particularly vowels (G). Encouraging an investigative approach, where children explore and discuss words and look at patterns of letters, will lay the foundations for the conventional spelling that children have to acquire.

Planning lessons and activities

The research on effective teaching of phonics and reading does not provide a definitive answer about the number of phonics lessons that children need to learn to read. There is natural variation in how quickly children learn to read. Some children do not require systematic phonics teaching at all, but the majority of children do. Interventions that have been shown to be effective in longitudinal research studies, reviewed in Chapter 4, "The Science of Teaching Reading and Writing", have varied in the number and duration of the lessons. Our best estimate is that one year of systematic teaching of phonological awareness and phonics should be sufficient for the majority of children, and some children will require considerably less than this.

Teachers should assess children's reading with real texts, and as soon as a child can decode unknown words with reasonable fluency (G), they should no longer have to be taught phonics for reading. This means that in a given class of children, gradually there will be fewer and fewer children who need the core phonics programme, a situation that will require teachers to plan for at least two groups of children: those who can use phonics to decode and those who cannot. The duration of lessons in the interventions that were part of research has also varied. Our model is based on the estimate that for children aged about five years old, 30 minutes per day for phonics lessons (that include other aspects of reading and writing) is the maximum amount of time.

When children can already decode and have a good early grasp of spelling, then more phonics lessons are not an optimal use of their time, which could be better spent on developing their reading and writing in different ways. If this time is not used efficiently, then children in any class or system will not be learning optimally. Teaching about morphemes and other word structures, which has some relationship to phonics knowledge, does need to continue until children are secure enough with conventional spelling.

The programme of lessons

The examples of lessons, and other aspects of teaching, that follow in the remaining chapters of the book centre on high-quality children's books and show how to develop children's knowledge of phonemes and letters alongside their comprehension and knowledge about writing. Links are also made to personal, social, and emotional development and children's understanding of the world where possible. The learning outlined in the examples links with, but is not exclusive to, the particular real books that are suggested as the basis of the lessons. By providing examples we hope that readers will be able to apply the teaching methods to other high-quality texts.

Building on the principles underpinning the examples is part of our view that teachers should develop their professional knowledge about using books in their education settings to support children's development of reading and writing. The content outlined in the following chapters shows how our balanced approach to reading and writing works. This is not the same as following a published programme or scheme. Our model is built on teachers developing their confidence and professional autonomy in the classroom so that they can best address the needs of the children they teach, who in many ways will be unique to that country, region, and school community.

Sessions are designed to be taught as part of what some people call Quality First Teaching (QFT). QFT emphasises high-quality, inclusive teaching for all pupils in a given class. It is driven by the teacher's knowledge of the children from their ongoing formative assessment (G), allowing them to differentiate appropriately and plan for the developmental needs of all children, including children working beyond the typical level of their peers; children with special educational needs; and those with English as an additional language.

Effective teaching addresses all children's developmental needs and enables all learners to make progress and achieve.

As part of understanding the balanced approach, teachers need to be confident with the knowledge required to teach reading and writing effectively, including phonics teaching. A small but important part of this knowledge is awareness of grapheme phoneme correspondences (GPCs), how blending and segmenting can be taught, and a suitable sequence for the teaching of GPCs. A suggested order for the teaching of these is outlined at the beginning of relevant chapters.

Planning teaching based on children's development

Children have different starting points and needs and have a wealth of different experiences in their lives. Effective teachers use their understanding of children's prior experiences to support them in moving to the next stage of their development as readers and writers. Understanding children's development on what is a continuum of oral language, reading, and writing is an essential reference point for teachers. The Centre for Literacy in Primary Education (CLPE) Reading and Writing Scales inform the sequences of teaching that the remaining chapters of this book address. The scales are a comprehensive account of children's development of reading and writing and hence cover more aspects than we are able to show in the examples of teaching in this book.

The Reading and Writing Scales of children's learning developed by CLPE are built on years of research and collaboration between literacy organisations in the UK. Originally developed over 30 years ago, the scales were first published as part of the CLPE Primary Language Record (PLR).[6] The PLR was widely used in primary schools in the late 80s and 90s, influencing language and literacy assessment in all parts of the UK and internationally. In 2015, the CLPE joined forces with the English and Media Centre (EMC), the National Association for Advisors in English (NAAE), the National Association for the Teaching of English (NATE), and the United Kingdom Literacy Association (UKLA) to update the scales and to make them freely available so that teachers could strengthen their understanding of children's development, strengthen their subject knowledge, and use the scales to assess children's reading and writing.

As can be seen in Figures 5.1 and 5.2, a child's development starts at the beginner stage, where learners are more dependent on adult support, then follows the stages of learning towards independence. The journey is not necessarily a simple linear progression for children, as they may progress at different rates. Each step on the scale provides a description of what a learner's reading and writing is like at a certain stage. Teachers draw on professional knowledge of their children through careful observation of their reading and writing behaviours in order to gain a picture of each child's development so that they can then plan the teaching needed next for the children to make progress. They reading scales are a formative assessment tool designed to aid teachers in planning an environment and curriculum that supports children's progress.

The scales include next steps for teaching for each point on the scale; they also incorporate practical ideas and strategies and outline the practice and provision which will enable pupils to make progress towards independence, and they are an essential tool for planning for the needs of pupils. Teachers often follow an 'observe, assess, plan and review' cycle to ensure they are clear on each child's progress and what provision needs to be in place for every child to succeed.

Chapters 6 to 13 provide detailed examples of how teaching is undertaken using the balanced approach to teaching phonics, reading, and writing. The final section of this chapter outlines, in Table 5.2, the teaching that is addressed in Chapters 6 to 13. For the purposes of explaining in detail the balanced approach, although each chapter has a main focus such as Cracking the Alphabetic Code the example lessons in each chapter include multiple components in line with The Double Helix of Reading and Writing.

Dependence → **Independence**

Beginning Reader | Early Reader | Developing Reader | Moderately Fluent Reader

Stage	Describing the Child's Reading Behaviours
Beginning Reader	The main feature of this stage is that readers are not yet able to access print independently and may not yet have awareness that the text carries meaning. They are likely to need a great deal of support with the reading demands of the classroom.
	Most children have favourites that they want to share and will be able to talk their way through a known book, drawing on picture cues and patterns of language remembered from hearing the book read aloud.
	Children may join in with simple nursery rhymes, poems, songs and rhyming texts, which should be an integral part of the curriculum at this stage. They generally enjoy listening to, sharing and joining in with a range of familiar texts. They react and respond to illustrations, character and narratives through questions and imaginative play.
	Children at this stage know how to handle books, are aware of directionality and how print works from being read to. Some children may be engaging with other kinds of texts, e.g. print around them, digital and media texts. They may know a few core words, letter names or sounds, often of personal significance, such as names or other words, letters or sounds of interest.
	Children engage with activities that develop their early phonological awareness through play with sounds, such as recognising sounds in their environment, using musical instruments and their bodies and voices to create a range of sounds.
	Reading at this stage relies principally on memory of the story and a willingness to perform, interpret and invent, based on what they have heard and recall.
	Older readers at this stage might have a limited experience of reading and may not choose to read for pleasure. Children at this stage are building up a repertoire of known texts to which they want to return again and again, as they are being read to and as they are developing as readers. Such readers may not yet have developed strategies to lift the words from the page. They are familiar with the storyline, the tune on the page and have a natural inclination to predict when working with memorable texts; so they become the storyteller and re-enact the text. It is this familiarisation that helps these children develop a growing awareness of what is involved in being able to do it themselves. On each occasion and over time, the children play a more active role in reading.
Early Reader	Early readers can tackle known and predictable texts with growing confidence but still need support with new and unfamiliar ones. They show a growing ability to make sense of what they read, drawing on illustrations, their knowledge of language and the world as well as the words on the page.
	Children within this stage are at an important transition from dependence on memory or on reading alongside an adult, to a growing independence in reading texts that are familiar but not known by heart. They are developing a growing enthusiasm for a wider range of reading material, which may include simple information books and picture books as well as text in the environment, in digital form and through media.
	Familiarity with a text provides a supportive framework of meanings and language patterns from which a child can draw, while beginning to focus more closely on print. They are beginning to evidence one-to-one correspondence, drawing on their developing phonic knowledge by linking graphemes and phonemes to help them decode simple words and recognition of a core of known words. They can read and understand simple sentences. As fluency and understanding develop children will begin to self-correct.
	With support, children reflect on their reading and respond personally to what they have read, making links to prior knowledge, significant experiences and popular culture. They begin to evaluate the books they meet, expressing likes and dislikes with reasons for their views.

The balanced approach to phonics, reading, and writing 97

	Older readers at this stage may have a narrow range of independent reading as they are still likely to be drawn to texts that are familiar and do not pose sufficient challenge in extending vocabulary and comprehension skills. Unfamiliar material can be challenging. However, they may be able to read their own writing confidently. They continue to need support with the reading demands of the classroom. Such readers could be over-dependent on one strategy when reading aloud, often reading word by word. They may be over reliant on phonics.
Developing Reader	A developing reader is gaining control of the reading process. Children within this stage link reading to their own experiences and are able to read simple texts independently. They show interest in a growing range of reading material and are able to branch out into a variety of books and other texts, which include simple information texts, poetry and picture books, as well as digital texts and print in the environment. Children apply their developing phonic knowledge when reading words containing known graphemes, recognising alternative graphemes for known phonemes and alternative pronunciations for graphemes, checking that the text makes sense. They read words containing common suffixes and contractions and understand their purpose. They have a more extensive vocabulary of sight words and fluency is beginning to develop through recognition of larger units within words. Children continue to develop self-correction strategies when reading does not make sense and are able to use more than one strategy. Children bring varied sources of information in order to enable them to make meaning of what they read. Their improved fluency enables them to comprehend more of what they are reading. Children reflect on their reading, respond personally to what they have read by drawing on personal connections to the texts. They evaluate the books they meet and are able to articulate views and preferences, making connections to other texts they have encountered. Older children at this stage are developing fluency as readers and are reading certain kinds of material with confidence, such as short books with simple narrative shapes and with illustrations. They will often re-read favourite books.
Moderately Fluent Reader	Moderately fluent readers are well-launched on reading. They read with confidence for more sustained periods, but still need to return to a familiar range of texts, whilst at the same time beginning to explore new kinds of texts independently. Children at this stage will be looking at larger units of words to help them to decode more effectively and read more fluently. Moderately fluent readers are developing confidence in tackling new kinds of texts independently. They are showing evidence of growing enthusiasm for a wider range of reading material that they self select; this may include but is not limited to information books, longer picture books, comics, graphic novels, age appropriate newspapers, short chapter books and a range of digital texts. They are likely to move between familiar and unfamiliar texts in their reading choices, linking new texts to others read, and to personal experiences. They are more confident to express opinions including likes, dislikes and challenges, as well as responding to the questions and listening to the views of others. Older readers at this stage may still need help with the reading demands of the classroom and especially with reading across the curriculum. As their reading experiences increase, children's reading strategies and the language cues of print begin to mesh and they take on more and more of the reading for themselves, bringing to the activity all they know and can do to make the text meaningful.

© The Centre for Literacy in Primary Education 2015-16

You may use this resource freely in your school but it cannot be reproduced, modified or used for commercial purposes without the express permission of CLPE.
The Centre for Literacy in Primary Education is a registered charity no. 1092698 and a company limited by guarantee no. 04385537

Figure 5.1 The CLPE reading scale

98 *The art of teaching*

Dependence →→→ **Independence**

Beginning Writer → Early Writer → Developing Writer → Moderately Fluent Writer

Stage	Describing the Child's Writing Behaviours
Beginning Writer	The main feature of this stage is that writers are not yet able to transcribe text conventionally. They may be able to talk about ideas that they would like to commit to writing, but are still at an early stage of understanding how language is written down and need support with transcription.
	They may be exploring and experimenting with mark making in a variety of forms. Marks are made to show ideas and children start to ascribe meaning to these. At the beginning marks may be large, circular and random. This develops into more letter-like shapes which may be interspersed with number-like shapes and drawing.
	Children at this stage can express ideas in simple sentences, though these may not always be complete and may use such grammatical over generalisations as 'I bringed a toy to school'. They have awareness that their voice is important for expressing and communicating needs and ideas to others.
	Children may be composing by trying out ideas through talk and dictating their ideas for writing to a facilitating adult or digitally recording their spoken ideas. They may also have some strategies for writing independently (e.g. drawing, mark making, copying, inventing own code).
	Older children at this stage may either appear to be reluctant to write or alternatively seek constant support and reassurance. Their experience as writers may be limited; they may be composing orally with confidence but be reluctant to write or avoid taking risks with transcription. Such writers need a great deal of support with developing their own texts (which are often brief) and with the writing demands of the classroom.
	In terms of composition, some children may be able to compose sentences orally that exceed their transcriptional abilities, whilst others require support with structuring their ideas and composing sentences orally prior to writing. Ideas for writing may be limited by their own range of experience and their lack of exposure to language and high quality texts. Transcriptional ability in this stage may be broad. Children may rely mainly on phonetic spelling strategies and memorised words, with few self-help strategies. Some children at this stage may have gaps in their phonic knowledge. They may still be writing in memorised letter strings, may not yet be making grapheme-phoneme correspondences and may seldom use punctuation to mark meaning. Some others may only hear initial and other predominant sounds in words.
Early Writer	Early writers are gaining confidence in using writing conventionally for a range of personal purposes (e.g. messages, notices, role-play). They can draw on their experiences of seeing language written down (e.g. in shared writing or as part of role-play) and demonstrate more understanding of the alphabetic nature of the English writing system. Children at this stage are willing to have a go at writing independently, using a few early strategies for spelling (e.g. use of initial letters, some known words, using letter strings as 'place holders'), so that writing can be read back more consistently.
	Children at this stage have a developing awareness of the fact that print carries meaning and make efforts to write with purpose e.g. in writing as part of role-play. They are able to speak in simple and compound sentences, ready for transcription. As their confidence increases, they are able to write more than one sentence and begin to join sentences with simple joining words such as 'and' and 'but'. They may use their oral language structures in their writing and so need support in developing appropriate written structures. Ideas for writing at this stage may be simple, based on direct experience or inspired by reading.
	At the beginning of this stage, children may write strings of legible letters of a more consistent size, including those in their name, and start to show a greater awareness of how writing works. As grapheme-phoneme correspondences develop, children start to represent known sounds, particularly at the beginning and end of words, and may start to write familiar words such as their name and other words of personal importance. Children at this stage may still mix upper and lower case, reverse letters and may not yet have developed an awareness of spacing between words. They begin to experiment with simple punctuation.
	Older children at this stage may still be at the phonetic stage of spelling where words are written as they sound. At the later stages, they may write sentences that no longer require mediation, with spaces between words and using simple punctuation. However, they continue to need support with writing across the curriculum. And their writing may lack detail and description to draw the reader in and help them to make meaning.
	Their handwriting is becoming increasingly legible at this stage and they may be exploring the use of simple punctuation.

Developing Writer	Developing writers can write simple sentences without the need for mediation, as they are able to represent sounds phonetically and know an increasing number of words that are exceptions to phonic rules. They are increasingly confident, writing independently within a familiar range of genres (e.g. letters, lists, brief narratives), but still need support with extending and developing writing. Children at this stage are able to rehearse their ideas orally prior to writing, expanding on ideas and adding detail and description. They draw on models from reading in structuring and developing their own texts. They are aware of the need to add description to their writing, using simple adjectives to expand noun phrases. They use an increasing range of common conjunctions, such as *and*, *but*, *so* and *because* to develop, link or expand ideas. These children may show awareness of alternative representations for phonemes, although these may not always be accurately represented in spelling. They develop strategies for spelling (e.g. known words, phonetically based invented spellings), that enable texts to be read by others. They are aware of the need for spaces between words and use simple punctuation such as capital letters and full stops and commas in lists. Their handwriting becomes of a consistent size and letters are generally formed correctly. They can read back their own texts consistently, checking for sense and meaning and are able to edit with support where necessary. Older writers at this stage write confidently in familiar genres (e.g. simple narratives) and try out different forms of writing, drawing on experience of the models available across other genres. They mainly use language and sentence structures that are close to speech and still need support with the writing demands of the curriculum. They display a greater awareness of the visual structures and patterns of words to move towards greater accuracy in spelling. Spellings of familiar words are generally correct and attempts at unfamiliar spellings reveal a widening range of strategies. They use sentence punctuation more consistently, including full stops and capital letters and may use question marks, exclamation marks and commas in lists. They may also experiment with speech punctuation. Handwriting is usually consistent and legible and they may be experimenting with joined handwriting.
Moderately Fluent Writer	Moderately fluent writers are writing more confidently and developing ideas at greater length in a few familiar forms. They have a growing ability to structure these texts and are willing to experiment with a wider range of writing. Children at this stage continue to rehearse and refine ideas prior to writing, through talk, drama and role-play, to ensure an authentic voice and appropriate language structures. They show a greater awareness of the reader by adjusting and developing language and content to suit the purpose and audience of the writing and help the reader to visualise. This may include the use of expanded noun phrases and precise vocabulary for effect or to add description. They are able to shape writing in familiar genres confident, drawing on their experience of reading. They demonstrate control over the conventions of writing and can develop and shape a variety of text types across narrative, non-fiction and poetry. They create developed pieces of writing, shaped and supported by planning structures such as notes, storymaps, storyboards, concept maps etc. They have an understanding of the different forms and layouts needed for different types of writing. They begin to write more extensively. They explore and experiment with a wider range of sentence structures, thinking carefully about how to extend and join parts of their texts using appropriate adverbs and connectives. Tenses are consistent and a wider range of punctuation is used appropriately, such as exclamation marks and question marks to support meaning. In addition children use inverted commas to demarcate direct speech. They read back their writing and, with support, revise their own texts to link and develop ideas coherently. Children's spelling is becoming much more accurate, with a wider range of exception words correctly spelt. They also have an awareness of a greater range of grapheme-phoneme correspondences, of words that contain these and of the basic rules for their use, which may be based on analogy. Advanced words may still be spelt phonetically. They draw on a wider range of strategies in spelling (e.g. common letter strings, awareness of visual patterns, as well as phonetically based spellings). Older writers at this stage are increasingly willing to take risks with both composition and transcription. They may find it difficult to sustain initial efforts over longer pieces of writing and may not be able to develop writing over a piece, losing momentum or cohesion towards the middle or not being able to draw writing to a satisfying conclusion.

©The Centre for Literacy in Primary Education 2015-16

You may use this resource freely in your school but it cannot be reproduced, modified or used for commercial purposes without the express permission of CLPE.
The Centre for Literacy in Primary Education is a registered charity no. 1092698 and a company limited by guarantee no. 04385537

Figure 5.2 The CLPE writing scale

Table 5.2 An outline of the content covered in the chapters of this book

Chapter and title	What's covered	Typical age	Indicative durations for teaching	Organisation and grouping
6 – Building the Foundations	The importance of reading for pleasure. Recognising individual starting points. Developing reader identity. Choosing and sharing texts with children. Developing language and literacy. Developing understanding of the purpose of writing. Early phonological development (G). Rhythm and rhyme. Engaging children through poetry. Linking the spoken word with the written word.	3 to 5 years	Embedded into text-level work throughout with additional provision as necessary for those children who need additional support	Whole-class reading aloud on a daily basis. Planned activities for different groups of children to target specific areas of development daily. Access to independent reading and writing daily in school and at home.
7 – Cracking the Alphabetic Code	Teaching the basic code. Teaching single phoneme-to-letter correspondences. Teaching the core skills of blending and segmenting. Using and applying knowledge and skills in reading and writing words, phrases, and sentences.	4 to 5 years	12 to 18 weeks of focused teaching	Whole-class taught sessions daily for approximately 20–30 minutes. Whole-class reading aloud on a daily basis. Planned activities for different groups of children to target specific areas of development daily. Access to independent reading daily in school and at home.
8 – Gaining Control	Extending knowledge of the basic code. Teaching digraphs, trigraphs (G), and consonant clusters. Developing children's ability in the core skills of blending and segmenting. Using and applying knowledge and skills in reading and writing words, phrases, and sentences.	4 to 5 years	12 to 18 weeks of focused teaching	Whole-class taught sessions daily for approximately 20–30 minutes. Whole-class reading aloud on a daily basis. Planned activities for different groups of children to target specific areas of development daily. Access to independent reading daily in school and at home.
9 – The Complexities of English	Teaching alternative letter representations for known phonemes. Teaching alternative phonemes for known letter representations.	5 to 6 years	24 to 32 weeks of focused teaching in Year 1	Whole-class taught sessions daily for approximately 20–30 minutes. Whole-class reading aloud on a daily basis.

The balanced approach to phonics, reading, and writing 101

	Making analogies between words. Using and applying knowledge and skills in independent reading and writing.		Planned activities for different groups of children to target specific areas of development daily. Access to independent reading daily in school and at home.
10 – Spelling	Understanding the orthography of the English language. Recognising morphological units. Developing an awareness of etymology.	6 to 7 years	Contextually embedded in whole-class taught literacy sessions. Targeted support for groups and individuals, where identified needs exist.
11 – Developing Fluency and Comprehension	Developing reading skills and strategies.	3 to 7 years and beyond	Small group and individual instruction where necessary, in addition to QFT, focused on specific identified needs of individuals and groups of children.
12 – Meeting the Needs of All Pupils	Understanding the needs of children. Addressing common issues: • Access to texts • Lack of motivation as a reader or writer • Composing writing • One-to-one correspondence • The ability to represent a written word for each individual spoken word in writing • Knowledge of letter-phoneme correspondences • Ability to blend and segment • Developing automaticity • Developing fluency • Letter formation and handwriting • Children who can already read.	All primary school years	Small group and individual instruction where necessary, in addition to QFT, focused on specific identified needs of individuals and groups of children.
13 – The Reader in the Writer	Understanding the purpose of writing. Developing writer identity. The development of writing. Using texts as models for writing. An authentic writing process.	3 to 7 years and beyond	Small group and individual instruction where necessary, in addition to QFT, focused on specific identified needs of individuals and groups of children.

In the next chapter we show how effective teaching can build the foundations of children's learning to read and write.

Notes

1 Wyse, D., & Bradbury, A. (2022). Reading Wars or Reading Reconciliation? A Critical Examination of Robust Research Evidence, Curriculum Policy, and Teachers' Practices for Teaching Phonics and Reading. *Review of Education*, 3. Retrieved December 1, 2023, from https://doi.org/10.1002/rev3.3314
2 GOV.UK. (2023). *Academic Year 2022/23: Schools, Pupils and Their Characteristics.* Retrieved October 26, 2023, from https://explore-education-statistics.service.gov.uk/find-statistics/school-pupils-and-their-characteristics
3 Bradford, H., & Wyse, D. (2020). Two-Year-Old and Three-Year-Old Children's Writing: The Contradictions of Children's and Adults' Conceptualisations. *Early Years*, *42*(3), 293–309.
4 Teresa Cremin has done excellent work on reading for pleasure: for example, Cremin, T. (2022). *Reading Teachers Nurturing Reading for Pleasure*. Routledge.
5 Wyse, D. (2017). *How Writing Works: From the Invention of the Alphabet to the Rise of Social Media*. Cambridge University Press.
6 Centre for Language in Primary Education. (1988). *The Primary Language Record: Handbook for Teachers*. Centre for Language in Primary Education.

6 Building the foundations

From their very earliest stages children are in search of meaning and communication. As babies they look to the facial expressions used by others and the intonation of voices around them to enable their needs to be met and to understand more about the world around them and their place within it. As they grow and develop they begin to learn how to use their own voices and actions as a means of communication, taking on and processing new vocabulary to communicate more with other people.

Most children first learn to decode printed words written in English, and comprehend the meaning of texts, between the ages of four and six. A minority of children will learn to decode words before they are four. A larger minority of children may not learn to decode and comprehend until after they are age six. The famous educator and originator of the Reading Recovery intervention, Marie Clay, was right when she said that if a child was not reading by the time they were age six, then they should get extra one-to-one support for their reading. At the earliest stages of learning to read, the child will be heavily dependent on adults and other more experienced readers such as siblings for support, but as they read more texts and learn the ways in which spoken language is represented in the words they see on the page, they gradually become fluent and independent readers.

Understanding the alphabetic code is one vital part of learning to read, but this is part of a range of understanding about reading that children have to acquire. A systematic programme of phonics teaching (G) is unlikely to be successful if prior experiences have not been assessed, then teaching and experiences planned and taught to develop children's motivation to read, their engagement with whole texts, their phonological development (G), and their understanding of print.

Any activity focused on developing young children's understanding of the correspondences between letters and phonemes (G) is built on their prior knowledge of oral language but also how print works in the real world. This prior knowledge includes understanding about the purposes for reading, including reading for pleasure, and understanding about writing as a means of communicating thoughts, ideas, and information. Young children are naturally curious about the world around them; this includes their curiosity about books and written language, but they need more experienced readers to help them to master new skills to grow their independence.

This chapter explores the kinds of activities and experiences that will typically support children as they enter a nursery setting at age three to four. We cover the kinds of approaches which lay the foundations for the successful implementation of a programme of literacy teaching that will in time include the systematic contextualised teaching of phonics and spelling. Activities will take place in a variety of nursery class contexts, for large and small groups, and for individual children. Our approach to the teaching of reading,

DOI: 10.4324/9781003442134-9

and of writing, always connects language and meaning. Rooting learning in language, including texts, allows children to see the whole point of reading and writing and the skills and strategies to which they will be introduced to support them on their journey to fluency (G). Teaching focuses on the end goal of achieving independence and maintaining children's motivation to persevere as they develop. Using real books and other motivating real-life texts from the outset supports children in gaining a sense of the multiple pleasures and purposes of reading and writing and helps children to see the point of reading and writing. If all goes well, children will maintain a lifelong engagement with reading and writing, long after their formal education ends.

Creating the conditions for learning

One of the key concerns with England's approach to synthetic phonics (G) delivered through validated phonics programmes is the de-professionalism of teachers and the focus on academic performance ahead of children's engagement, well-being, and play. In their earliest years children learn through play. It is key to their personal, social, and emotional development, as well as encouraging key skills that lay the foundations for the future through communication, teamwork, curiosity, problem-solving, resilience, risk-taking, creativity, and empathy.

The examples of teaching and learning exemplified in our approach aim to impact positively young children's learning. We set high expectations within a model that develops children's literacy holistically, using creative and play-based approaches encouraging young children to:

- be curious and inquisitive;
- explore and investigate;
- be imaginative and creative;
- question and seek to clarify;
- extend their thinking around the concepts, themes, and meanings of texts;
- develop and extend their learning through play.

This needs to be set within a cycle of ongoing, formative assessment (G), where teachers:

- observe children to ascertain what they know and what they can do;
- assess their development against age-related expectations;
- identify next steps to support development;
- plan appropriate activities and provision with these next steps in mind;
- review the impact of the teaching and learning.

For some children their needs and next steps will relate mainly to academic development, looking at what knowledge and skills they need to progress to their next phase of learning. For others there will be a mix of academic, social, and emotional needs. A tired, hungry, insecure, or unhappy child will not learn as effectively as those who have these basic needs met, so careful observations and interactions of all elements of a child's learning and development must be considered in identifying needs and in determining next steps.

The importance of reading for pleasure

Any successful programme of literacy hinges on the importance of children understanding the value of literacy to them. In respect of reading, this includes the understanding that reading is a pleasurable activity and that the benefits experienced from reading are worth the effort it takes to learn to read.

Over the last 20 years the value of cultivating a reading for pleasure culture has been a constant feature of discourse in the primary education sector. Extensive studies have indicated the multitude of benefits that reading for pleasure can afford both in terms of the academic gains and those that go well beyond the classroom. Alice Sullivan and Matt Brown's work based on cohort research studies highlighted the capacity for reading for pleasure to raise standards and combat social exclusion.[1] They found that reading for enjoyment was a more significant contributor to a child's educational success than their family's socio-economic status. Reading was more of an influence on children's cognitive development between the ages of 10 and 16 than their parents' level of education. We know that being literate not only sets the foundation for better academic and socio-economic outcomes but also that reading can support personal, social, and emotional development, enabling better mental health and greater capacity for empathy and critical thinking, as evidenced by the Reading Agency.[2] Children who do not learn what it is about reading that makes other people engage for pleasure are unlikely to choose to read independently.

What we must understand is that reading for pleasure is not a bolt on, added extra, or series of activities to tick off. It is an act, a coming together of skills, knowledge, and attitudes, which does not happen after a phonics programme is complete or when children achieve fluency; it begins from the moment a baby has their first encounter with a text. Children are far more likely to read for pleasure when they can read, when they have texts available that make them want to read and they are aware of the inherent pleasures that reading offers to them, resulting in the intrinsic motivation to read for themselves.

With this in mind, the practical approaches and strategies outlined in this chapter, and the chapters that follow, are designed to ensure that young learners are able to develop motivation for reading and writing, making sense of their learning from the start, constructing meaning from experience, and being actively engaged in their learning through playful approaches that inter-connect learning. Our approach, as you have seen in prior chapters, draws on evidence of the most effective ways in which young children learn and develop. Talk, reading, experimenting with writing, and play are the most important elements of literacy development at these earliest stages of learning to read and write and will be embedded throughout the learning opportunities described in the next chapters.

Developing reader identity

Sharing, reading, and talking about books with children is one of the most important things that an adult can do with a young child and should happen on a daily basis. It immediately engages children with written language. Reading aloud also creates a bond between the adult and child, fostering a sense of togetherness and belonging, and, with well-chosen texts that match the needs and interests of a child, builds their identity as a reader, allowing them to see that this is a place and a space for them. As Kathy Goouch and Andrew Lambirth[3] recognise: "it is the human connection between reader and text and teacher that consistently provides the reading lesson."

This personal connection is a key component to supporting a deeper and more meaningful engagement with texts, so it is paramount to ensure that all children have access to a range of texts that have the particular qualities needed to encourage them to become happy, enthusiastic readers and writers with all of the benefits this brings. Affirming the identities and languages that children use is key in selecting books to share. In schools, homes, libraries, and bookshops, children need to meet texts with characters that look like them, sound like them, and have the same interests and experiences, in texts that reflect their needs, interests, and experiences, as well as texts that authentically show them the lives of others in wider society. As the work of Sims Bishop (1990)[4] highlighted, the affirming power of seeing ourselves and being seen across all art forms and areas of life is integral to our collective healthy development as individuals and as a wider society. If books do not reflect the realities of the readership and the wider world, they can also serve to suggest that reading and writing are only for some groups of people, not others. In the worst cases, some texts contribute to the 'erasure' of certain groups in society through marginalisation or present questionable and racist representations.

The Centre for Literacy in Primary Education (CLPE) in London reports on the availability of inclusive and diverse reading materials for all children on a yearly basis in their *Reflecting Realities* survey.[5] This work was developed in consultation with the Cooperative Children's Book Center of the School of Education at the University of Wisconsin–Madison to glean insights from their practices and protocols as developed over the last three decades. The statistics in the initial report, published in 2017, showed that children from racialised minorities in the UK were facing bookshelves where they saw little or nothing that ensured they were visible in their literary world. Since then, mirroring the trend seen in the US, CLPE's annual reporting shows an increase in the number of children's books published featuring a minority ethnic character from 4% in 2017 to 20% in 2021. The percentage of books published with a main character from a racially minoritised background has risen year on year but remained extremely low at 9% in 2021. The CLPE reports go further than reporting the statistics; they also provide adults engaging with children's literature with a purposeful framework for discerning the quality of representation in texts published in the UK, with examples of key texts that highlight quality representations for readers across the primary years.

When choosing books, teachers have to consider the implications of how children might internalise what they see and read about and how this might shape their impressions of the literary space and their engagement with it. It is important to provide a wide range of real books, which feature diverse and representative characters, enabling children to connect with their own lives and the lives of others.

At the very early stages of reading, texts such as the Lenny series by Ken Wilson-Max, Anna McQuinn's Lulu and Zeki series (Lola and Leo in the US), and the works of Nathan Bryon and Dapo Adeola have been consistently identified in CLPE's reports as excellent examples of texts with high-quality representation to share with a wide variety of readers.

Reading a wide and representative range of texts aloud to children is one of the most important ways that children are motivated and supported to become readers. It enables children to experience and enjoy stories they might otherwise not meet, enlarging their reading interests and providing access to texts beyond their level of independence as readers. This also helps children to broaden their repertoire as readers, becoming familiar with a wider range of genres and the work and voice (G) of particular authors. By reading well-chosen books aloud, teachers also help children to become part of a community of readers, sharing in the rich experience of a growing range of books they enjoy, get to know well, and talk about. Reading is a social process: conversations about books read will help children to explore and reflect on texts in ways that are made meaningful, personal, and pleasurable.

Opportunities for re-reading a book that they have previously listened to, or read for themselves, help all children to engage more deeply with it. Reading and re-reading known texts is important for all readers, but particularly so for less experienced readers or those for

Figure 6.1 Interior page spread from *Lenny Has Lunch* by Ken Wilson-Max[6]

Figure 6.2 Interior page spread from *Lulu's Nana Visits* by Anna McQuinn, illustrated by Rosalind Beardshaw

whom English is an additional language. Re-reading helps children to become more familiar with a text, enabling them to read it more confidently and fluently and with greater attention to the meaning. This is explored more extensively in Chapter 13.

Engagement with other kinds of print is also important.[8] Children encounter print all around them as part of everyday experiences. Many will be able to recognise the names of shops or restaurants they visit frequently; the names of favourite characters, programmes, or films in comics or on TV guides; words associated with particular hobbies, interests, or fascinations, such as the names of animals or dinosaurs; place names or instructions on a road sign or a map; a favourite dish on a menu or in a recipe book; or the names of common products, if shopping lists or packaging are available. It is therefore important that a variety of text be displayed and made available throughout the setting and be used and to support young children's motivation to read and knowledge of how text works.

Developing understanding of the purpose of writing

As well as fostering a culture of reading for purpose and pleasure, it is important to engage in activities that share with children how print functions in writing. From the earliest stages, children need to understand that writing is an important form of communication and can be used by them to record and express their thoughts, ideas, and experiences. An enabling environment for writing will provide children with the means, inspiration, and motivation to write. This includes a well-stocked writing area, with materials to write, suited to children's age and stage of development, which are accessible and portable so that writing can happen in any place at any time.

Teachers and assistants also model writing, sharing opportunities and purposes for writing throughout the setting and regularly engaging in active demonstrations of writing. This might include things like making a shopping list, labelling equipment or belongings, making handmade books to record children's invented or retold stories, making song or rhyme cards (including for children's own compositions), creating maps and plans, writing instructions for everyday experiences such as cooking or making playdough, creating signs or informational writing to display for others to read, and making score boards or sheets for sports and games. This, as recognised by Wyse et al.,[9] gives young children opportunities to "test their hypotheses about the forms and functions of writing."

At this stage children will be heavily dependent on adults, but as they learn more about the purpose of writing and develop their knowledge of the writing system, they will gain in independence and fluency. At the early stages, children may want adults to scribe their ideas for them, but then, as they learn more about written language, they will take great pleasure in sharing their growing mastery of new skills. Children's writing will begin at the mark making stage, using an increasing variety and sophistication of marks as their fine motor skills develop, before using and applying their growing knowledge of letters, the phonemes they represent, and the spelling patterns found in the English language. From an early stage, children should be supported to be aware of how words sound but also how they look, what they mean, and how they are constructed. This will provide them with a rich knowledge of how language works and an ability to orchestrate a wide range of strategies to support their success as writers and as readers.

In our Double Helix Model of teaching, reading and writing are intertwined: children's increasing knowledge about how words are spelt will be influenced by their knowledge of how to read words, and vice versa. It is therefore important to draw children's attention to patterns in words through sharing texts and analysing words together, extending children's understanding of the written word and creating an investigative fascination with written language and spelling.

It is also important to encourage talk, reading, and writing in other languages spoken by children, particularly if English is not their first language. Language proficiency in a home language supports the development of talk, reading, and writing in English, so adults should ensure that they know as much as possible about a child's prior language experience, including their speaking, reading, and writing proficiency, as they enter an educational setting. This information should then be used to validate and extend this experience in the classroom setting through environmental print; texts published in other languages; and opportunities and support to think, speak, read, and write in languages other than English.

Early phonological development

To be able to effectively read and write, children need to be able to analyse the sounds they hear and see in words and know how these can be represented in writing. To support them in developing the prerequisite skills for this, adults engage children in a wide range of activities which will help to develop both their phonological awareness, supporting their awareness of the sounds of language and their phonemic awareness (G), their awareness of phonemes, the smallest units of sound in language. Before launching into learning the letter-phoneme correspondences and the skills of segmenting and blending words, it is important that children be engaged in the pleasures of reading and writing and for adults to foster and support children's early phonological development, tuning them in to listening to, recognising, making, and discriminating sounds. This awareness of language that is rooted in whole texts provides the essential context for understanding about the smaller units of language.

Phonological awareness requires an ability to use finely tuned auditory discrimination. To ensure children are prepared for this, teachers engage children in activities that support their understanding of how to recognise and describe sounds in the environment. Sharing a book such as *Quiet!* by Kip Alizadeh[10] will support children in understanding how to listen to and recognise sounds. The title itself demonstrates how to set the conditions for listening, with the child protagonist holding a finger to their lips as a sign for this. The opening page spread addresses the reader directly, telling them to "Sssh! Listen" and asking them "What's that noise?" We then follow them on a journey of discovery of the different sounds that can be heard in their home, such as "the bubbling of the pan and the humming of the fridge" (pp. 8–9) in the kitchen and "the laptop whirring and the pitter patter of the rain against the window" (pp. 14–15) in the living room. As can be seen from the text quoted so far, the book provides an excellent example of rich and descriptive language to enhance and extend children's own vocabulary. The illustrations in the text connect the onomatopoeic (G) words used to describe the sounds with their corresponding objects, inviting children to ascribe the printed word to its context and meaning. Children will relish in joining in with each sound as the text is read and re-read. These onomatopoeic words, like "click", "slosh", "bang", "crunch munch", and "blah blah blah" also allow plentiful opportunities for children to explore and experiment with voice sounds, exercising a range of vocal movements that will eventually support the precise articulation of phonemes.

The structure of the text can be used as a playful and purposeful context to engage in listening activity in the child's own environment, with adults asking supportive questions to draw the children in to listening in their own environment: What can they hear in different rooms? How would they describe each sound? Is it a loud or soft sound? It is a long or short sound? What word could they write down to represent the sound? Teachers and assistants can replicate the format of the original book with children, taking the children on a walk to different places to listen to sounds, drawing each place visited, and labelling the sounds heard next to the objects that made the sounds. These could be bound together as book to share with the children themselves as well as wider audiences, creating a purposeful and authentic outcome and developing children's identities as writers as well as readers.

Rhythm and rhyme

The work of Peter Bryant, Lynette Bradley,[11] and Usha Goswami[12] drew our attention to the crucial role of rhythm, rhyme, and analogy (G) in learning to read. They found that rhythmic abilities are associated with language-related abilities such as reading, or precursors of reading, and that rhythmic timing is essential for both motor skills and language development. Music, song, and rhyme play a vital role in the development of children's language and literacy. Hearing and joining in with songs, rhymes, and poems should be a regular part of a child's daily experience. They provide a distinctive way of encouraging children to focus on the sounds, patterns, and rhythms of language, a vital step in learning to read. They also give children a valuable opportunity to play with language and vocabulary. Opportunities to explore and savour the sounds in words help children to form the different sounds in language, paving the way for and strengthening children's awareness and articulation of phonemes. Playing with sounds and rhyming patterns in words supports the development of the vocal apparatus in the mouth, pharynx, and nose, supporting speech and language development as well as paving the way for the articulation of phonemes.

There is increasing evidence of links between music and language for reading[13] and writing,[14] for example, in synchronising spoken stressed syllables with clapping and with a musical accompaniment. Sharing a book like *The Drum*, by Ken Wilson-Max,[15] with young children provides a wonderful context for understanding the relationship between spoken syllables and music. The whole text is a rhythmic exploration of language where the syllable patterns of the words can be played as music on a drum by an adult, with the children joining in, clapping the spoken stressed syllables alongside. This can then be extended to clapping out each syllable in the words, fitting this into the beat pattern. The words of the text, which begin: "This is the drum. This is the beat. Clap your hands. Stamp your feet," invite children to become involved with the musical language with their whole bodies.

Tanka, Tanka Skunk, by Steve Webb,[16] is an open invitation to engage with music and syllabification. Children can follow the rhythmic refrain in the text: "Skunka Tanka Skunka Tanka Tanka Tanka Skunk" by clapping along or tapping claves or rhythm sticks. They are introduced by the narrator of the text to the idea that the names of the animals involved are composed of different numbers of beats, identifying the syllables in each word: "This is kangaroo. His name has three beats, like this . . . kan-ga-roo" (pp. 8–9). Children can explore and experiment with identifying and beating out the names of the other creatures in the book, either on drums, as the characters do, or by clapping or tapping rhythm sticks or claves. This book is a good example of a text that will enrich and extend children's vocabulary. There are well-known animals, such as a tiger and a duck, and perhaps less well-known animals like a lemur and a llama. Children can also talk about the similarities and differences between animals which are more closely related, like a beaver and an otter or an ox and a yak. Throughout the text, there are plentiful opportunities to engage children with a range of language and literacy opportunities, such as identifying the alliteration in the text; grouping animals whose names start with the same phoneme; developing grammatical knowledge; incorporating adjectives to describe the animals, like the "big gorilla" or the "tiny little hairy spider"; investigating onomatopoeia in the sounds made by the animals to practise the articulation of a range of voice sounds, "quack quack oink oink COCK-A-DOODLE-DOO!", whilst also investigating how letter case and punctuation help us to understand how words should be read aloud.

Tuning into sounds in words

As children tune into the sounds of language, they will start to be able to recognise where different words start with the same letter sound, identifying examples of alliteration. This is a commonly used device, often used to capture children's attention in the names of characters like *Mickey Mouse*; in product names like *Freddo Frog*; or in book titles, such as *Billy's Bucket* or *Lenny Has Lunch*. Children generally find it easier to hear and recognise simple initial sounds in the first instance, before moving on to simple onsets (G) and rimes (G). As children begin to tune into the way letters look on the page, letters and increasingly letter-like forms will begin to appear in their emergent writing. As listening skills develop they will also tune into sounds in the medial position (G), including examples of assonance – repeated vowel (G) sounds. Reading and exploring texts which emphasise repeated sounds will help children to identify and play with these sounds for themselves. Books such as *Ravi's Roar* by Tom Percival;[17] *Rita's Rabbit* by Laura Mucha, illustrated by Hannah Peck;[18] and *Octopus Shocktopus* by Peter Bently, illustrated by Steven Lenton[19] are excellent examples of texts which would be appropriate for early readers.

Children with a good awareness of rhyme tend to become better readers and spellers.[20] As they begin to understand the complex orthography (G) of the English language, children with a good knowledge and experience of rhyme will be able to use analogy to analyse and match sound and spelling patterns for greater accuracy in both reading and spelling words;[21] for example, if they know how to spell 'cake', it will be easier for them to learn to spell 'bake', 'make', 'take', and 'shake'.

The vital role of rhyme and poetry

Nursery and playground rhymes are part of most cultures, so children will likely bring with them an experience of rhymes and songs to the educational setting, which they have had shared and sung with them in the home environment. These will often be children's first experience of fictional narrative: many rhymes create mini-stories through carefully chosen words, introducing children to characters in settings where problems occur and resolutions are found.

Asking parents and carers to share favourite songs and rhymes from the home environment, including those in home languages, will help the children to see the universality of rhyme and increase their repertoire of known rhymes and songs. Parents could create audio recordings of children's favourites to share in the setting, supporting children to see their personal experiences and home cultures and languages as valued and valuable.

Children could be invited to identify and discuss the similarities and differences between songs and rhymes shared, looking at common themes, characters, or patterns of language. Rhyme cards and bags can be created with the children, recording the words of favourite rhymes and songs and collecting props that will help them to recall and perform these for themselves or alongside others. These could also be lent out to share at home, enabling families to engage in rhyme together and children to become confident in remembering and retelling favourites. In the Froebel Trust's Baby Room Project,[22] it was found that singing also had a wide range of benefits, including the promotion of intimacy and connectedness and practitioner well-being.

Engaging in rhyme is often a formative experience for children joining in with language and group interaction. Indeed, with babies, using sounds or signs to join in with songs and rhymes is an important form of pre-verbal communication. It is therefore crucial that children experience a rich repertoire of rhyme, song, and poetry in the early years and beyond, helping them to learn the tunes and patterns of language, hear and understand new language in context, and understand how to communicate meaning through words.

Poetry also provides an opportunity to focus children's attention on rhyme. *Big Green Crocodile: Rhymes to Say and Play* by Jane Newberry, illustrated by Carolina Rabei,[23] introduces a range of rhymes to engage and delight the youngest children, supporting them to connect language with meaning. Wibble Wobble Clown, one of the rhymes in *Big Green Crocodile* (see Figure 6.3), with its direct invitation to "Stretch right UP and flop right DOWN", links words to meaning and encourages children to savour the sounds and shapes of words. Such rhymes introduce a focus on the rhythm and lyricism of poetry, encouraging children to chime in with repeated phrases and patterns, engaging with the language they hear and say and moving physically to poetry, feeling the rhythm in their bodies and building the foundations for writing, drawing, and counting.

High-paced action rhymes like "Wibble-Wobble Clown" are placed alongside quieter rhymes like "Plane Spotting", which invite us to join with the subject of the poem to "lie, looking at the sky, watching all the aeroplanes as they fly" (p. 17), imagining where they are going. Through rhymes such as this, children learn that they can use language to recreate and make sense of direct experiences in their own lives.

Blow a Kiss, Catch a Kiss by Joseph Coelho, illustrated by Nicola Killen,[25] is a carefully considered collection for the very young, full of poems which catch and reflect their emotions and interests. Many of the rhymes actively encourage children acting out parts of the text, as in the poem "Eye Caterpillars": "Eyebrows up/Eyebrows down/Eyebrows wiggle/Eyebrows frown" (p. 9). This is an excellent way of consolidating understanding of language and vocabulary and supporting the understanding that print carries meaning. The short length of the poem on the page also invites children to engage in one-to-one correspondence between oral and printed words by pointing to the words as they say the lines.

The Journey Game, also from the *Blow a Kiss, Catch a Kiss* collection[26] (p. 19), provides an excellent way into natural adult/child interactions focused on looking at and describing the world, with its encouragement to join in the response in the lines: "When you see a tree say . . . Treetreetree/When you see a cow say . . . Moomoomoo". After reading the poem, children and adults can play at making their own lines up, with adults asking appropriate questions to engage children's imagination, such as: What could you say when you see a bus? A dog? This kind of wordplay introduces the shapes and sounds of words, essential precursors to forming, articulating, and recognising speech sounds, as well as connecting words with meaning. The final verse: "When you see a cloud say/What'cha doing up there?/What'cha doing up there?/How did ya get so high/High up in the air?"

Figure 6.3 Page spread of sharing the poem "Wibble Wobble Clown" from the book *Big Green Crocodile*[24]

invites adults and children to play at asking questions of objects around them. Adults can invite children to pick objects from around them, like a tree or a fly, and consider questions they want to ask. This allows them to experiment with the prosody (G) and phrased expression needed for questioning, modelled by the adult reading aloud the original lines in this way. The text also offers a good example of the differences between oral and written language in the phrase "What'cha", including alternative meanings.

As children begin to focus more closely on the details of print, they will begin to take an interest in the shapes and structures of words and will notice similarities between them. Poems with strong rhyming patterns enable adults to draw children's attention to the patterns in rhyming words, highlighting words with the same rime pattern in a rhyme, song, or poem they are familiar with. This can then be developed by exploring sets of rhyming words and making collections of words with similar rimes, helping them to read and spell new words by analogy.

Linking the spoken word with the written

As children's ability to discriminate sounds develops, adults can demonstrate how to synthesise sounds to read words in demonstrations of reading. This will prepare children for the next stage of learning, where they will be introduced to letter-phoneme correspondences and how to segment and blend words for reading and spelling, and demonstrates from the start why these skills are important in gaining independence in reading. This should be naturally built into times when texts are shared, without overly interrupting the flow of reading. For example, in a text like *Mr Gumpy's Outing*, by John Burningham,[27] many of the animal names are easily broken down into constituent phonemes, which the children can be supported to blend together, such as cat – /c/ /a/ /t/, dog – /d/ /o/ /g/, pig – /p/ /i/ /g/, sheep – /sh/ /ee/ /p/, and goat – /g/ /oa/ /t/. All the animal names come at the end of a repetitive sentence, such as " 'I'd like a ride,' said the cat," so the adult is able to sound out the animal name whilst pointing to the representative letters in the text and pose a question to the children, which enables them not to lose the meaning of the text, such as 'Who else wanted a ride in Mr Gumpy's boat?' At first, the running together of the sounds in their natural form in spoken words will need to be more artificially demarcated by the adult, but as the children gain a sense of how this works, they will become increasingly independent in their ability to discriminate phonemes. It's important not to overdo this: little and often in a range of books is best so that children begin to gain a sense of how the marks on the page represent the sounds in the spoken words.

Demonstrations of writing will also be a key context for adults to model how spoken words are broken into their constituent parts to write them and how to draw on existing knowledge and understanding of wider language to spell unfamiliar words. Writing should take place regularly, throughout the setting, both indoors and out for a variety of different purposes matched to the children's interests and endeavours. This shares the purpose and pleasures of writing and builds on their understanding of how to transcribe words onto the page.

Providing places and spaces for children to display and celebrate their own writing consolidates children's understanding of the purpose of writing to communicate and record thoughts, feelings, experiences, and information, making writing meaningful to the children and increasing motivation to write.

The most important lessons to be learned in these first formative years are about the satisfaction and pleasures of reading, the joy of the rhythms and patterns of language, and the meaning carried by print, exploring this in relation to their own lives and experiences and the lives and experiences of others. They should understand that words written or printed link to spoken words and that writing can be used as a means of communication – to express or record thoughts, feelings, ideas, and experiences. This will not only support the development of children's comprehension but will also help them to begin to master the complex skill of lifting the words from the page and continue to preserve and maintain motivation throughout the journey to being an independent reader and writer.

Notes

1. Sullivan, A., & Brown, M. (2015). Reading for Pleasure and Progress in Vocabulary and Mathematics. *British Educational Research Journal, 41*(6), 971–991. Retrieved December 1, 2023, from https://doi.org/10.1002/berj.3180
2. The Reading Agency. (2015). *Literature Review: The Impact of Reading for Pleasure and Empowerment*. Retrieved December 1, 2023, from https://tra-resources.s3.amazonaws.com/uploads/entries/document/2277/The_Impact_of_Reading_for_Pleasure_and_Empowerment.pdf
3. Goouch, K., & Lambirth, A. (2016). *Teaching Early Reading and Phonics: Creative Approaches to Early Literacy* (p. 8). SAGE.
4. Bishop, R. S. (1990). *Multicultural Literacy: Mirrors, Windows, and Sliding Doors*. Retrieved October 19, 2023, from https://scenicregional.org/wp-content/uploads/2017/08/Mirrors-Windows-and-Sliding-Glass-Doors.pdf
5. Centre for Literacy in Primary Education (CLPE). (2023). *Reflecting Realities Research*. CLPE. Retrieved October 19, 2023, from https://clpe.org.uk/research/reflecting-realities
6. Copyright © 2023 Ken Wilson-Max, from *Lenny Has Lunch*. Written and illustrated by Ken Wilson-Max. Reproduced by permission of Alanna-Max Books, London, N4 4NL www.alannamax.com
7. Text Copyright © 2023 Anna McQuinn Illustrations, Copyright © 2023 Rosalind Beardshaw, from *Lulu's Nana Visits*. Written by Anna McQuinn and illustrated by Rosalind Beardshaw. Reproduced by permission of Alanna-Max Books, London, N4 4NL. Retrieved December 1, 2023, from www.alannamax.com
8. Stainthorp, R., & Hughes, D. (1999). *Learning from Children Who Read at an Early Age*. Routledge.
9. Wyse, D., Bradford, H., & Winstanley, J.-M. (2023). *Teaching English, Language and Literacy* (p. 177). Routledge.
10. *Quiet!*. Written and illustrated by Kip Alizadeh, Child's Play International (2017).
11. Bryant, P., & Bradley, L. (1985). *Children's Reading Problems: Psychology & Education*. Basil Blackwell.
    Bryant, P., Bradley, L., Maclean, M., & Crossland, J. (1988). Nursery Rhymes, Phonological Skills and Reading. *Journal of Child Language, 16*, 407–428.
12. Goswami, U. (1990). A Special Link between Rhyming Skill and the Use of Orthographic Analogies by Beginning Readers. *Journal of Child Psychology, 31*(2), 301–311.
13. Degé, F., Kubicek, C., & Schwarzer, G. (2015). Associations between Musical Abilities and Precursors of Reading in Preschool Aged Children. *Frontiers in Psychology, 6*(1220). Retrieved December 1, 2023, from https://doi.org/10.3389/fpsyg.2015.01220
14. Wyse, D. (2017). *How Writing Works: From the Invention of the Alphabet to the Rise of Social Media*. Cambridge University Press.
15. *The Drum*. Written and illustrated by Ken Wilson-Max, Tiny Owl Publishing Ltd. (2018).
16. *Tanka Tanka Skunk!* Written and illustrated by Steve Webb, Red Fox Picture Books (2004).
17. *Ravi's Roar*. Written and illustrated by Tom Percival, Bloomsbury Children's Books (2019).
18. *Rita's Rabbit*. Written by Laura Mucha and illustrated by Hannah Peck, Faber and Faber (2021).
19. *Octopus Shocktopus*. Written by Peter Bently and illustrated by Steven Lenton, Nosy Crow (2020).
20. Bradley, L., & Bryant, P. (1985). *Children's Reading Problems*. Blackwell.
21. Goswami, U., & Bryant, P. (2016). *Phonological Skills and Learning to Read: Classic Edition*. Routledge.

22 Powell, S., Goouch, K., & Werth, L. (2015). *Seeking Froebel's 'Mother Songs' in Daycare for Babies.* Retrieved October 19, 2023, from https://tactyc.org.uk/pdfs/Sacha%20Powell.pdf
23 *Big Green Crocodile: Rhymes to Say and Play.* Written by Jane Newberry and illustrated by Carolina Rabei, Otter-Barry Books (2021).
24 Text Copyright © 2021 Jane Newberry. Illustrations Copyright © 2021 Carolina Rabei, from *Big Green Crocodile: Rhymes to Say and Play.* Written by Jane Newberry and illustrated by Carolina Rabei. Reproduced by permission of Otter-Barry Books, Hereford, HR1 3QS www.otterbarrybooks.com
25 *Blow a Kiss, Catch a Kiss: Poems to Share with Little Ones.* Written by Joseph Coelho and illustrated by Nicola Killen, Andersen Press (2022).
26 *Blow a Kiss, Catch a Kiss.*
27 *Mr Gumpy's Outing.* Written and illustrated by John Burningham, Red Fox (2001).

7 Cracking the alphabetic code

In the early stages of learning to read, children need to develop their understanding of the alphabetic code. Teaching the alphabetic code, known as phonics teaching (G), plays a vital role in helping children understand how spoken words are represented in text so that they can read and write them. This phonics teaching should be contextualised through the whole texts and sentences that are the building blocks of written language so that children make connections between smaller and larger units of language and understand how reading and writing really work.

Most children develop their awareness of phonemes (G) and letters between four and five years of age. However, there are some children who develop this awareness later and who may need additional support in the foundations of reading (see Chapter 12). There are other children who will have knowledge of the alphabetic code earlier, as will be seen from their ability to read simple unknown texts independently. These children will not need phonics teaching for reading but will benefit from some phonics and other teaching related to writing and spelling words.

Although the emphasis in the teaching of reading at this stage has a clear focus on the alphabetic code, this needs to be systematically contextualised in whole texts and authentic and meaningful purposes for reading and writing. Phonics teaching needs to be set in a literacy-rich curriculum enabling children to benefit from their developing knowledge of phonemes and letters when applied in their reading and writing. By 'literacy-rich', we mean that lessons[1] where phonics is a main focus explicitly build on and directly link this teaching with real texts to support the development of language, reading, and writing. This is not the same as planning separate phonics lessons at a different time from 'literacy-rich' lessons. Some lessons may use a text once; at other times, a number of sessions will be planned to explore a text in detail over an extended period of time.

Using real books to teach phonics

At the start of a taught lesson, or series of lessons, the first thing the children experience is the wonder of a real book. This will begin with purposeful talk about the possibilities the text might hold by introducing the front cover and talking about the text and illustrations they see. The focus text may be read as a whole or may be unfolded over a series of lessons to build motivation and engagement; explore predictions and hypotheses about the text; develop children's comprehension; and explore opportunities for talk, writing, and extended activities related to the text. However the text is introduced, lessons will always involve the teacher reading some or all of the text aloud to the children, stopping at key points to discuss or ask questions about the text, clarify language and concepts, assess comprehension, activate children's prior knowledge about concepts and ideas explored, and engage the children in hypotheses about the text. Sometimes, the children will be so rapt by the reading, there may be no discussion.

Children's intense engagement with the multiple meanings created by an author through the special mixture of text and pictures is one of the many things that makes children's literature, and primary teaching, such a pleasure. And it is the main reason and purpose for teaching reading. If we lose sight of this, for example, through a too-narrow focus on the alphabetic code, children will be less motivated to read and will fail to grasp the essence of reading and learning to read.

Real texts used should be displayed large enough for the children to be able to see and follow as a group. This may mean using e-books alongside a physical copy of the book for the children to return to individually or in groups or placing the text under a visualiser, so that every child can clearly see the text and be able to closely read both the text and illustrations alongside the teacher. Sections of the text will be read and re-read aloud by the teacher, allowing them to model and demonstrate specific knowledge and skills related to reading, including one-to-one correspondence between spoken words and words in print; the use and application of phonics at the point of reading words; and how to read with fluency (G), including the use of expression and intonation and reading punctuation. Skilled teachers also need to be able to formulate questions about texts or sections of texts which develop children's comprehension, moving from the literal towards being able to infer, deduce, and evaluate.

Using real texts in this way ensures that children explore rich language, vocabulary, and grammatical concepts and structures from reading, which they can use and apply in talk and writing (Nation et al., 2022).[2] It also gives teachers the opportunity to contextualise the use of reading skills and strategies at the point of reading and exemplify why phonics is a key strategy for gaining independence.

Real texts build children's motivation from the start, with engaging storylines, subject matter, and illustrations. In time they also imbue writerly knowledge, teaching children much about purposes and forms for writing, as well as the appropriate and varied use of language and grammar for specific purposes and audiences, enabling pupils to learn much about the work of authoring texts.

The links between phonics, reading, and writing

As part of our model, the Double Helix of Reading and Writing, we make it clear that children's writing supports their knowledge about how words work in reading. At the same time as children are learning to read words, they are also learning how to use their knowledge of sound and spelling patterns to be able to write down spoken language for themselves. As children are supported to write independently, through purposeful, meaningful, and engaging contexts, they will begin to pay close attention to the sounds and patterns within words and how these are represented. In this way they learn more about relationships between phonemes and letters and how these apply to reading words.

Contextualised phonics teaching at this stage will focus on:

- children understanding that spoken words and their phonemes are represented by letters;
- the introduction of letter-phoneme correspondences, including the enunciation and articulation of phonemes;

120 *The art of teaching*

- knowing the names of letters and understanding how these letters are formed in writing;
- teaching the skills of blending or synthesising phonemes for reading and segmenting words for writing, first orally, then in texts;
- how to read and write words that do not conform to letter-phoneme correspondences taught, particularly commonly used words.

This teaching will be linked to themes and ideas explored in a focus text (including through illustrations) as part of the focus on phonemes, words, and sentences found in the text.

Extended classroom activities can be planned around themes and ideas shared in the text, encouraging children to be imaginative and creative; giving them the opportunity to incorporate and consolidate language, vocabulary, reading, and writing across areas of learning and providing time and space for children to develop their independence in reading and writing.

A contextualised approach to teaching the basic code

This chapter explores the first phase of systematic phonics teaching in primary schools, assuming that the foundations are in place, as we explained in Chapter 6, "Building the Foundations". The phonics teaching at this stage, and all stages, is contextualised in a real book, which involves teaching single letter-phoneme correspondences but also linking these to a text and its illustrations. Based on experience working with a range of four- to five-year-old children, we recommend that this stage of learning typically be delivered over approximately five to six weeks, with children being introduced to letter-phoneme correspondences at the rate of approximately four to five per week.

The suggested order in which to teach the letter-phoneme correspondence in this initial phase is based on the frequency in which the phonemes appear in words. The more common phonemes enable children to discover a larger range of words with which they can use and apply their growing knowledge in order to read and spell.

At the start of this phase the focus will be on introducing single letters which correspond to phonemes and consolidating children's knowledge and understanding of how to orally blend and segment phonemes in words. As soon as they know enough letter-to-phoneme correspondences (e.g. S /s/, A /a/ (short A phoneme), T /t/, P /p/, I /i/),[3] they will begin to blend and segment words using the letter-phoneme correspondences they have been taught. In each session, the teacher supports the children in revisiting and revising previously taught letter-phoneme correspondences. High-frequency words which do not conform to letter-phoneme correspondences taught are also discussed, as well as introducing new letter-phoneme correspondences. This helps to consolidate and extend knowledge during every session, allowing the children to continue to practise and extend their ability to blend and segment in order to read words, phrases, and sentences, supporting their independence as readers and writers.

Throughout this phase, as children continue to learn more letter-phoneme correspondences, they will continue to practise and gain greater independence in the skills of blending and segmenting with an ever-increasing variety of words, including those with consonant clusters at the beginning and/or end of words. They will also independently read phrases and sentences containing words which are decodable using the letter-phoneme correspondences taught and read high-frequency words which do not conform to the letter-phoneme correspondences taught.

Table 7.1 Suggested order to teach letter-phoneme correspondences

Week	Letter-phoneme correspondences to be taught	Example words that can be decoded/encoded with taught letter-phoneme correspondences (the speaker's accent may result in different phonemes in some words)	Common words to be taught alongside which are not phonetically decodable using the letter-phoneme correspondences children will have been taught
1:	s, a, t, p, i	Words with two phonemes: at, it Words with three phonemes: sat, tap, pat, sap, pin, pit, pip, tip, sip, sit Words with four phonemes: past	I, a, as, is
2:	n, m, d, g, o	Words with two phonemes: an, in, on Words with three phonemes: dad, dam, din, dim, dip, dig, dog, dot, gag, gap, got, mad, man, map, mat, nag, nan, nap, not, pad, pan, pad, pig, pod, pot, sag, tag, tin, tan, top, sad, sin Words with four phonemes: damp, mask, mast, mint, mist, pond, sand Longer words: stamp, stand	said do, to no, go, so
3:	c, k, e, u, r	Words with three phonemes: ask, cat, can, cog, cot, con, cop, cup, cut, dug, gum, gun, gust, gut, men, mud, mug, mum, mad, net, nun, nut, peg, pen, pet, pug, rag, ram, ran, rat, red, rid, rig, rim, rip, rod, rot, run, rum, rug, set, sun, sum, ted, ten, tug, tum, top Words with four phonemes: camp, cask, cast, cost, crag, cram, crib, croc, crop, drag, drip, drop, drum, dump, dust, gasp, mend, mink, must, nest, pest, pink, pump, ramp, rink, rank, rest, risk, rust, sink, task Longer words: cramp, crept, crest, crimp, crisp, crust, drank, drink, scram, script, stink, sunset, trust	the come, some, done
4:	h, b, f, l, j	Words with three phonemes: bad, bag, ban, bap, bat, bed, beg, bet, ban, big, bin, bit, blot, bob, bog, bond, bonk, bop, bot, bud, bug, bun, bus, but, fab, fad, fan, fat, fib, fin, fit, fog, frost, had, hag, ham, hand, has, hat, hem, hen, hip, him, his, hit, hog, hop, hot, hug, hum, hut, jab, jam, jet, jig, jog, joy, jug, jut, lab, lad, lag, lap, lid, lip, lit, lug, mob, pub, rob, rub, sob, tub	of like

(Continued)

122 *The art of teaching*

Table 7.1 (Continued)

Week	Letter-phoneme correspondences to be taught	Example words that can be decoded/encoded with taught letter-phoneme correspondences (the speaker's accent may result in different phonemes in some words)	Common words to be taught alongside which are not phonetically decodable using the letter-phoneme correspondences children will have been taught
		Words with four phonemes: band, bank, best, blast, blip, blab, bled, blob, blog, blub, bulb, bump, blub, bump, brag, bran, brat, brim, clad, clam, clan, clap, clasp, clip, clog, clot, club, crab, craft, daft, drab, fast, flag, flan, flat, flip, flit, flop, fond, frog, hand, hump, jest, jump, junk, just, lamp, land, lank, last, limp, lisp, lift, link, lint, lisp, list, lump, milk, plan, plug, raft, slab, slam, slap, slat, slob, sled, slog, slop, slot, slab, slap, slam, slat, slid, slip, slit, slug, slum Longer words: blank, blimp, blink, bland, blend, blond, clamp, clank, clink, clonk, clump, clunk, drift, slept, slump	
5:	v, w, x, y	Words with two phonemes: ox Words with three phonemes: van, vat, vent, vet, wag, wax, web, wet, wig, win, wit, wag, tax, fix, max, mix, six, box, fox, yak, yam, yap, yelp, yes, yet, yob, yum Words with four phonemes: vest, went, wept, west, wimp, swag, swig, swam, swim, swop, twig, twin, next, vast, yank Longer words: swept, twist, exit, cravat	want, was with we, he, she, be, me
6:	z, qu	Words with three phonemes: zap, zag, zig, zip, zit Words with four phonemes: quid, quip, quit, quiz Longer words: quest, quest, quilt, squid, squint	you my, by, why

Words that do not conform to letter-phoneme correspondences taught

High-frequency words are common words which appear most often in written English. Some of these, like 'in', 'of', 'at', and 'an' are decodable at this early stage of phonics teaching, but others, like 'a', 'the', 'to', 'no', 'go', 'we', and 'he' are not decodable using the letter-phoneme correspondences children will have been taught at this stage. These words that are not as straightforward to decode can be explored with the children in a way that enables them to understand some of the differences in letter-phoneme correspondences. It is important to register how the letters they see in these words do not match the phoneme correspondences that will have been taught.

Teachers ensure that these words can be seen by children at all times – for example, as word-cards on a display of 'words we see a lot' and/or written in a class book of 'words we use a lot', for children to refer to in reading or writing. Printed versions of these word-cards may be sent home for the children to display on a wall or on the refrigerator to practise reading and writing.

Looking at words with similar phoneme and spelling patterns is also helpful, relating this to children's knowledge of rhyme and analogy (G), drawing attention to patterns in words, for example, in: be, he, me, she, and we; go, no, and so; by and my; some and come. When exploring words in this way, children with a good knowledge of rhyme and analogy may also suggest other words which follow similar sound patterns. Some of these may follow the same spelling patterns; others may not. For example, if we take the same groups of phonemes in the previous words, the following words use different letter patterns: tea, owe, lie, or gum.

The following example is our first detailed explanation in the book of how a lesson can be taught. It then shows how a sequence of contextualised phonics lessons would be taught.

A lesson introducing initial grapheme-phoneme correspondences

Consistent with our approach, we begin with a real book. A recommended text for this series of example lessons is *Stanley's Stick* by John Hegley, illustrated by Neal Layton.[4] This is a highly relevant book for children at this stage of learning, showcasing the power of children's imaginations, as we delight in all the things that Stanley, a young boy, does with a stick. The wonderful figurative language by poet John Hegley exemplifies the delights of language and the sounds in words, including plentiful examples of alliteration to draw children's attention specifically to the sounds in words. Thoughtful illustrations by Neal Layton provoke thinking, evoke empathy, and extend children's thinking beyond the text on the page.

This is an ideal text to begin a programme of phonics teaching, as it offers opportunities to see, hear, and use the initial set of letter-sound correspondences taught (S /s/, A /a/, T /t/, P /p/, and I /i/) in the context of words and sentences that form part of an authentic, engaging, and motivating story.

The book is so rich with ideas and opportunities for children to engage with extended work around the text that we would recommend using it across an extended period of learning, where the text is slowly unfolded over time, offering the children the chance to be introduced to a series of letter-phoneme correspondences in context and engage in important reading activities such as predicting, hypothesising, and summarising. This approach builds motivation for reading over time as well as allowing children to spend more time with a story and get to know the characters, illustrations and plot in-depth through discovering the meanings in both the text and illustrations.

124 *The art of teaching*

Lesson 1: Introducing the book

The teacher starts the lesson by sharing the book's front cover (Figure 7.1), giving time and space for the children to look closely at and discuss the illustration. The teacher encourages them to make connections with their own lives and experiences they have had by asking a range of questions about the front cover, such as What can you see? What do you think you know about this character? Where do you think they are? What are they doing? Does it remind you of anything you have seen or done before?

As the children discuss the text, it is important for the teacher to scribe some of the ideas in a way that children can clearly see the teacher's writing. This demonstrates the links between oral language and written language and allows the teacher to assess the children's prior learning with regard to some of their vocabulary and comprehension. It also makes clear to children that writing is a way of recording and communicating our thoughts and ideas for others.

If the children haven't done this already, the teacher can also discuss the accompanying text, asking whether they recognise any of the words. They may, for example, already recognise the name of the character, author, or illustrator, particularly if there is a child with this name in the group or if it is a name known by any of the children in the class.

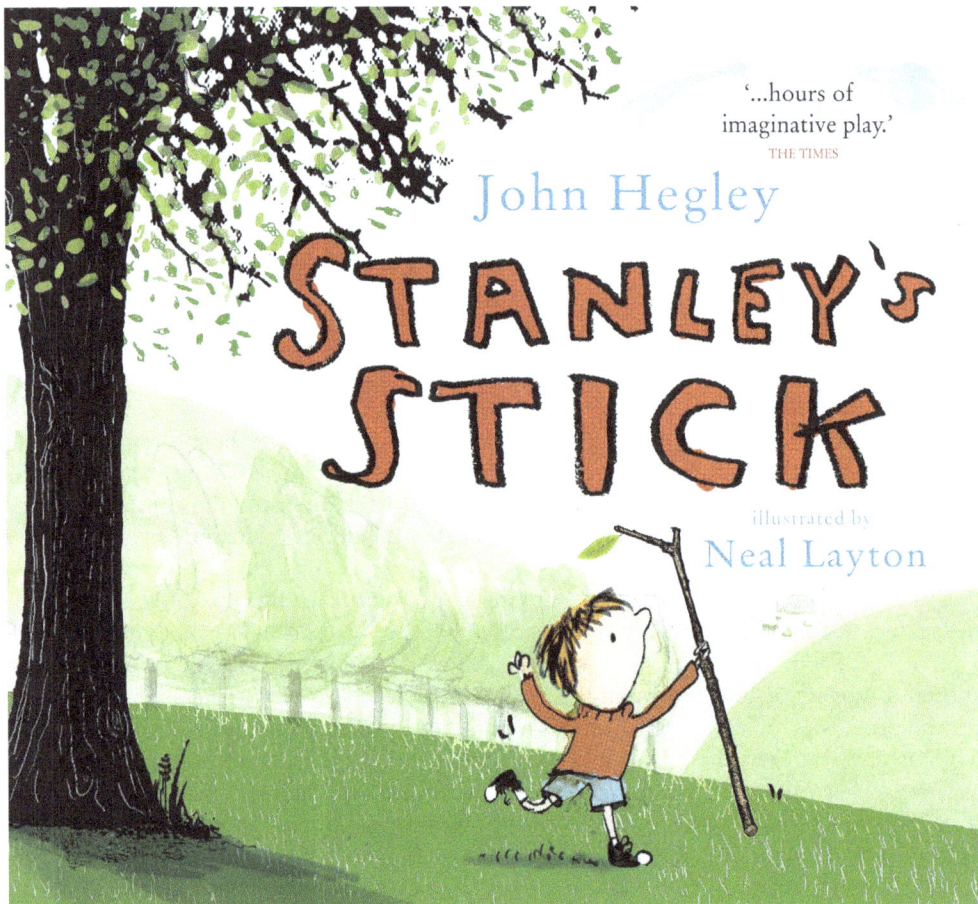

Figure 7.1 Front cover of the book *Stanley's Stick*[5]

Cracking the alphabetic code 125

The teacher can read the title aloud and open discussion and speculation around it, by asking questions such as: What do you think a book with this title might be about? If this is *Stanley's Stick*, how might he have come to have the stick? What might he do with it? How do you think he feels about the stick? Why might this be? What might happen to Stanley and the stick in the story?

The teacher can then re-read the title aloud, encouraging the children to join in, by pointing to each word to demonstrate one-to-one correspondence between oral and written words. They can ask the children to identify the phoneme at the start of each word, repeating the words again and emphasising this. The children can then be introduced to a letter-card, which shows the letter, S, which represents this phoneme, /s/. This should be of a size that can clearly be seen by all children in a whole class session and may range from A6 to A4 in size (Figure 7.2). These can be bought pre-made or can be easily handmade from pre-cut card, with a clear representation of the letter written in thick marker pen. This is preferable, so that the children can see how this letter is formed when written as opposed to the slightly different formations that result from computer-generated letters (something that children also need to learn to appreciate in time). Letters should be handwritten in lowercase. It would also be useful to share the uppercase version on the back of the letter-card for reference.

The letter-card can be used to demonstrate where the letter can be seen in the words Stanley and Stick and at the end of Stanley's. It is important that children be able to correctly enunciate each phoneme taught. The children can be encouraged to repeat after the teacher, who demonstrates how to enunciate the phoneme clearly. Teachers can talk about what happens in the mouth as the phoneme is formed – with /s/, the teeth sit together, the tongue sits behind the teeth, and air passes between the gaps in the mouth cavity and lips. Using small safe mirrors will allow the children to see what this looks like for themselves. Children also need to be clear that some phonemes are voiced and some, like this one, are unvoiced. In active demonstrations, teachers can encourage children to place two fingers lightly onto their throat. If they voice the phoneme, they will feel the vibrations on their fingers; if it's unvoiced, there will be no vibrations.

It's important for children to understand the difference between the name of a letter and any phoneme it represents, as well as being aware of how to form the letters in writing for themselves through clear demonstrations by the teacher, who can talk about the position and movement of the strokes as they demonstrate, so the children can follow. Depending on the stage of fine motor development, the children can engage with the letter formation themselves in a variety of ways. They could use their index finger to trace the letter shape in the air or to trace it on the ground in front of them. If they are confident

Figure 7.2 Example of a letter-card for the taught letter-phoneme correspondence

and able to secure the tripod grip on a pencil or pen, whiteboards and appropriately shaped pens can be provided.

Objects seen in the text or illustrations representing simple two-, three-, or four-phoneme words which start with the focus phoneme can be highlighted to practise the skills of oral blending and segmenting. Appropriate objects to refer to in the illustrations of *Stanley's Stick* might be of a sun, spoon, stick, slug, sand, sea. Verbs could be referred to as well, to describe Stanley's actions, such as sit or stand. It is important for teachers to be able to confidently model and demonstrate how to take a word, such as 'sun' and segment it into its constituent phonemes, such as /s/ /u/ /n/, enunciating each phoneme clearly and correctly. More overt demonstrations will be necessary at the initial stages to show how to synthesise these phonemes.

Teachers should also be able to model and demonstrate how to say a whole word, such as 'sand', and listen for and say the phonemes in the word in the order in which they occur, such as /s/ /a/ /n/ /d/. At the early stages, it is important to say the word slowly and clearly to support the children, encouraging them to count the phonemes on their fingers as they hear them, as well as being able to repeat the sounds back to the teacher and blend them to form the whole word. Demonstrations of how to write each word on a word-card as they segment the phonemes will provide encouragement for the children to do this for themselves and to read the word-cards independently after the taught session.

Extended activity for a session like this could focus on children hearing and recognising initial phonemes in their own name and other objects independently. The title of the book can encourage the children to think about the initial phoneme in their own names by asking these kinds of questions: What phoneme does their name start with? Can they say this phoneme for themselves?

The teacher should ensure the children are aware when they are identifying the initial *phoneme* in their name, as opposed to the *name* of the first letter in their name, demonstrating this with their own name (or with another name if they are not comfortable sharing this). For example: 'in my name, Charlotte, the first phoneme is /sh/'. After isolating the initial phoneme, they can be encouraged to think of an object which starts with the same initial phoneme. Again, it is helpful for the teacher to demonstrate this with their own name, such as 'Charlotte's shell'. The teacher could go on to say, 'The first phoneme in Charlotte's name is seen in the letters C and H.'

An extension activity could involve the teacher working with the children to create a display with photos of the children and objects related to the initial phoneme in their names.

Lesson 2: Building engagement with the text and understanding of ideas within it

The children are re-oriented to the book by revisiting the front cover and title page before the teacher reads aloud the first double page spread of the book: "Stanley stands on Stockport Station with his stick. Stanley always carries his stick with him" (p. 6–7) (Figure 7.3). This spread can be used to share multiple examples of the letter-to-phoneme correspondence, S and /s/, in context.

The children can be encouraged and given time to closely read the illustration on this page before the teacher opens a discussion about this spread by asking these kinds of questions: Where is Stanley? Does anyone know where Stockport is? Has anyone been there before? Why might Stanley be at Stockport Station? How do you think he is feeling? What tells you this? Who do you think is with him? What makes you think this? The children's responses to these questions can be recorded by the teacher, as seen in Figure 7.4. Each

Cracking the alphabetic code 127

Figure 7.3 Opening page spread from the book *Stanley's Stick*[6]

128 *The art of teaching*

Figure 7.4 Teacher's scribing of children's responses to the initial page spread from *Stanley's Stick*

child's contribution is labelled with their name, enabling the teacher to refer to these to assess children's language, understanding of the text, and links to their prior knowledge and real-life experiences.

The teacher can then re-read the second sentence aloud: "Stanley always carries his stick with him," before continuing to encourage speculation and personal connection with the text and ideas, and assessing children's understanding using questions such as: What is he carrying? Why do you think he does this? What might this tell us about the stick? Do you have an object that is special to you, which you take to different places with you?

The teacher can then carry on reading aloud, up to "There is game after sticky game" (Figure 7.5) (p. 11). The spread introduces the word 'activity', which can be connected to the new letter-phoneme correspondence letter A with phoneme /a/. To clarify comprehension of language and concepts, the teacher also asks questions, such as: Stanley has a lot of stick activity. What does this mean? What activities does he do with his stick on these pages?

To make the connection between phonics and writing, the teacher could write Stick Activity at the top of a large sheet of paper and say the word 'activity' again, emphasising the initial phoneme and asking the children: What phoneme can be heard at the start of this word? This new letter-sound correspondence A /a/ can be introduced and with it the skills of enunciating the phoneme and recognising and forming the letter which represents it through the use of a letter-card and letter formation activity, appropriate to children's fine motor skill development. In this case, /a/ is a voiced phoneme. So that the children can ensure the phoneme is voiced, the teacher encourages children to place two fingers lightly onto their throat. If they voice the phoneme, they will feel the vibrations on their fingers.

Words heard and seen in the text can be used to allow children to see and hear the letter-phoneme correspondence in context. If examples can't be found in the text or illustrations, teachers will need to come up with words of their own. With this text, words like axe, add, ant, apple, ankle, adult could be used. Children can then practise saying the words, alongside the teacher, focusing on clearly enunciating the phoneme at the start of each word.

To introduce children to high-frequency words which do not conform to letter-phoneme correspondences taught so far, the teacher can turn back to the spread in the book where Stanley is standing on Stockport Station with his stick (p. 6–7) and use this illustration to model how to use a new high-frequency word 'a' in the context of a sentence, such as

I can see a man reading a newspaper.

I can see a dog on a lead.

These sentences can be spoken and also shared as written sentences, with the focus high-frequency word underlined to draw children's attention to the word in context (see Figure 7.6). Teachers can read and display these in the context of the related illustrations and activity so that children can see and refer to these words in the context of the text.

They can then share a pre-prepared word card with the word written on it, at least A5 in size so that it is clearly visible to the children (Figure 7.7). This can be introduced and displayed in the setting for children to reference in their independent reading and writing activity.

In this case, the teacher can explain that as well as being a letter that represents the phoneme /a/, this is also a word, showing the word card to the children and sharing how it is read differently to the phoneme they just learned. This will also involve how this word is pronounced in sentences, whether this is like the letter name A, or the schwa sound /u/.

It is also important to contextualise each word in a sentence. To encourage the children's independent ideas, the teacher can encourage the children to offer their own suggestions for alternative sentences incorporating the word 'a', introducing and modelling the fact that they need to use 'an' rather than 'a' if the word precedes a word which starts with a vowel (G).

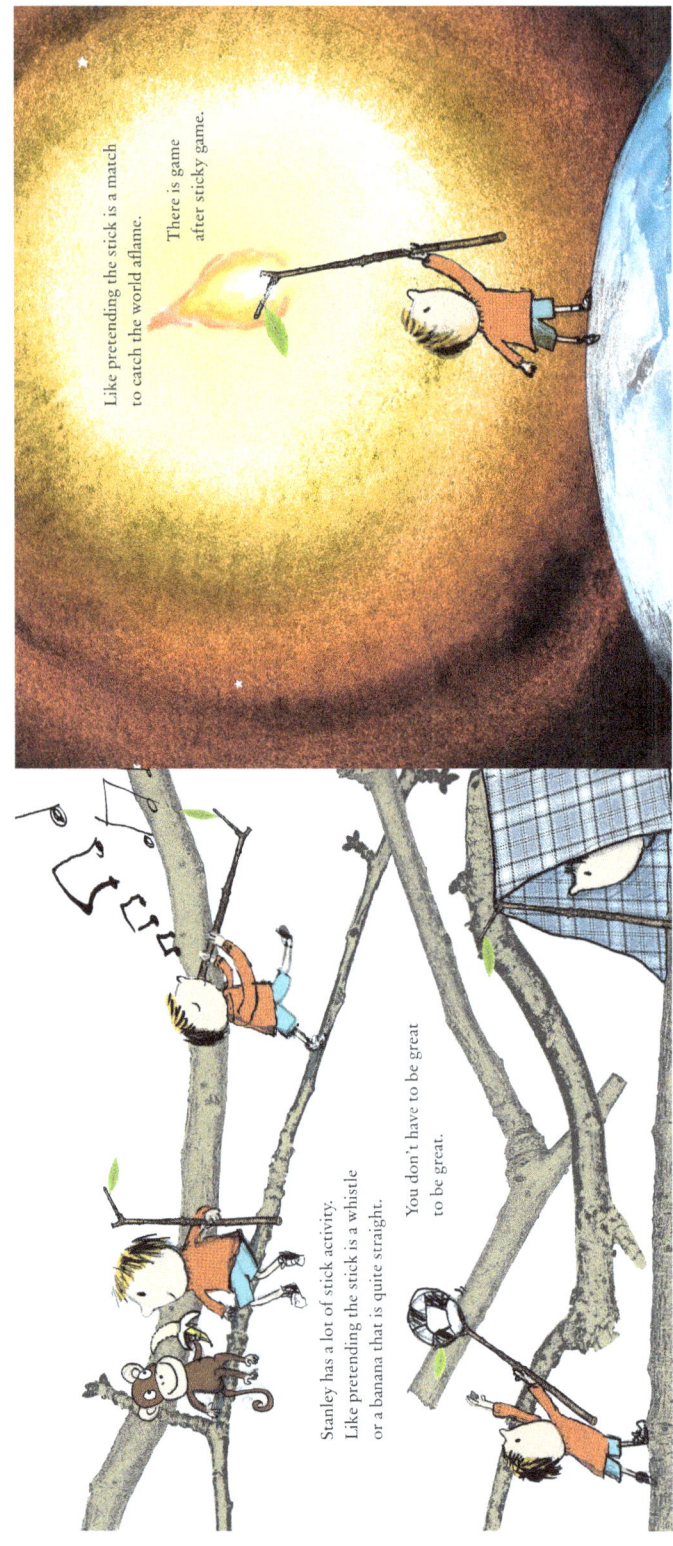

Figure 7.5 Second page spread from *Stanley's Stick*[8]

> *I can see a man reading a newspaper.*

> *I can see a dog on a lead.*

Figure 7.6 Sentences with focus high-frequency word underlined

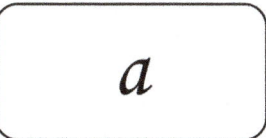

Figure 7.7 Example of a word-card, handwritten by the adult

The teacher scribes the children's sentences, underlining the word 'a', so that it is visible in context, and places these sentences around a copy of the illustration, alongside those already shared by the teacher.

A second word card can then be introduced, with the word 'as' written on it. The teacher can demonstrate how to use the letter-phoneme correspondences learned as a strategy for decoding the word. It will need to be noted that, in this word, the letter S makes a slightly different voiced phoneme. The teacher says the phoneme, which is /z/, for the children to repeat orally. The children can then repeat this alongside the teacher.

As an extension to the activities so far, the teacher can show the children a real stick to encourage children to offer words that describe it, taking the opportunity to use the word 'as' in context, building on the words the children offer, such as 'My stick is as bendy as a banana', 'My stick is as straight as a ruler'.

The teacher can scribe the children's sentences, underlining the words 'a' and 'as' when used, so that they are visible in context, and place these sentences around a display of photographs of the children with their sticks. These words could also be sent home with the children on printed word-cards to practice reading and writing. We prefer that these not be referred to as 'tricky words' because this could create a psychological barrier for the children. They are not tricky; the letter-phoneme correspondences just vary from the basic code they have been taught.

To extend the activity beyond the taught session, teachers and teaching assistants can work with the children to collect a selection of sticks of a variety of lengths and weights to use for various stick activities, stimulated by ideas from the text. Children could be encouraged to bring in a stick from home for further discussions about similarities and differences and to reinforce the phoneme-to-letter correspondence that has been learned. Large sticks are perfect for children to involve their whole body to move the sticks to construct dens and for larger projects. Shorter straight sticks of any length will work well as flagpoles, wands, swords, and so on and to use in smaller imaginative play and creative activity.

Ideas for using the sticks can be scribed on the sheet of paper titled Stick Activity, so children can refer to these and continue to add ideas over time. This gives an opportunity to model how to set out the writing in a list form, with one idea on each line. It would also

132 *The art of teaching*

be pertinent to talk about what shouldn't be done with the sticks to ensure that the stick activity is fun and children use the sticks safely. The children's comments can be used to make a stick safety poster to hang in the environment, such as 'No waving sticks about in the air near other children,' 'No fighting with sticks.'

Adults can work alongside the children to carry out a range of activities with sticks, including in the outdoors; for example:

- providing googly eyes and other embellishments to glue on to sticks and creating stick creatures, which they can create stories and go on adventures with;
- opening up a woodwork area to create with sticks using hammers and nails;
- lighting a bonfire or a fire pit with the children to watch how the sticks burn and then use the charcoal when cooled to write some sooty messages (Figure 7.8);
- building a den, making a tent, or constructing a shelter;
- using a pile of sticks make a habitat pile in the outside environment to attract insects;
- taking photographs and video of children engaging in stick activity to stimulate talk and reflection.

Activities such as these provide children with engaging real-life experiences, which stimulate language and talk around and beyond texts shared in taught sessions.

Figure 7.8 Photograph of children watching a fire created from sticks as part of their stick activity related to *Stanley's Stick*[9]

Lesson 3: Using letter-phoneme correspondences to blend and segment words

When slowly revealing a text in a series of phonics and reading lessons, it is important to begin each session by re-reading the text shared so far. In lesson three the teacher can read on to: "Stanley's stick is good for writing in the sand in languages only Stanley can understand" (p. 16). Time and space should be given for close reading and discussion, opened up through questions such as: Do you understand Stanley's secret language? What do you notice about the letters he has written? Some children might note that he has written "Stanley woz ere!" backwards in the sand. This can be explored, perhaps using a mirror to see the text the right way round. The way Stanley spells the words 'woz' and 'ere' can be discussed, looking at how these words are spelt conventionally and how his spelling might give clues to how he says these words when he talks.

Picture books benefit from being read multiple times. With each new encounter a child picks up additional detail and with it new layers of meaning. The teacher can encourage this by flipping back through the pages so far to reflect on *Stanley's Stick*, asking questions such as: What does Stanley's stick look like? How could you describe it? What different things does he do with his stick? New ideas can be added to the Stick Activity list.

The tall tree on the page spread, "Stanley's stick was once part of something grand, and it will never return" (p. 8), provides an opportunity to introduce a new phoneme, /t/. The teacher can ask the children: Where did Stanley's stick come from? What is the tall and grand thing that the stick was part of? These kind of questions help children to develop their reading comprehension. The words 'tall' and 'tree' enable children to hear the focus phoneme in context. The teacher can ask the children to look at the illustration, point to the tree and say the sentence: 'A tall tree.', encouraging the children to listen to and identify the phoneme at the start of the words 'tall' and 'tree' – clear enunciation is key, particularly in 'tree'.

The teacher repeats the process of enunciating the phoneme, looking at the letter correspondence on a letter-card, and learning how to form the letter in writing, in order to introduce the children to the name of the letter and the phoneme it represents. It is important to continually connect this back to the language, using the sentence 'a tall tree', so that the children can see and hear the letter-phoneme correspondence in context.

As soon as the children know enough letter-phoneme correspondences, the children can start to use these to segment and blend written words. They would now, for example, be able to decode phonetically the words 'at' and 'sat'.

Teachers must be confident to model this process explicitly, taking each word in turn and demonstrating how to recognise the phoneme each letter represents, saying the phoneme out loud while pointing to each letter, and then demonstrating how to blend the phonemes together to read each word in turn. At first, this will need to be done explicitly; then as children gain more experience they will be able to decode more fluently.

It is crucial to ensure children are clear on the meaning of the word as they read it, so the word should be presented in a spoken sentence after blending successfully, such as 'I woke up **at** seven o'clock this morning' and 'I **sat** on the chair to read a book.'

Such words can then be displayed under a heading such as: 'Words we can sound out', alongside sentences containing these words for the children to see and refer to independently. Copies of these can be sent home with the children to practise recognising the taught letter-phoneme correspondences and blending the sounds to read the words with parents, carers, and family.

134 *The art of teaching*

In extended activities related to the text which follow this lesson, activities to develop pull and pinch grip, supporting muscle development for handwriting, can be planned through a range of activities, such as:

- using sticks to write using paint on rolls of paper;
- using sticks to write in the sand, in the mud, in shaving foam, gloop and so on;
- decorating sticks with ribbons, string, chalk, and paint (Figure 7.9);
- taking a sketch book and art materials outside to make a sketch of the trees;
- making line drawings of the sticks in pencil or charcoal (Figure 7.10);
- making twig art inspired by the work of artists who work with nature as a medium, such as Andy Goldsworthy;
- stringing sticks together to make wind chimes, giant picture frames, or frames for an outside display or to weave through with ribbons.

Figure 7.9 Photo of child aged four to five engaged in weaving sticks with wool and string as a stick activity[10]

Cracking the alphabetic code 135

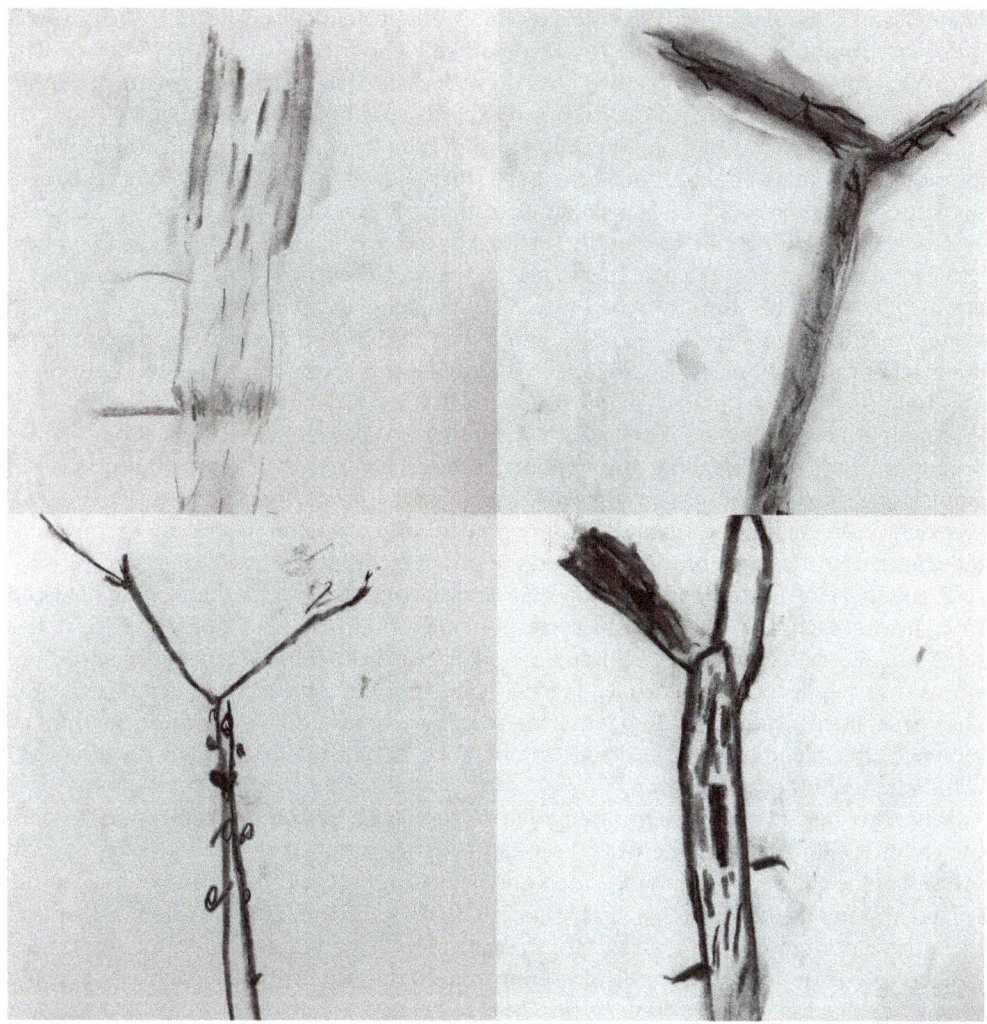

Figure 7.10 Examples of observational drawings of sticks produced by children aged four to five[11]

Lesson 4: Developing deeper connections with a text

The teacher begins the session by re-reading aloud the text covered so far in the lessons and on to: "'Because the fish are pretend, no fish get hurt,' says Bertie" (p. 19). At this point, some children might see that the letters used to represent the /ee/ phoneme at the end of Stanley and Bertie are different. This would be a good observation which can be discussed with the children. It is an important feature of the English language that in some words, different letters are used to represent the same sound. If you have other children in the class with names that follow either of these patterns, draw out this knowledge by writing the names down, such as Stanley, Harley, Finley, Audrey, Abbey, Bertie, Freddie, Emilie, Jamie, Lily, Ashlee, Daphne, or Chelsea. Linking this to children's own names and clearly enunciating the final phonemes before looking at name cards to see the letter or letters which represent this phoneme is a good way to introduce the rich orthography (G) of English.

Specifically targeted questions will support children's ability to summarise parts of the text and to use their personal experience and imagination to come up with new ideas.

Examples of these might be: What do you know about Stanley and Bertie? What do you think they might be like? Do you think you'd like to be friends with them? Why or why not? What sorts of things did the two boys do with their sticks? Can you think of any other things to do with sticks, based on your own experiences of playing with them?

The teacher can also support the children to develop their skills of prediction by asking them what they think might happen next in the story and why. They can make a note of these suggestions to come back to as you continue reading to see if these predictions were correct.

Teachers should be able to identify sections of the text suitable for introducing a new letter-phoneme correspondence. In this part of the text, the page: "And four times now, he has used it to pick up slugs from pathway, platform and pavement, thus saving them from a fate worse than feet" (p. 17) is ideal. Before focusing in on the repeated /p/ phoneme, the teacher can encourage the children to infer what this action might tell us about Stanley, using questions such as: Why do you think Stanley picks up the slugs with his stick? What might have happened if he had left them there? What might we learn about Stanley because of this? By re-reading the sentence, the teacher can then repeat the process of enunciating the /p/ phoneme in the words in which it appears, looking at the letter correspondence using a letter-card, and learning how to form the letter in writing, to introduce the children to the name of the letter and the phoneme it represents.

It is important for teachers to know and demonstrate new words that can be read and written with each new letter-sound correspondence that is taught. For example, at this stage, the words tap and pat could now be added to the children's existing repertoire of words they can decode and encode. Teachers can continue to model and demonstrate the skills of segmenting and blending, ensuring words are repeated in the context of a spoken sentence after blending the word successfully, such as 'Give yourself a **pat** on the head.' 'The water comes out of the **tap**.'

Where words have multiple meanings, these should be explored and investigated with the children. For example, the word 'tap' can be a noun but can also be a verb. Practical investigations will support an embedded understanding: sticks can be used to tap out the syllabic rhythm of the words, such as '*Stanley's Stick*' – 'tap tap, tap'. Children can tap out the syllabic rhythm of their own names, for example, 'Benjamin's stick' would be, 'tap tap tap, tap' as Benjamin has three syllables, compared to the two in Stanley. Meg's stick would simply be, 'tap, tap' as Meg only has one syllable.

To extend activity from the taught session, the teacher can work with small groups of children to choose a stick with an unusual shape and texture, pass the stick around, and collect the words the children come up with to describe the stick, writing these down as they say them. If they struggle to come up with ideas, they can be encouraged to look closely and say what they see or to use their wider senses to describe what it looks or feels like or what it reminds them of. The teacher can then use the children's ideas and words to compose a group poem with the children, supporting them to expand on, structure, and transcribe their ideas in a demonstration of the writing process in action (Figure 7.11).

In order to develop children's motivation and independence to write, the children can be encouraged to write their own poems or lists of stick activities during group/guided writing activity or as an independent writing activity. A supportive environment for writing, including a wide range of media and tools for writing that are freely available for children to access at all times, will facilitate this. Providing a focused area for children to display and celebrate independent work will ensure they understand that writing leads to 'published' outcomes that can be shared with a wider audience.

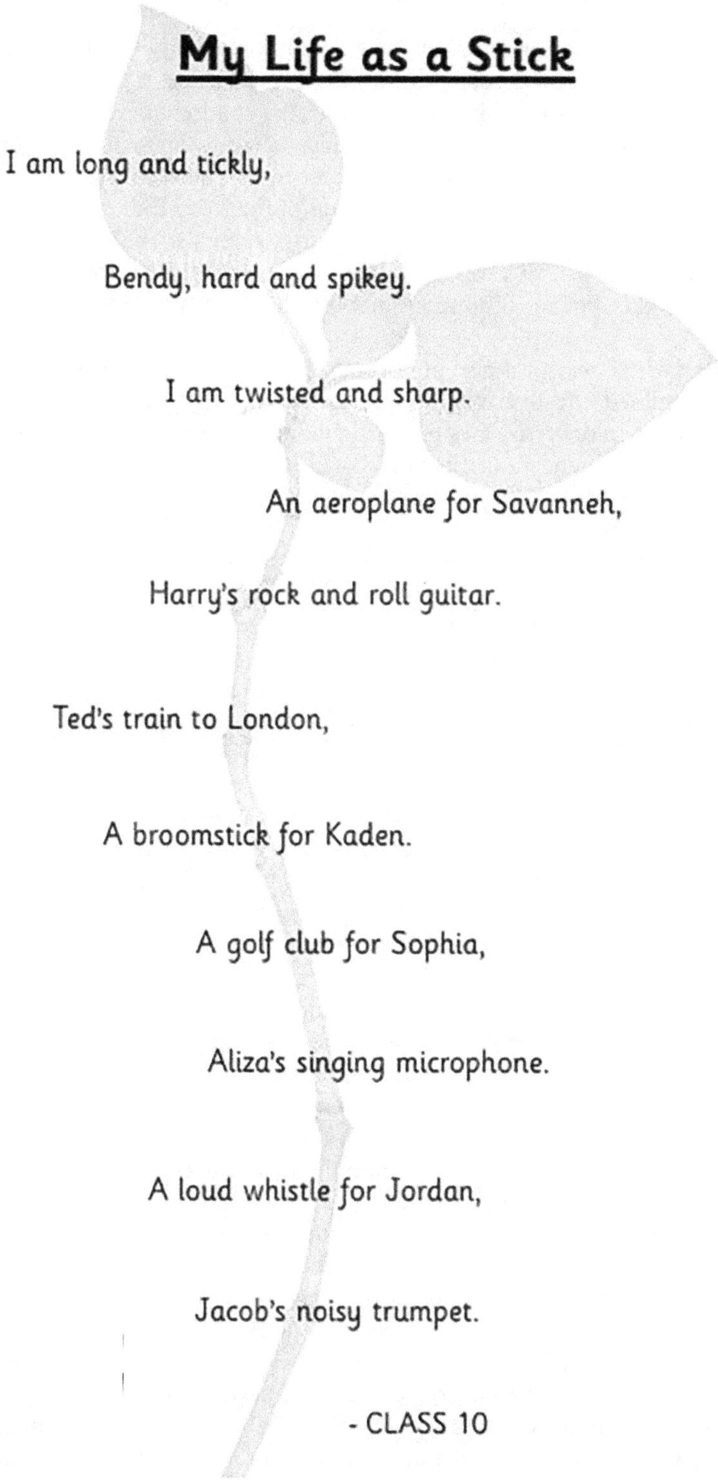

My Life as a Stick

I am long and tickly,

Bendy, hard and spikey.

I am twisted and sharp.

An aeroplane for Savanneh,

Harry's rock and roll guitar.

Ted's train to London,

A broomstick for Kaden.

A golf club for Sophia,

Aliza's singing microphone.

A loud whistle for Jordan,

Jacob's noisy trumpet.

- CLASS 10

Figure 7.11 Group poem by children aged four to five years[12]

Lesson 5: Reading the whole book and extending comprehension

In the final session the teacher can read the whole book from beginning to end. Hearing whole texts read aloud is a fundamentally important experience. If the text has been slowly revealed in the way demonstrated in these sessions, the children may be able to join in with reading parts of the text, which by now are familiar to them. The point after reading is key for assessing and developing comprehension. Teachers will need to ask a range of questions to clarify and extend the children's understanding of the story they heard, from the literal to the more inferential, such as What happened to Stanley's stick? Were you surprised by this? Why do you think the stick was so special to Stanley? Why do you think he made the decision to throw the stick into the sea? What did this make you think about? How did it make you feel?

After reading whole texts it is also important to assess readers' responses. Aidan Chambers (1993)[13] outlined effective ways to engage children in book talk, opening a forum for discussion about initial responses to texts, talking about their likes, dislikes, questions they are left with, and connections they make with the text, personally, or linked to books they've read or things they have seen. With a text like *Stanley's Stick*, teachers might ask things like: Which part of the book stays in their minds most vividly? What will they tell their friends about this book? Do they have any questions about the story? How might we answer them?

To introduce a new letter-phoneme correspondence it is important that teachers are able to find words in the text which contain the new letter-phoneme correspondence in practice. To introduce the phoneme /i/, the words 'is' and 'in' in the following sentence are ideal: "So here is Stanley standing on the station, taking his stick for a short stay at the side of the sea with his mum and dad. The train pulls in" (p. 20). When the text is shared, some children might also hear or see this in the medial vowel position in the word 'his'.

Once again, the teacher can then repeat the process of enunciating the phoneme in the words in which it appears, looking at the letter correspondence using a letter-card and learning how to form the letter in writing, to introduce the children to the name of the letter and the phoneme it represents. It is important to continually connect this back to the semantic context by reading the whole sentence again.

The skills of segmenting and blending can then be developed by looking at further words, which children will be able to decode and encode with the letter-phoneme correspondences that they have learnt thus far. By now, the children will know enough letter-phoneme correspondences to have a go at segmenting words for spelling. It is important to say each word in turn, articulating the phonemes in the words carefully so that children can hear each phoneme clearly. It may also be useful for them to count how many phonemes they can hear on their fingers. They can then indicate the letter that represents each phoneme they can hear. This might include using the letter-cards displayed in the room, on a frieze showing the letter-sound correspondences, using magnetic letters and boards, and/or by writing the letters corresponding to the phonemes with dry wipe pens on individual whiteboards. Children should be encouraged to say and write the sounds in order, going back to say them again and blend the word to check for accuracy.

As before, these skills will need to be more explicitly modelled by the teacher at this stage, but as children gain more experience they will be able to do this independently. It is vital to ensure the children are clear about the meaning of the word when the teacher reads it and that the word is contextualised in a spoken sentence after blending the phonemes in the word successfully.

As children's skills progress, consonant clusters at the start and ends of words can be incorporated. For example, this could be done with a word such as 'spit'. At first these will be introduced as separate phonemes to blend and segment, but in time the children can be encouraged to recognise common clusters of letters as larger units.

When introducing high-frequency words, ensure that any patterns that help the children see the relationship between groups of words are made explicit. For example, as the letter-sound correspondence for /i/ is introduced, the high-frequency word 'is' can be introduced, alongside the relationship with the word 'as', which children have already explored. In this word, as in the word 'as', the letter s represents a slightly different voiced phoneme, /z/. Say the word together, enunciating the sounds within it clearly for the children to hear and repeat back.

It is important to come back to this word in the context of a sentence, ideally from the book: "It is called. . . . Fantastick. Stanley's fantastick" (p. 30–34). This can then be used to investigate the wordplay used, through questions such as: What does fantastic mean? Why do you think he calls his stick fantastick? What fantastic things have you done with your sticks while we have been reading this book?

Children can also be introduced to the word 'I'. As they saw with the word 'a', as well as being a letter that represents the phoneme /i/, this is also a word. The teacher reads the word to the children, sharing how it is read differently to the phoneme they just learned. It is also important to recognise the fact that as a word, this is always written as a capital letter, wherever the word comes in a sentence. This is best exemplified in the context of some example sentences, written on strips, with the focus high-frequency word underlined, and placed around appropriate illustrations. To incorporate the word 'I', these sentences could be written from the perspective of Stanley, such as 'Bertie and I sat on the log.' 'I hurled my stick into the sea.'

To extend children's composition, the teacher can model a sentence for the children to demonstrate how to use the word in a sentence by recalling some of the stick activity that has taken place, such as '**I** wrote in the sand with my stick,' before inviting the children to orally compose their own sentences beginning with the word 'I' to share what they have done with their sticks, like 'I built a den with the big sticks.' 'I made a stick creature.' These sentences should be scribed by the adults and/or written by the children themselves, depending on their stage of development, to display alongside photographs of the children engaged in their stick activity.

To extend this activity further, beyond the taught session, the teacher could support the children to make a class book about their own stick activity using photos or drawings made by the children as a means of communicating to others about their sticks and the activities they have engaged in with them, with the children writing their own captions and thought bubbles. Photos could be also be imported into simple video creation software or apps and children could narrate their 'stick activity'.

More experienced writers will be able to draw and write their own accounts of their stick play or to write their own stick stories using words and illustrations, which could be presented in simple handmade books; developing writers could narrate their accounts for an adult to scribe.

Celebrating the learning throughout the time working with the book through creating an ongoing display of work (Figure 7.12) will enable the children to see the value of their learning and contributions made, as well as encouraging further talk and activity around the text.

Figure 7.12 Photo of display of a variety of children's work inspired by *Stanley's Stick*[14]

Cracking the alphabetic code 141

The example series of lessons outlined in this chapter can be used and drawn upon as a demonstration of how to plan in this way when introducing other single letter-phoneme correspondences and sharing how to contextualise the teaching of letter-phoneme correspondences, as well as words which could be used to develop children's skills of segmenting and blending to facilitate their independence in reading and writing words. There are also suggestions for incorporating the teaching of high-frequency words in an order that facilitates an investigative approach to the way such words are read and spelt.

As teachers read real books, they will need to be able to recognise opportunities to contextualise the teaching of phonics in similar ways to develop children's understanding of why and how phonics supports them in their ability to read and write independently.

Notes

1 When we use the word 'lesson' in this book, we recognise that the words 'session' or 'activity' may be more appropriate for some contexts of education, such as early years.
2 Nation, K., Dawson, N. J., & Hsiao, Y. (2022). Book Language and Its Implications for Children's Language, Literacy, and Development. *Current Directions in Psychological Science*, 31(4), 375–380.
3 Capital letters are used to refer to a letter name. Phonemes are represented with lowercase letters surrounded by forward slashes, such as: the letter S often represents the phoneme /s/.
4 Layton, N. (2011). *Stanley's Stick*. Written by John Hegley and illustrated by Neal Layton. Hachette Children's UK.
5 Text Copyright © 2011 John Hegley Illustrations Copyright © 2011 Neal Layton from *Stanley's Stick*. Written by John Hegley and illustrated by Neal Layton. Hachette Children's Group London, EC4Y 0DZ. Retrieved December 1, 2023, from https://www.hachettechildrens.co.uk/. Reproduced with permission of the Licensor through PLSclear.
6 Hegley, *Stanley's Stick*.
7 Reproduced with permission from Staplehurst Primary School, Kent, UK.
8 Hegley, *Stanley's Stick*.
9 Reproduced with permission from St Stephen's School, Richmond, UK.
10 Reproduced with permission from Ysgol Maes Y Mynydd, Wrexham, UK.
11 Reproduced with permission from St Stephen's School, Richmond, UK.
12 Reproduced with permission from Easterside Academy, Middlesbrough, UK.
13 Chambers, A. (1993). *Tell Me: Children, Reading and Talk. Stroud*. The Thimble Press.
14 Reproduced with permission from Virginia Primary, Tower Hamlets, UK.

8 Gaining control

As children learn an increasing amount of letter-to-phoneme (G) correspondences and continue to practise the essential skills of segmenting and blending words for reading and writing, their progress, confidence, motivation, and independence as readers and writers will grow. Situating this learning in the context of real texts and extended learning experiences which develop children's understanding, as shown in the previous chapter, is the most effective approach which also brings learning to life. This learning engages children and sustains their motivation to read and write for real purposes and for pleasure.

Thus far, children will have been taught the single-letter representation for a range of common phonemes. This supports them in understanding the concept that written letters relate to phonemes in spoken words and that learning these correspondences, along with the ability to segment and blend using these letter-phoneme correspondences, will help them to read and write words.

Contextualised phonics teaching (G) at the next stage for children's learning focuses on the following key ideas:

- in some cases phonemes are represented by more than one letter (e.g. /sh/ in ship);
- the need to increase proficiency in the skills of blending and segmenting to read and spell words;
- the need to increase proficiency in reading and writing words containing consonant clusters (e.g. trip);
- how to read disyllabic (two-syllable) words, including those with double letters at the syllable juncture (e.g. rabbit);
- how to read and write sentences using words containing letter-to-phoneme correspondences that have been taught;
- increasing knowledge of how to read and write a wider range of words that do not conform to letter-to-phoneme correspondences taught so far, particularly high-frequency words;
- children using their growing knowledge to independently make phonetically plausible attempts at words which contain different letter-phoneme correspondences than those already taught;
- being aware of children's development through their self-teaching.

Taught sessions will continue to use real texts which support children to grow in their knowledge of language and continue to motivate them to read for pleasure and for a range of different purposes. The teacher will read aloud such texts, taking the weight of the

DOI: 10.4324/9781003442134-11

reading work, and allowing the children to enjoy and learn from texts that may be beyond their current independent reading level but well within their listening comprehension and interest level. Using these texts, as we showed in the previous chapter, teachers will also continue to model and demonstrate where phonic knowledge can be used and applied in context, using words from the text to demonstrate knowledge and skills, and will continue to focus on developing children's comprehension of the texts through engaging them in dialogue about the texts and their responses to the texts.

There will be differences in the texts that children will hear read to them and those which they use to practise reading for themselves. To support children to grow as independent readers at this early stage of reading, teachers may choose to use highly decodable texts so that children can directly practise phonic skills, experience success in word reading, and work on reading comprehension using a text which is directly matched to what they have been explicitly taught.

The choice of texts for teaching reading is one of the defining features of the reading debates. For decades reading schemes and phonics schemes have been designed to fit the prevailing policies on reading. In the last decade the focus on narrower phonics schemes has come to dominate. As a result a considerable number of companies have made significant profits out of the teaching of reading in primary schools. There is, of course, an alternative. As we showed in Chapter 3, "How Texts Teach What Children Learn", real books not only provide an opportunity for children to practise their decoding but offer so much more in relation to the meanings created by authors through their text and illustrations. The profits from these books when used in schools also go to publishers, but the authors will receive their royalty payments and in so doing will be able to keep writing. A key question, then, is whether you would prefer the education system to encourage authors of real books or encourage producers of commercial phonics schemes.

With the increasing emphasis on phonics as a core strategy for reading, which in England included the requirement for validated phonics programmes to provide "sufficient decodable reading material to ensure children can practise by reading texts closely matched to their level of phonic attainment and that do not require them to use alternative strategies to read unknown words",[1] decodable texts have flooded the educational market in recent years. It is important for teachers to understand that no decodable reader will provide the richness of narrative, language, and engagement as the kind of books that we recommend to support the teaching of reading. It is logically argued that scheme books with controlled selections of words can provide opportunities for children to repeatedly encounter words for which they have learned the phoneme-letter correspondences. This may lead to fluency (G) with these words. However, the effectiveness of using scheme books versus real books to teach reading remains unproven by research.[2]

If teachers do decide to use scheme books, it is necessary to review the quality of the books, because some are far better quality than others. For example, some of the higher-quality scheme books have been written by authors and/or illustrated by illustrators of real books for children, and as a result the illustrators take children beyond the limited text on the page so that the storylines are more satisfying. Non-fiction scheme books tend to be better than fiction books. As ever, teachers also need to review the representation of characters in whatever books they choose to ensure that the resources in the classroom show diverse and representative images of the societies that we live in.

It is also important for teachers to know when such texts have fulfilled their purpose. Evidence indicates that once children have learned a core set of grapheme-phoneme correspondences, they get no more opportunity to practise these in decodable books (G) than they do in other books they might be reading and that once children move beyond the very early stages of reading, the benefits of decodable readers are likely to be outweighed by their limitations.[3] So it is important that teachers monitor reading regularly and recognise when to move children on to texts that continue to support their growing knowledge of reading whilst developing the motivation to read.

The Learning to Read collection, part of the CLPE Corebooks[4] database of books, provides a supportive guide for teachers to draw from at this stage. These are books which are particularly beneficial to children in the early stages of learning to read, with a particular focus on helping children to gain control as readers. The books often have these features:

- memorable texts that feature repetition and encourage predictions;
- texts in which rhythm and rhyme are important;
- texts that allow children to practise and apply their phonic knowledge;
- books with strong story shapes and structures;
- texts which positively reflect children's interests and backgrounds;
- books with supportive illustrations;
- books that draw attention to written language and to the ways books work.

The Learning to Read collection for readers aged 7 to 11 (Key Stage Two in England) has been specially chosen to support the reading of older children who are still inexperienced readers or who are having some difficulty in reading by including texts with meanings pitched at an appropriate level for their age.

In these early stages of learning to read and write, the role of the teacher is to ensure that children build a rich and varied vocabulary, consolidated by concrete experiences, and build sophistication in their spoken and written language. Children are taught to recognise when utterances are complete, such as 'The baby is asleep in the cot', as well as when they are incomplete, such as 'Mummy gave it'. Adults should work first on children's oral language, recasting in complete utterances where these are incomplete and modelling how to write in complete utterances when demonstrating writing. Providing children with a wide range of experience with texts will also help to build understanding of how written language works in different forms and for different purposes.

Children's fluency in reading requires not only that they can decode words but also that they can read whole sentences with full understanding of their meaning. Early teaching about phonemes, letters, and words is always contextualised in whole sentences and whole texts. However at this stage of gaining control, it is even more important to include an explicit focus on phrases and sentences.

For many children the concept of a sentence is not sufficiently explored, so as they pass through their education they lack the understanding to punctuate sentences effectively and face the continued feedback of 'Don't forget your full stops and capital letters'. However, defining a sentence is something that even linguists don't have full agreement about, yet all proficient readers and writers can recognise a written sentence when they see one. One important feature of sentences is that they make sense on their own: sentences are units to which syntactic 'rules' or classifications, such as distinguishing 'words', 'phrases', and 'clauses', can satisfactorily be applied. A sentence also is not reliant on larger grammatical constructions to express its meaning.[5] Syntax (G) refers to the ways in which words are arranged to make larger meaningful units like phrases and sentences. So, the use of a capital letter at the beginning and a full stop at the end of a written sentence are not trivial features because these demarcate what written sentences are. Sentences as part of oral language are even less easy to identify because the grammar of oral language differs in important ways from the grammar in written language.

To build children's independence as readers and writers, teachers will need to be able to provide and use models of decodable sentences for children to read and write in taught sessions, linked with the context of the real books being used. Incorporating the writing of dictated sentences containing words which are decodable with the letter-phoneme correspondences taught will support children to achieve success as independent writers, building confidence and motivation. Children should also be encouraged to use and apply their phonic knowledge to write phonetically plausible attempts at unknown words.

Phonemes represented by more than one letter

This crucial next stage in learning helps children to understand that more than one letter can be used to represent a phoneme. This will include digraphs (G) and trigraphs (G), as outlined in Table 8.1.

For teachers, understanding the difficulty that can occur in recognising when two or three letters work together to represent one phoneme and being equipped to support this knowledge in practice is essential. As children progress in this next phase of their learning, it is important

Table 8.1 Letter-to-phoneme representations

Name of element	Letters-to-phoneme representation	Examples in words
Consonant digraphs	CK /ck/	pick, sack, luck
	FF /ff/	huff, off, sniff
	LL /ll/	bell, fill, smell
	SS /ss/	hiss, mass, stress
	ZZ /zz/	fizz, buzz, frizz
	CH /ch/	chip, chat, champ
	SH /sh/	ship, shed, shrimp
	TH /th/	**voiced**: this, that, then
		unvoiced: thin, thick, think
	NG /ng/	bang, spring, clung
Vowel (G) digraphs	AI /ai/	maid, paint, sprain
	EE /ee/	seed, green, sweep
	OA /oa/	road, croak, coast
	OO /oo/	**long**: too, mood, spoon
		short: good, foot, crook
	OI /oi/	join, oink, spoil
Digraphs made of vowels and consonants	OW /ow/	now, down, crowd
R-controlled vowel digraphs	AR /ar/	park, sharp, spark
	OR /or/	torn, snort, storm
	UR /ur/	fur, turn, burst
	ER /er/ (also known as the schwa [G])	river, bitter, tender
Trigraphs	IGH /igh/	sigh, night, bright
	AIR /air/	pair, chair, unfair
	EAR /ear/	tear, clear, appear
	URE /ure/	pure, cure, unsure

146 The art of teaching

that teachers spend enough time on the essential skills of blending and segmenting whilst introducing the children to these digraphs and trigraphs. The teaching also helps children to consolidate their understanding of the differences between these and the common consonant clusters at the beginnings and ends of words which they have already begun to encounter.

When encountering digraphs and trigraphs, learners need to recognise and recall these as multiple letters which are representative of one phoneme and that the individual letters that they are composed of do not represent phonemes in the same way that they would if they were blended and segmented separately. This requires seeing and using these diagraphs and trigraphs in practice on a regular basis and practise in recalling the letter-phoneme correspondences to segment and blend the phonemes in order to read and write words. Strong proficiency in using this knowledge, and rapid recall and recognition of these new letter-phoneme representations, will ensure children's continued progress towards independence. Although approaches based on memorisation of words have come under repeated criticism, there is no getting away from the fact that these digraphs and trigraphs have to be memorised. Fortunately children's capacity for learning words orally is innate, so the teacher's role is to provide experiences that enable children to connect their natural learned oral language with reading and writing.

Consonant clusters, as outlined in Table 8.2, in contrast, are units made up of separate phonemes to be blended and segmented. There is no new knowledge when

Table 8.2 Consonant clusters

Element	Representation	Example words:
Common consonant clusters at the start of words	**Two letter:**	
	bl-	blob, blink, bluff
	cl-	clap, clunk, cloth
	fl-	flag, flick, flush
	gl-	glad, gloss, gloom
	pl-	plug, plain, plump
	sl-	slip, sling, slurp
	br-	bran, braid, brown
	cr-	crab, crisp, cross
	dr-	drip, drown, drank
	fr-	frog, fresh, frost
	gr-	grip, greed, grain
	pr-	prop, print, press
	tr-	trip, train, trust
	sc-	scan, scarf, scrub
	sk-	skip, skill, skunk
	sm-	smack, smart, smooth
	sn-	snip, snoop, snail
	sp-	spin, spoon, split
	st-	step, stand, stain
	sw-	sweep, swing, swift
	tw-	twig, twang, twist
	Three letter:	
	scr-	scrap, scram, screen
	str-	string, strain, struck
	spl-	splat, splash, split
Common consonant clusters at the end of words	–nt	hunt, point, burnt
	–nk	bank, think, shrink
	–sp	lisp, wisp, crisp
	–st	just, roast, chest

learning to read and spell consonant clusters, just an extension of the skills of blending and segmentation. However, as children become more accustomed to encountering these in practice, they will begin to recognise and recall these as common strings and no longer need to blend and segment each individual phoneme to support the journey to automaticity.

Earlier work on syllabification, as outlined in Chapter 7, "Cracking the Alphabetic Code", will support children in reading and writing disyllabic (G) words to extend their word reading skills. Here, as children gain the knowledge that more than one letter can represent a phoneme, teachers can introduce double letters at syllable junctures, as outlined in Table 8.3. These are letters that are doubled at the point where two syllables meet and will be introduced in words that will be decodable with the letter-phoneme correspondences taught within this stage of learning, such as rabbit, carrot, letter.

When reading disyllabic words, teachers can begin by reading the word as a whole before supporting the children to break the word into syllables by covering parts of the word to separate the syllables and modelling how to read each part in turn, then putting the word back together as a whole. When writing such words, teachers should model how to break the word into the two syllables and then how to break each syllable down into its constituent phonemes, representing these with the correct graphemes (G), including doubling consonants at the syllable juncture where relevant. When the word is complete, teachers model how to read the word as a whole (in the context of a sentence), making sure to read any doubled consonants as single phonemes.

In addition to this, children's reading and awareness of texts will raise their awareness of the complexities of the alphabetic code. For example, they will become increasingly aware that a phoneme can be represented by different letters (e.g. their and fair), and a letter or group of letters can represent different phonemes in different words (e.g. the E in elephant). It would not be accurate to teach the idea that a letter only represents one phoneme. Fortunately in time children use the general principle that letters represent phonemes to self-learn, including their increasing ability to recognise whole words fluently. It continues to remain important to reiterate the depth of English orthography (G) by talking to children about words where letter representations do not match the phoneme correspondences they have currently been taught and linking alternative representations to other known words so that children are aware of patterns between groups of words.

Differences in dialect and accent may mean that phonemes are pronounced in different ways by different speakers. For example, the words 'bath' and 'path' are pronounced differently in regions of England. In the north of England, the letter A in 'bath' and 'path' represents the /a/ phoneme, whereas in the south of England, the A represents the /ar/ phoneme. This will need to be taken into account, depending on the dialect of the speaker.

Table 8.3 Disyllabic words

Element	Representation	Example words:
Common double letters at syllable junctures	BB /bb/ DD /dd/ NN /nn/ MM /mm/ RR /rr/ TT /tt/	rabbit, rubber ladder, sadder tennis, manner hammer, summer carrot, horrid better, glitter

Introducing consonant digraphs and developing blending and segmenting skills

The phase of systematic phonics teaching explained in this chapter as ever is contextualised within real books. Based on experiences of working with a range of four- to five-year-old children using this approach, we recommend that this stage of learning should be delivered over approximately 12–18 weeks, with children being introduced to letter-phoneme correspondences at the rate of approximately four to five per week.

As in the previous phase, in each lesson the teacher should support the children to revisit and revise the letter-phoneme correspondences that have been taught and high-frequency words which do not conform to letter-phoneme correspondences taught, as well as introducing new letter-phoneme correspondences and high-frequency words. This helps to consolidate and extend knowledge during every lesson allowing the children to continue to practise and extend their ability to blend and segment in order to read words, phrases, and sentences, supporting their independence as readers and writers.

Throughout this phase the key learning aims will be for children to recognise and use letter-phoneme correspondences where more than one letter represents a single phoneme. The children will also gain greater independence in the skills of blending and segmenting with an ever increasing variety of words, including those with consonant clusters at the beginning and/or end, as well as independently reading phrases and sentences containing words which are decodable using the letter-phoneme correspondences taught and the high-frequency words which do not conform to the letter-phoneme correspondences taught.

The following examples describe how a sequence of lessons contextualising phonics at this stage in a programme of literacy would be taught.

A recommended text for this series of lessons is *Peck Peck Peck* by Lucy Cousins (Walker Books, 2014). This book tells the story of a young woodpecker, who after being taught to peck a tree by its father, finds many more objects to practise its pecking skills on! Its vibrant and engaging illustrations consolidate and develop children's understanding of the text on the page and beyond, including the die-cut holes emphasising the activity of the little woodpecker. The pace of the pecking increases throughout the story until each page is covered with holes. The story finishes with the baby bird proudly sharing its achievements with its father before being rewarded with kisses. This is a highly engaging and motivating text, excellent for reading aloud and supporting children's understanding of what fluent reading sounds like. The story also supports children to empathise with a character who, like them, is growing in independence. This book supports teachers to introduce the concept of a consonant digraph, starting with CK to represent /ck/ and SS to represent /ss/. The book will be shared over three sessions, enabling children to have the time to focus on reading and writing sentences using their knowledge of the new letter-phoneme correspondences and to focus on the skill of reading and writing disyllabic words.

Lesson 1: Introducing the book and a new consonant digraph

The title words and front cover illustration, with its punched holes, provide the perfect context for introducing the letter-phoneme correspondence CK to /k/, in the context of the meaning of the word 'peck' used in the text.

Before the session, the teacher should pre-prepare two sentence strips for pairs of children to share, one which says 'I peck the hat' and one which says 'I peck the mat'.

The teacher begins the lesson by sharing the front cover (Figure 8.1), including the novel feature of the punched holes. Focusing on the illustration first will enable children

Gaining control   149

Figure 8.1 Front cover of *Peck Peck Peck* by Lucy Cousins[6]

to work from a common level, orienting themselves with the possible subject matter of the text and being able to draw on prior knowledge and understanding they may have that relates to what they see, whether they can independently read the words or not. The teacher encourages this by asking a range of questions designed to encourage the children to share their prior experience and understanding: What can you see? What do you know, or think you know, about the creature that you see? Do you know what kind of bird this is, or anything about them? Why do you think there are holes in the cover? What do you think they show or tell us? What do you think might happen in this story?

As the children contribute their ideas, it remains important for the teacher to scribe their responses to demonstrate the links between oral language and written language. This also validates the children's ideas by recording them in writing and enables the teacher

150 *The art of teaching*

to return to the written responses in order to assess and build on children's language and understanding of concepts being explored.

The teacher can go on to direct attention to the words on the front cover, inviting the children to share whether they already recognise them or can read part or all of them using the letter-phoneme correspondences that they already know. The children may notice that in this title, the words are represented in uppercase letters or recognise that the same word is repeated multiple times. Using their knowledge of letter-phoneme correspondences, they may also be able to attempt to segment and blend a word to read it. It will be important to clarify the meaning of this word by asking the children what they think the word 'peck' means and elaborating on this by discussing the actions of the character: What has the bird done? What has happened because of the bird's pecking? Do you know what this bird is? If the children are not aware of this, the teacher should share the name, woodpecker, discussing this together: How do you think this bird got its name? How does its name connect to its behaviours? Have you seen a woodpecker before? What was it like, and what was it doing? Watching a video of a real-life woodpecker alongside this discussion will increase the children's understanding of the creature and its behaviours in its natural habitat.

Looking at the word allows an opportunity to introduce the consonant digraph CK, which represents the phoneme /k/. Drawing attention to the word on the cover, the teacher should identify the letters C and K that are used to represent this phoneme and explain that when these letters appear together in a word, they work together to represent one phoneme, /k/. This is the same phoneme in words like 'cat', 'can', 'kid', and 'kin'. The teacher should support the children in understanding that when this sound comes at the end of a word, it is usually represented by the letters C and K together. Clear explanations that support children to see orthographic patterns from the start will facilitate children's understanding of the choices they make when they attempt to spell words.

Introducing handwriting letter joins at this stage may help children to remember the relationship between the two letters. Continuing to introduce these new letter-phoneme correspondences on a letter-card will support children in seeing the two letters working together. Because of the fact that the letters in this title are written in uppercase, it would also be useful to include the uppercase representation on the back of the word card (Figure 8.2). Teachers can illustrate the connection further by drawing a connecting line between the two letters to support children in visualising that the two letters are representing one phoneme.

The teacher can then return to the words in the title, demonstrating how children can use and apply their phonic knowledge to segment and blend each word that they see. They should point to each letter in a word in turn, encouraging the children to say the phoneme each letter represents, including the digraph /ck/ at the end of the word and blending this together to read the word 'peck'. Having the word cards for P and E with the lowercase letter on the front and uppercase letter on the back available, so that the children

Figure 8.2 A letter-card showing the consonant digraph /ck/

can connect the uppercase letters with the phonemes, might be useful if children do not recognise these automatically.

The teacher can then encourage the children to read the three words fluently together, '*Peck Peck Peck*', by returning to the title, pointing to each word in turn, modelling one-to-one correspondence between words in oral and written language, which will support their knowledge as independent readers.

The teacher then reads the book aloud, up until the page that says, "And now I'll peck this big blue door then go inside and peck some more" (p. 14–15). The word 'peck' is repeated numerous times during this section. Pointing to the word and encouraging the children to join in each time it occurs will encourage the children to join in as active participants in the reading experience and see that they are able to use their phonic knowledge to read this word for themselves, developing automaticity as they see the word repeated on multiple occasions. At each stopping point, teachers take time to assess the children's listening comprehension and to connect the book with their own lives and experiences through questions such as: What do we know about the woodpecker? Who was it with? What was its daddy trying to teach it? How did its daddy feel when it pecked the tree? Can you think of a time when a family member taught you how to do something new? What was it? How did they feel when you did it? How did it make you feel?

The teacher then re-reads the final sentence of that section, using this as an opportunity to re-engage the children with the text and in hypothesising and predicting what might happen next: What do you think the woodpecker will peck when it goes through the big blue door? This expanded noun phrase (G) is a good example of book language that has the potential to be a model to encourage children to expand their own descriptive vocabulary. Teachers can build on this by using and encouraging children to use such phrases in context, such as talking about 'the long red ladder' when climbing on the physical equipment or the 'small wooden block' in the construction area.

Next, the teacher can turn the page to the page spread shown in Figure 8.3. This spread provides an opportunity for children to directly use and apply their growing phonic knowledge in the context of the text, including the extension of knowledge in how to read two-syllable words.

The teacher can share this spread large enough for all the children to see, either projected on a large screen or with the help of a visualiser, giving pairs of children the pre-prepared sentence strips, one which says 'I peck the hat' and one which says 'I peck the mat', to look at for themselves. The teacher can draw children's attention to the match between the sentence strips and the first two lines of the text on the page, allowing time and space for the children to have a go at re-reading these in pairs, using their knowledge of high-frequency words and letter-phoneme correspondences to support them. If children are failing to recognise the digraph, the teacher can draw a line under the two letters to remind children that these represent one phoneme. At this stage, some children may need additional support to do this independently: encourage these children to sit near an adult, who can point to the words and sounds and model the skills of letter-phoneme correspondence and how to say each sound in turn and blend to read each decodable word.

This page spread also offers an opportunity for the teacher to introduce how to read the disyllabic words 'tennis', 'racket', and 'jacket'. The teacher can model how to sound these out, noting that the letters NN represents the single phoneme /n/ in tennis. When the individual words have been read, the teacher should encourage the children to re-read the whole page alongside them. The children will see how the letter E in the words jacket and racket represents the /i/ phoneme when read fluently in context.

152   *The art of teaching*

Figure 8.3 Internal page spread from *Peck Peck Peck* by Lucy Cousins (pp. 16–17)[7]

In extended work linked to the text, the children could be encouraged to engage with imaginative play inspired by the story. They could make finger puppets of the woodpecker by cutting out copies of the bird printed onto cards and attaching a ring of cardboard to the back so that it fits onto their finger, or attach a stick to the back to create a stick puppet. Using scissors to cut is another excellent way of developing fine motor control and grip strength to support the muscles in the hand and wrist needed for pencil grip. The children could then take their bird around the setting as they work and play, finding different things for it to peck. Adults can take photos of the children engaged in this imaginative play and print these out for the children to describe their bird's actions, using the supportive structure from the book: 'I peck the . . .' These ideas could be scribed onto speech bubbles, either by the adults or the children themselves, and displayed for the children to see.

Lesson 2: Responding to the book and developing segmenting skills to write sentences

As illustrated in the previous chapter, when using a text over more than one session, it is important to begin each session by re-reading the text so far. In this next lesson, the teacher can then read further on, up to "PECK PECK PECK a tangerine, a nectarine, a green bean, an aubergine, some margarine and seventeen jelly beans" (pp. 24–25). Once again it is important for the teacher to point to and encourage the children to read along with the word 'peck' each time it appears. The children could think about how they might read this word, to imitate the sound and action of the word's meaning, using appropriate intonation to bring this to life as they read.

At this particular stopping point, astute readers may pick up on the many rhyming words contained in the text, as well as the fact that these words use different spelling variations to represent the rime (G) /een/: for example, in words like 'magazine', 'Geraldine', 'tangerine', 'nectarine', 'aubergine', 'sardine and 'margarine', 'green' and 'seventeen', and 'bean(s)'. It is important to continue to discuss these variations, if the children notice this, encouraging them to note the patterns in different groups of words. This lays the foundation for the next step in learning, that phonemes can be represented in different ways in different words.

The teacher can use this next stopping point to assess the children's comprehension, asking questions to check their understanding of the story events referring to both the text and illustrations and to clarify vocabulary has been understood: Which rooms in the house did the woodpecker go into? What objects did the woodpecker peck? Did you hear any new words while I was reading? What were they? What did they mean? If you're not sure, what do you think they might mean?

The teacher can then revisit the new digraph /ck/ and its letter sound correspondence with the children, using the letter card to support recall. Explore other decodable words containing this letter-phoneme correspondence, focusing the children's attention on the fact that this representation usually occurs when this phoneme is heard at the end of a word. The children can read these words in the context of new sentences, linked to the storyline in the book and printed out on sentence strips for them to read in pairs, such as 'I peck the truck.' 'I peck the sack.' 'I peck the brick.' Acting out the sentences using the real objects and one of the bird puppets made by the children will help consolidate understanding of the meaning of each sentence after it has been read. To develop expressive reading, teachers could focus on how the bird feels as they peck each different thing and how this would affect the way the sentence is read, supporting children's understanding of the prosodic (G) and phrased reading which supports the development of reading fluency.

To support the development of children's writing, the teacher can prepare some picture cards with different household items that the bird could have pecked, the names of which are decodable using the letter-phoneme correspondences the children have learnt so far. These allow children to practise a range of the letter-phoneme correspondences taught to this point, as well as the new digraph /ck/, and could include items such as a bed, a cot, a pan, a pot, a carrot, a tap, a mug, a pen, a clock, a rubber duck. It would be engaging for the children if a peck hole were punched into each picture card, as in the original text. The teacher can support the children in using the repetitive structure of the text: 'I peck the . . .' to compose a written sentence to accompany one of the chosen photo cards, modelling and demonstrating how to recall and write the high-frequency word 'I' and how to segment the word peck, counting the phonemes on their fingers to support this and writing down each letter correspondence in turn, including the digraph CK at the end of the word. They can also demonstrate how to recall and write the high-frequency word 'the' as part of this sentence, as well as how to segment and write the word on the picture card, isolating each phoneme and writing the corresponding letter representation.

Another picture card can then be shown as an opportunity for the children to independently write the accompanying sentence onto sentence strips or individual whiteboards. The teacher can dictate the sentence to the children, clearly enunciating each word, and repeating multiple times to aid recall as the children write. Some children may require more adult support at this stage. Teachers could provide magnetic letters to support children whose pen grip hampers them from the physical act of writing or have a group of children near them who need extended support to segment words and recall the correct letter-phoneme correspondences. The letter-phoneme correspondences taught should be displayed prominently in the environment on a frieze or chart and should be highlighted regularly as a scaffold to draw upon when needed.

To extend work around the text, the teacher can encourage the children to think about what else the woodpecker might peck. Photo cards of appropriate decodable household objects could be provided as a stimulus. The children can then paint their own scene of the woodpecker pecking the object, in the style of author/illustrator Lucy Cousins, looking at her distinctive bold colours and black outlines, and explore how to achieve this effect in their own work. When their paintings are dry, children can develop their grip strength and fine motor skills by using a single hole punch to punch out the spot where the woodpecker has pecked, as in the original book. Confident writers could write a sentence to accompany their illustration. Developing writers could have a go at this, with support from an adult to help them sound out the words, recognise the graphemes they need to represent the phonemes, or scribe their spoken sentences, depending on their level of development.

Lesson 3: Introducing a new digraph for reading and writing

In this final lesson the teacher reads the complete narrative from beginning to end. It is important that the children have the chance to hear the whole story uninterrupted and read fluently. The teacher can then continue to assess children's comprehension by asking questions that move the children from literal to more inferential reflections: What was the door of the house like? What objects did the woodpecker peck in the bathroom? How many jelly beans were pecked? Do you think that the woodpecker did practise hard? How do you know? Why do you think the woodpecker was tired at the end of the story? How do you think the people who own the house might feel when they get home? What makes you think this?

It would be beneficial to provide time for a more open discussion where the children can discuss what they liked and disliked about the book, any questions they had after reading, and any connections they make with their own lives or other things they have read or seen. They might, for example, continue to talk about things they have learned to do, moments where adults have been proud of them, their own favourite activities, or their own bedtime routines.

The teacher can end the session by revisiting the final page of the book (Figure 8.4), re-reading the text aloud and looking at how the story ends. The final illustration and accompanying text provides the opportunity to introduce the phoneme /ss/, as seen in the word 'KISS.' As with /ck/, the teacher can discriminate between how this phoneme is represented differently at the beginnings and endings of words and introduce this new letter-phoneme correspondence, using a letter-card. Children can also practise forming the letters that represent this phoneme with whiteboards and pens as their fine motor skills develop. The teacher can then return to the final spread in the book to look at the word 'kiss' in context. On a pre-prepared sentence strip, model how to read the sentence: "He got a big kiss from Dad."

The teacher can talk with the children about the nest the woodpecker sleeps in, asking the children if they know what birds use to build their nests and how they do this. A video of this could be used to support the children's understanding. It would be good to have twigs, moss, feathers, and mud available so that the children can see the real materials birds use to build their nests. These connections made between the text and real contexts and objects improve children's learning by using experiential learning techniques. The teacher can use this knowledge to introduce a second sentence strip to the children, which they can read themselves using the letter-phoneme correspondences and high-frequency words they know: 'I see mud, twigs and moss in the nest.'

The teacher can then revisit the two-page spread showing the laundry room with multiple peck holes (pp. 26–27) and use this as a context to model how to write the sentence: It was a big mess! As before, they can show the children how to say each word in turn, recognise each phoneme, and write its corresponding letter representation, including the double letter to represent the phoneme /ss/ at the end of the word mess. As the teacher writes, they can model how to leave spaces between each word, how to correctly form each letter, and how to re-read as you go for sense and meaning and to identify the next word to be written. At the end of the sentence, they could discuss appropriate punctuation, looking at the difference between using a full stop and an exclamation mark, and what effect this has on the sentence when it is read aloud. The children can discuss which punctuation they think is most appropriate and why.

On their own whiteboards or on sentence strips, the children can be given an opportunity to practise writing a dictated sentence in the same way. They can consolidate their understanding of consonant clusters in a sentence linked to the final illustration in the story, 'It went to bed in the nest'. Selected examples of the children's written sentences can be photocopied if completed on whiteboards or pinned up if on sentence strips around a copy of this final illustration.

Figure 8.4 Final page spread from *Peck Peck Peck* by Lucy Cousins (p. 32–33)

Gaining control   157

In activities extended from the text, teachers can focus the children's attention on looking and caring for birds in the local environment. This could involve:

- weaving nests from natural materials;
- making bird cakes or bird feeders to hang in the garden area of the education setting;
- setting up birdwatching hides with binoculars, spotter guides, sketchbooks, and drawing/writing equipment;
- providing photographs of different birds for the children to draw and paint – developing children's artistic skills by using watercolours and thin brushes for details;
- labelling diagrams of birds;
- sharing knowledge about birds through making own guides and posters;
- building a wide vocabulary to describe and compare birds seen in local environment.

By the time children have learned one representation for each of the phonemes at the end of this stage, they should be able to independently read and write decodable words, phrases, and sentences, as well as having the motivation to read and write in a range of contexts and for a range of purposes. They should be able to form most letters correctly and, inspired by a range of texts read, write in different styles for different audiences. The example of writing in Figure 8.5 shows a child who is able to use and apply phonic knowledge at this stage independently. In a self-initiated activity, they decided to make some rules for the rest of the class to follow, outlining how to use the classroom toilets responsibly. In the sample of writing, there is clear evidence of their ability to match letters to sounds but also in mastering the voice (G), style, and form for a set of instructions.

In the sentences written by the child, there is clear evidence of them using and applying their knowledge of both consonant and vowel digraphs as well as consonant clusters, common words that do not conform to letter-phoneme correspondences currently taught, and wider knowledge of spelling patterns from reading, for example:

- the /ll/ digraph in 'well';
- the /sh/ digraph in 'shut', 'flush' 'wosh' (wash), and 'finishd' (finished);
- the /ee/ digraph in 'eet' (eat), 'seet' (seat);
- the /ow/ digraph in 'down', 'now' 'owt' (out), 'alowd' (allowed);
- the /ai/ digraph in 'chain' and the known alternative in 'play';
- the common words that do not conform to letter-phoneme correspondences taught: you, your, to, the, there, all, go.

This child has a good awareness of the form and language appropriate to instructional texts but also of their audience, addressing them directly and using techniques to maintain their interest across the writing: "good, you now (know) them all. There's mor (more) to go", and motivating readers with "well dun (done)!" to conclude the writing. They are clearly ready to move on to the next stage of learning, consolidating their knowledge of known sounds and how to punctuate sentences and extending their existing knowledge to learn a wider range of common words that do not conform to current letter-phoneme correspondences, a wider range of representations for sounds to increase spelling accuracy and morphological (G) patterns for verb endings.

At this stage of learning, teachers will need to be monitoring and evaluating the progress of children, looking at where children need to be moved on and stretched, and where

Figure 8.5 Writing sample from a child age five: "Toilet rools"

they might need additional support, providing this to individuals and groups with similar needs as necessary. Identified areas for support for children might include:

- retaining and recalling taught GPCs;
- orally forming and enunciating phonemes accurately;
- forming letters in writing;
- oral blending and segmenting of words;
- matching some phonemes to letters for blending;
- matching some letters to phonemes for segmenting;
- one-to-one correspondence when reading words in phrases and sentences;
- ascribing meaning to what has been read or written.

Additional support at this stage will involve individual, paired, or group work targeted at reinforcing specific knowledge or skills at a slower pace and going beyond the regular class teaching. Teachers should provide a wide range of reading experiences, including reading aloud, small group and individual reading, and using texts matched to children's needs and interests, including texts designed for children to use and apply phonic knowledge.

For children needing support with fine motor skills for writing, including letter formation, teachers ensure that there are a range of gross and fine motor development opportunities in the extended and continuous provision (G). This will include:

- moving and travelling in different ways, including with equipment to develop arm and shoulder strength and endurance;
- opportunities for dance and movement, including cross-body work, to develop bilateral co-ordination;
- throwing and catching activities to develop hand-eye co-ordination and visual tracking;
- opportunities to use a range of tools and equipment throughout the setting, including the provision of malleable activities to develop grip and pinch strength.

For children who can already read, it is important to ascertain whether phonics sessions will support their continued progress. An important part of teachers' assessments is to look at whether children's knowledge of how to write words matches their ability to read them. If not, a programme of phonics teaching modified particularly to support writing is likely to be useful.

If some children are able to use and apply phonics for reading and for writing above the level expected at this stage, reading and writing words automatically, the teacher continues to support their reading and writing development in targeted sessions instead of phonics lessons. To ensure they are still connected to the rest of the class, this learning can be built around the same focused texts, shifting the emphasis from these children being read to, to them reading independently. The level of their comprehension is extended by providing appropriate questions during and after reading, which target a range of reading skills, including creative responses to texts read, including through their writing. These children also write in response to what they have read and experienced, providing a range of opportunities and materials to facilitate this.

Observing and assessing children's progress as part of taught and independent activity is vital in looking for how well children are achieving against age-related expectations, as is knowing how to effectively intervene with children who are not developing at the same rate as their peers. This will enable teachers to ensure that every child's needs are appropriately met.

Notes

1 Department for Education (DfE). (2023). *The Reading Framework*. Department for Education.
2 Pugh, A., & Kearns, D. (2023). Text Types and Their Relation to Efficacy in Beginning Reading Interventions. *Reading Research Quarterly*, 1–23. Retrieved December 1, 2023, from https://doi.org/10.1002/rrq.513
3 Castles, A., Rastle, K., & Nation, K. (2018). Ending the Reading Wars: Reading Acquisition from Novice to Expert. *Psychological Science in the Public Interest*, *19*(1), 5–51. Retrieved December 1, 2023, from https://doi.org/10.1177/1529100618772271
4 Centre for Literacy in Primary Education (CLPE). (2023). *The Corebooks Collections*. Centre for Literacy in Primary Education (CLPE). Retrieved October 23, 2023, from https://clpe.org.uk/books/corebooks/corebooks-collections
5 Crystal, D. (2010). *The Cambridge Encyclopedia of Language* (3rd ed.). Cambridge University Press.
6 Copyright © 2013 Lucy Cousins. From *PECK PECK PECK*. Written and illustrated by Lucy Cousins. Reproduced by permission of Walker Books Ltd, London, SE11 5HJ. Retrieved December 1, 2023, from www.walker.co.uk
7 Cousins, *PECK PECK PECK*.

9 The complexities of English

Teaching the basic alphabetic code is based initially on the idea of a one-to-one correspondence between a phoneme (G) and a letter. Learning these correspondences is at the heart of systematic phonics, which addresses the most common letter-phoneme correspondence and how words containing these can be read and written using knowledge of how to blend and segment words. However, the spelling system, or orthography (G), of the English language is complex: what some people call 'irregular'. Many English words do not represent phonemes with one letter: they use more than one letter to represent phonemes, and the same phonemes can be represented by more than one combination of letters. For example, the phoneme /ay/ is represented in the word 'made' with the letter A (modified by the final letter E in the word), but in the word 'say', the phoneme is represented by the letters AY.

Typically from the age of five onwards (Key Stage One in England's national curriculum), children will begin to learn that the same phoneme can be represented by different letters in different words and that the same letters can represent different phonemes in different words. Our approach to teaching phonics, reading, and writing based on real texts will by this stage have enabled children to see examples and have conversations about this aspect of the English language already, equipping them with an understanding of the complexity of English orthography from the very start. Many commercial phonics programmes limit this knowledge, ensuring children only see one representation of each phoneme as they progress, restricting children's experience of seeing words containing alternative representations in their reading and using these in their writing in taught sessions, Children who have had a wide range of literacy experiences from the start, including a supportive environment for language use at home; access to a broad range of real texts; and adult support for choosing, reading, and discussing texts that have been shared and read will have had more access to the complexities of the English language as part of their stronger foundations for learning to read and write.

This next stage of learning requires a careful balance of pairing growing phonic knowledge with knowledge about vocabulary and word structure. Although children's spelling development typically consists of a limited number of recognisable stages, this is not a simple linear progression because young children are able to draw on a range of phonological, orthographical, and morphological (G) knowledge from the early stages of writing and spelling. Many children see patterns in words early on, particularly in words that have a significant meaning to them. For example, in hearing, seeing, and using the words mummy, daddy, and baby, many children will recognise the fact that the /ee/ phoneme is represented by the letter Y at the end of these words, a pattern which they may also link with other words such as 'bunny', 'very', and 'happy'.

DOI: 10.4324/9781003442134-12

162   *The art of teaching*

At this stage teachers should be aware that any benefits of decodable texts are now likely to be outweighed by their limitations. Children will need to increasingly understand the variations in English orthography, enabling them to read and write a broader range of letter(s)-to-phoneme correspondences. This gives children access to a much greater range of texts and more satisfying and authentic storylines in real books, which, crucially, they can now begin to read for themselves as well as hearing these read to them by teachers, other adults, and family members.

Phonological awareness, orthographic awareness, and morphological awareness contribute to word reading.[1] Learning at this stage therefore moves from a reliance on phonics to a more analytical and investigative approach, exemplifying and encouraging children to look at how words are written, taking note of patterns which help them to remember how the different letter-phoneme representations are used in different words. At this stage more emphasis will be given to the relationship between spellings and word meanings, not only the links between phonemes and letters. Teaching focuses on the connections between words represented by patterns of letters.

Key to this is understanding that onset (G) and rime (G) provides a fundamental insight for children into the links between how words are spoken and how they are represented in writing, something which is developed from the initial stage of hearing these in words, as explored in Chapter 6, "Building the Foundations", towards exploring how these are represented in written words. Rime is a fundamental element of consistency[2] which allows children to begin to see relationships and consistent patterns between groups of words rather than seeing each word as an individual unit, which aids both reading and spelling accuracy. This knowledge supports children to begin looking at larger units in words. As children internalise rime analogies, they spend less time on decoding, and the blending of new words can become an easier task. This in turn helps them to decode text more easily so that their attention can be focused on understanding the text read.[3]

Case study research has revealed that children who learn to spell relatively easily are interested in all aspects of language and literacy. The children in Olivia O'Sullivan and Anne Thomas'[4] study enjoyed reading, read a wide range of books at home and at school, and saw their reading as a source of learning about vocabulary and spelling. The experiences of these case study children suggest that a continuing focus on reading complete real texts, and focusing on comprehension, continues to be essential. Children can be helped to explore word meanings and make connections between the spellings of a range of words from which to draw on to make analogies (G) in both reading and spelling.

The wide variety of pronunciations for vowels (G) poses a particular challenge for children in reading and spelling words: "Vowels are the most unpredictable element in the English language and the major reason why 'sounding words out' is not an easily workable strategy in English."[5] Initial consonant representations are consistent across approximately 96% of words and final consonant representations across approximately 91% of words.[6] However, consistency of vowel representations only stands at 51% across different words. This is where the importance of investigating rime patterns comes to the forefront. When the entire rime is considered, consistency rises to 77%, showing the benefit of children being supported to make analogies between words with the same rime. For example, if you look at the phoneme represented by the letter A in the words 'fall', 'father', 'fan', 'face', and 'fare', the pronunciations are all different, whereas if you look at 'fall', 'call', and 'small', the pronunciations of ALL in each word are all the same. Looking at the larger rime structure rather than the individual phoneme is most beneficial. Likewise, if a child recognises how to read and spell the rime in the words 'make' and 'cake', they can use this knowledge to read and spell words like 'bake' 'shake', and 'mistake'. The multiple ways of representing vowel phonemes in spellings in English, and in significant numbers of consonant phonemes, highlight the challenge of learning to read and write and also why making analogies between words is a useful strategy for increasing accuracy in both the reading and spelling of words.

If we take the phoneme /ai/, there are many different combinations of letters that can be used to represent this speech sound. Some are influenced by where the phoneme appears in the word; for example, the AI representation is much more likely to come in the middle of a word as in 'rain' or 'paint', whilst the AY representation is much more likely at the end of a word, as in 'play' or 'away'. Some letter combinations provide a different indication of how to pronounce the vowel represented, for example, the letters A-E, also known as the split vowel digraph (G), in words like 'make' and 'came' denotes the long vowel pronunciation. Some letter combinations are influenced by how words entered our language, for example, in words like 'ballet', 'sorbet', and 'crochet', all derived from words in the French language. Other letter combinations link to relationships between the meanings of words, for example, in prey linked to predator or pray linked to prayer. This is particularly important in exploring homophones (G) and the spelling patterns chosen to represent these words, which are pronounced in the same way.

At this stage of learning, teaching will focus on teaching children the most common alternative letter representations for phonemes building on the one representation they have been taught in learning the basic code, focusing on some of the more apparent generalisations and patterns, and looking at which representations are most and less common (see Table 9.1). It is important for teachers to have a good knowledge of the relationship between how words are spelled and the rules and patterns behind written representations, not least to be able to support pupils who are working beyond age-related expectations.

Table 9.1 Phonemes and their representations by multiple letter combinations

Phoneme	Basic representation	Alternative representations	Example words
/ai/	AI – 'rain'	AY – common at the end of words	day, play, stay
		A_E – split vowel digraph	came, take, bake
		EIGH	eight, weigh
		EY	hey, grey,
		EI	
/oi/	OI – 'join'	OY – common at the end of words	boy, toy, enjoy
/ee/	EE – 'seen'	Y – common at the end of words	mummy, daddy, baby
		EA	mean, bead, beat, speak, teach, cream, beast
		E_E	even, these
		IE	field
		EY	key, money
		EO	people
/ie/	IGH	IE – common at the end of words	tie, lie, pie
		Y – common at the end of words	by, why, cry, reply
		I_E	line, slide, prize
		I	find, mind, wind, behind

(*Continued*)

Table 9.1 (Continued)

Phoneme	Basic representation	Alternative representations	Example words
/oa/	OA – 'boat'	OW – common at the end of words	blow, grow, snow
		OE	toe, woe, foe
		O_E	woke, pole, home, stone, note
		O	go, no, so, cold
/oo/	OO – 'moon'	UE – common at the end of words	blue, true
		U_E – split vowel digraph	clue, true, flute,
		EW	crew, chew, blew, threw
		OU	you
		UI	
/yoo/		UE	cue, due, queue, statue
		U_E – split vowel digraph	tune, cube, cute
		EW	new, due, stew, few
/oo/	OO – 'book'	U	put
		OUL	should, could, would
/ow/	OW – 'town'	OU	out, our, ouch, round, count, mouth, proud
/ar/	AR – 'farm'	A	father, bath, past
		AL	half
/ur/	UR – 'turn'	IR	girl, bird,
		ER	her
		EAR	heard, early
/or/	OR – 'born'	AW	saw, draw, claw
		AL	all, walk, hall
		AUGH	caught, naughty
		OUR	your, four, court
/ear/	EAR – 'dear'	ERE	here
		EER	deer
/air/	AIR – 'hair'	ARE	care, beware, stare
		EAR	bear, pear, tear
		ERE	there, where
/e/	E – 'bed'	EA	head,
/i/	I – 'bin'	Y	gym, crystal, pyramid
/o/	O – 'pot'	A	was, what, wand,
/u/	U – 'fun'	O	son, worry, brother
		O_E	come, some
/w/	W – 'win'	WH	when, whether, which
/f/	F – 'fin'	PH	elephant, dolphin, phonics
/c/	C – 'cat', K- 'king' CK – 'tick'	CH	school
		QU	
		X	
/sh/	SH – 'shell'	S	sure, sugar
		CH	chef
/ch/	CH – much	TCH	catch
		TURE	picture, nature, mixture
/s/	S – 'sit'	SE	house, grease, loose
		C	cent
		ST	rustle, whistle
/j/	J – 'jet'	G	giant
		DGE	edge, judge

(Continued)

Table 9.1 (Continued)

Phoneme	Basic representation	Alternative representations	Example words
/l/	L – 'lid'	LE	castle, purple, table
/m/	M – 'mat'	MB	lamb,
/n/	N – 'nut'	KN	knight
		GN	gnat, sign
/r/	R – 'rip'	WR	wrap, wrist
/v/	V – 'van'	VE	have, love, give
/z/	Z – 'zip'	SE	cheese, noise

The links between reading and writing have been recognised for some time, influencing our approach and the model for literacy developed in this publication. For example, "Progress always entails word knowledge derived from reading and from applying the knowledge through purposeful writing. Spelling is thus pivotal to both reading and writing: in this sense it is central to the meaning and acquisition of literacy."[7]

Developing children's understanding of alternative letter-phoneme representations

Based on experiences of working with a range of five- to six-year-old children, we recommend that this stage of learning be delivered over approximately 24–36 weeks, with children being introduced to alternative letter-phoneme correspondences to see and investigate why and how the different letter-phoneme representations are chosen and used in different words.

In each lesson the teacher supports the children to revisit and revise the most common letter correspondences for phonemes previously taught and the high-frequency words which do not conform to letter-phoneme correspondences which have been taught up to this point, as well as introducing alternative representations for phonemes, pronunciations for letters, and new high-frequency words. This helps to consolidate and extend knowledge during every lesson, supporting the children's whole word recognition, and hence their fluency (G), in reading a wider range of words, phrases, and sentences, supporting their independence as readers and writers.

The following examples describe how a sequence of lessons contextualising phonics and word study at this stage in a programme of literacy teaching would be taught. A recommended text for this series of lessons is *The Great Paint* by Alex Willmore.[8] This is a humorous yet thoughtful story perfect for young readers from five to seven, which tells the story of a frog who loves to paint but who one day loses inspiration. He goes out into the wider habitat with his tools to create, but not everyone is so enthusiastic about the art he adds to the surroundings! The text conveys important messages about pursuing different interests and hobbies whilst giving children the opportunity to view behaviours and actions from different perspectives as well as focusing on attributes such as kindness, acceptance, friendship, and empathy. The text offers much to discuss in terms of children's personal, social, and emotional development alongside supporting children's ongoing literacy development.

In addition to its merits as a whole text, this book can be used by teachers to introduce different representations for the vowel phoneme /ai/. Children will be able to revisit and

166 *The art of teaching*

revise the common representation AI, which they will have already been introduced to, as well as being introduced to common variations. Alongside this, they will also be able to look at how morphological and etymological approaches to word reading and spelling can support their growing understanding of how words are spelled and linked to meanings. To enable children to become deeply invested in the text, the book is shared over a series of lessons, enabling a focus on reading and writing using knowledge of the new letter-phoneme correspondences and to focus on reading and writing longer texts.

Lesson 1: using and applying phonic knowledge at the point of reading and writing

The teacher shows the children an enlarged picture of the cover image with the title covered so that they focus first on engaging with the illustration to comprehend the potential overall meaning of the text and its themes. This kind of focus is also vital for children's oral language development through discussion. Children are invited to share their first impressions of the character they see and what this character is doing. The teacher can turn to the front endpapers of the book (Figure 9.1) to reflect on how this expands the children's initial thoughts and ideas. Questions are asked which enable the children to share their overall impressions from looking at these illustrations, such as Who is this character? What do you think you might know about them? What is the character doing? How would you describe its movement and energy? How is the character feeling? Do its feelings stay the same throughout? How do you know? Why do you think this might be? What ideas do you have about the story that this character is involved in? The teacher encourages the children to offer answers to the questions and notes things that the children say by writing ideas down around a copy of the illustration as a record of children's prior knowledge and base vocabulary.

As the teacher listens to the ideas that the children share, they take the opportunity to clarify and extend children's responses and language choices, if necessary, to support them in expressing their ideas fully. For example, to talk about the way in which the frog is using the paint (wipe, mix, brush); how the frog moves his body, its position and directionality (swish, swing, stretch, shimmy, glide); or how the paint travels or lands (dribble, splash, splosh, splatter, trail). As they scribe the ideas, the teacher models the skill of using and applying phonic knowledge learned up to this point. This can be done by writing captions or sentences related to this illustration, including polysyllabic words and those containing adjacent consonants. They can support fluency in children's spelling by using known letter-phoneme correspondences, incorporating consonant clusters, and writing whole words with increasing automaticity, moving from sounding out individual phonemes to looking at larger units in words, for instance: 'mixing' 'm-i-x-i-ng' . . . 'mix-ing' . . . mixing or 'splash' . . . 's-p-l-a-sh' . . . 'spl-ash' . . . splash.

The teacher turns to the back cover, modelling how this helps us to learn more about the book before reading. They should provide time for the children to explore the illustration before reading the blurb aloud. This can provide an active demonstration to share how we can use the cover matter to help us to browse and choose books for reading, looking at whether what they see on the cover appeals to them and inspires them to read the book. The children can be invited to share their initial responses through carefully targeted questions, such as: Is this what you expected? Does what you saw or heard confirm any ideas you already had about the character and their story? What further insights are we given about Frog's character and potential behaviour? Who are these new characters and

Figure 9.1 Front endpapers from *The Great Paint* by Alex Willmore (p. 2–3)[9]

how do you think they are feeling in this moment? Why might that be? Do we think they are 'friends' with Frog? What makes you think this?

To provide further insights into the thoughts and feelings of these new characters, the teacher can arrange the children into groups of four and invite them take on the role of one of the animals shown in a silent tableaux of the scene portrayed: Frog, Bird, Fox, and Rabbit. To allow them to step into the shoes of their character, the teacher can ask the children: What might your character be thinking or saying at this moment? The children should be given time to compose and prepare their ideas, holding their poses. They can then be invited to articulate their thoughts aloud, with the teacher actively listening and taking time to clarify incomplete utterances and support children by modelling how to reframe these into complete ideas or sentences.

As an extension, the children can be invited to write their ideas down, using and applying their phonic knowledge when writing and drawing on their knowledge of common words which do not conform to the letter-phoneme correspondences taught so far in the teaching programme. They can be encouraged to decide whether the characters are thinking these things or saying them out loud, showing this by drawing a thought or speech bubble around their writing. The children can also be encouraged to read aloud what they have written to each other, using their voices in different ways to indicate the feelings of their character and reading aloud with expression, supporting the development of fluency, before coming together as a group to perform their scene to the wider class audience.

The teacher can then return to the front cover and ask the children to think about what this book might be called. The teacher can reveal the book title, encouraging the children to recognise the common word 'the', and to introduce the word 'great', which does not conform to the letter-phoneme relationships learnt up to this point. The teacher also supports the children to use and apply their phonic knowledge to read the word 'paint', which includes the common representation AI for the long vowel phoneme /ai/, and to carefully discriminate between and enunciate the adjacent consonants 'n' and 't' in the consonant cluster at the end of the word.

The teacher clarifies understanding of concepts and language and opens up further hypothesis about the story which lies ahead: How does the title link to the ideas they already had? What do you think a 'great paint' might mean? This can open up talk about the dual meanings of this word – for Frog the act of painting might be great, the painting Frog engages in might be of an excellent quality, or it might link to the scale of the painting Frog engages in. What other predictions do these meanings provoke about the story? Does anything we have seen remind you of any other stories you know? What questions do you have about what you have seen or what might happen?

Lesson 2: Encouraging the development of fluent reading and engaging in creative acts

The teacher begins the session by reading aloud the first page of the text: "This is Frog. And this is his swamp" (p. 6–7). As they model the reading they demonstrate how most of the sentence can be decoded, including the word frog, with its initial consonant cluster /fr/, and recognising the fact that in the word swamp, the letter 'a' makes the /o/ sound, as it does in 'frog'. Allow time for the children to re-read this initial spread alongside the teacher, who can run their finger across the words to engage the children in a choral reading of the sentence. Rehearse this a few times to consider the pace and intonation needed to draw the reader in to the story and share the meaning of the words read. The children can then be encouraged to reflect on the words and illustration: Is this all that could be said about Frog? What else might we say about him from what we have learned already and from this particular illustration?

The teacher then re-reads the first part of the sentence, with the children, and models how to draw Frog on a large piece of paper, as seen in the illustration, making explicit observations about his body position, facial expression, and gaze. They can then scribe the children's ideas about Frog around this illustration, supporting them to use precise and descriptive vocabulary. The teacher models, as necessary, how to take the children's descriptions and questions about the character into a range of sentence-types such as: Frog is an artist. He is enthusiastic about life. Frog is cheerful in the morning. Where does Frog like to paint? When Frog paints he feels happy.

Now the teacher re-reads the second sentence: "And this is his swamp", looking again at the fact that the letter 'a' makes the /o/ sound in the word when we read it, as in 'frog'. They should ask the children to share what they know about swamps, either from their prior knowledge from the accompanying illustration, scribing their thoughts and observations around a copy of the illustration, supporting their thinking and prompting responses with questions such as: What are your initial impressions of Frog's swamp? Do you like it? Why? Why not? What would it feel like to be there? How would you describe its atmosphere? What is this habitat like? What features does it have? What details do you notice, looking more closely? Do you have any questions? What connections are you making with real life or other stories? Do you recognise the other animals who share this habitat with Frog? If the children's prior knowledge is limited, sharing an age-appropriate clip from a nature film about swamps can enhance children's knowledge, understanding, and ideas.

In extended activity around the text, the teacher can provide art materials so that the children can begin to sketch their own interpretations of Frog in the swamp habitat, drawing on what has been seen and discussed. Before engaging in the art, teachers encourage the children to look back at the original illustration to discuss specific features in Frog's swamp that they might like to include in their drawing, both above and below water: how light, colour, and tone are used to create atmosphere and mood and how pattern and line convey features and atmosphere. Teachers can draw alongside the children, thinking aloud what they observe and how they are interpreting this in their own sketches. They can then model how to annotate the artwork with descriptions about the habitat, its features, or its residents, drawing on any language heard in films seen if appropriate, and encourage the children to do the same.

The teacher can create a gallery area for the children to pin or peg up their artwork in the learning space and invite the children to conduct a gallery walk in which they are given opportunity to look at and comment on each other's sketches: what they notice and find interesting or striking.

They could go on to focus on the atmosphere created by the sounds of the swamp, by returning to any film clips shared, or by playing the children a swamp sound clip and asking them to listen carefully to the sounds they hear. This will immerse them in the story setting whilst also further developing their early phonological awareness. The teacher can encourage them to differentiate and describe the environment sounds in terms of pitch, dynamics, and prosody (G). Are they high or low sounds? Long or short? Repetitive or patterned? What rhythms can be heard? They can also model the language they might use to describe the sounds they have identified, such as expanded noun phrases (G) like: gurgling water, croaking frog, chirping bird, hooting owl.

This can be brought together in a final piece of performance by organising the children so that they are responsible for making the sound of a chosen feature or animal in the swamp and given time to decide on how to vocalise this sound individually. Small groups of children first, then gradually the whole class, can create a layered soundscape, taking cues from ideas discussed or from the teacher acting in role as a conductor.

Lesson 3: shared reading to demonstrate and develop reading fluency

The teacher should begin the session by re-reading the story from the beginning, up to page 9: "He needed to find some inspiration" (Figure 9.2) (pp. 8–9). This is a good place to pause to allow the children to share their initial responses to this moment: What is happening here? How is Frog feeling and how might this differ from what we have seen so far? Do they agree that his swamp is dull? What does "find some inspiration" mean? They should encourage the children to draw on evidence from the text to understand what is happening and to begin to summarise their understanding of Frog's current situation. What do they think will happen next?

The teacher should then read aloud the next page spread (pp. 10–11), modelling the phrasing of fluent reading, which will add meaning, and giving the children time to reflect and explore the illustration, supported by questions such as: What is Frog planning? Where do you think he is going? What do you think of his behaviour here? What might the bees or Moose think or feel about it? What more does it tell us about his character? Do you have any questions about what has happened so far?

The teacher can then hand over control of the reading to the children, preparing them to share in the reading of this spread, exploring how to convey Frog's movements and behaviour in the reading. The words 'Pinch!', 'Crack!', 'snap!', and 'Yoink!' can be explored together, looking at the letter-phoneme correspondences to read these words or to draw on their knowledge of known words like 'oink' within a word like 'yoink'. This is a perfect way to introduce the concept of onomatopoeic (G) words, which is another concept about how words communicate meanings, connecting these examples with any others the children already know. The children should be encouraged to look at the punctuation as well as the difference in font size, considering what this might suggest about the way in which these words should be read aloud.

The teacher and children can then re-read this spread together, with the teacher supporting the children to develop reading fluency in their use of phrased expression and in playing around with pace to convey Frog's energy in this scene.

Lesson 4: Developing understanding of language and vocabulary

The teacher begins the lesson by re-reading the story from the beginning until, "Frog took out his brush and got to work!" (p. 13), encouraging the children to join in alongside where they feel confident, practising their phrased expression. The teacher should pause here to give the children time to share their initial responses: How has the landscape changed during Frog's short walk to Bear's cave? Frog describes the cave as "dark, drab, bland . . . lacking a certain something." Do you agree? Do you think Bear would agree with this description?

The teacher then can read on to reveal Frog's finished artwork and Bear's reaction (pp. 14–15): How is Bear feeling? How do you know? Is this what they expected? Why or why not? How is Frog feeling in this moment? How do you know? How did he think Bear

The complexities of English 171

But Frog's swamp was so dull!
He needed to find some inspiration.

Frog was an artist.

Their colours, their shapes . . .
he saw the beauty in
everyday objects.

He saw things differently.

Figure 9.2 Internal page spread from *The Great Paint*[10]

would respond to his artwork? The children should then be encouraged to explore each of the two characters' viewpoints in more depth through the language used in the story: Which words tell you how Bear likes his cave to be? How does his description "my lovely dark cave" compare with Frog's "dark, drab, bland . . . lacking a certain something"? The children can then be invited to engage in debate and discussion around whether they think the cave looked better before or after Frog got to work: What do they like about Frog's finished artwork? What could they say to Bear, so that he might appreciate Frog's efforts and what he has created for him? Conversely, they should also be encouraged to discuss what effect this might have on Bear: How might it be upsetting or even damaging to his needs? Should you be able to make art anywhere you choose? Can you imagine someone coming in to your home or your and redecorating it without asking? How would you feel? What would you say to them?

The teacher can then continue to read on to "Some people just don't appreciate fine art!" (Figure 9.3) (p. 16), encouraging the children to closely read the illustration of Bear and Frog: How is Frog feeling when Bear tells him to get out of his cave? How do we know? Which words tell us this? How does he show his feelings in his body position, facial expression, and gaze? The children can be invited to stand up and physically adopt Frog's stance, emulating his pursed lips, narrowed eyes, and backward glance. They can also look back at his expressions on the previous spread when creating his artwork and when faced with a distressed Bear and ask the children to re-enact these moments, talking about how they compare and contrast, providing a good opportunity to explore, clarify, and extend the children's vocabulary around feelings.

The teacher should take time to discuss the range of emotions that are being conveyed by Bear and Frog across this section of the text, modelling vocabulary they might use to describe these beyond 'happy' and 'sad', linking to words used in the book which help us to infer how a character is feeling, such as the verbs 'shouted' or 'growled': How does someone usually feel if they are shouting? How have Bear's feelings changed over the page when he growls? How would you read "OUT!" to convey the emotion in this moment? What about Frog – what does 'huffed' mean? What does it say about his emotional state and how he would express himself right now? Teachers can continue to draw on drama to reinforce and develop language, inviting children to take on the role of the different characters and to talk about what they might be thinking and feeling and re-enacting conversations between the characters, reading lines with expression and intonation and increasing fluency as they build familiarity with the text.

Throughout this section of the text there are ample opportunities to investigate past tense representation of verbs through the context of those introduced in these scenes: told, shouted, growled, muttered. Teachers can explore the spelling patterns with children, looking at what most of these words have in common, that is, the –ed suffix and establishing that 'told' does not fit that pattern, as it is an irregular verb (see Table 9.2). The three others with the same spelling pattern – shouted, growled, muttered – can be used to explore their morphology (G), identifying and highlighting each of their root words, their present perfect tense. Note together that in the case of these three words, you simply add '-ed' without the root word changing. Children who are more experienced at spelling can now more closely investigate other words where the root word is changed before adding '-ed'. This could be recorded in a chart to enable the children to explore the morphological patterns in other verbs that may have been used in response to these unfolding scenes: pinch, crack, snap, yoink, lack, carry, swish, splash, splosh, love, do, walk, climb, appreciate, spot, enjoy.

Figure 9.3 Internal page spread from *The Great Paint*[11]

Table 9.2 The '-ed' suffix

Root word – verb form	Suffix				Irregular verbs
	add 'ed'	double consonant then add '-ed'	'- E' then add '-ed' or add 'd'	change Y to I then add '-ed'	
Shout	Shouted				
Growl	Growled				
mutter	Muttered				
Tell					told
splash	Splashed				
Carry				carried	
Snap		snapped			
See					saw
Love			loved		

As these words are explored, it is important to ensure that children are encouraged to listen carefully to how the suffix sounds to the ear, despite having the same spelling pattern: /id/ in shouted; /d/ in growled; /t/ in splashed. These words can be collated according to each of these corresponding phoneme patterns (/id/, /d/, /t/) so that children can begin to make generalisations as to what they might have in common with regard to the phonological pattern in the rest of the word.

Irregular spelling patterns in past tense verbs like 'told' and 'saw' should also be highlighted. As drawing on morphology is not useful here, the teacher could explore the etymology or origin and journey of such words where relevant to find out why they are spelled like this. Taking an interest in spelling rather than dismissing the word as 'tricky' leads to a positive relationship with the English language, within which the children will meet interesting irregularities of all kinds.

The children should be invited to investigate the spelling patterns of past tense verbs in their wider reading and literacy activities, adding to the chart as they find new examples. This could also be extended to the suffix '-ing', exploring the morphology in the same way, drawing comparisons and making generalisations regarding alterations to the root word: seeing, lacking, swimming, loving.

The text in this section of the book also gives the opportunity to investigate opposites created by contractions and their meaning and spelling pattern, such as in do and don't. Such words can be added to a word bank upon which the children can draw on in their own talk and writing.

Lesson 5: Extending sentences from simple sentences to compound sentences

The teacher begins the lesson by re-reading the text so far and on to "But it seemed that Snake did not agree" (p. 19).

There are ample opportunities in this part of the text to use and apply phonics and spelling in the context of this high-quality text. Teachers support children to explore the different ways the /ai/ phoneme is represented on the page (see Table 9.3), in words like great, paint, shapes, everyday, inspiration, cave, appreciate, Snake, taste, say. The children could be invited to hold their thumbs up when they hear the /ai/ sound in a word as the

Table 9.3 Alternative representations of the /ai/ phoneme

ai	ay	a-e	a	ea	ey	eigh
paint	everyday say	shapes cave appreciate Snake taste	inspiration	great		

teacher notes each of these words on a Post-It note to stick up on the board – these could be prepared in advance to maintain the pace of reading. These can then be sorted and categorised according to their spelling pattern:

Children are supported to make connections by analogy with words they can relate to these spelling patterns, such as paint, faint, saint, taint, day, say, play, ray, snake, cake, bake, fake, lake.

The teacher encourages the children to add words they encounter in their wider reading and literacy activities to this chart, discussing which spelling pattern(s) are the most common and which rarer. They can then support the children to begin to make generalisations which will help with their independent spelling decisions, for instance, spotting that the /ai/ phoneme at the end of a word would most often be represented by the letters AY, and /ay/ if in the middle of a word is much more likely to be represented by AI ('crayon' being one of the exceptions).

Teachers could also use this section of the text to explore the alternative pronunciation of the letter A in a range of words, such as: swamp and was (/o/), inspiration (/ai/), a (the schwa [ə] /u/). The teacher can set up hypotheses for the children to investigate connections and patterns, such as Does an A after a W or WH always make an /o/ sound, as in was or what?

After reading, the children should be given time to talk about their responses to Frog's actions: How does it make them feel about him? Do they think Frog should be so pleased with himself? He sees the beauty in everyday objects, but what is he not seeing? The teacher can continue to draw attention to the two characters' contrasting emotions and how this mirrors what has happened before with Bear and Frog, if the children do not do this for themselves.

In extended work around the text, the children can then be given the opportunity to look at the image of Snake asleep in her tree and the new image of her, asking the children to spot the similarities and differences between the two and to annotate each image with their observations. The teacher can then model how to take two observations from the annotated illustrations to create one compound sentence, using the conjunction but. They can start by choosing a particular aspect of Snake's appearance, such as her body shape or facial expression, and composing a sentence for both 'before and after' Frog, such as 'Snake's body was smooth and plump.' 'Snake was folded like thin paper.' Or 'Snake was enjoying a sleep on her branch.' 'Snake was cross.'

Through shared writing, the teacher can demonstrate how to use a conjunction to link the two sentences together and perhaps substitute the proper noun 'Snake' for a pronoun 'he' or 'she' to avoid repetition, such as 'Snake's body was smooth and plump but now she was folded like thin paper.' Or, 'Snake was enjoying a sleep on her branch but now she was cross.' Other conjunctions, like 'so' or 'until', could also be introduced. The children could then be given opportunities to try this for themselves, to articulate their observations into a compound sentence that can accommodate a comparison and write this on a sentence strip to accompany the 'before and after' illustrations.

Lesson 6: Extending knowledge of letter-phoneme correspondences and developing empathy through reading

The teacher begins by re-reading the whole of the book so far and on until "'Hmph! They just don't understand!'" (p. 26), encouraging the children to focus on the illustration in which Frog is sitting glumly on the tree stump and inviting them to consider the thoughts and feelings he might be experiencing in this moment and why he might be feeling this way. The teacher could support the children to look back over the artwork that Frog has created over the course of his journey to help them to tune into his feelings: Which pieces do they like best? What do they like about them? Does it matter whether they or Frog like this artwork? What is wrong about it?

The teacher can support the children to reflect on how Frog's emotions have changed over the course of the story, exploring and identifying together the words and pictures that show he has been excited, confused, crestfallen, pleased, and frustrated. The teacher can list the children's ideas, supporting them with making precise language choices to describe these feelings to add to their growing repertoire. The children should be encouraged to relate this to their own experiences, sharing personal narratives to strengthen their empathy for Frog in these moments and exploring how this kind of emotion might make someone act on the outside or feel on the inside.

This is a good opportunity for the children to use and apply their growing knowledge in a further range of potentially decodable words (depending on their current knowledge) and high-frequency sight words that they will have encountered in the book. For example:

- the alternative pronunciations of the letter A in: art, great, paint, swamp;
- the alternative representation of the /o/ phoneme in opening, show, own, hope, going, suppose;
- the /u/ (schwa) (G) phoneme representations in touch, colour, sculpt, cut, marvellous, understand, idea, colourful, wonderful, suppose;
- the /ee/ phoneme representations in appreciate, differently, beauty, needed, ready, agree, excitedly, seemed;
- the /igh/ phoneme representations in idea, trying, like, I, right, excited.

The children should be supported by the teacher to investigate words that share the same spelling patterns as these words through rhyme and analogy. They can go on to categorise the words so that they can spot generalisations such as the /ee/ phoneme at the end of words most often being generated by 'y' and /oi/ at the end of a word usually being represented by 'oy'.

The teacher then reads on to "'Oh how can I put this right?!'" (p. 27), concealing the last sentence. At this point, the children can be invited to think about how Frog could put right his actions, encouraging them to connect this situation to their own experiences and to reflect on a time when their behaviour upset someone else and what they did to make it right, including but beyond apologising.

Now the teacher can continue reading up to "My Great Art Show!" (p. 31), inviting the children to consider whether they think this is a good way for Frog to resolve the situation. The teacher will need to pre-prepare a handwritten copy of the text from Frog's invitation in the illustration and look at this with the children, asking them to consider how it works as an invitation: What would they usually expect to find in an invitation, in their experience? If the children's experiences are limited, provide them with real-world examples from which to reference and clarify new print concepts like 'RSVP'. Working together, the teacher and children can establish that there may not be quite enough information in it, for example, his friends might well remember where he lives but they won't know when to arrive, how long the event will last, what they might bring, who it involves or what to expect. The teacher can work with the children to create an agreed-upon set of text features that they think would be helpful for the other animals receiving the invitation and that are commonly used, such as an opening line to describe the event followed by headings to include: date, time, place, and who to RSVP to. The children could decide what other details they could include about the event that would be of interest to Frog's friends. They can also make individual decisions about the decorative presentation of the invitation, imagining how Frog would have liked it to look.

The teacher can also explore the written voice (G) with the children, reading the invitation aloud again and discussing whether they think he has been persuasive enough. The children might feel that the phrases 'grand opening' and 'Great Art Show' will generate lots of excitement, but others may feel Frog should have written a covering letter, apologising for his actions and telling them he wanted to make it right.

In extended work around the text, the children can then be given the time and resources to create an invitation each for Frog to distribute to his friends. They could create this using digital software so that the same invitation could be replicated once published or distributed online or by using paper and art materials and posting their invitations in the class post-box.

The teacher can then re-read the spread again, showing the children the illustration in which all of Frog's friends begin arriving at Frog's Great Art Show. The children could help Crocodile by making a list from which to check off each animal as they arrive, drawing on their phonic knowledge to segment for spelling their names, such as 'B-ear', 'R-a-bb-i-t' or (if at a more fluent spelling stage) breaking each word up into larger parts, such as 'Sn-ake', 'Ra-bbit'. Encourage the children to check the spellings of animal names like 'Tortoise' which are more unusual, perhaps showing them how to use a simple infant dictionary or encyclopaedia for support.

Lesson 7: Reading and reflecting on the text as a whole

The lessons can then be drawn together by reading the book as a whole and giving the children the opportunity to discuss their likes, dislikes, questions they have about the text as a whole, and connections they make with other texts or experiences. A broader range of questions can then be asked to facilitate a deeper level of reader response such as:

- How long do you think the story took to happen?
- Think about where the story happened – could it have been set anywhere or did it need to happen in this setting? Where else could this story take place?
- How did you feel about the ending? Were you satisfied by it or were you expecting a different ending? Did you want to know more? Did you feel that there was a message in the story or a lesson that the author wanted the reader to take away from it?

- How did the illustration and layout from page to page support us to understand what was happening? When did they give us any more information than we got from the text? How did they show the character's emotions or personality, for example?
- What did you notice or like about the language: the way it sounded, its patterns, any words or phrases that you found particularly memorable or vivid? How did it add to our understanding of a moment or a place?

The children can be invited to engage in a wide variety of writing outcomes from the text. As they develop independence, children should be given a degree of choice about what and how they write and be supported by the teacher as a practising writer to understand the purpose, form, and audience for their writing in order to achieve success. They might want to write:

- their own retelling of the story – perhaps in a different form like a comic;
- a re-telling of the story from the perspective of one of the characters;
- a news report on what Frog did and how it affected the animals;
- another story about Frog or one of the characters inspired by their exploration of the character in this story;
- a note of advice to Frog or one of the other characters;
- a script to turn the story into a play to perform;

This text can also be linked to a wider range of cross curricular experiences, such as a focus on animals and their habitats, with a wider range of reading and writing opportunities available for the children to research a wide range of animals and their habitats and opportunities for the children to engage in scientific and non-chronological report writing about animals and habitats of interest and how ecosystems work and thrive.

If children continue to be introduced to a wide range of texts, across a variety of genres, which allow them to contextualise their growing understanding of how the English orthography works in practice, they will be able to link spoken words with written words and the way these are represented. This knowledge will enable them to draw on a growing repertoire of vocabulary developed from exposure to a greater range of words from real texts to make analogies between words they know and unfamiliar words, to commit a greater range of words to memory, increasing reading and spelling fluency. This, coupled with rich discussion around texts read and opportunities for children to practise reading for themselves, will ensure that children develop as independent and engaged readers, able to lift words from the page and to understand the meaning of what has been read. Real books, such as those outlined in the teaching sequences exemplified, will also allow children to investigate how texts are constructed in different forms and for different purposes and audiences, enabling them to develop as writers as well as readers.

Notes

1. Kim, Y.S. (2023). Simplicity Meets Complexity Expanding the Simple View of Reading with the Direct and Indirect Effects Model of Reading. In S.Q. Cabell, S.B. Neuman, & N.P. Terry (Eds.), *Handbook on the Science of Early Literacy*. Guilford.
2. Goswami, U. (1995). Phonological Development and Reading by Analogy: What Is Analogy, and What Is It Not? *Journal of Research in Reading, 18*(2), 139–145.
    Goswami, U., & Bryant, P. (2016). *Phonological Skills and Learning to Read: Classic Edition*. Routledge.

Goswami, U. (1999). Causal Connections in Beginning Reading: The Importance of Rhyme. *Journal of Research in Reading*, 22(3), 217–240.
3 Ehri, L. (2009). Grapho-Phonemic Enrichment Strengthens Keyword Analogy Instruction for Struggling Young Readers. *Reading and Writing Quarterly*, 25(2–3), 162–191.
4 O'Sullivan, O., & Thomas, A. (2007). *Understanding Spelling*. Routledge.
5 O'Sullivan & Thomas, *Understanding Spelling*, p. 15).
6 Treiman, R., Mullennix, J., Bijeljac-Babic, R., & Richmond-Welty, E. D. (1995). The Special Role of Rimes in the Description, use, and Acquisition of English Orthography. *Journal of Experimental Psychology: General*, 124(2), 107–136.
7 Henderson, E., & Templeton, S. (1986). A Developmental Perspective of Formal Spelling Instruction Through Alphabet, Pattern, and Meaning. *The Elementary School Journal*, 86(3), 304–316.
8 Willmore, A. (2022). *The Great Paint*. Written and illustrated by Alex Willmore. Tate.
9 Copyright © 2022 Tate. From *The Great Paint*. Written and illustrated by Alex Willmore. Reproduced by permission of the Tate Trustees.
10 Willmore, *The Great Paint*.
11 Willmore, *The Great Paint*

10 Spelling

Being able to spell effectively is closely connected to understanding of language more generally, and fluency in standard spelling enables written composition and hence creative processes. Language is multisensory and draws on all our experiences of words: hearing them, saying them, seeing them written down, and the movement patterns we make as we write them. Effective teaching of spelling builds on these essential understandings about language, not least the central place of meaning in all language learning.

Orthography is the term that means the conventional spelling system of a language. Like all aspects of written language, the main purpose of the orthography is to represent the meanings of spoken words in written language. The orthography of the English language is often presented as being irregular, but it is actually now largely consistent because, like all similar languages, it has been standardised over hundreds of years. However, the English language does have what is called a 'deep orthography' (G). This means that the relationship between spoken sounds and single letters is not one-to-one. In a brilliant analysis and bravura paper about functional illiteracy in the USA and Canada, published as long ago as 1988, linguist Julius Nyikos analysed the use of the letter U and found 50 graphemes (G) representing the phoneme (G) /oo/. Building on this analysis he calculated that the most common English words used 1120 graphemes to represent the phonemes of English. This figure is far greater than indications given by synthetic phonics advocates as they try and convince you that teaching most phoneme-to-grapheme correspondences is the only rational approach. The paper cast doubt on "phonics-first" approaches and emphasised the need for children to be taught to check that pronunciations "make sense in the context".[1]

In some other languages that we describe as having shallow orthographies, such as Spanish or Turkish, the relationship is much more direct, so there is a more consistent link between spoken sounds and single letters. In shallow orthographies it is more straightforward to teach spelling using synthetic phonics (G). In deep orthographies, such as English, a combined method by which children learn basic alphabetic decoding procedures but also look at whole words and spelling patterns within words, and at the same time develop a sight vocabulary of familiar words, is needed.

The main reasons that English has a deep orthography is its history, which is a rich and complicated one. For those readers interested to learn more about the history of written language, Dominic Wyse[2] includes a chapter devoted to this. For a shorter account more directly relevant to teaching English, language and literacy readers could try Dominic Wyse, Helen Bradford, and John-Mark Winstanley and Winstanley's book *Teaching English, Language and Literacy (5th Edition)*.[3] These two sources refer to many other authors who have worked on the history of the English language, including the linguist

DOI: 10.4324/9781003442134-13

David Crystal, whose work has included collaboration with the British Museum that also publishes important accounts about reading and writing related to its special exhibitions.[4]

Teaching spelling requires teaching of the idea that letters *sometimes* represent single spoken sounds and not suggesting that one letter always equals one spoken sound. Even for letters where the relationship is usually with a particular phoneme, there can be other relationships, such as the letter B's contribution to the phoneme /t/ in the word 'debt', which is sometimes called a 'silent' letter. If phonics is emphasised too much or too narrowly, for example, is used beyond learning of some basic phoneme-to-letter combinations that we call 'the basic code', then the approach is not optimal and risks teaching an incorrect picture of the English language.

The less common representations of phonemes can in time become a source of fascination and amusement. For example, the word 'mnemonic' includes the letter M used to represent two different phonemes in one word: /n/ and /m/. The word 'pneumatic' includes the letter P, which represents the /n/ phoneme in this word. In the French language, the word for tyre is 'pneu', and the first phoneme is pronounced /p/!

The central importance of meaning to drive teaching reading and writing also applies to teaching spelling. In order to teach spelling, including the early stages of teaching the basic code, the teacher maintains an emphasis on the meaning of words in sentences and on the meanings of parts of words. The successful teaching of spelling has been hampered for too long by an undue narrow focus on correction and testing rather than on increasing children's understanding and enjoyment of words and how they have come to be constructed. Although learning spellings comes naturally to many children, all children can be helped to improve their spelling by analysing the different parts of words and through a focus on meaning. Some simple examples of how parts of words represent meaning include compound words such as 'cupboard' that consist of two words, each meaning something different, that were brought together to represent one meaning. Other examples include the way that words are built from meaningful units. For example, the word 'present' could be seen as consisting of 'pre' and 'sent'. A fanciful meaning might be the idea of a gift being posted, or pre-sent. The prefix 'pre' is used for many words such as 'prepare' and typically has the effect to modify the meaning of a base word. As it happens, the word 'present' can also change its grammatical function depending how it is used in a sentence, for example, 'I present' (I offer to you), 'a present' (for your birthday), because 'I am present' (I am here now).

Letters rarely operate in isolation to make meaning, unless they are letters that also represent words such as A (as in 'a dog') or I (referring to myself). Confusingly, some letters sound the same as words: B (an insect); C (I see you, and then there is ICU which sounds the same but has a completely different meaning!). To learn to spell it is helpful to understand every part of a word as a means to supporting visual memory, and therefore teaching will include a focus on each segment of a word. A focus on analysing words including their etymologies is also intrinsically fascinating for many people, including through the fun of word games, which are another good resource for learning.

Discussions about the meanings and structures of words should also link the teaching of writing with the teaching of reading. Regular reading gives children practice in reading common and familiar words whose letter-phoneme correspondences will at first not conform with their developing knowledge of phonemes and letters. Increasing word reading ability and fostering understanding of orthography, text conventions, and reading strategies all come together to support reading comprehension (Perfetti & Stafura, 2014).[5]

The interconnectedness of reading and writing is key: the more children see words written down and encounter the way they are spelled in their reading, the more readily they will begin to use these words and spellings in their own writing. However, although this happens naturally for many children, all children benefit from teachers who explicitly demonstrate some of these links between reading and writing. In the ongoing teaching of literacy, it is therefore crucial for teachers to strengthen knowledge and understanding of the written forms of words alongside the sounds and meanings of words and the relationships between these aspects. As children progress from about age four to five years old (Early Years in England) up to the age of seven (Key Stage 1 in England), using the approaches shown in the previous chapters, most children will be able to decode and encode basic words with increasing accuracy. They will also be learning common letter sequences that can be found in words, for example, the /ake/ in 'bake', 'shake', and 'mistake', that help them to understand the use of letter representations for phonemes, increasing their ability to decode and encode words with greater accuracy and fluency. An important part of this learning is to discount alternative patterns that are unlikely to occur, such as /aik/. Working in this way builds children's knowledge and experience of orthographic mapping[6] – the process competent readers use to store words in memory and link with printed words so that they can be recognised automatically, leading to increasing fluency in reading.

Introducing children to visual patterns in words

There are many ways that patterns within and between words can be introduced to children to help their spelling, reading, and writing. For example, there are patterns in the way words sound such as in 'go', 'no' and 'so', or 'he', 'we', 'she', and 'be'. And there are patterns of meaning in words like 'them', 'they' and 'their', or 'where', 'here', and 'there'. Learning how to see patterns in spelling, including the relationships between meaning in words, supports comprehension as well as spelling. A focus on rhyme and analogy (G), as explored in Chapter 6, "Building the Foundations", also supports children.

Recognising word families

Exploring the construction of words can unlock understanding of how words are spelled and hence aid the learning of spellings. Take the number two: the silent w in the middle of the word is not as common as the pattern /too/. However, when explored alongside words such as 'twin', 'twice' 'twelve', and 'twenty' where the w is pronounced, it will help children to see the connections in the meanings in this family of words and therefore why they are spelled as they are.

Introducing compound words

Compound words are words which consist of two base words, which were originally combined to form a new word. Each base word is spelled exactly as it would be as an independent word. No modifications are made when they are joined together to make a compound word. When introducing and exploring compound words, it is important to explore the meanings of base words and the new meaning of the compound word and how this relates to the original base words, as in a word like 'playground', composed of 'play' and 'ground' – an area in which people (predominantly children) play. The names of many ball sports are compound words, such as 'netball', 'football', and 'volleyball'. Exploring the meanings of these base words can unlock understanding of the pattern the way that these sports are played – all with a ball.

Segmenting words into larger chunks – syllables and parts of words

To increase fluency in both reading and spelling, children will need to move on from identifying and sounding out each individual phoneme to looking at larger chunks in words. This may start with clusters of consonants, then move on to syllables; other word structures that make small changes in meaning – such as the singular to plural by adding S (morphological (G) units) – and recognising words within words. Many children become 'stuck' or over-reliant on basic phonics for too long. This stilts their reading because they continue to sound out individual phonemes instead of recognising larger chunks of words and whole words, something that impedes fluency in reading and writing.

Using *The Way Home for Wolf* to teach concepts

A recommended text to support children in moving on from decoding words by individual phonemes to looking at parts of words is *The Way Home For Wolf* by Rachel Bright and Jim Field.[7] The book tells the story of Wilf, a fiercely independent young wolf cub who wants to find his own way home. But when he becomes lost, he relies on the help of a band of new friends to guide his way. This rhyming text offers support for early readers in developing reading fluency, and the storyline links to themes of independence, community, and friendship, supporting children's personal, social, and emotional development. It is also an exciting adventure story, taking children to a range of different locations and meeting a rich variety of characters that support children in developing empathy and understanding of the situation faced by the main protagonist.

Consistent with other lessons that we have described, the teacher can begin by introducing the front cover of the book, sharing the title and the front cover illustration (Figure 10.1). The children would be encouraged to think about the character of the wolf and the potential story in the book. The phrasing of the title also provides rich opportunity for deeper thinking and discussion through questions such as: 'The book is titled *The Way Home for Wolf*. What does this make us think about? Where might wolf be on the way home from? What might the way home be like? What stories might unfold on the wolf's way home?' Further insights might be gleaned from gaining a sense of the character of the wolf from the illustration used on the cover: 'What do you know or think you know about the wolf from what you see here? What do you think this wolf is thinking about or feeling? What might be making it think or feel this way? Where is the wolf looking? What does this make you think about or feel?'

The inclusion of the footprints and the shadow is a deliberate choice by the illustrator, intended to add additional meaning. The teacher would draw the children's attention to these features, if they don't already notice them, provoking thinking through further questions such as: 'What do you notice about the footprints? What might this suggest? What sense does the shadow give you? What might it suggest about the story?'

There is much to discuss in the phonemes represented in the words used in the title: the AY representation of the /ai/ phoneme in 'way', commonly used when this sound comes at the end of a word; the long vowel (G) representation of the /o/ sound in the word 'home', an alternative representation to the OA letter-phoneme correspondence the children have been introduced to, also found in 'dome' and 'gnome'. This could also be linked to looking at the words 'come' and 'some', which have the same OME letter string, but this time representing the short vowel /u/ phoneme. The word 'wolf' is also interesting to discuss; in Old English, this would have been spelled 'wulf', perhaps matching more closely children's phonetic understanding of the word, also seen in middle Dutch and middle low German versions of the word 'wolf'.

The teacher can then read aloud the first double page spread of the book (Figure 10.2). The first focus of the lesson is on children's engagement with the text and its meanings. The teacher allows time for the children to consider what they have heard and read and to orient themselves with the text and illustration. Questions can be asked to develop children's understanding of the text and the narrative, such as: 'What is happening at the start

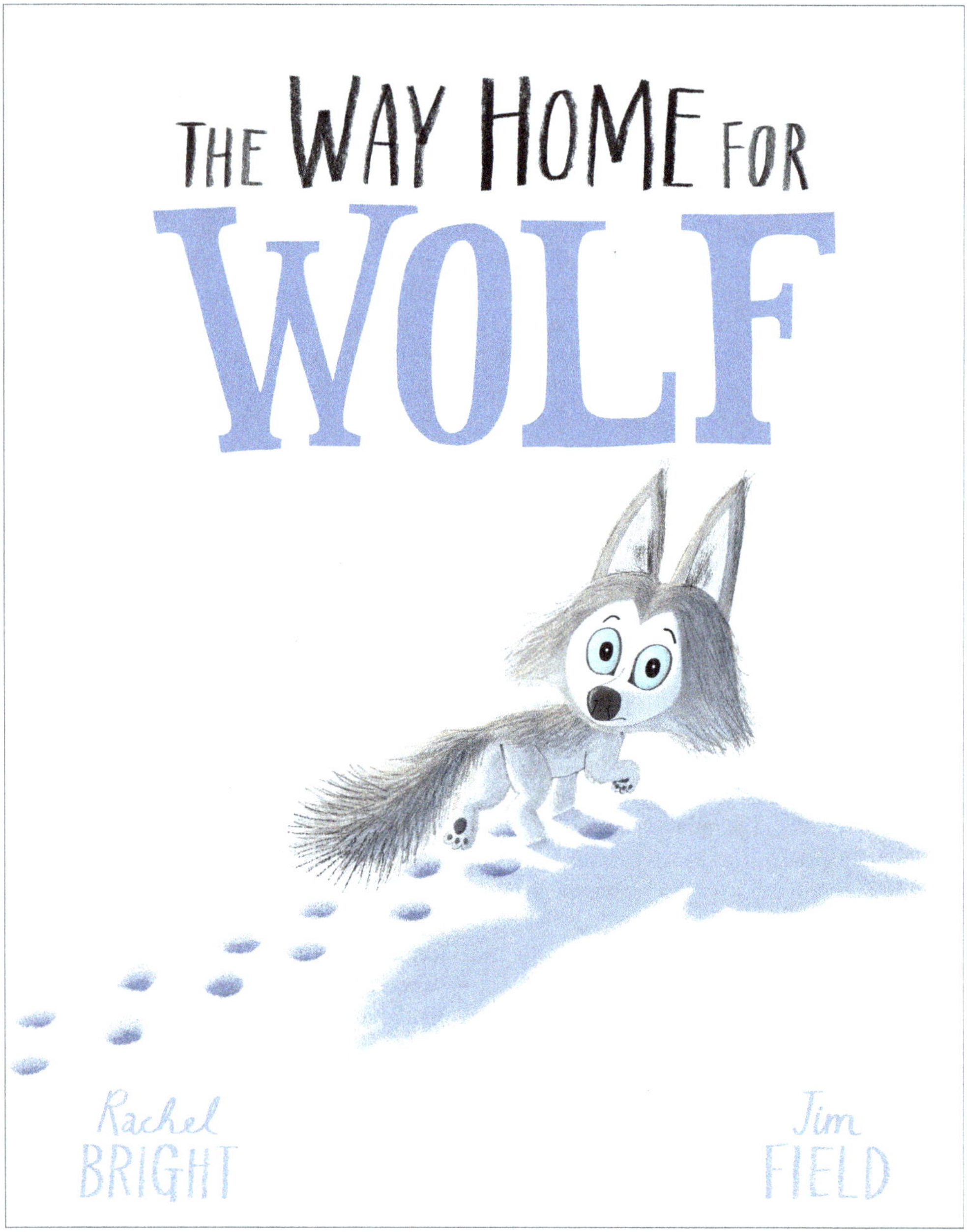

Figure 10.1 The front cover of the book *The Way Home for Wolf*[8]

Figure 10.2 First double page spread of *The Way Home for Wolf*[9]

186 *The art of teaching*

of the story? When is this happening? What tells us this? What is the place that the start of the story is set in like? How might you describe it to someone else?' The teacher can give pairs or small groups of children a copy of this illustration which they can discuss and annotate with their thoughts, ideas, and observations. This can provide the teacher with a knowledge of the children's initial and prior understanding of the themes and concepts explored and an assessment of children's vocabulary.

The teacher can enhance children's understanding and sense of the setting through watching an age-appropriate video sharing the setting. In the illustrations, the Northern Lights are seen, something that few children will have had the opportunity to see directly. The scale and sense of the mountains and trees and vastness of the landscape could also be brought to life in this way. After the children have discussed and collected language and vocabulary about the setting, they could go on to write a description which could be displayed alongside a copy of the illustration.

This first page spread contains many opportunities to explore and read words in different ways. For example, the compound word 'rainbow' could be explored and discussed. Writing this out onto a word card, which can be folded in half to look at each part of the word separately, exploring how it is read and its meaning, and then unfolded to look at the whole word and its meaning is a useful way of demonstrating how this word can be read in larger chunks (see Figure 10.3). For children still at the point of needing to segment and blend constituent phonemes, this can be modelled with each part of the word: /r/ /ai/ /n/ to read 'rain' and b/oa/ to read 'bow', before reading the word as a whole.

There are also lots of verbs in this section of the story. The morphological units can be isolated, looking at how these can be read as larger units in 'flickered', 'dusting', 'whipping', 'whistled', 'howling', and 'shimmering', looking at any changes in the base word as the verb suffix is added. The plural endings of 'lights' and 'wolves' can also be discussed, looking at any changes in the base word as the plural suffix is added. The rhymes in the text also offer opportunities to explore and investigate different representations of vowel phonemes, for example, the IGH representation of /igh/ in 'lights' and 'night' compared with the I_E representation in 'ice' and 'white' and the I representation in 'wild'. 'Wild' and 'wind' can also be looked at alongside each other to explore and investigate the two different phonemes represented by the letter I – the long vowel /igh/ in 'wild' and the short vowel /i/ in 'wind'.

Providing children with vocabulary books where they can collect words they have explored to refer back to will help them to continue to tune into the ways words sound and are spelled. These could be divided into sections, for example, to collect:

- words with alternative representations of the same sounds;
- words where the same letter(s) represent different sounds;
- common high-frequency words that do not conform to children's current phonic knowledge;
- words that each individual child needs to focus on;
- words of personal interest.

Figure 10.3 Word card for the compound word 'rainbow', showing fold in middle

The rest of *The Way Back Home for Wolf*, which can be explored over a series of subsequent sessions in the ways outlined in the previous chapters, offers an opportunity for the children to become emotionally engaged with an adventure narrative, following the small wolf's journey as he strays from the pack and becomes lost in the tundra. There is further opportunity for the children to investigate story setting, looking at how this influences narrative, including the introduction of additional characters linked to the setting and how to structure and pace a narrative in words and pictures. The book has a rich and varied vocabulary, offering an opportunity to enrich and enlarge children's stock of words, from the introduction of the technical word 'tundra' for the setting, to the creatures that live there and help wolf on his way, the 'sea unicorn' ('narwhal'), 'walrus', 'musk-ox', 'arctic fox', 'goose', 'moose', and 'bear-moth'. Each character also offers an opportunity to investigate the sounds and spellings in their names. There is a rich stock of verbs, regular and irregular; plurals; and superlatives, allowing different suffixes to be explored for both reading and spelling. There is also a variety of compound words and words with alternative representations for known phonemes. Exploring these words regularly will increase children's understanding of the ways in which words can be broken up to read, as well as how to spell words with increasing accuracy.

Creative approaches such as response to illustrations, visualisation through illustrations, small world play (G), drama and role play, writing in role, and producing writing related to the text should be built in to the teaching throughout, in the ways that have been explored in previous chapters. This may include writing in different genres, such as non-fiction writing about the habitat of the tundra and the creatures which live in this environment or children's own adventure narratives or stories of being lost.

Exploring morphology

Morphology and phonology interact in the English spelling system. Morphology introduces us to the units of meaning which make up words, known as morphemes (G). The main meaning of a word is represented by its base and is usually, but not always, a free morpheme – that is, it can occur by itself as a complete word. Bound morphemes, which are known as prefixes and suffixes, can be attached to the base element. In order for children to understand the structural aspects of spelling, as their knowledge of words progresses, they begin to attend less to the sounds of words and more to the ways in which words are structured, so a focus on highlighting the morphological structures of words is a useful way of supporting children's development.

Using *Unfortunately* to teach concepts

Unfortunately, by Alan Durant and Simon Rickerty,[10] offers a supportive context to explore morphological units in the context of a rich and engaging text. This humorous adventure story recalls the series of lucky escapes faced by a young boy as he makes his way through a jungle. Fortunately for him, he avoids being eaten by a lion, a starving snake, a man-eating hunter, a bear, and a venomous spider. The text and full of action illustrations will engage and delight young readers, drawing their attention to the written word as they look for patterns in the language used, and ignite their imaginations with ideas for story scenarios of their own.

The front cover illustration and placement of the title text are an immediate route into opening up a discussion about the meaning of the title, *Unfortunately*. The teacher can ask the children for their ideas about what unfortunate events might occur in the pages of the book to follow, drawing on the cover illustration for ideas. (Figure 10.4).

Figure 10.4 Front cover of Unfortunately[11]

Table 10.1 Base words and morphological changes

Base	Prefix	Suffix	Changed word	Grammar	Meaning of changed word
fortune	–	–	–	noun	luck
fortune	–	ate	**fortunate**	adjective	being lucky
fortunate	un	–	**unfortunate**	adjective	being unlucky
unfortunate	–	ly	**unfortunately**	adverb	in an unfortunate manner

The teacher can then look at the word 'unfortunately' in more depth with the children, breaking it down into its constituent morphological units and looking at the changes to the base word and its meaning when the different affixes (G) are added (see Table 10.1).

The teacher can model how to write the word 'unfortunately' onto a word card, exploring and explaining the constituent parts as they write. This knowledge can then be brought back to the front cover of the book to discuss what unfortunate incidents might happen in the story which is about to be read.

The opening double page spread of the book offers an opportunity to explore the –ing suffix as well as a further incidence of the –ly suffix (see Figure 10.5).

The teacher reads aloud the text on the page before discussing the text and accompanying illustration with the children, using questions such as: Where is this? What is happening here? How do you think the boy is feeling? How do you know?, encouraging the children to use the text and details in the illustrations to provide evidence for their responses. The children could look again at this scene, using this as an opportunity to step into the shoes of the boy.

The teacher can draw out with the children the verbs that tell us what the boy is doing: 'walking' and 'whistling' and the adverb which shows us how he is walking: 'happily'. The teacher can share with the children the base words 'walk', 'whistle', and 'happy' and the suffixes '–ing' and '–ly' and look at how these combine to make the words in the text. For example, with 'walk', there is no change to the base word when the suffix 'ing' is added. With 'happy', the letter Y changes to an I as the '–ly' suffix is added, and with 'whistling', the E is removed before the 'ing' suffix is added. The teacher can write the sentence from the text on a large sentence strip, explaining the changes needed to the root words as they add the suffixes.

Sometimes the focus on text can be enjoyed outside of the classroom, as this can help the children's motivation for reading by exciting them with a new scene for their reading. The group of children and the resources of the sentence strip and the 'unfortunately' word card would be taken to a large space, ideally an outdoor space to mirror the outdoor nature of the scene in the text, or alternatively a school hall or gym would suffice. The children are encouraged to step into role as the boy and walk happily through the space, whistling as the teacher reads the text from the sentence strip. At a given point, the teacher would hold up the 'unfortunately' word card and read this word aloud. The children are then given time and space to think of something unfortunate that could happen to the boy. They raise their hands if they have an example, and the teacher selects a child to share their idea. This can be modelled by the teacher if necessary, such as 'Unfortunately, a tiger jumped out from behind a tree.' The children then might freeze in a pose that shows how the boy might react and what his facial expression might look like. This can be done a few times to allow multiple children to share their ideas and different 'unfortunate' scenarios to be explored.

As the children return to the classroom space, the teacher can read aloud the next page spread from the book (Figure 10.6). This spread provides a good model for the teacher to talk about the use of language and grammar for effect on the reader. The functions of words (e.g. verbs, adjectives and adverbs) are explored to see how effectively they have been used by the author to build tension and drama around the unfortunate incidents that occur.

As part of good-quality contextualised teaching of language and grammar, children will be best supported by teachers and other adults who can:

- analyse and name the grammatical features in authentic texts;
- explain grammatical concepts accurately through examples from high-quality texts;
- talk about the impact and specific effects created by an author's language and grammar choices;
- support them to transfer this knowledge into their own writing, such as how to make meaning through word choices;
- know how to consolidate and build on children's existing knowledge about language.

Figure 10.5 Opening page spread from *Unfortunately*[12]

Figure 10.6 Second page spread from *Unfortunately*.[13]

Children become more competent language users when they have had opportunity to experience language in action and to learn how language can be chosen to achieve a specific effect on the reader; how different written forms have different voices (G), and how the use of language is different. Children are supported to internalise these aspects of texts to draw on familiar devices and structures in their own writing. This is the way that more experienced readers become more competent in a wider range of written forms.

After reading the spread aloud, the teacher will discuss with the children what happened in the spread, how it made them feel, and what made them feel this way. The children might talk about:

- the way that the functions of words (such as adjectives and adverb) are used to describe the lion in the sentence: "'**Unfortunately**' he met a big, scary lion with very sharp teeth." and what this made them think and feel about the lion;
- the verb choices in the sentence: "The lion ROARED and leapt at the boy", such as the way the text was presented on the page, with the word 'roared' in capital letters, and what this made them think and feel about what was happening;
- the adverbs and verbs used in the sentence: "**Fortunately**, the boy quickly climbed up a tree and escaped" and what this made them think and feel about what was happening;
- the choice of words and punctuation used in the boy's direct speech: "Can't catch me!" and what this might tell us about the boy's feelings and character.
- the choice to end the spread with the single word, "**Unfortunately** . . .", punctuated with ellipsis (G).

If the children do not notice these things themselves, the teacher models by introducing this language in action and when appropriate will describe words using the appropriate grammatical terminology as they are discussed. However, the focus should be on the effect of the language use rather than finding and naming grammatical parts and structures.

As part of the investigations the teacher can also reinforce the suffixes used in 'roared', 'fortunately', 'quickly', and 'escaped', looking at any changes needed to the base word as suffixes are added, as well as the irregular verbs 'met' and 'leapt' and how these are spelt.

In extended work based on the text the children could go on to make their own predictions of what might happen in the next spread of the book and what they might see in the text and illustrations, drawing on their knowledge of what they have seen in this spread. They can think about how they can use what they have learned about using verbs, adverbs and adjectives to add detail, drama, and suspense and how to show the change of emotion in the boy between when something unfortunate and fortunate happens.

The rest of the book provides ample opportunity to continue to explore language, grammar, and punctuation for effect, as well as learning much about a repetitive narrative structure and continuing to learn rules and patterns for using different morphological units. This could support the children in going on to create and shape their own adventure narratives. Some may be encouraged to use the supportive structure of the original story, perhaps thinking about how a different setting could change the story – for example, what if the story were set in the Arctic instead of the jungle? Others may want to draw on their wider knowledge of narrative structures to draft a different type of adventure, leaning how to use language, grammar, and punctuation for effect on readers of their own.

Exploring etymology

Etymology explores the relationship between a modern version of a word and its historical origins. Exploring etymology can include the interconnectedness between words and how words relate in meaning to each other as a result of common origins.

Astrogirl by Ken Wilson-Max[14] is an excellent text for children to explore family and identity. It is centred on the theme of space, a popular topic of interest for young children, and introduces concepts and ideas including orbiting the Earth, what astronauts eat, the concept of zero-gravity, the experiments that astronauts undertake on their missions, and the idea of the isolation and possible loneliness of space travel. The book ends with the realisation that the main character, Astrid's mother, is an astronaut. This is a text rich with possibilities for deeper exploration over a longer period of time around the topic of space but also giving the children a chance to share their own interests, fascinations, and inspirations, potentially writing their own personal narratives or non-fiction texts about their own interests, hobbies, or fascinations.

Through using this text in a series of lessons, children can be introduced to base words, word origins, and how words have developed, linked to their meaning over time. The front cover of the text and the title of the book introduce a natural focus on the form 'astro', borrowed from both Latin and Greek, related to space, the planets, stars, or other objects in space or to the structure of a star. When discussing the title of the book and in opening up discussions around the illustration on the front cover (see Figure 10.7), children may already note the clothing and the props given to the character and may already predict that the girl they see is an astronaut. The setting painted in the background of the illustration gives further clues to the meaning.

The opening spread of the book (Figure 10.8), which can be read aloud and explored with the children, can then be used as the basis to discuss the topic of space and stars in relation to the main character in the story. This page introduces the main character's name, Astrid, and gives us, as readers, an insight into her interests and fascinations. The teacher needs to provide a large-scale version of the text and accompanying illustration, for example, by using a 'visualiser'.

The teacher reads aloud the next page of the text, which contains the words 'astronaut' and 'asteroid' (Figure 10.9). The word astronaut can be written by the teacher, alongside the words from the title, 'Astro Girl', comparing the spellings at the start of the word 'astronaut' with the 'Astro' from *Astro Girl* and discussing the possible meaning of the word related to the word they are more likely to know, astronaut. The teacher can write both word forms, 'astro' and 'aster-', and explain their meanings before relating these to the words 'astronaut' and 'asteroid' and exploring the meanings of these words, including any prior knowledge the children have about these words and their meanings.

Exploring homophones, homographs, and homonyms

In English orthography there are a number of words which are pronounced the same but have different meanings: these are called homophones (G): words like sea and see, mail and male, for and four. The spellings of these words will usually relate to their origins and meanings, so what is most important when learning to spell these words is that they always remain connected to the meaning of the word in its particular context. In any set of homophones, spellings of one or more of these words will inevitably fall outside of the

Figure 10.7 Front cover of *Astro Girl*[15]

Figure 10.8 Opening page spread from *Astro Girl*[16]

Figure 10.9 Internal page spread from *Astro Girl*, containing the focus words astronaut, Astrid, and asteroid[17]

most common phonics patterns. These are often the most challenging words to spell correctly, even for the most advanced learners, so time should be taken to explore spellings and meanings in multiple contexts and over time.

Homographs are words which are spelled the same but which are not necessarily pronounced the same. This is more of a challenge when reading than when spelling words. Once again, the way in which the word should be pronounced is intrinsically linked to meaning, so such words must always be viewed in context. Consider a sentence that begins: 'We were asked to take a bow . . .' and which continues '. . . to play the violin'. This can only be read correctly if the reader has read the complete sentence; otherwise it could be assumed that the physical act of lowering the body in 'taking a bow' was intended in the first part of the sentence. This is why a firm focus on language comprehension and meaning is crucial from the very earliest stages of reading and why words should be connected with a sentence context. The same can be said of homonyms, which both sound and are spelled the same, like the word 'can' in sentences such as: 'I can do this' or 'I opened a can of soup.'

Emphasising investigation

Prevalent cultures of testing spelling, and over-emphasis on correcting spelling, in primary education means that many children become fearful of making spelling mistakes and therefore lack confidence to experiment with spellings of words for which they don't know the conventional spelling. The problem with this is that it often discourages children from using words in their writing which could be more interesting choices, deferring instead to simpler options of words that they already know how to spell. In any classroom setting it is therefore important to have an open and investigative approach to spelling.

Words which do not conform to regular patterns should be discussed and investigated, leading to a greater understanding of why these words are spelled as they are. Children should always be encouraged to have a go and attempt spellings of unknown words with no immediate pressure to get these right, to use what they know and to invent spellings if they need to, to maintain fluency and flow in their independent writing, highlighting in some way when they are aware they are uncertain of a spelling. Such words can then become the basis for investigation, finding out how the word can be spelled correctly and why it is spelled in this particular way. This allows the potential for a much greater interest in the English language as a whole, and for children's understanding of why words are spelled as they are, drawing on the rich history of the language and how it has developed over time. This approach to spelling can be linked to the effective teaching of writing as a process that includes different drafts that require different levels of correctness.

Age-appropriate dictionaries and thesauruses should be freely available for children to use at any time and these should be regularly updated to address linguistic developments over time. If a child doesn't know how to spell a word, finding it in a dictionary may prove challenging, but if they know the meaning of the word they want to use, and can link it to another known word with a similar meaning, a thesaurus might prove more fruitful. Teachers should demonstrate ways to use these reference books in practice in ways which will support the children to achieve greater independence and confidence as they progress in their journey towards fluency. Children should also experience writing first and subsequent drafts using word processing applications. In time they should also learn about using 'spell-check' within these applications.

When looking at children's writing, teachers need to be adept at recognising and analysing errors and looking at common patterns in misspellings and the commonalities and differences between children's understanding. Teachers can then incorporate their assessment of individuals and groups of children into their planning for and teaching of a whole class, a group, and individuals. Sometimes teaching involves going back over prior learning and understanding; sometimes it may mean incorporating an approach that has not been explored before – for example, looking at morphological units, particularly if there has been an over-emphasis on phonics.

When monitoring children's spelling in a piece of writing, it is useful to note which words they are spelling with accuracy and what is most prevalent in the errors they are making. For example:

- Are the errors associated with the structure and meaning of words or the visual aspect of spelling?
- Are the children showing awareness of the overall structure and meaning of the word in their attempt, like 'comeing' for 'coming' or 'tommorow' for 'tomorrow'?
- Do children attempt to represent most of the sounds they hear in a word? Are they showing awareness of the phonemes in the word? For example, 'kichen' for kitchen, or 'litl' for 'little'?
- Is the attempt showing a lack of understanding of the spelling system? For example, 'tat' for 'turtle' or 'lein' for 'licking'?

Once this is analysed, teachers can look at where children need more specific support. Sometimes this will be on an individual basis; at other times groups of children or even the majority of a class might be making similar errors. Teaching around areas identified for support can then be planned into the literacy provision and across the curriculum, drawing on appropriate words from shared texts and curriculum topics to broaden children's knowledge and awareness of spelling patterns and strategies.

The English spelling system has evolved over centuries of linguistic and social changes, all of which have had an impact on the way in which words have been written down. The best way to equip children with the knowledge of how to spell with increasing accuracy is to ensure they have an understanding of the basis of the English spelling system, age-appropriate understanding of how and why it has evolved, and knowledge of the common patterns and irregularities within it. English spelling continues to evolve, particularly as new words are added, including the use of dialect in writing. This can be seen in the writing of many poets, who often choose to use dialect to convey a particular voice, for example, in the Caribbean dialect used in the picture book *Fruits* by Valerie Bloom (Figure 10.10).

The conventional spelling system is important, but so is children's knowledge that spelling is a linguistic and more importantly a socio-linguistic phenomenon. Children need to be aware of how the written word has evolved from the spoken word, the variations in spellings that exist, and why there are variations and be equipped to engage in investigations and explorations of vocabulary, including how and why words are spelled in particular ways. In this way, they master control of *their* language rather than developing a fear of language.

O ne guinep up in the tree
Hanging down there tempting me.
It don' mek no sense to pick it,
One guinep can't feed a cricket.

Figure 10.10 Opening page spread from *Fruits*[18]

Notes

1 Nyikos, J. (1988). A Linguistic Perspective of Functional Illiteracy. In S. Embleton (Ed.), *The Fourteenth LACUS Forum 1987*. The Linguistic Association of Canada and the United States (LACUS). p. 162. The paper also explores the known variations in total number of phonemes in the English language, and used the conservative estimate of 40 phonemes as the basis for its analysis.
2 Wyse, D. (2017). *How Writing Works: From the Invention of the Alphabet to the Rise of Social Media*. Cambridge University Press.
3 Wyse, D., Bradford, H., & Winstanley, J. (2023). *Teaching English, Language and Literacy* (5th ed.). Routledge.
4 Crystal, D. (2010). *Evolving English: One Language, Many Voices*. The British Library.
  Clayton, E. (Ed.). (2019). *Writing: Making Your Mark*. The British Library.
5 Perfetti, C., & Stafura, J. (2014). Word Knowledge in a Theory of Reading Comprehension. *Scientific Studies of Reading*, 18(1), 22–37.
6 Ehri, L. (2014). Orthographic Mapping in the Acquisition of Sight Word Reading, Spelling Memory, and Vocabulary Learning. *Scientific Studies of Reading*, 18(1), 5–21.
7 *The Way Home for Wolf*. Written by Rachel Bright and illustrated by Jim Field. Orchard (2018).
8 Text Copyright © 2018 Rachel Bright. Illustrations Copyright © 2018 Jim Field, from *The Way Home for Wolf*. Written by Rachel Bright and illustrated by Jim Field. Hachette Children's Group London, EC4Y 0DZ. Retrieved December 1, 2023, from https://www.hachettechildrens.co.uk/. Reproduced with permission of the Licensor through PLSclear.
9 Bright, *The Way Home for Wolf*.
10 *Unfortunately*. Written by Alan Durant and illustrated by Simon Rickerty. Orchard (2010).
11 Text Copyright © 2010 Alan Durant. Illustrations Copyright © 2010 Simon Rickerty, from *Unfortunately*. Written by Alan Durant and illustrated by Simon Rickerty. Hachette Children's Group London, EC4Y 0DZ. Retrieved December 1, 2023, from https://www.hachettechildrens.co.uk/. Reproduced with permission of the Licensor through PLSclear.
12 Durant, *Unfortunately*.
13 Durant, *Unfortunately*.
14 *Astro Girl*. Written and illustrated by Ken Wilson-Max. Otter-Barry Books (2019).
15 Text and illustrations Copyright © 2019 Ken Wilson-Max, from *Astro Girl*. Written and illustrated by Ken Wilson-Max. Reproduced by permission of Otter-Barry Books, Hereford, HR1 3QS. Retrieved December 1, 2023, from www.otterbarrybooks.com
16 Wilson-Max, *Astro Girl*.
17 Wilson-Max, *Astro Girl*.
18 Text Copyright © 1996 Valerie Bloom and illustrations Copyright © 1996 David Axtell, from *Fruits*. Written by Valerie Bloom and illustrated by David Axtell. Reproduced by permission of Macmillan Children's Books, Hampshire, RG24 8YJ. Retrieved December 1, 2023, from https://www.panmacmillan.com/mcb

11 Developing fluency and comprehension

Teaching children to read is driven by the goal to enable them to comprehend text. Even in the early stages, where for many children phonics is being taught more intensively, teachers do not lose sight of this goal. In addition to learning to decode words, it is important that children make progress in all aspects of reading and writing, including vocabulary development and comprehension, as well as spelling, which helps children understand how words are formed and how these can be broken into constituent parts. Children's early success at decoding enables them to comprehend texts appropriate for their stage of development. However, this reading is not fluent at first.

Reading fluency (G) involves reading words accurately and automatically, at a fluid speed to enable comprehension, and without undue effort, as well as use of appropriate prosody (G) – an understanding of suitable stress and intonation appropriate to the meaning of the text. Fluent reading requires reading accuracy, which facilitates an appropriate reading speed, leading to the reading feeling effortless and the reader deploying changes in volume, pace, and phrasing, sounding interested and engaged when they read text aloud. Fluency means that the reading effort can be re-directed from lifting the words from the page to comprehending the meaning of the text at increasingly deep levels. Fluency tends to develop between the ages of 6 and 12 for the majority of readers – and the fluency that, for example, includes professional presentation skills in public can be a life-long process of development. For older readers with reading difficulties, it is important to remember that they may still need some continued focus on letter-phoneme (G) correspondences and the core skills of blending and segmenting to be able to decode effectively and recognise larger chunks of words and an increasing amount of whole words automatically, as well as developing understanding of the meanings of texts. Chapter 12, "Meeting the Needs of All Pupils", provides more information on how children with reading difficulties can be supported. Reading widely and often allows children to encounter words that they may not encounter in other everyday language contexts. This is particularly important given that, for example, in the Oxford Language Report in 2020,[1] teachers were especially concerned about low levels of vocabulary in the transition from primary to secondary education, which they believe is a barrier to learning for almost half of pupils.

Reading comprehension "is the essence of reading because it entails readers understanding the written word expressed in texts."[2] It is important that teachers understand that comprehension is an act – a coming together of many skills and strategies that a reader could use to make sense of what they read or have read. These skills and strategies can be taught and demonstrated to children but do not act in isolation and will be drawn upon in different ways and at different times, depending on the text read, the reader who

DOI: 10.4324/9781003442134-14

reads it, the context in which they experience it, and the experience they bring to the reading at any given time. At the earliest stages of reading, comprehension begins with children making sense of texts which have been read aloud to them. This is the foundation for comprehending written text. Reading comprehension develops over time, into secondary education and beyond. To comprehend text, we relate what has been read to our experiences and the knowledge of the world we currently have, so our ability to make sense of texts inevitably changes as our life experience and knowledge and understanding of the world develops. Every reader brings a different variety of personal and life experience to any text read, which means that although there will inevitably be shared understandings between pupils, they will make sense of the text in unique ways. In socially and culturally diverse classrooms, it is important to ensure that a particular view of the world is not dominating others and that all readers' interpretations are explored and taken into account.

When teaching reading,

> our central concern is with learning to read for meaning. Reading is not just pronouncing written words . . . children who become avid and accomplished readers focus on making sense from the start: they develop a habit of mind that expects the words they decode to make sense. This allows them to monitor their own performance from an early stage, and to make corrections when they misread.[3]
>
> (p. 4)

In order to do this effectively, children will need to use a diverse range of skills and knowledge to understand what has been read, drawing on their understanding of language and the context of the text read so far.

There are three key aspects that teachers should focus on to support children's reading fluency:

- understanding the meaning of what has been read, including to support appropriate prosody (G) when reading aloud;
- knowing and using strategies to effectively decode words;
- reading with increasing automaticity – recognising the majority of words quickly: sometimes called a 'sight vocabulary'.

As reading fluency develops, so will children's ability to monitor what they are reading and self-correct when they make a mistake. Comprehending text moves from mainly understanding literal meanings towards increasing ability to make inferences and to evaluate the qualities of texts that have been read.

Reading comprehension skills and strategies should be taught through modelling and demonstration as part of any reading experience. All of the lessons demonstrated throughout this book show how comprehension can be incorporated into everyday literacy teaching. Table 11.1, adapted from the work of Wayne Tennant, David Reedy, Angela Hobsbaum and Nikki Gamble,[4] outlines key strategies that should taught. Although each strategy will need to be defined, explored, and understood by the children, they are likely to interrelate and should not be focused on solely in isolation, instead forming part of a holistic approach to exploring a text. These are broad strategies, which work across texts.

Table 11.1 Comprehension skills and strategies to be taught across planned reading experiences

Strategy	What it means
Predicting	Being able to draw on prior knowledge and experience to make an educated hypothesis about the text. This may be done prior to reading a text by discussing the front and back cover of a book as part of an introduction to a text or at various stopping points throughout the reading of a text.
Re-reading	Repeated reading through a text (forwards and backwards) in order to self-correct; clarify understanding of ideas, themes, concepts, or vocabulary; to connect ideas, themes, or topics; and to make connections within the text.
Clarifying	Identifying and consolidating understanding of unfamiliar vocabulary, ideas, or concepts raised in the text.
Discussing	Talking about what has been read after reading a section of a text, or the whole text, to draw together what has been understood and begin to form opinions. This can be repeated over the course of reading a complete text to enhance understanding as ideas develop over time.
Visualising	Forming, creating, and developing a visual picture of a text or part of it. Creating art work derived from a text could be an extension of this.
Summarising	Discerning and drawing out the most important points, the main ideas and details, and/or events in a text and paraphrasing and sequencing these effectively.
Questioning	Answering and asking questions to come to a greater understanding about a text, ranging from literal through to inferential and evaluative responses.
Empathising	Having the ability to 'walk in someone else's shoes': think as the other person thinks and feel like the other person feels.
Skim-reading	The ability to skim the text to gain a sense of the text and understand the context.
Scanning	The ability to search through the text at speed to find particular language, ideas, or information.
Close reading	Reading in depth to take on every aspect and detail of the text and its language. This will include close reading of illustrations in illustrated texts.
Developing understanding of the text-type	Identifying the linguistic and organisational features of a particular text-type and the understanding this gives about a forms of text, their purpose, and any intended audience.

The reading curriculum encompasses planned opportunities for different kinds of reading, all of which will contribute to the development of reading fluency and comprehension. These include:

- Children being **read to** by an adult, using texts which are mostly those that are above the level which the children can comfortably access independently.
- Adults **reading with** children, where teachers or other supportive adults explicitly focus on reading skills and strategies with children, targeted to their developmental needs using texts at an instructional level.
- **Reading** being done **by** children, where children are engaged in independent reading practice using texts that closely match their independent reading ability.

Reading aloud

Reading aloud is one of the most important thing that teachers and other supportive adults can do to develop young children's understanding of what fluent reading sounds like, as well as their motivation to read and their listening comprehension.[5] Reading aloud should be a frequent and regular part of each school day, as well as being promoted to parents and carers as an essential activity outside of school. It was argued, in Jim Trelease's classic book aimed at parents, that children's reading comprehension does not catch up with their listening comprehension until the age of 12–13;[6] if so, reading aloud remains a core activity for children at least throughout their primary schooling.

Reading aloud slows written language down and enables children to hear and take in the tunes and patterns of a variety of texts. It enables children to experience and enjoy stories and other reading materials that they might not otherwise meet. In the real books which are read aloud to children as the foundation of our approach, children will encounter a broader and richer range of vocabulary, full of more novel words which will enable them to learn new orthographic (G) forms which will support reading and spelling knowledge.

Reading aloud is best done by a fluent reader, in front of a child, but in an increasingly multi-modal society this can also be experienced in a range of different ways which support children to hear a range of different reading voices (G) and styles and an increasingly wide range of material. Videos of authors reading their books aloud, or poets performing poetry such as those produced for the books in the Centre for Literacy in Primary Education's (CLPE's) Power of Pictures programme[7] and the CLPE Poetry Award (CLiPPA) shortlisted titles[8] are incredibly supportive for children in gaining insights as to how to read fluently and for impact on an audience, taking into account the meaning of language and texts and how to convey this effectively to an audience.

Audiobooks, with a printed text to follow along with, can be hugely beneficial for children to hear good examples of reading with appropriate prosody. Readers of these will have thought carefully about how to read at a rate that is best for the audience to follow along with; how to introduce and develop characters, settings, and storylines; and how to use their voices effectively to pace the narrative and imbue the appropriate emotion into the storyline at different points to maintain the interest of the listener. Examples chosen by teachers should include audiobooks read by readers with a variety of dialects and in the home languages of children in the class. These could be recorded by parents, carers, and community volunteers if they are not available commercially.

Reading aloud seems like a straightforward activity, but to be done well it needs careful consideration. It is always best if the reader has read and experienced the text for themselves before reading this to their audience. That way they are aware of the overall shape and structure of the text, where the rise and falls are and therefore how to use their voice to ensure appropriate meaning is enhanced by the way in which the text is read. Teachers and adults need to ensure that the reading is well paced. This should mean that the reading is fluent and fluid, read at a slightly slower rate than normal speech so it doesn't sound rushed but isn't read so slowly that it sounds unnatural.

At the earliest stages of reading, where children are more heavily dependent on a teacher or other adult to gain access to texts, reading aloud is an essential part of the reading programme. Real books read aloud lift children to the level of a text they cannot yet access independently whilst sharing the joy of an engaging text. The weight of the reading 'work' in terms of decoding and word recognition is removed from the reader, allowing them to focus on meaning and to develop listening comprehension. Teachers can also model specific skills and strategies as part of the experience, including:

- how to decode words;
- looking at increasingly large chunks of text until automaticity is achieved;
- how to read on fluently across lines where sentences have been broken by line breaks;
- acknowledging and reading the punctuation used in different texts;
- acknowledging other text conventions such as italicisation and emboldening of text and use of varied print size and layout and raising children's awareness of what these devices tell us as readers about how the text should be read.

Barbara Throws a Wobbler by Nadia Shireen[9] is an excellent example of a text where every element of the text and illustration is designed to imbue meaning and support the reader to read the text to get to the heart of the intended meaning. This empathetic yet brilliantly funny story tracks a day in the life of Barbara, whose bad mood at the start of the day gets worse and worse until it becomes all encompassing. The power of this particular story is that it's up to Barbara herself to solve the situation; no adults come in to save the day. Every child will relate to being overwhelmed by their emotions, and, in *Barbara Throws a Wobbler*, the story reflects this, offering children the chance to consider and empathise with the difficulties of self-regulation.

As readers our eye is immediately drawn to the central protagonist (Figure 11.1), Barbara, and the mood conveyed by her facial expression and body position. This is confirmed by the opening sentence: "Barbara was in a *very* bad mood." The scale of the mood is emphasised not only in the choice of the quantifying adjective 'very' but the choice to italicise this word and present it in a larger size than the rest of the sentence. To read this aloud, we are then clear that this is where our emphasis should be placed. The use of the speech bubble makes it clear to us when Barbara is speaking, so modify their voice to signify this, as well as the emotion needed to convey the text, "I am NOT" before reverting to the narrator voice for the words, "she said." The capitalisation of "NOT", its larger font size, and the choice to punctuate this statement with an exclamation mark indicate again where the stress of the sentence should be placed but also how this word might be read. The dynamics, tempo, and pace can all be discussed and played with, looking at the different effects that can be created and in what different ways before deciding which best reflect the feelings of the character at this point in the story.

The final nod from the narrator is purposely presented in brackets, telling us that this is an aside, just for us as the reader and not for Barbara. This page is a masterclass in the complex simplicity that can be conveyed in a picture book and teaches us much about the meanings created and shared between the author, the text, and the reader. This kind of text allows readers to orchestrate everything they see and read to engage with the text and make meanings from it. Reading is often portrayed as a studious, silent, and solitary activity, but this is a book which encourages engagement, play, and interaction with each decision that has been made by its skilled author/illustrator.

The next page spread in the book (Figure 11.2) invites us further into the world of Barbara's story and the underlying cause of her bad mood.

In this spread the reader is introduced to cohesion in sentences, invaluable knowledge for both a reader and a writer. The reader needs to be able to read ahead, and remember what has been read, to effectively link the parts of narrative across the spread as a whole.

Figure 11.1 Opening page spread from *Barbara Throws a Wobbler*[10]

Developing fluency and comprehension 207

Then Barbara stepped on a crack, which she had been trying *very* hard not to do. Things were going from bad to worse.

It had started in the morning, because of a sock problem.

And at lunchtime there had been a strange pea.

Figure 11.2 Second page spread from *Barbara Throws a Wobbler*[11]

Connecting words and phrases at the start of the sentences such as "It had started in the morning", "And at lunchtime", and "Then" are used to build the action over a series of events. The ambiguity of the "sock problem" pushes the reader to step inside the story to try to figure out what this might be, to both understand what is happening and to empathise with Barbara more fully. The addition of the adjective in the phrase "a strange pea" provides drama and, on the final page of the spread, the varying lengths of the two sentences add detail and tension. All of this needs to be understood alongside the prompts in the way that the text is punctuated and presented, for example, in the spacing of the sentences, which allows for reflection after each event is presented and the repeated italicisation of 'very', for the reader to understand just how this should be read aloud.

This would be a good text to use for repeated readings by the children, after the teacher has read it aloud as a model, taking parts of the text, re-reading these, and exploring in pairs or small groups different ways to read these aloud, the effects that can be created through using the voice in different ways, and how this enhances or detracts from our understanding of the story.

The importance of re-reading

Re-reading is an important and valuable reading behaviour and one which should be celebrated and supported. In a classic book for teachers, the importance of what was called the "Bedtime Story Cycle", carried out by parents in almost all homes, was highlighted because of the empowerment that repeated readings of the same story can give to children's ability to join in with, comprehend, and increasingly remember the language and patterns of words in the book.[12] This is an important first step into reading. Sometimes adults can become frustrated that a child wants to read the same story over and over again, thinking that they need to continuously move on to new books and experiences, but re-reading is an essential way for children to engage with and control the reading process.

In the classroom, sections of the books which are shared and read aloud to children should be made available to them to re-read for themselves, to consider how meaning is being shaped and how to convey this in their own re-readings. Children's understanding of meanings is developed by giving audible voice to the printed words, trying out variations, and evaluating effects. Pairs or mixed groups of children can pick out and present sections of a text shared after rehearsing and practising the reading together. Mixed ability pairings or groupings will allow those more proficient in decoding and word recognition to support those needing further practice and development in this area, and children can work together to evaluate the effectiveness of the reading.

Providing opportunities for discussion about texts

Children need frequent, regular, and sustained opportunities to talk together about the books that they are reading as a whole class. The more experience they have of talking together like this the better they get at making explicit the meaning that a text holds for them. These social interactions with texts support children's oral language, vocabulary, and their confidence to bring individual perspectives but also share in common understandings.[13] This 'book talk' is supportive of all readers and writers, but it is especially empowering for children who find literacy difficult. It helps the class as a whole to reach shared understandings and move towards a more informed debate about ideas and issues.

Discussions and questions around texts read should be based on open frameworks, which explore a range of questions designed to explore all aspects of comprehension, such as those outlined by Chambers (1993).[14] Once they have heard a book read aloud, a class is encouraged to begin to explore their responses to it with the help of what Chambers calls "the four basic questions". These questions give children accessible starting points for discussion:

- Was there anything you liked about this book?
- Was there anything that you disliked?
- Was there anything that puzzled you?
- Were there any patterns or connections that you noticed?

The openness of these questions, unlike questions that prompt single-word answers, encourages every child to feel that they have something to say. It allows everyone to bring their own connections and interpretations of a text without the fear of the 'wrong' answer.

As children respond it can be useful to write down what they say under the headings: 'likes', 'dislikes', 'puzzles', patterns'. This written record helps to map out a view of the important meanings in the text and is an aid to returning to ideas later in the lesson. Asking these questions will inevitably lead to a fuller discussion using more general questions. In an illustrated text, this will incorporate discussion around the illustrations as well as to the text.

Chambers' approach also contains suggestions for 'special' questions to use after the initial conversations have begun. These are questions which direct children's attention more closely to themes or ideas that are important to an understanding of the text but which might otherwise be overlooked.

Dramatising reading

Sections of a text or a text as a whole can be prepared by the teacher for dramatisation by children or prepared through collaboration between the teacher and the children. This can range from role play, re-enactment through 'small world play' (G), and using puppets and props through to improvisation and dramatisation of story scenes or events to fully dramatised scripted performances. This type of performance allows children to become more deeply involved in the literature, stepping inside a story. In engaging in a dramatic performance of a text, they learn much about setting, characterisation, dialogue, sequencing and pacing of events and about the emotional journey of a text or part of it: "meaning is more fruitfully seen not as residing in the text according to the intention of the author but as a function of the active meaning-bestowing activity of the reader."[15]

Dramatising reading is of equal importance for children as readers and writers. Drama can provide ideas and stimulus to develop ideas in writing, to write within and beyond a text, and to write in role as characters. As a teacher on CLPE's Power of Reading programme recognised in their evaluation comment: "Children's focus is shifted from the process of writing to its content. Quite often they forget they are writing! They seem to enjoy writing so much more when preceded by drama."

Scripted performances allow children as writers to see how a playscript is constructed to learn more about the purpose, form, and conventions of this type of text and to engage with how these work in practice. Seeing performances in a theatre or from a visiting theatre company provides valuable insights into how texts are brought alive in this way and teaches children much about how to present a piece for an audience. Reading and re-reading a script or practising and honing an improvised piece for performance and considering how to bring characters and events to life teach children much about how to convey meaning and use voice to engage an audience, which are both vital for the development of reading fluency.

Reading and performing poetry

Poetry is a perfect vehicle for engaging more reluctant readers and for tuning more confident readers into paying attention to the multiple meanings of words on the page. A focus on rhyme helps children to look at patterns within words and how they are formed, supporting word recognition and spelling. Playing with sounds and rhyming patterns in words supports the development of the vocal apparatus in the mouth, pharynx, and nose, supporting speech and language development, and for the precise articulation of phonemes. The crucial nature of rhyme, song, and poems in any Early Years curriculum is in building children's recognition of alliteration and rhyme, exploring and identifying patterns in language, and enhancing and enriching children's language and vocabulary.[16]

Reponses to poems depend on what the reader brings to the experience and what connections they make with the text; a poem is not a puzzle to be solved. In this way, there is no right or wrong when talking about poems or sharing opinions about what they are listening to or reading. Poetry opens a realm of the possible, extending children's interpretive skills and ability to infer and deduce beyond the literal. The brevity of text on the page and the rhythms, tunes, and patterns of the language support children in developing reading fluency. The space on the page left between lines and stanzas for the reader to make their own interpretations develops comprehension.

Poetry plays with language but also encourages us to make our own sense of it. Writers of poetry make pragmatic and judicious choices in the way they use words and punctuation for the ultimate effect on the reader. Reading well-written poetry allows us to look at ways to compose ideas effectively, using the best language, the most thought-through layout, and most appropriate punctuation to convey meaning. Having relatively quickly heard a whole poem, children can more quickly discuss authorial intent, understanding why choices have been made and the effects these have. These are high-level skills for readers and writers.

Poetry also supports the development of children's emotional literacy. They can learn to reflect on and manage their emotions, feelings, and behaviour very effectively through drawing on experiences they hear about in poems. Well-chosen poems can help children to make sense of experiences, feel connected with others, and also to learn that poetry can give them a voice, if they engage as writers themselves.

Learning poems by heart for performances, recitals, or competitions engages children in many of the reading behaviours which support fluency. They will need to read aloud and re-read the poem, on multiple occasions, to gain a sense of the rhythm of the language and to get to the heart of the meaning of the poem and consider the feelings evoked by it. It is only then that they will be able to make the appropriate decisions as to how to use their voice to convey this effectively to an audience. As they experiment with and consider the choices they make through rehearsal, they are able to evaluate the effectiveness of their performance and consider how it can be enhanced.

A poem such as "My Shell" by Matt Goodfellow, (Figure 11.3) from the book *Caterpillar Cake*, offers much to a young reader in terms of developing reading fluency and

Figure 11.3 The poem "My Shell", from *Caterpillar Cake*[17]

comprehension. The bright and engaging illustration draws the reader into the moment being described from the outset. We are introduced to the setting for the poem's narrative and the narrator or 'I' in the poem and can use this to start to make connections of our own with this experience – this might include being at the beach, feeling the warm sun, being happy, or finding something special.

The choice of the pronoun 'my' in the title creates an immediate connection with the poem; as the reader we know that this shell belongs to someone, it's not just a random shell, which creates an emotional investment. The rhyme structure used in the poem supports the flow of reading; children can connect the rime (G) patterns in words like 'beach' and 'reach' and 'name' and 'same' to support them in recognising and reading these words. Language is judiciously chosen and used to give us a sense of the story behind the relationship between the narrator and the shell. The choice to describe the shell as "alone on the beach" evokes empathy, along with the description of where it lays "over the sand dunes and out of my reach", creating a sense of longing. Over the course of the poem, we are taken on the emotional journey of the protagonist, from this longing to the anticipated excitement of achieving the dream of having the shell.

Children can look at how to create this in their own performances, looking at how to pace the reading of the poem as well as how to use their voices to bring out the meaning and emotions. Fluency isn't about reading fast; it requires knowledge and understanding of when the pace needs to change to reflect the meaning and emotional of a text.

The final verse needs to leave the reader with the overall sense of awe and wonder experienced by the poem's protagonist. Children will need to explore through repeated re-readings how to capture this effectively.

Using picture books with children of all ages

Much like poetry, the brevity of the text in picture books provides a welcome context for children to practise key skills that support the development of reading fluency, language, and comprehension, and these should be made available to children of all ages.

Shorter texts such as these allow children to focus on being able to read ahead to support fluency and to read with the punctuation in mind. Additional details in the illustrations can give vital information about characters' thoughts and feelings and specific details about story events that will support children in understanding the meaning of the text and to be able to read with this in mind, considering how to use pace, expression, and intonation to enhance the meaning in their reading.

Picture books are an important genre of children's literature and not just a step on the route to longer books. Far from being an easy read, the multimodality of such texts facilitates the development of sophisticated reading skills, enabling children to develop comprehension alongside reading fluency and to learn about narrative structure and character development in an accessible way, which impacts children's understanding about narrative writing.[18]

Specific reading skills and strategies are needed to read multi-modal texts like these. Teaching children how to closely read pictures, understanding that every mark and decision made by the illustrator contributes to the meaning of the text, as much as the choice of language and crafting of the text by the author, helps children to develop deeper levels of comprehension from additional opportunities to infer, deduce, think critically, empathise, and make personal connections within and across texts and real-life experiences.[19]

There is a huge range of picture books on the market now, aimed at all ages. Some work for children at all ages and stages of development. Indeed, when older children read a picture book, they bring to it a broader range of life experience that supports them to more deeply understand the themes and meanings imbued in what can, at first look, seem like a simple story.

This is evident in a text like *Grandad's Island* by Benji Davies, a moving story about a young boy, Syd, and the relationship he has with his Grandad. The story initially presents as a fantasy journey to a tropical island where Grandad eventually decides to stay as Syd travels home alone, but older children recognised the deeper layers of subtext to reveal the true themes and meanings of the narrative. As one teacher observed, in feedback on one of our professional development sessions, whilst she had been reading the text with her class:

One of our boys, who barely writes, was able to discuss Grandad at length, the need for his stick as he was becoming vulnerable. One of the children introduced the word 'dementia', which was described with some sadness by many of the children. The vocabulary became richer as time went by.

Presenting informational writing

Videos of famous speeches, well-chosen documentaries, and informational programming share a range of ways of bringing written material to life for an audience and can demonstrate a range of purposeful skills for children, such as how to use the voice in a variety of ways to convey meaning or emotion, pausing for effect or impact, or to leave space for the listener to reflect or consider.

Arguments, debates, and persuasive writing require careful thought before presenting to an audience of peers to make sure that an audience is engaged, that points are presented clearly, and that the audience is led to form an opinion on what they have heard. The children in the audience can then be questioned about what they have learned, what opinions they have formed, and what helped them to form these.

A range of instructions can be used across the curriculum to support paired or group reading practice, encouraging children to work together to read and follow recipes, construction plans, and directions for a range of processes from art and design projects to scientific experiments. These can be discussed, talking about the ease with which they could be followed and identifying any areas for clarification.

Informational writing on a range of topics can be presented to audiences in a variety of ways, such as recording a narration for a nature documentary or creating a visual presentation on a particular topic to present to others. Oral presentations of informational writing support children to become fluent in reading technical language and exploring the different grammatical structures used in such writing. Scripting the presentation first will allow the presenter to consider how to best present the content to their audience to keep them engaged. Scripts and notes can either be learned through repeated readings or held onto to read from or refer to during the presentation. Encouraging the audience to prepare questions about the presentation allows children to take control of this important tool for assessing comprehension, allowing the adults to assess both the quality of the questions and the answers.

Opportunities for children to read independently

Children's independent reading of books requires teachers to provide books in which children can access the vast majority of the text for themselves so that they can both decode and understand what has been read in order to further develop reading fluency. In Chapter 3, "How Texts Teach What Children Learn", we explored the kinds of texts that should be available to children to select from. As models of engaged readers, teachers will need to support children in the skills of browsing and choosing appropriate texts for independent reading. This will include how the front and back covers can be used to gain a sense of what is to be read and reading the first few paragraphs or pages of text to ensure it can be accessed independently at the rates necessary to achieve fluency, as well as ensuring the book is a sufficiently motivating read for a child. It can be a very important lesson to demonstrate to a child that they can put down a book that is not motivating them without having to finish it and to select a more motivating choice instead.

Careful decisions and interventions will need to be made with readers who still need support at the decoding stage. Books chosen for these readers to select from must be of a high interest and at an appropriately challenging emotional level. These readers must not feel like the books they can access are for children much younger than them; this can be exceptionally demotivating: they must be able to be engaged and motivated by the text and its illustrations.

Motivation for texts can be very difficult to achieve in decodable and scheme texts, which are written to narrow guidelines and criteria, so although they may be helpful for children to practise specific skills in relation to word recognition, they will need to be provided alongside a range of rich and engaging real books that are suitable at the child's level. The Learning to Read collections in CLPE's Corebooks selections[20] provide a range of examples of suitable books and are invaluable to draw on when creating selections for classrooms.

It is crucial for teachers to know which children are read to at home and which children have opportunities to read to someone on a regular basis. Repeated reading practice by children using appropriately chosen texts is essential for developing fluency. Children who do not have regular opportunities to read to someone else must be given additional access in the classroom. This could be through planned activities such as:

- one-to-one reading with the teacher or another supportive adult.
- reading with a reading buddy (G) – such as a fluent reader from an older class;
- reading to a reading volunteer – this could be a parent/carer or other adult who comes into the classroom for this specific purpose;
- the setting up of a particular reading experience such as a reading breakfast or reading café, where invited adults read one-to-one with children as part of a social experience.

Teachers should make time to read one to one with children on a regular basis to be able to:

- discern whether a book is at the right instructional level for a child;
- monitor reading fluency;
- observe and identify strategies used by the reader;
- make informed decisions about future teaching;
- monitor a child's reading progress over time.

Keeping simple notes on an observation of a child's reading will provide a wealth of information for a teacher in understanding a child's reading behaviours and in looking at what to plan for future learning to support their continued progress. Behaviours noted during observations of children's reading can help teachers discern what these tell them about a child's future needs. These observations can also be useful in highlighting areas of the reading curriculum that have been under- or over-emphasised in teaching, resulting in children becoming over-reliant on particular strategies.

Whilst listening to a child read, a teacher may also choose to time the reading so that they can assess the words per minute rate of reading as a measure of reading fluency. They can also ask the child questions about the text or section of text that has been read so that word recognition, fluency, and comprehension can be assessed as part of the process. When observing children's independent reading, teachers may want to note:

- whether the books chosen are at an appropriate reading level for the child, as measured by the number of words read correctly;
- words which the children still need support to decode, ones they still need to sound out or break down in other ways, and how they attempt to do this. This can be a positive reading behaviour, but teachers should note if a child is over-reliant or under-reliant on phonics and support them in developing strategies to allow them to read with increasing automaticity;
- words which children read incorrectly – whether these are substituted for other words and whether this affects the meaning of what has been read. If the word makes sense in the context, this could indicate that the child is comprehending what they read. If the word looks similar to the written word but does not make sense in the context, this could indicate a lack of self-monitoring or a need to develop comprehension. At extreme levels this could indicate possible visual difficulties;
- whether the child inserts additional words that don't appear in the text. The child may be reading too fast and not paying enough attention to the words on the page. This may also be because they have experience of the text or one like it in another telling or format and be adding additional language remembered and recalled. This may also indicate an issue with one-to-one correspondence or visual tracking;
- whether the child self-corrects when they read a word or section of the text incorrectly. This is a positive reading behaviour; it shows that the child is self-monitoring and knows when what they have read is not correct. If a child is having to self-correct regularly, they may need to be encouraged to slow down their rate of reading if this seems rushed or to pay more attention to the letters in the words;
- words which the child is unclear on the meaning of and how much this affects their understanding of the text;
- whether they re-read any sections of the text: this is a positive reading behaviour showing that the child may be actively monitoring the reading for sense and accuracy. The child may need to re-hear what was just read to be able to continue;
- whether the child is able to read with appropriate prosody and phrasing, including an ability to read the punctuation and to read with appropriate expression where necessary.

If a particular strategy needs to be taught for a number of children, this could be addressed through targeted teaching in a reading group.

There are other more structured ways of assessing children's reading. For example, standardised tests of reading can be used, but these should always include a comprehension measure because this is the essence of reading. Standardised tests are useful because they can augment teachers' knowledge of which children need more support. Children with reading difficulties will need one-to-one support for their reading and writing. A small number of children may need to be assessed by a specialist to see if they meet the criteria for dyslexia (G) and hence qualify for more specialist support.

To support children's developing reading fluency and comprehension, teachers need a full and holistic view of all elements of reading and how the written word connects with the spoken word. They need to know and understand where each child is at on their journey towards fluency, their ability to make sense of what they have read, and the texts and reading experiences that will support their future development. They will be able to use their knowledge to create a curriculum which enables children to develop word reading and comprehension effectively, using regular assessment for learning, through observing children's reading and assessment of reading through appropriate assessments, which enable them to identify areas for development and know how to incorporate these into future planned experiences.

Notes

1 The Centre for Education and Youth. *Bridging the Word Gap at Transition: The Oxford Language Report 2020*. Oxford University Press. Retrieved December 1, 2023, from https://fdslive.oup.com/www.oup.com/oxed/wordgap/Bridging_the_Word_Gap_at_Transition_2020.pdf?region=uk
2 Wyse, D., Bradford, H., & Winstanley, J.-M. (2023). *Teaching English, Language and Literacy* (p. 147). Routledge.
3 Dombey, H., & United Kingdom Literacy Association (UKLA). (2010). *Teaching Reading: What the Evidence Says*. Retrieved December 1, 2023, from https://ukla.org/product/teaching-reading-what-the-evidence-says-2/
4 Tennent, W., & Reedy, D. (2016). *Guiding Readers – Layers of Meaning: A Handbook for Teaching Reading Comprehension to 7–11-Year-Olds*. UCL IOE Press.
5 Centre for Language in Primary Education (CLPE). (1991). *The Reading Book*. CLPE.
6 Trelease, J. (2013). *The Read Aloud Handbook*. The Penguin Group.
7 CLPE. *The Power of Pictures Book Selections*. Retrieved October 25, 2023, from https://clpe.org.uk/books/power-of-pictures
8 CLPE. *Poetry Video Archive*. Retrieved October 25, 2023, from https://clpe.org.uk/poetry/videos
9 Shireen, N. (2020). *Barbara Throws a Wobbler*. Penguin Random House.
10 Illustrations from *Barbara Throws a Wobbler* by Nadia Shireen. © Nadia Shireen 2021, published by Jonathan Cape. Reproduced by permission of the Random House Group Ltd.
11 Shireen, *Barbara Throws a Wobbler*.
12 Holdaway, D. (1979). *The Foundations of Literacy*. Ashton Scholastic.
13 Roche, M. (2014). *Developing Children's Critical Thinking Through Picturebooks*. Routledge.
14 Chambers, A. (1993). *Tell Me: Children, Reading and Talk*. The Thimble Press.
15 Fleming, M. (2017). *Starting Drama Teaching*. Routledge.
16 Whitehead, M. (2010). *Language and Literacy in the Early Years 0–7*. SAGE.
17 Text Copyright © 2021 Matt Goodfellow. Illustrations Copyright © 2021 Krina Patel-Sage, from *Caterpillar Cake*. Written by Matt Goodfellow and illustrated by Krina Patel-Sage. Reproduced by permission of Otter-Barry Books, Hereford, HR1 3QS. Retrieved December 1, 2023, from www.otterbarrybooks.com
18 Maine, F. (2015). *Dialogic Readers: Children Talking and Thinking Together about Visual Texts*. Routledge.
   Hacking, C. in CLPE (2020). *The Power of a Rich Reading Classroom*. SAGE.
   Arizpe, E., Noble, K., & Styles, M. (2023). *Children Reading Pictures: New Contexts and Approaches to Picturebooks* (3rd ed.). Routledge.
19 Doonan, J. (1993). *Looking at Pictures in Picture Books*. The Thimble Press.
   Michaels, W., & Walsh, M. (1990). *Up and Away: Using Picture Books*. Oxford University Press.
20 CLPE Corebooks Database. Retrieved October 26, 2023, from https://clpe.org.uk/books/corebooks

12 Meeting the needs of all pupils

At the heart of high-quality teaching is the teacher. Excellent knowledge of the subject and curriculum, and a thorough understanding of how learning develops in all aspects of literacy is essential, but this must work hand in hand with sensitive understanding of children's development through assessments of their learning. Children in any age group can experience difficulties with reading, writing, and spelling, for a wide variety of reasons. Some of the causes include physical problems with vision and or hearing, a particular special educational need such as dyslexia (G), inappropriate teaching programmes, poor quality teaching, lack of alignment between teaching and children's development, and factors external to the school that are part of children's lives. Generally there is not one straightforward cause of reading and writing difficulties. Every child has individual needs, resulting in different kinds and degrees of difficulty which, if not supported by appropriate teaching, will hamper their progress.

Some patterns of reading and writing difficulties include children who may be:

- making progress in reading and writing but progressing more slowly than their peers;
- experiencing difficulties in reading and writing as well as difficulties in other areas of learning;
- experiencing more acute difficulties in reading, writing, and/or spelling;
- experiencing difficulties in one area more than others, for example, decoding, comprehension, and/or spelling.

Interventions to augment regular teaching are needed for children with reading and writing difficulties: additional one-to-one teaching is one of the most effective strategies. However, there is a risk that schools have a 'deficit mindset' about children. This is a way of thinking summed up in phases such as 'Oh, these children have got no language' or 'Well, what would you expect coming from that background?' A more balanced mindset is seen in schools that recognise that children are at different stages of reading and writing development and that they progress at different rates for a variety of different reasons. High expectations, for example, the expectation that children should be able to read texts appropriate for their age at the latest by age six, are important, but there also has to be sensitivity in how to encourage and support all children. Undue pressure and a narrow curriculum are not the most appropriate ways to help children who struggle.

Every child will have different prior experiences of language and literacy. Each will have been brought up in a particular familial and linguistic context and will have their own personality, tastes, specific interests, learning styles, and levels of confidence. As we know from the work of Iram Siraj and colleagues,[1] children from deprived backgrounds who succeed

DOI: 10.4324/9781003442134-15

"against the odds" are those whose home learning environment (HLE) includes parents actively engaging with their children's learning, including reading and writing. There are also clear advantages for children who have books in their home, are read to, and are taken to the library. Through discussion with their pupils, teachers need to assess which children are likely to have had key prior experiences and, most importantly, which children have not. These are the children teachers need to concentrate their efforts on in school if both attainment and equality gaps are to be closed. Partnerships with parents are a key part of any action taken to support children with difficulties.

Effective intervention for children with reading or writing difficulties involves thinking carefully about what we can do to make sure these children are not missing out on the resources and experiences that lead to future success. This involves dialogue with parents and carers and carefully fostered relationships that enable the school and home to work in an effective partnership around the needs of the child and family. Teachers work with parents and carers to garner information about children's reading experiences so they are better able to support children's development. One part of the support given to children is the nature of texts and their access to them. Given that motivation to read is so important, children need access to texts where their identities are reflected and affirmed by the books they have on offer to them.

Children for whom English is an additional language

Many children speak more than one language. It is crucial that the process of learning to read and write in an additional language not be conflated with seeing children as having a language deficit. On the contrary, children who speak more than one language have greater understanding of language in general. As Jim Cummins[2] recognised, "the assumption that students (bilingual or monolingual) underachieve because they are 'learning disabled' or have low IQs deflects attention from the educational programme and preserves inappropriate pedagogy from critical scrutiny." Intervention with children who use English as an additional language involves first ensuring that these children gain basic interpersonal communicative skills (BICS) to achieve conversational fluency (G), which, if new to English, takes about two years. These skills are best developed in a curriculum rich in social interaction, through contextualised tasks and practical activities, allowing them to "become actively involved in *using* language for meaningful self-defined purposes."[3] It will take much longer, five to seven years or more, to achieve proficiency in the language of the classroom and curriculum which Cummins calls cognitive academic language proficiency (CALP). Strong support of literacy in children's first language(s) will enable them to be more successful in acquiring academic English and achieving in subjects across the curriculum.

Teachers need to be aware of:

- any other languages spoken by children;
- children's level of development in any languages spoken;
- whether they read in languages other than English and their level of development;
- whether they write in languages other than English and their level of development.

It would additionally be beneficial to gain an understanding through parents or other language support services of how spoken language, reading, and writing in these languages are similar to and differs from English, such as grammatical structures and type of script, including directionality. Sourcing texts in children's first languages, either through families providing these from home or by ordering texts from specialist providers like Mantra Lingua, a UK-based publisher of award-winning multilingual education resources, will be key in fostering children's language and literacy development in English and in first languages.

If children have joined the setting from another country, it is also useful to know their experience of formal schooling. Many countries begin formal schooling later than in the UK, at six to seven years old, and may have prioritised a play-based approach up to this age. The context rich-experiences and creative and play-based approaches outlined in our approach provide the ideal context for children learning English as an additional language to thrive and make progress socially and academically.

Ensuring access to texts

In the early stages of learning to read, children will want to hear their favourite books and other texts read time and again, so it is important for teachers to establish which these are and then to build up a stock of well-loved books for children to draw upon in the school setting, in addition to providing a range of texts that are new to children.

In thinking about support for the children who do not have a wide range of reading and writing opportunities, it is important for schools and teachers to plan how to provide these. Extra one-to-one reading opportunities with a teacher, a reading buddy (G), or other reading partner, with an appropriate book matched to their current stage of development, give valuable opportunities for children. Visits to and support for parents to join local libraries and the opportunity to borrow books from the school provide additional ways of accessing texts.

As well as facilitating access to books at home, teachers should also look at the books on offer to children in the school environment, evaluating whether they are appropriately up to date and interesting for the children; whether they are displayed and presented in a way that is easy for children to access and self-select; and whether they speak to the identities, experiences, and interests of the current group of children. It's also important for teachers to give time to reading, taking time at different parts of the school day, in planned and unplanned experiences in and outside of taught sessions, reading to children, reading with children, and hearing reading being done by children. Real books should also be made readily available for children to take home to share with enabling adults to read and discuss together.

Books for children to read independently should be pitched appropriately at the child's current level of development. As was mentioned in Chapter 8, some of these books might be decodable texts closely matched to the letter-phoneme (G) correspondences children are learning, in addition to other texts which offer appropriate support for the children's developmental needs, such as those from CLPE's Learning to Read Collections,[4] matched to different age-phases.

Recognising and responding to children's needs

In terms of children's reading, writing, and spelling development, it will be important to observe and assess children as readers and writers over a period of time and during a range of different activities and experiences to get a clear picture of what each child knows and can do and the nature of any difficulties they have. Important things to look for at the early stages of reading and writing are shown in Table 12.1.

Table 12.1 Key indicators for assessing children's reading and writing

Reading	Writing
Motivation for reading.	Motivation for writing.
Access to texts at home.	Access to materials for writing at home.
Knowledge of basic book handling skills, awareness of print and text conventions.	Ability to exercise fine motor control, form letters, and develop a legible and fluid handwriting style.
Application of one-to-one correspondence: linking a spoken word to each written word they see on the page.	The ability to represent a written word for each individual spoken word.
Ability to comprehend what has been read.	Ability to compose ideas for writing.
Ability to read ahead to maintain flow.	Ability to hold ideas so that thoughts can be maintained whilst they are written down.
Ability to read aloud according to the punctuation used.	Knowledge of how to punctuate writing effectively.
Appropriate prosody (G) and phrasing when reading aloud, showing an awareness of meaning.	Awareness of appropriate language, form, and style for the type of writing.
Ability to read words with increasing automaticity – not needing to sound words out.	Ability to write words with increasing automaticity – not needing to sound words out.

Reading and Writing

Knowledge of how to segment words into larger units, syllables, clusters, morphological units.
Knowledge, recall and application of letter-phoneme correspondences taught.
Ability to segment and blend, first orally using spoken sounds, then using letter-phoneme correspondences.
Knowledge, recall, and application of the fact that some phonemes are represented by more than one letter.
Ability to recognise that different letters may represent different phonemes in different words.
Children's ability to attempt to read and write common high-frequency words and other words which do not conform to the letter-phoneme correspondences children have been taught.

Once a teacher has identified an area of difficulty, appropriate additional support needs to be put in place to work on these areas. The support needed and the way in which this is planned will be dependent on the level of the children's needs. With children who are working just below age-related expectations, some additional focused teaching on specific areas of need in small group scenarios is likely to be most effective. Paired or very small group work may be useful to attend to more social aspects of learning. With children with more significant levels of need, support will be more effective if it is based on thorough assessment of children's needs and finely tuned support at a one-to-one level. If, having assessed children, teachers are concerned that a child may have dyslexia, then they will need to work with specialist professionals to test for dyslexia.[5]

Lack of motivation as a reader and/or writer

Children's lack of motivation to read or write often results from a lack of access to a wide enough range of texts and experience of reading and/or writing in a range of everyday contexts, or children not having enough choice, voice (G), and agency (G) over what they read and/or write. Teachers should ensure they share, read aloud, and give children access to a variety of different text types, which share writing for different purposes and audiences. These are important motivators for both reading and writing.

For children who are not motivated to read, this is often because they have not found the right book to interest them. It's important here to know your children well, what they have been exposed to in the past and why this hasn't motivated them, what they like and dislike, who they are as individuals, and what their hobbies and interests are. Significant amounts of time should be spent with these children in order to find the books that will begin to motivate them. Support them in browsing books that are on offer, talking about what interests them and what doesn't and reading alongside them to support them in developing tastes and preferences. When teachers find a book that a child likes, they seek to understand what the book might say about the child's preferences and therefore what might be good to recommend next. If printed texts are not engaging children, then an audiobook might be a good starting point. Hearing texts brought to life in this way can offer new motivation to engage with and read along with the printed form. Digital texts can offer children new ways of seeing what reading is and what it can be, particularly for a wider range of non-fiction reading.

For children who are not motivated to write, this is often because of a lack of understanding about the processes of writing, including how choice and voice are important in writing. Pre-determined learning outcomes, although planned with progress in mind, may be demotivating if a child has different ideas and motivations for writing. Where possible, move away from fixed to flexible outcomes, allowing space for children to independently choose the content and/or form their writing could take. Retelling a known story in the form of a graphic novel instead of an extended narrative or being able to independently decide the focus for a newspaper article meets the same purpose whilst opening up a different and more engaging way to write for some children.

Composing writing

Just as with reading, teachers learn to identify children with writing difficulties by understanding typical patterns of development. They look at the children who can and do write, what experiences they have had, what knowledge and skills they have and can draw on, and how this builds and shapes their growing ability and identity as writers. Teachers ensure that children understand that writing is a means of communicating thoughts, ideas, and experiences and that they are given plenty of opportunity and agency to understand that their thoughts, ideas, and experiences matter and that these can be communicated in writing for others to engage with. Children need to see the different purposes of writing, from making a shopping list to making books and stories of their own. They need to hear the different voices, language, and patterns of different forms of writing and to be aware of how different types of writing are communicated and presented to readers.

The range and breadth of texts and genres across the curriculum includes: access to songs, rhymes, and poetry; traditional tales and stories; classic and contemporary fiction in picture books; graphic and other novels; and high-quality information texts, including the use of multimodal texts. Using quality non-fiction texts helps children to bridge the gap between texts and real-world experiences, deepens children's engagement and understanding, and accelerates their acquisition of new vocabulary.

Books like *Yucky Worms* by Vivian French and Jessica Ahlberg teach children a wide variety of new language and terminology about a subject well within their grasp and interest whilst also sharing how to present writing in a range of different ways: an account with labelled diagrams and factual statements and descriptions. Page spreads like those seen in Figure 12.1 show what a high-interest non-fiction text can look like, with precise technical language and writing modelled in different forms to convey information to the reader.

222 *The art of teaching*

Figure 12.1 Inside page spread from *Yucky Worms*[6]

Teachers ensure that children have access to rich and engaging experiences to draw on for inspiration for their own writing. This, of course, includes a rich repertoire of texts read aloud but also opportunities to draw and create art, to engage with music and drama, and to engage in quality real-life experiences such as engaging in the natural world, going on trips and visits or inviting visitors into the setting to stimulate curiosity and ideas for writing.

Teachers plan a range of writing experiences and opportunities for writing as part of a high quality writing curriculum, including shared, group, and individual writing and a range of purposes, contexts, and materials for children to engage in independent writing for their own pleasure and for a range of different purposes. Teachers model the intention of different pieces of writing across the curriculum; they also look at how and why writing supports learning and communication and demonstrate how to follow an authentic writing process from ideation to publication, as we show in Chapter 13.

Visiting writers, such as authors, illustrators, poets, playwrights, and journalists, can share with children what an authentic writing process looks like, engaging in writerly behaviours such as drawing or notetaking to stimulate and record initial ideas and working up writing to a finished outcome, drawing on their own experiences as writers. This is an incredibly motivating experience for children, which sows the seeds of making a living as a writer in a variety of ways.

Developing fluency

Regular exposure to words through reading and writing builds children's ability to recall words with increasing automaticity. As children gain more knowledge and understanding of letter-phoneme relationships, they become increasingly aware of a wider range of spelling patterns that occur within the English spelling system. In time this allows them to process print more rapidly and to recognise familiar patterns, even in words that at first they are not familiar with. They may still revert to earlier phonics strategies when new words do not reflect letter patterns that children are familiar with. At this stage children need practice in consolidating their knowledge and skills as readers and spellers and to be supported to continue to develop an interest in the structures and meanings of words.

Time for adults to read aloud, modelling what fluent and phrased reading sounds like, alongside time for reading in groups, pairs, and with individuals and time for personal independent reading should be a regular part of the class reading programme. Some children may need additional opportunities above and beyond this. As enabling adults, teachers engage children in discussion about books, responding to what they have read or to what has been read to them, focused on clarifying understanding and meaning. Fluency can only be achieved when children have both the skills to lift words from the page and the ability to understand the meaning imbued in the text read. As children become more confident readers, teachers look out for those with the ability to self-correct and those children who don't.

Children who don't self-correct their errors sufficiently will need further support in self-monitoring, listening for and realising when the words they read do not make sense in context, drawing on and orchestrating a full range of cues, and cross-checking between them for increasing accuracy. Teachers should support children to articulate their processes, such as: 'Why did you go back and change that word? How did you work out how to read it? How did you know that wasn't the right word?' They can also support children to articulate their developing knowledge about word structures and patterns through introducing, discussing, and using appropriate terminology such as prefix, suffix, or root word.

Developing comprehension

Listening comprehension is the precursor to reading comprehension, which fully develops when children acquire the skills to both lift words from the page, monitor their reading as they read, and interpret meaning from what has been read. Reading aloud real books to children, talking about texts, and asking children questions about texts, from those that assess literal retrieval to those which require children to infer, deduce, and evaluate, will provide the foundations for children to expect text that they read themselves to make sense and to always approach text with a search for meaning.

Working one to one and in small guided groups with children with significant difficulties will allow teachers to pick texts which motivate specific groups or individuals as well as providing opportunities to engage in reading, practising their reading, and developing their comprehension. It is important for teachers to encourage children to acknowledge when they read a word that they do not know the meaning of and provide opportunities and strategies for clarifying the meaning of unknown words in relation to the context of what has been read. If the word is not in the child's oral language vocabulary, then the teacher helps them learn a new word. More experienced pupils make use of sources such as dictionaries, both printed and digital.

Providing opportunities for children to re-read texts or parts of texts allows a second focus on the meaning of text after the initial focus on decoding the words. Asking children to read text aloud, or to perform it, allows them to hear the words being read and therefore to self-monitor more closely, checking for sense and meaning.

Activities which encourage children to summarise what they have read after reading focus their attention on recalling what they have read in a manageable way, centring on the main points, ideas, or events and on memorable language or vocabulary. Asking children to create drawings in response to reading, either text which has been read to them or text which they have read themselves, is another way of assessing children's understanding. Teachers might ask children to visualise a specific character, setting, or event from a written description and use this as an opportunity to fine tune children's focus on the meaning of the words on the page. Other creative responses that involve transforming a text in a particular form to a text and/or artwork in a different form give multiple opportunities for comprehension and composition that require secure understanding of the source text.

Letter formation and handwriting

For children needing support with fine motor skills for writing, including letter formation, teachers ensure that there are a range of gross and fine motor development opportunities in the extended and continuous provision (G) of the classroom. This will include:

- moving and travelling in different ways, including with equipment to develop arm and shoulder strength and endurance;
- opportunities for dance and movement, including cross-body work, to develop bi-lateral co-ordination;
- throwing and catching activities to develop hand-eye co-ordination and visual tracking;
- opportunities to use a range of tools and equipment throughout the setting, including the provision of malleable materials such as play dough to develop grip and pinch strength.

These opportunities may be necessary for older as well as younger writers and should be planned into group and individual activities where necessary.

Children should be provided with a range of writing implements and materials that help them to master grip, to follow common line and shape patterns that lay the foundations for letter formation and handwriting, and have plenty of opportunities to practise and develop fluidity in letter formation and handwriting. Teachers should ensure they use appropriate letter formation and model fluid handwriting as part of teaching and in creating materials in the setting. The efficiency offered by technology often leads to a reduction in children seeing teacher's own writing as a model for learning. Schools should decide on and maintain fidelity to the script chosen to model letter formation and handwriting, including the introduction of joined handwriting. The National Handwriting Association[7] offers support and guidance on this, rooted in a range of research.

One-to-one correspondence

To help children develop their one-to-one correspondence between spoken and written words, teachers may choose to plan extra shared, group, or individual reading sessions. Teachers and assistants might model for children how to finger point at specific words read to identify words clearly in the text. Some children find lolly stick pointers helpful as they look at simple texts for themselves, pointing to each word in turn as they read it. Rhyme cards showing the lyrics to well-known rhymes, with accompanying illustrations, could be placed in the reading area of the classroom or, similarly song cards in the music area to encourage children to link written text with words spoken or sung.

Signs, labels, and other environmental print should be an integral part of the learning environment, with adults in the classroom referencing and pointing to print as they read words. This should also include print in common home languages spoken in the class, for example, in food packaging in the home corner (G), in books in children's home languages in the reading area, and in welcome signs, which share greetings in community languages. In unplanned, incidental reading in the setting, adults should be clear on which children need to focus one-to-one correspondence and model this at any time during reading. During free reading opportunities, children who can read in more than one language should be encouraged to do so, investigating the similarities and differences between these languages and English in terms of directionality, characters, and word and sentence structures.

Support for one-to-one correspondence in writing involves extra shared, group, or individual writing sessions, which model the process of composing ideas for writing and the process of transcribing these ideas onto the page. Teachers and assistants model:

- how to translate spoken ideas into a form ready for the page;
- how to isolate, say, and write each word individually, including modelling and demonstrating the use and application of phonics and other word knowledge at the point of writing;
- how to write appropriately for the form and intended audience, including choosing and using appropriate language and grammatical structures;
- and how to read back written compositions, pointing to each individual word as they read to check for sense and meaning.

Adults should also draw attention to appropriate punctuation to be used, how this is used, and why this has been chosen. Writing in different forms and for different purposes should be displayed throughout the setting, sharing the different purposes for writing and the different forms that writing can take. Children are actively encouraged to write in different contexts and for different purposes and audiences throughout the setting and have the tools, media, and inspiration to do so, in both indoor and outdoor learning environments. They are also given agency to display their writing around the classroom. In incidental writing that is part of the classroom provision, adults should be clear on which children need focus on this particular skill and model this during any writing opportunity. During free-writing opportunities, children who can write in more than one language are encouraged to do so, investigating the similarities and differences between these languages and English in terms of directionality, characters, and word and sentence structures.

Knowledge of letter-phoneme correspondences

Children's independent use and application of the phonic knowledge and skills they have been taught can be supported by clearly displaying the letter-phoneme correspondences taught for children to see and reference throughout their learning. This can be done in multiple ways, on a large frieze, on letter-phoneme correspondence charts that are accessible in the writing area and which can be borrowed and used throughout the setting, and/or by displaying letter-phoneme flash cards clearly. Teachers can plan specific group or individual activities for children needing extra practice in their recall of letter-phoneme correspondences, such as letter-phoneme match bingo games or quick recall of spoken and written phonemes using 'letter fans'. Ping-pong balls with letter-phoneme correspondences (see Figure 12.2) can be placed in a water tray with mini fishing nets, or letter-phoneme pebbles can be buried in a mud or sand tray with mini trowels or spades and buckets, enabling children to see and recall letter-phoneme correspondences in a wide variety of situations and practise letter-phoneme recall, as well as developing grasp, pinch, and grip strength to support fine motor control for writing.

In shared, group, individual, and independent reading and writing activities, teachers should support children to recognise and recall letter-phoneme correspondences. If children struggle to remember that two or more letters can sometimes represent one phoneme, they can be helped to recognise this by identifying where these occur by underlining these in words read or written and corresponding them to written representations on letter-phoneme flash cards, charts, friezes, or fans.

Selecting a letter-phoneme correspondence as a focus and creating a sound table as an interactive display and encouraging children to find objects in the setting or to bring in objects from home that start with the focus letter-phoneme correspondence are ways of stimulating further interest in phonemes and their letter representations.

Ability to blend and segment

Children often struggle with blending and segmenting written words because they have not secured the skills of orally blending and segmenting before written letter-phoneme representations are introduced. Extra group or individual input on oral blending and segmenting, alongside taught phonics sessions, will be key for any children in need of extra support to consolidate this specific skill. Planned activities should be playful and engaging, such as blending bingo, where an adult segments a word matched to pictures on a bingo card, and if children blend the word correctly and have the picture on their card, they can place a token on the object. Children can win for a line or a full house. In the outdoor environment, children can engage in the 'crossing the river' game. A large sheet of blue

Meeting the needs of all pupils 227

Figure 12.2 Letter/phoneme ping-pong balls and pebbles to support knowledge of letter-phoneme correspondences[8]

fabric can be laid in waves between the adult and the children. Each child can be given an object which can be orally segmented into two or three phonemes. The children can ask: 'Teacher, teacher, can we cross the cool, blue river?', to which the teacher can respond: 'Only if you have the /h/ /a/ /t/ ', orally segmenting one of the objects for the children to blend. If the child has the object and successfully blends the word, they can join the teacher on the other side of the river. In shared, group, and individual reading and writing sessions teachers should also select words with two or three phonemes, which the children can be asked to segment or blend whilst reading or writing, as in the example in Chapter 6, "Building the Foundations", drawing on *Mr Gumpy's Outing*. It's important that the emphasis on phonemes not be overdone to the point that this distracts from the story or writing but instead draws on judiciously chosen examples which allow children to practise these skills in authentic contexts.

When oral blending is secured, the focus can then shift to the children being able to blend and segment words and phrases using the letter-phoneme correspondences they have been taught. The same games can be played, but this time, the children will have the words and the adult will have the pictures or objects, and instead of the adult modelling the blending and segmenting, the children should attempt this for themselves, with adults modelling and demonstrating the act of segmenting and/or blending as required.

Developing automaticity

Many of the words that children encounter in books which are shared and read to and with them at the early stages of reading and many of the words they may wish to use in their freely chosen writing will contain letter-phoneme correspondences which do not conform to those which they have learnt in taught sessions. As is highlighted throughout the example lessons shared in this book, it is important to recognise the parts of words which do and do not correspond to children's current understanding of phonemes and to build on this by raising awareness of visual patterns in words. Displays of common high-frequency words in groups that draw children's attention to common patterns within them, such as he, she, we, be and me, my and by, so, no, and go can be a useful resource. Teachers draw children's attention to such words in shared, group, and individual reading and writing experiences, looking at where alternative representations occur and how these are read or written in these words. Teachers draw children's attention to common rime (G) patterns in words, making collections of words with common letter strings. Some practices are based on the links between handwriting and children's spelling development.⁹ The links between the spelling patterns in words and the way letters are joined together can be a focus of shared and group handwriting practice, focused on particular patterns within words.

Phoneme charts and friezes are revised as children's knowledge progresses and they learn the most common alternative representations for phonemes. These charts highlight and share analogies (G) between words which use the same representations by illustrating patterns. For example, the letters AY that represent the phoneme /ai/ or the letters OY that represent the /oi/ phoneme are most likely to occur at the end of words, whereas the AI and OI representations are most likely in the middle of words. Teachers highlight and talk about the range of representations as words occur in shared, group, and individual reading and writing opportunities.

Children who can already read

For children who can already read, it is important to ascertain what will support their ongoing progress. The first thing to look at is whether their knowledge of how to write words matches their ability to read them. If not, a programme of phonics teaching (G) should be focused on writing. If children are able to use and apply phonics for reading and for writing, reading and writing words automatically, then teachers support their reading and writing development in targeted sessions in place of phonics. To ensure they are still connected to the rest of the class, learning for these children is built around the same focus texts. The teaching changes the emphasis from these children being read to, to them reading themselves.

Teaching that develops children's knowledge of morphological (G) units may still be beneficial to continue to build their ability to decode unknown words (see Chapter 10). Children can be encouraged to read aloud to others and perform poetry to improve reading fluency. Reading comprehension is extended by providing appropriate questions during and after reading, which target a range of reading skills, including creative responses to texts read. Children are encouraged to write in response to what they have read and experienced, providing a range of opportunities and materials to facilitate this. Alongside this, teachers take the time to conduct a wider, more holistic assessment of their reading ability (see Chapter 11, "Developing Fluency and Comprehension"), checking whether they read fluently, comprehend literally and increasingly inferentially, and are able to self-correct, using multiple cues for cross checking.

In summary, effective intervention will most likely consist of carefully planned teaching opportunities which are based on thorough observations and assessments of individual children's reading and writing development and the knowledge, skills, and strategies they draw on to support their learning. This will take into account their motivation, their confidence and independence, and their prior knowledge and their knowledge of letter-phoneme correspondences and spelling patterns in words. This kind of teaching that is tailored to individual needs will be more beneficial than pre-determined schemes and programmes and will also fit alongside activities in which the rest of the class are engaged.

Planning and providing a rich and interesting literacy curriculum also enables children to join in with their peers, at times supporting their peers' development rather than being separated, which has social consequences.

Notes

1. Siraj-Blatchford, I. (2009). Learning in the Home and at School: How Working Class Children 'Succeed Against the Odds'. *British Educational Research Journal*, 36(3), 463–482.
2. Cummins, J. (1984). *Bilingualism and Special Education: Issues in Assessment and Pedagogy* (p. 5). Pro Ed.
3. Cummins, *Bilingualism*.
4. Centre for Literacy in Primary Education (CLPE). (2023). *The Corebooks Collections*. Centre for Literacy in Primary Education (CLPE). Retrieved October 23, 2023, from https://clpe.org.uk/books/corebooks/corebooks-collections
5. International Literacy Association. (2023). *Research Advisory: Dyslexia*. International Literacy Association. Retrieved October 30, 2023, from https://www.literacyworldwide.org/docs/default-source/where-we-stand/research-advisory-dyslexia.pdf
6. French, V., & Ahlberg, J. (2012). *Yucky Worms*. Walker Books.
7. National Handwriting Association. (2023). *Homepage*. Retrieved November 13, 2023, from https://nha-handwriting.org.uk
8. TTS Group: Phonics Ping Pong Balls. Retrieved December 1, 2023, from https://www.tts-group.co.uk/phonics-ping-pong-balls/1001477.html TTS Group: Phonic Pebbles. Retrieved October 26, 2023, from https://www.tts-group.co.uk/phonics-pebbles/LI01232.html
9. Sassoon, R. (2003). *Handwriting: The Way to Teach It* (2nd ed.). Paul Chapman Publishing.
    Cripps, C., & Cox, R. (1996). *Joining the ABC: Teaching Handwriting and Spelling Together*. LDA.

13 The reader in the writer

One of the most important parts of our new approach to teaching literacy is the integration of language, reading, and writing, including all the key building blocks of children's literacy development. In research, practice, policy, and the media, the teaching of reading has had more of a focus than writing. This book has made the case for a balanced approach, with writing an equal partner to reading. We have argued that when important elements such as phonics, spelling, vocabulary, grammar, and punctuation are taught discretely, children will not learn as well as they could. A thorough understanding of how these aspects support children's reading and writing and an ability to contextualise the teaching of these elements is essential for teachers. With this knowledge, teachers are able to ensure that the curriculum they construct enables children to develop as confident readers and writers and to thrive as literate people. This chapter of the book has a strong focus on writing and the kinds of writing that are possible as children progress through the whole of their primary education.

The best teaching is driven by the concept of writing as a means to communicate, to record ideas, express thoughts, and entertain readers. Much like reading, children who have had positive prior experiences with writing gain valuable knowledge and understanding about the value and process of writing which lays the foundations for later success.[1] In homes where parents and carers talk with their children about texts, this leads to better outcomes in schools. However, just as writing has been neglected in research policy and practice, compared to reading, so it can be in homes.[2]

An unduly narrow and separate focus on the building blocks of writing, such as spelling, punctuation, and grammar, often neglects the idea of writing as a creative act that enables all writers to express themselves by communicating their thoughts, ideas, and emotions in a way that can be understood by others. To neglect the writer's task to communicate original ideas is to miss a fundamental characteristic of what writing is.

Developing writer identity

As well as the knowledge and skills to compose writing, children also need to develop positive attitudes to writing. They need to understand the purposes and pleasures of writing and see themselves as writers: with valuable things to say, with confidence to have a go at writing, with resilience to persevere when aspects of writing become challenging, and then to experience the satisfaction that is achieved when writing is completed. These are things that practising writers experience and that maintain their motivation and inspiration to write. A great deal of focus in the classroom is placed on the technicalities of writing, but we must, as teachers of writing, remember that developing writer identity is an essential element of teaching writing. As Henrietta Dombey noted, "engaging in the act of writing builds a cultural identity for the writer, an authorial persona. To write is to extend one's relationship with the world and one's role in it."[3]

In this book we have shown how policies on teaching reading and writing in England have become extreme. Yet the history of education in England has numerous examples of much more balanced policies and reports. For example, in 1975 a memorable government-commissioned report called *A Language for Life* noted that,

> No child should be expected to cast off the language and culture of the home as he [sic] crosses the school threshold, nor to live and act as though school and home represent two totally separate and different cultures which have to be kept firmly apart.

The committee that produced this report was set up by Margaret Thatcher, who was to become prime minister four years later. The evidence of conservative governments from 2010 onwards has shown that such a report would not now be written, mainly because of an ideological commitment to 'Standard English' as dubiously defined in the national curriculum of 2014.[4] Consequently we find a lack of encouragement for children to bring their culture and experiences to the classroom, for example, through their writing. In his essay in *The Good Immigrant*,[5] Darren Chetty recalls the experiences he had with his multi-cultural Year 2 class in East London, in particular how challenging the children found it to incorporate protagonists of colour in their stories, despite being encouraged to draw on the people in their own life and community for inspiration. When a child attempted to do this and shared their work with the class, a peer said, "You can't do that! Stories have to be about white people." As part of CLPE's the Power of Poetry project,[6] a teacher reported a Year 4 child being awestruck after watching a video performance by poet Valerie Bloom and stating, "I didn't know poets can be black people too. I thought Valerie Bloom was white."

These two examples provide evidence of an underlying belief that books and the literary space were understood by these children to be an exclusive domain for white characters and authors. Consequently their identity as writers was restricted.

Our approach to teaching reading and writing is designed to support the needs, identities, and experiences of all children, particularly those whose backgrounds and cultures are too often not reflected in texts, nor in the national curriculum. A key part of this support is choosing and using texts in the classroom which include diverse characters and which are produced by a diverse range of creators, showcasing a range of ways to use language effectively and authentically.

The complexities of writing

What we ask of children in producing writing is an immense task and an ability to put together so many different aspects of learning and knowledge concurrently. There are a multitude of different elements that a child must consider when they come to write, which can make the task of writing overwhelming for children. Not only must they have an idea of what is to be written and how to translate their thought to words on the page, they must also consider how it will be received by the reader. This includes knowledge about the purpose of the writing and how it will be organised; an awareness of the audience for the writing and the voice (G) and style it should be written in, including knowledge of appropriate language and grammar; knowledge of letters, sounds, and spelling; letter formation for handwriting or typing or dictation skills for digital texts; and the ability to check and edit writing for sense, meaning, and clarity and to evaluate the potential reaction of a reader.[7]

There is also a need to consider the time needed for writing, compared to talking, listening, and reading. A young writer must have the ability to hold ideas in their minds and slow their thinking to produce writing at a manageable rate. The more children can automatically commit words to memory, the easier this will become. In addition to quick recall of spellings, fluent handwriting also contributes to fluent composition of writing. Sometimes, even older children will need additional opportunities to develop gross and fine motor skills to support efficient grip of writing implements and the development of a fluent writing style. Developments in dictation features in computer programs can support children for whom the physical labour of writing is a particular challenge.

The teacher is the person who guides the young writer to understand the purpose and practices of writing and models the process involved in a way that helps pupils at each stage of the process. This is crucial in gaining an understanding of the labour and process of writing and in understanding and empathising with the challenges that young writers face when they are tasked with writing. Being able to model writing live to children is key to this.[8]

Teachers model, in an organic way, real writing in progress, not a model which has been prepared in advance. They show the children how to move from an idea to an oral composition and then how to manage the stream of ideas to translate the oral language into written text. Teachers also build the skills and processes of handwriting, spelling, and so on (the transcription side of writing) so that these do not impede children's composition of ideas for their writing.

Teaching writing therefore needs to explore a range of activities, as shown in the lesson sequences in the previous chapters. A mixture of tightly focused activities encouraging children to directly use and apply phonic knowledge in writing prepared words, phrases, and sentences, which teachers dictate for children to write independently during the taught sessions, focuses children's energy on transcription. In contrast, more loosely structured activities are also suggested.[9] These use real books to provide contextualised purposes and contexts for writing and opportunities for children to use and apply their phonic knowledge to compose writing of their own, based on the texts read. This gives children valuable opportunities to use and apply their phonic knowledge independently whilst making choices about their writing – what it contains and how it is composed. As an extension of these sessions, the combination of working with the book and independent writing opportunities offered alongside the book provides a foundation for even more creative work, for example, using the process approach to writing that gives children choices about what to write and how.

Reading as a model for writing

In the CLPE research project and publication *The Reader in the Writer*, Myra Barrs and Valerie Cork[10] set out to explore the changes which took place in children's writing when teachers introduced them to challenging literature in real books and provided time for the discussion and study of literature in the classroom. The research established a clear link between children's involvement with literary texts and their development as writers, giving evidence of children's growing ability to write from within a fictional situation, to be attuned to literary styles and rhythms, to imagine a likely reader, and to work to influence this reader's response. Although initially conducted as a small-scale research project with six classes of 10- and 11-year-olds (Year 5 in England), this work still inspires much of the work done now at CLPE, including the Power of Reading Programme, which looks at how to teach a book-based literature curriculum to children from 3–11 years.

The most recent evaluation of the impact of the Power of Reading Programme in England included analysis of statutory test data for children aged 10 to 11 from the schools involved; teacher evaluations of the training days; quality assurance visits to schools to investigate the effectiveness of the implementation of the training in practice; and New Salford Reading Age Tests for baseline, interim, and final assessments of pupils. One of the recommendations of the evaluation was to "encourage the use of Power of Reading as an effective intervention for reading and catalyst for developing Quality First Teaching."[11] This exploratory evaluation has been augmented by a robust RCT of The Power of Pictures approach, as you will see later in this chapter.

Real books provide children with examples of writing crafted by professional writers for their intended audience. Such texts offer children the opportunity to explore language in action, judiciously chosen and used for impact on their intended audiences. This also offers a way to explore and incorporate a contextualised focus on grammar. Reflecting on the effectiveness of grammar teaching for improving writing, Dominic Wyse and Carole Torgerson found that:

> Small group and whole class teaching that includes a focus on the actual use of grammar in real examples of writing (including professionally produced pieces, realistic examples produced by teachers, including 'think aloud' live drafting of text, and drafts of pupils' writing) may also be more effective.[12]

As part of contextualised teaching of language and grammar, children will be best supported by adults who:

- know how to consolidate and build on children's existing knowledge about language – including the children's languages and dialects spoken;
- talk about the impact and specific effects created by an author's language and grammar choices;
- explain grammatical concepts clearly through examples from quality and authentic texts;
- support children to transfer this knowledge into their own writing and how to make meaning through language and grammar choices.

Children will become competent language users when they have had opportunity to see language in action, exploring how language can be chosen to achieve a specific effect on the reader, how different written forms have different voices, and how they sound different. They internalise these voices and draw on familiar structures in their own writing – the more experienced reader being more competent in a wider range of written forms, having gained implicit understanding. As Margaret Meek noted: "if we want to see what lessons have been learned from the texts children read, we have to look for them in what they write."[13] Only when a child is competent in using language in this way will they be able to absorb the terminology used to describe the choices that they and other authors make and, in turn, make successful writing choices of their own.

Example of a writing lesson

Controlling writing choices can be explored in practice through the use of a text, in this instance *Growing Frogs* by Vivian French, illustrated by Alison Bartlett[14] The text provides children with an introduction to technical and subject-specific vocabulary and precise use of language in phrases like "in the middle of each jelly shell", "no giant frogs here!", and "scooped a little of the frogspawn" (see Figure 13.1). The text has a dual purpose: the main text provides information through a fictional narrative, based on a character's experiences of nature; the accompanying text around the illustration delivers information pertinent to the narrative. The change in style and tone allows young children to see the shift and differences between narrative and informational writing, modelling the voice and style of each effectively.

The examples we give here resulted from the use of this text with four- and five-year-old children (Reception class in England). The activities included a range of real-life experiences such as an opportunity to engage in pond dipping, keeping a tank of frogspawn in the classroom, and observing the changes as the eggs hatched to tadpoles and the tadpoles grew into froglets before releasing these back into the wild, and reading a wider range of information and story texts on the subject of frogs and other lifecycles. The examples of writing shown in Figures 13.2 and 13.3 are drafts of writing, initially composed on dry-wipe whiteboards, in preparation for writing information for visitors to the classroom to learn more about the tadpoles that were housed in the tank.

From the writing samples we can see that both children have been engaged by the topic and text stimulus, gaining knowledge, understanding, and vocabulary from the text read and practical experiences they have engaged in. Both have a strong authorial voice, understanding how to use language to convey information, and are not afraid to engage with complex vocabulary for which they did not know the conventional spellings. Both children showed awareness that meaning can be conveyed in both text and illustrations, both choosing to include an accompanying illustration linked to their writing.

The children appeared to be confident to use and extend their knowledge of letter-phoneme (G) relationships and the skills of blending and segmenting, as well as their wider knowledge of words, to attempt to spell 'surrounded', 'jelly', and 'suddenly'. The child in Figure 13.2 showed their awareness of the vowel (G) digraph (G) /ee/ in the way in which they coloured in the letters, signalling their connection.

The next steps for both children are evident from looking at the samples. The focus for the child in Figure 13.2 would be on the words that did not conform to their letter-phoneme knowledge: words such as 'are', 'by', and 'they'. The child in Figure 13.3 showed understanding of such words, spelling 'the', 'so', and 'they' correctly. The focus for this child would be on hearing and representing spoken sounds correctly in writing, using the correct letter-phoneme correspondences, particularly in representing clusters and digraphs in words like 'strong' and 'back'.

These examples illustrate the effectiveness of our approach in action. The real text and rich experiences provided, coupled with contextualised teaching of phonics, contributed to authentic, confident, and independent early writing and learning about a natural biological phenomenon. This is the level of deep engagement and attainment that we want to see from children in the Early Years as part of a developmentally appropriate, creative curriculum.

The reader in the writer 235

Figure 13.1 Internal page spread from *Growing Frogs*[15]

236 *The art of teaching*

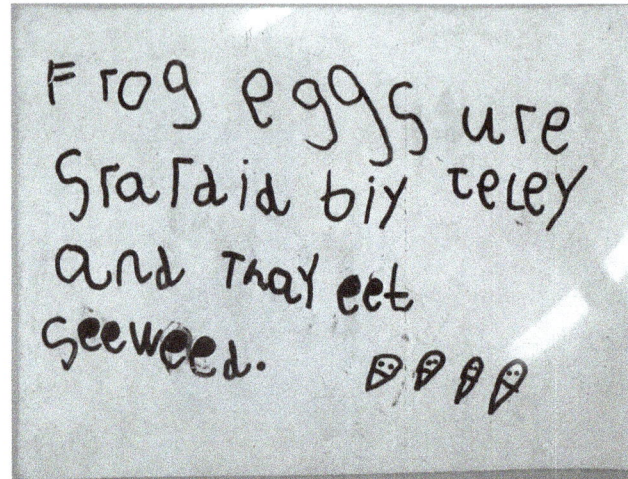

Figure 13.2 Writing sample by a child aged five: "Frog eggs are surrounded by jelly and they eat seaweed."

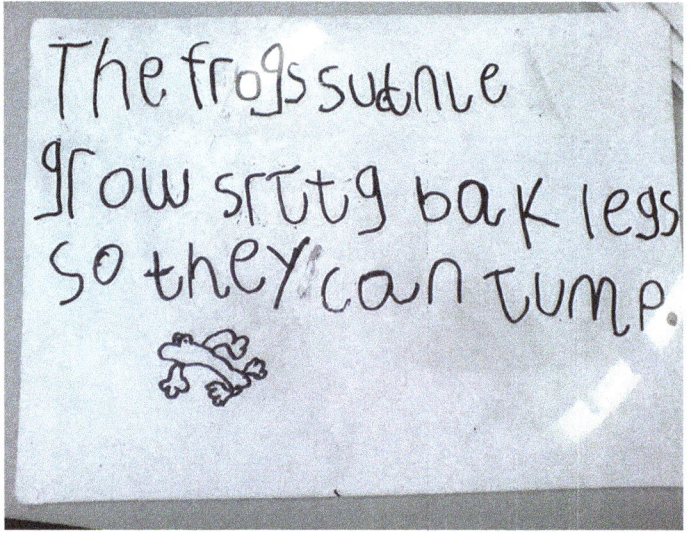

Figure 13.3 Writing sample by a child aged five: "The frogs suddenly grow strong back legs so they can jump."

Following an authentic writing process

Creating an authentic model of writing in the classroom allows students to feel what it is like to be a writer. It is so much more than simply 'doing' writing tasks. An authentic process results in well-developed pieces of writing: pupils follow a truly creative process and have the impetus to write for themselves. The core focus of an authentic writing process is on giving pupils a credible opportunity to develop their own voice, have a choice about what they want to say and how they say it, and have the chance to write with freedom. The Double Helix of Reading and Writing has the composition of writing at the centre of the model. In Chapter 4, "The Science of Teaching Reading and Writing", we explored the research showing the effectiveness of the process approach to writing. We now turn to another practical example of teaching the processes of writing.

The writing process outlined in Figure 13.4 was developed by CLPE, in partnership with published author-illustrators as part of their Power of Pictures professional development programme. The Power of Pictures was borne from insights from CLPE's Power of Reading programme about the impact of picture books and artistic approaches on children's reading and writing. The Power of Pictures aims to raise children's reading and writing skills by enhancing teachers' understanding of the writing process, using picture books as a medium. Published author-illustrators work with teachers to explore the author's writing processes, looking at how this can be translated into the classroom with children from age 3 to 11. Pupils also connect with the author-illustrator through specially produced videos which introduce the author-illustrator to the pupils and share them reading one of their books and how to illustrate a key character, as well as giving insights into how they developed the focus picture book. Lesson plans support teachers in exploring a focus picture

Figure 13.4 CLPE's model demonstrating the core components of an authentic writing process[16]

book by the author-illustrator to understand how the story has been created and shaped before encouraging pupils to use this knowledge to develop their own picture books.

The following writing process model describes the steps a practising writer goes through so that this process can then be replicated in the classroom. Each circle represents a different stage of the process. A writer will often work through each of the stages in sequence, but the continuous line between each small circle aims to show how a writer will often have to go back and forth through the steps as work is developed over time and the writing progresses from ideation to publication.

At its centre the model shows that a classroom needs to work as a community of writers: a place where the writer identity of all pupils is fostered, developed, and celebrated. The teacher adopts the dual positions of a teacher who is an active and practised writer, addressing the skills and knowledge about writing, and a writer who teaches the craft of writing. In a purposeful writing community, pupils and adults work together to support each other to develop, reflect on, and celebrate writing.

Ideation is the process of generating and developing new ideas for writing. Teaching and demonstrations of writing will focus on where and how we get ideas from in the real world of writers and writing. Children will be provided with the time, space, stimuli, and resources to begin to form ideas for their own writing for real purposes and audiences. Ideas could be stimulated by stories, books, and information read or seen; personal experiences and feelings; real-life events; or a specific stimulus such as music, art, drama, film, or dance.

Teachers can support children by modelling and sharing how to come up with ideas for their own writing by reading to them and encouraging them to read widely and often; to spend time thinking; to draw and doodle; to talk with others; to watch or listen to different kinds of media or performances; or to engage in cultural experiences, such as art, theatre, music, and dance.

Instead of writing straight into set exercise books, children could be provided with writing journals or sketchbooks with the purpose of using these to explore and play with ideas prior to writing. Drawing remains a key part of the writing process and is encouraged: drawing, sketches, and visual organisers can be used by writers to map, explore, and develop ideas. As author Gill Lewis explains, and as can be seen in her sketches in Figure 13.5:

> I have to draw before I start writing. Drawing unlocks the mind. When words are hard to find, drawing bypasses the two-dimensional tickertape language centre of the brain. Thinking visually fills the head in glorious technicolour. The mountains of the mind fill the void. Rivers roar and landscapes unfold in three dimensions. Characters walk in, demanding adventure. We step onto the path of infinite possibilities where stories begin to happen. When scribbles and doodles fill the page, words soon follow.

Creation is the act of writing. The initial ideas are shaped with a purpose, audience, and form of writing in mind. Teachers can model different ways to capture, work up, and develop ideas in the journey towards publication, such as through the use of notes, drawings, visual representations, and voice recordings. Sharing the processes of real writers, for example, through images of their journals, notebooks, and sketchbooks, is a valuable part of this process. This shares how the creation process begins rough and messy; that writing is shaped, developed, and becomes ordered over time through re-working; and that this is a positive practice, as can be seen in the examples from author-illustrator Ed Vere in Figure 13.6.

Figure 13.5 Preparatory sketches for the novel *Moon Bear*, sharing the development of Gill Lewis' initial story ideas[17]

240 *The art of teaching*

Figure 13.6 Preparatory work from Ed Vere for *How to Be a Lion*[18]

At this stage of writing, it is important that children be given time and space to play with and work up ideas, supported by teachers modelling and demonstrating this in their own writing.

Reflection is the act of reviewing the writing produced in order to make sense of the content and to make appropriate changes if they are required. Through shared demonstrations of their own and the children's writing, teachers and children can work together to look at where ideas are working well, drawing on their knowledge of what they have seen as being effective in published texts they have read, and where challenges or sticking points arise. The focus here should primarily be on the content and overall structure of the writing and whether this fits the purpose, audience, and form, rather than the technical handling of the writing system (spelling, punctuation, etc.).[19] Reading the writing aloud is a crucial part of this process, so that writers can hear how the words sound and flow off the page.

Children are provided with opportunities to work with a supportive peer or teacher to gain an audience for their writing. With younger or less experienced writers, scaffolds for the kinds of questions that could be asked to prompt thinking and develop ideas can be used, for example:

- Does the story make sense?
- Do you engage with the characters?
- What parts make sense; what parts could be refined or improved?
- Does the story flow?
- Are you engaged as a reader; would you want to turn the page and find out what happens next?
- Are you emotionally engaged with the story?

Understanding that ideas that are not working can be discarded can be liberating for young writers. They will also need to see, through teacher modelling, how to edit work effectively, adapting and improving sections of their work rather than simply re-writing the whole piece.

Drawing on the experiences of real life writers is key. Picture book maker Chris Haughton takes up to two years to realise a picture book. Author S.F. Said works through multiple drafts of each novel he writes. Whilst understanding that this is impractical in a classroom context, this teaches valuable lessons about the time and space needed to craft writing. Many of the teachers on the Power of Pictures programme independently talked about the idea of 'slowing things down to speed things up', recognising the depth and quality that can be achieved by children when this is realised in the classroom:

> It's helped me appreciate the importance and difficulty of the writing process. It has changed my perception of editing, i.e. that this is part of the creation process. It has also helped me understand lots of the difficulties that children have; namely generating ideas, considering audience, understanding the structure of writing. More time needs to be given to the ideation process and support with structuring texts. Children just need time to produce quality.

Publication is the means to present writing in a way that is most appropriate for the purpose, audience, and form. This may be through the spoken as well as the written form and may also involve digital communication, if appropriate. Prior to publication, writers should work with a supportive partner to polish the work ready for publication, proof-reading work and checking for spelling and punctuation accuracy.

Access to resources and materials that facilitate the most appropriate forms of publication, reflecting those used by practising writers, should be provided to give children the full sense of the satisfaction that publishing and presenting writing can bring, including using appropriate technology for specific forms and techniques for making and binding handmade books and for digital formats. A focus on the use of legible handwriting at this stage appropriately supports children to present their work effectively for an audience.

Opportunities to display and present work allow children to gain a sense of the satisfaction of publishing work for an audience, who can be prompted to offer responses on the effect the writing had on them.

The page from a child's picture book in Figure 13.7 shows an example of published writing in an achievably conceivable classroom context at its full effect. Its seven-year-old writer generated their own idea for a picture book story. They were able to write fluently, with correct spellings appropriate to their age and stage of development, including words with common suffixes. Sentences are appropriate to the form, effectively composed and punctuated, and the storyline and way in which the text is presented introduce the narrative in a way that effectively engages a reader.

Impact on teachers and pupils

In 2019 the Power of Pictures approach was tested at scale as part of an evaluation jointly funded by the Education Endowment Foundation (EEF) and the Royal Society of Arts (RSA), evaluated by the Institute of Education, University College London, and the Behavioural Insights Team.[21]

The evaluation design was a randomised controlled trial (RCT) and implementation and process evaluation which included 1264 pupils in 51 schools using the approach. 1410 pupils in 50 schools acted as a comparison group. The evaluation found that:

- pupils who received the Power of Pictures (PoP) programme had, on average, higher writing scores (equivalent to one month of additional progress) as compared to children in the control group;[22]
- among children eligible for free school meals (FSMs), those in schools where PoP was delivered in also made one additional month's progress.
- children in PoP schools had higher writing self-efficacy and writing creativity (ideation) scores than those from schools in which the programme was not taught;
- the visual element of this programme attracted learners who traditionally have difficulties engaging in literacy activities;
- teachers reported high levels of engagement with the programme, not only from the pupils and themselves but also from the senior leadership team (SLT) at their schools.

CLPE's work has gone on to explore and test the effectiveness of this model in a range of other writing genres, including poetry and extended narrative. When teachers are able to provide and draw on real text examples of the kind of writing being explored in lessons and draw on resources which exemplify and allow children to replicate processes used by practising writers, children have a greater understanding of the purpose of writing and a greater sense of engagement in the process and show greater independence and originality

Figure 13.7 Example of a page from a published picture book by a seven-year-old pupil on CLPE's the Power of Pictures programme[20]

in what they produce. As part of CLPE's internal evaluations of its work, reflections about the programme from teachers are often like these:

> Working alongside creatives has improved our student's engagement as they love seeing them in the videos and feel a personal connection to them. Working with creatives has vastly improved our knowledge and understanding of an authentic writing process – hearing the way they gather ideas, plan their pieces, how they work in rough and then refine has been so valuable.
>
> Everything has a purpose – we're always talking about who this is for, who do we want to impact. Children are creating their own picture books in Year 1 now, having high level discussions about impact on their readers, even in the youngest year groups. Children are making choices based on what impact they want to achieve. We're seeing the sophistication of choices starting to come through. Adopting the authentic writing process model has already had a massive impact on children and what they think writing is for.

Tensions caused by England's national curriculum and assessment frameworks for writing and teachers' confidence in allowing children to have choice and voice in their writing were, however, identified as a potential barrier towards this way of working, as the process evaluation of the PoP evaluation showed. Many teachers on the project cited 'National Curriculum requirements' and 'expectations for assessment' as barriers, but they were also aware that the approach led to more original and independent writing than those that were being produced in many classrooms.

Voice, choice, and agency (G)

The children involved in the PoP were able to gain a greater sense of self-efficacy and investment in their work, as they created picture books independently. The ideas for the characters and storylines came from and were developed by them, with the support of teachers and peers. The extensive exploration of the key text taught them how a picture book narrative could be achieved. The opportunity for children to be truly creative was significant to the teachers involved, many of whom reported that this was the first time their children had written an entire narrative, devised from their own ideas, independently. As this project teacher reflected:

> The children were not used to creating something they have such ownership over. They embraced the opportunity to create something using largely their own ideas. They were engaged and had increased pride in their work, they wanted to share it with lots of teachers. Teachers of other year groups were impressed and motivated by the lesson outcomes.

This approach can also be used with other forms of writing, for example, newspaper reports through understanding the authentic processes of journalism before compiling independent news stories on topics of the children's interest.

When children have experience of the function and purpose of different kinds of writing and the ways in which writing of different text types can be developed and composed, supported by the study of how this is realised in authentic texts by practising writers, they will have the knowledge and experience to choose and use a variety of different forms to write based on their own ideas and motivations. Young children benefit from a well-stocked dedicated area for writing in the classroom, access to a range and breadth of texts, and time and space put aside for children to write of their own volition.

A purposeful writing classroom, which develops the reader in the writer and the writer in the reader, is one which:

- gives prominence to writing and writers in the classroom, understanding the integral relationship between language, texts (including the producers of the texts), readers, and writers;
- showcases a variety of different purposes for writing using examples of real-life texts and those produced by the adults and children in the space;
- balances the compositional and transcriptional elements of writing in effective demonstrations of and interventions in writing;
- provides opportunities and choice for writing in own time, independently and collaboratively;
- provides choice in how children shape and design their own texts;
- includes a range of resources and media for writing at each different stage of the process, such as models and inspirations, a wide variety of writing tools and paper stock, word processing and other appropriate technology and media to present writing in authentic ways, handwriting guides, special pens, and bookmaking materials;
- allows support, space, and time for children to discuss, gain responses to, and edit their work prior to publication along with the resources and technology to support this part of the process, such as word banks, dictionaries, and thesauruses – published and classroom made, highlighters, different-coloured pens for editing, and large Post-It notes for re-drafting sections;
- celebrates the written work of children through display, performance, and publication, allowing children to see the full purpose of writing and feel a complete sense of authorship.

To effectively enable children to develop the knowledge, skills, and attitudes to write, they must be provided with an environment and provision in which they readily identify as writers and which develops them as authentic writers from the start. If children see and understand that writing is a means of communication, which allows them to explore ideas and to express themselves, then the teaching of the technical skills, including phonics, spelling, and punctuation, becomes a real and relevant experience to enable them to become more skilful and proficient writers. Without developing children's intrinsic motivation to write and their sense of identity as a writer, writing becomes a secretarial activity, and children's enthusiasm to write for a range of purposes and audiences and in a variety of forms is lost.

In understanding the crucial interrelationship between reading and writing, and in developing an understanding of language and how it can be used in a variety of contexts, children learn the effects that writing can have on them as a reader, gaining a sense of authorial intent from the start of their education.

This chapter of the series of chapters that have exemplified how the balanced approach to teaching phonics, reading, and writing can be implemented by teachers has focused on the fundamental idea of children having their own identity as readers and writers. Although the sequence of the chapters of a book suggest a linear progression, respect for children's identities in all sorts of ways is essential from the first time a teacher meets a new class of children and begins one of the most satisfying parts of being a primary teacher:

unlocking the power of reading and writing, a gift for the whole of each generation of children's lives. In the next and final chapter of the book, we look to possible futures.

Notes

1. Dunsmuir, S., & Blatchford, P. (2004). Predictors of Writing Competence in 4- to 7-Year-Old Children. *British Journal of Educational Psychology, 74*(3), 461–483. Retrieved December 1, 2023, from https://doi.org/10.1348/0007099041552323
2. Bradford, H., & Wyse, D. (2020). Two-Year-Old and Three-Year-Old Children's Writing: The Contradictions of Children's and Adults' Conceptualisations. *Early Years*. Retrieved December 1, 2023, from https://doi.org/10.1080/09575146.2020.1736519
3. Dombey, H. (2013). What We Know about Teaching Writing. *Preschool & Primary Education, 1*(1), 22–40. Retrieved December 1, 2023, from https://doi.org/org/10.12681/PPEJ.40
4. Wyse, D., Bradford, H., & Winstanley, J.-M. (2023). *Teaching English, Language and Literacy* (5th ed.). Routledge.
5. Shukla, N. (Ed.). (2017). *The Good Immigrant* (p. 96). Unbound.
6. CLPE. (2018). *The Power of Poetry Research Summary*. Retrieved December 1, 2023, from https://clpe.org.uk/system/files/The%20Power%20of%20Poetry%20Research%20Summary%202017.pdf
7. Gregg, L., & Steinberg, E. (2018). *Cognitive Processes in Writing*. Routledge.
8. Horner, S. (2010). *Magic Dust that Lasts. Writers in Schools – Sustaining the Momentum*. Arts Council England. Retrieved December 1, 2023, from https://www.suehorner.com/resources/ACE_published_version_of_Magic_Dust.pdf
9. For a figure showing a continuum of loosely structured to tightly structured writing approaches see p, 190 of Wyse, Bradford, & Winstanley, *Teaching English*.
10. Barrs, M., & Cork, V. (2001). *The Reader in the Writer: The Links between the Study of Literature and Writing Development at Key Stage 2*. Centre for Language in Primary Education.
11. Doherty, J. (2019). *Strategic School Improvement Fund (SSIF): Round 2 Diminishing the Gap for Disadvantaged Pupils in Key Stage 2 Reading* (p. 36). Centre for Literacy in Primary Education (CLPE).
12. Wyse, D., & Torgerson, C. (2017). Experimental Trials and 'What Works?' in Education: The Case of Grammar for Writing. *British Educational Research Journal, 43*(6), 1019–1047. Retrieved December 1, 2023, from https://doi.org/10.1002/berj.3315
13. Meek, M. (1988). *How Texts Teach What Readers Learn* (p. 48). Thimble Press.
14. *Growing Frogs*. Written by Vivian French and illustrated by Alison Bartlett. Walker Books (2000).
15. Text © 2000 Vivian French Illustrations © 2000 Alison Bartlett. From *Growing Frogs*. Written by Vivian French and illustrated by Alison Bartlett. Reproduced by permission of Walker Books Ltd, London, SE11 5HJ. Retrieved December 1, 2023, from www.walker.co.uk
16. Centre for Literacy in Primary Education (CLPE), & Hacking, C. (2020). *The Power of a Rich Reading Classroom* (p. 106). SAGE.
17. Reproduced with permission from Gill Lewis from preparatory work for *Moon Bear*, written by Gill Lewis, Oxford University Press (2014).
18. Reproduced with permission from Ed Vere, from preparatory work for *How to Be a Lion*, written and illustrated by Ed Vere, Puffin (2018).
19. Richmond, J. (2015). *English, Language and Literacy 3 to 19: Writing 7 to 16*. Owen Education and UKLA.
20. Reproduced with kind permission from Summercroft Primary School, Bishop's Stortford, UK.
21. Although Dominic Wyse was part of the research team, he was not at that time working with Charlotte Hacking. EEF-funded evaluations have separate teams for evaluation and intervention: Anders, J., Shure, N., Wyse, D., Barnard, M., Abdi, F., & Frerichs, J. (2021). *Power of Pictures: Evaluation Report*. Retrieved December 1, 2023, from https://educationendowmentfoundation.org.uk/projects-and-evaluation/projects/power-of-pictures
22. The report makes clear the standard statistical uncertainty about the precise amount of the gains.

14 A better future for children's education

Amongst all the different views that are part of the debates about teaching phonics, reading, and writing, there is a common cause: the vital importance of children learning to read and write. For many people the ideal of children becoming life-long lovers of language, reading, and writing is what drives their passion for better teaching. The main disagreements in the debates are about the best ways to ensure that *all* children achieve not only the basic skills of reading and writing but also progress way beyond the basics. If children are to be well served by education systems, then reconciliation of the reading wars and collaboration by researchers, teachers, and policy makers is the best way forward.

This book has presented the case for a new evidence-based approach: a balanced approach to teaching phonics, reading, and writing that is needed to ensure that all children make optimal progress in education and consequently in their future lives. This case for the balanced approach has been made theoretically through the new model of the Double Helix of Reading and Writing, which draws on the most robust research evidence about effective teaching. We have exemplified the new approach with detailed examples of practice, and these chapters of the book also alert readers to many principles of practice that can be adapted by teachers to meet the specific contexts of the classes and schools that they teach in.

We have identified an international trend of increasing pressures to adopt narrow forms of synthetic phonics (G) based on what has been called 'the science of reading', but close scrutiny of these claims shows that the research on effective teaching does not support narrow approaches. Strong policy agendas mandating a single approach such as synthetic phonics, driven by influential individuals and based on partial understandings of the full research picture, will result in inappropriate distortions in national, state, and school curricula. Contrary to what are no doubt well-meaning efforts, these policies are in danger of harming children's education because their implementation is not sufficiently close to the strong research base that already exists.

In England the policies on teaching reading became the most extreme, particularly compared with New Zealand, Canada, Ireland, and the other countries of the UK. The history of England's extreme approach can be seen in a key report from 2006,[1] strongly influenced by one disputed research study, which laid the ground for changes that would by 2022 be seen as unique in the context of 100 years of primary education in England.[2] These policies were championed through the self-declared "obsession" of a Member of Parliament.[3] This obsession appeared to have influenced a whole government department, the Department for Education, to instigate a range of policies that in combination came to reflect the highest level of direct control of the teaching of reading in primary education ever seen. This same politician also came to influence education in Australia.

DOI: 10.4324/9781003442134-17

The publication of a 176-page government manual on the methods for teaching reading and writing[4] demonstrated an unprecedented level of interference in the work of teachers as professionals. No authors apart from the Department of Education were credited for the document. Knowing who authored any publication is vital for understanding potential biases. While this manual cited *some* strong relevant studies, its selection was partial and the reasons and methods for selection of research unexplained; consequently there were significant omissions.

The capacity for governments and individual politicians to assume so much control over any element of the curriculum and teaching methods is highly problematic. Policies on teaching reading and writing, and indeed the whole curriculum, need to be built through sustained collaboration by groups of people with the most appropriate expertise. This expertise needs to reflect multidisciplinary perspectives. With regard to teaching reading and writing, such experts include researchers, teachers, teacher educators, and policy makers. Government direction on the minutiae of teaching, which includes the vetting of phonics schemes, is not appropriate: more general guidance is what is needed in education policies. Undue influence on the methods of teaching that are matters for professionals to determine is inappropriate and counterproductive. The 18-year trajectory of policies on teaching reading in England needed to change. Most of all, narrow ideologically driven aspects of the national curriculum required change. Our argument is that policies and practices for teaching reading and writing should more closely reflect the balanced approach to teaching phonics, reading, and writing that we have advanced in this book.

The apparent need for simplicity in political messaging, a problem caused by experience of engagement with some elements of the media, translates badly into the necessarily subtle practices that expert teachers can bring to evidence-informed teaching and which need to be acknowledged in curriculum policies. Although confident, experienced teachers and head teachers routinely mediate the negative aspects of education policies, the policies should be better in the first place, by which we mean evidence informed and built on rigorous consensus between an appropriately wide range of relevant stakeholders. As we wrote this early in 2024 a general election was imminent, and evolution of the curriculum in England, rather than revolution, looked like a potentially bold policy for an ambitious new government. Measured changes to the policies of the national curriculum and associated guidance, based on a wide range of appropriate research, had the potential to be transformative in so many ways.

National curriculum development appears to work well when a body that is to some degree independent of government acts in a coordinating and leading role to ensure that policies are developed that reflect a balanced review of evidence and are agreed upon through collaboration and consensus: for example, Ireland has led the way in this kind of curriculum development through its National Council for Curriculum and Assessment and the development of its primary national curriculum. Sufficient time to develop policies is vital. There need to be mechanisms that allow for incremental change in policies that transcend the relatively short-term cycles of governments, for example, four- to five-year terms of office, that can be an impediment to sustained development and implementation, particularly when a new political party comes into power. New Zealand and Ireland had achieved this longevity in national curriculum policies.

One of the main characteristics of this book is that its theory, research, and practice reflect the academic discipline of education and the fields of education policy and practice.[5] There have been many books about the teaching of reading which have promoted a science of reading, often arising from psychology and neuroscience, sometimes as the basis for negative critiques of teachers and teaching methods; teacher training; and education research, policies, and practices. Our book draws on some of the important work in psychology and neuroscience, but it also draws on work in other academic disciplines: as such, the account is multidisciplinary. However, most important of all, this book puts forward a view rooted in the academic discipline of education, and in educational practice, commensurate with authors who have both researched and directly experienced teaching and learning in primary schools, and the shifting sands of education policies, over several decades.[6] We hope that the approach we have taken in this book has some of the characteristics of what has been called a "Translational Science",[7] which is a systematic way of bridging robust research and educational practice and policy. There are many research contributions to education by people with similar expertise to ours that simply haven't had the influence in policies that they should have, sometimes for ideological and political reasons.[8]

The balanced act

Assuming that robust evidence, sufficient timescales, and consensus were the main drivers of curriculum reform, what might an evidence-based approach to teaching reading and writing look like? More than ever, in the 21st century, children's voices and agency (G) should be at the heart of their education.[9] The balanced approach is centred on children's interests and their development, including the experiences children bring from the home lives. The cultural variety of families in school communities and in countries across the world, and existential challenges that we face including climate change, provides a pressing need for supporting children's agency as a means for them to have the confidence to create their own futures. Entitlement to a broad and balanced curriculum, and appropriate pedagogy, does not mean the same curriculum for all children. True entitlement is built on recognising the need for *different* curriculum experiences to match the diversity of children in schools.

The vital importance of motivating children to read and write is foundational to the balanced approach presented in this book. It begins with engaging children through some of the best texts written for them. It extends into motivational activities that arise from these texts. This is a far cry from narrow synthetic phonics lessons, which, even when taught expertly, simply haven't the same appeal for children. The balanced approach assumes agentic teachers as professionals who are passionate about education and confident to use teaching methods that they know are effective on the basis of research evidence and the evidence from their own teaching. Narrow synthetic phonics teaching (G) is the opposite: children have no agency, and their teachers and teaching assistants have to 'follow the script'. The balanced approach is firmly based on the most robust research evidence; extreme forms of teaching such as narrow discrete approaches to synthetic phonics are not and hence should be rejected in primary and early years education. Time and again, in countries around the world, extreme forms of phonics teaching have been implemented through major political reforms, and time and time again they have not succeeded.

First and foremost the approach to teaching phonics, reading, and writing should be focused on the use of and creation of real books and other texts. Instead of the drive to support money-making from synthetic phonics schemes, our approach puts the work of authors of books for children centre stage. The potential for pure enjoyment of the best of these books, but also the uniquely wide range of learning that these books provide, which 'decodable books' (G) simply cannot provide, is reason enough. But also we think it is appropriate for the creativity of authors to be rewarded for their work in education more than developers of phonics schemes.

While changes to national curricula and curricula at the level of states and other regions urgently need improvement in some places, and while it is necessary to take the time to do this well, in some countries there is no time to wait. When policies are too narrow it falls on teachers to find ways to resist and mediate the curriculum and high-stakes testing systems, in the best interests of children. In seminal research on creativity, the metaphor of immunisation against the negative effects of high-stakes tests was astutely used in defence of creativity, and this was built on the idea that schools in the UK in the 1970s and 80s were some of the most creative places in the western world.[10] In the same way that the genetics of human beings enable them to resist viruses, so the Double Helix of Reading and Writing could help to resist GERMs.[11] The balanced approach that we advocate can be achieved now in classrooms everywhere.

Many people invoke the metaphor of the pendulum to reflect changing attitudes to education and ways of teaching. Extreme swings of the pendulum are indeed a serious problem when many of the important aspects of teaching reading and writing have been shown to be effective by robust research but each swing of the pendulum results in extreme practices taking hold. Our interpretation is that the strongest and most extreme movements historically have been towards narrow forms of teaching reading and writing. As far as the teaching of reading is concerned, this has nearly always been in the direction of phonics, and increasingly synthetic phonics. And while approaches such as the whole-language approach have generated much commentary, the reality is that such approaches have never been the majority of classrooms and schools around the world.

The balanced approach has not to date had the influence and traction that it deserves in policy and practice. Our conviction is that if serious progress were made towards the adoption of the approach, children's education and hence lives would be enhanced. The passion and commitment that are part of the reading debates need to fuel a new movement for change: a paradigm shift to a balanced approach to teaching phonics, reading, and writing.

Notes

1 Rose, J. (2006). *Independent Review of the Teaching of Early Reading: Final Report*. DfES Publications.
2 Wyse, D., & Bradbury, A. (2022). Reading Wars or Reading Reconciliation? A Critical Examination of Robust Research Evidence, Curriculum Policy, and Teachers' Practices for Teaching Phonics and Reading. *Review of Education*. Retrieved December 1, 2023, from https://doi.org/10.1002/rev3.3314
3 Wyse, D. (2023, 20th October). *Teaching Synthetic Phonics and Reading: PIRLS of Wisdom?* Retrieved December 1, 2023, from https://blogs.ucl.ac.uk/ioe/2023/10/10/teaching-synthetic-phonics-and-reading-pirls-of-wisdom/
4 Department for Education (DfE). (2023). *The Reading Framework*. Department for Education.
5 A case for the importance of education as an academic discipline is made in this paper: Wyse, D. (2020). Presidential Address: The Academic Discipline of Education. Reciprocal Relationships between Practical Knowledge and Academic Knowledge. *British Educational Research Journal*, 46(1), 6–25. Retrieved December 1, 2023, from https://doi.org/10.1002/berj.3597
6 Wyse, D., Bradford, H., & Winstanley, J.-M. (2023). *Teaching English, Language and Literacy* (5th ed.). Routledge.
7 Solari, E., Terry, N., Gaab, N., Hogan, T., Nelson, N., Pentimonti, J., Petscher, Y., & Sayko, S. (2020). Translational Science: A Road Map for the Science of Reading. *Reading Research Quarterly*, 55(S1), 347–360.
8 Fazackerley, A. (2023). *'Shocking' Scale of UK Government's Secret Files on Critics Revealed*. Retrieved November 18, 2023, from https://www.theguardian.com/politics/2023/nov/18/shocking-scale-of-uk-governments-secret-files-on-critics-revealed

James, M. (2012). *Background to Michael Gove's Response to the Report of the Expert Panel for the National Curriculum Review in England*. Retrieved March 30, 2022, from https://www.bera.ac.uk/bera-in-the-news/background-to-michael-goves-response-to-the-report-of-the-expert-panel-for-the-national-curriculum-review-in-england

9 A topic addressed by this longitudinal study: retrieved December 1, 2023, from https://www.ucl.ac.uk/ioe/departments-and-centres/centres/helen-hamlyn-centre-pedagogy-0-11-years/childrens-agency-national-curriculum

10 Hennessey, B. (2010). Intrinsic Motivation and Creativity in the Classroom: Have We Come Full Circle? In R. Beghetto & J. Kaufman (Eds.), *Nurturing Creativity in the Classroom* (pp. 342–365). Cambridge University Press.

11 Global Educational Reform Movement. Fuller, K., & Stevenson, H. (2019). Global Education Reform: Understanding the Movement. *Educational Review, 71*(1), 1–4.

Glossary

Affix   an element such as a prefix or suffix added to the base form of a word in order to modify its meaning or create a new word.
Agency   people's capacity to act, including making choices over things that affect them.
Analogy   comparing similar patterns in words, such as the rime 'ake' in 'make', 'shake', and 'mistake'.
Continuous provision   classroom provision, often play-based, that enables children to select areas and activities inside or outside the classroom and to use and apply learning in a more flexible way than is the case for teacher directed lessons.
Decodable books   specially prepared books that are part of commercial phonics schemes. The books are mainly composed of words that are restricted to those that include the phonemes that children will have learned about as that are part of their phonics teaching.
Digraph   a group of two letters representing a single speech sound.
Disyllabic   a word consisting of two syllables.
Dyslexia   a persistent difficulty in reading and writing, particularly in relation to word-reading and spelling.[1]
Ellipsis   punctuation marked by three evenly spaced dots to indicate an incomplete thought or where words have been intentionally omitted.
Expanded Noun Phrase   a phrase where one or more adjectives are used to add detail to the noun, for example, 'a big, blue door'.
Fluency   in oral language, refers to a smooth and easy flow when speaking. Reading fluency means reading aloud accurately, with appropriate speed of reading and with appropriate prosody.
Formative assessment   forms of assessment that enable teachers to make decisions about next steps for children's learning. These assessments are often ongoing daily assessments including feedback and marking.
Grapheme   a letter or letters (or other visual symbols) that represent a phoneme or phonemes. The smallest meaningful unit in written language.
Home Corner   the area of an early years classroom where imaginative play happens. This may be in the form of a replica of a home environment but can be any kind of recognisable environment which inspires play.
Homophone   a word which sounds the same as another word but which has a different spelling or meaning, for example, bear and bare or so and sew.
Medial position   in the middle of a word, usually referring to a phoneme in the middle of a word.
Morpheme   the smallest meaningful unit of linguistic expression. Morphemes can be words (free morphemes) but also affixes (bound morphemes). For example, the word unhappiness is formed of three morphemes; the base 'happy', with the addition of the prefix 'un-' and suffix 'ness'.
Morphology/Morphological   the forms and structures of words.
Onomatopoeia   the act of creating or using words that include sounds that are similar to the noises the words refer to, for example, 'crash', 'whoosh'.
Onset   any consonant sounds that come before the vowel in a syllable (e.g. c̲/at, **b**/at, **m**/at).
Orthography   the conventional spelling system of a language.
Peer review   the process where experts independently read proposed research papers, and sometimes chapters or books, to determine if they think that they merit publication.
Phoneme   the smallest unit of spoken sound in a language that can distinguish one word from another, for example, /b/ in the word 'bit' versus /p/ in the word 'pit'. There are 44 phonemes in the English language.

Phonemic Awareness   the ability to identify and manipulate individual sounds (or phonemes) in spoken words.

Phonics Screening Check (PSC)   a national test consisting of words and pseudowords used in England to test children's reading. A similar test is also used in Australia.

Phonics Teaching   a range of teaching approaches that involve teaching phonemes and their representations by letters.

Phonological Development   children's development of their understanding of the ways that oral language can be divided into units of sound.

Prosody   the rhythm and intonation of a language when spoken.

Psycholinguistic   an aspect of linguistics that focuses on psychological processes that are part of how language and literacy develop and how they are used.

Reading Buddy   a more experienced reader who is partnered with a less experienced reader in order to support their continued development. A reading buddy may read to their designated reader or act as a support as they listen to their designated reader read to them.

Reliable/Reliability   the idea proved by the results from a research study that if an intervention were to be tried with another sample of similar participants (e.g. pupils), it would have the same kind of effects.

Rime   the vowel and any consonants that follow the onset in a syllable (e.g. c/**at**, m/**at**, b/**at**).

Schwa   the most common vowel sound in the English language, typically unstressed. This sound can be heard at the start of 'about' and at the end of 'hammer'.

Small World Play   children using figures and resources in miniature to build stories and play imaginatively.

Split Vowel Digraph   a vowel digraph which is split by a consonant when represented in a word, for example, the /oe/ in 'toe' is split by the /n/ in 'tone' (which historically has been called 'the magic E').

Syntax   the arrangement of words to create sentences.

Synthetic phonics   a particular approach to teaching reading that strongly emphasises separately teaching phonemes and their representations by letters as the way to help young children learn to read.

Systematic phonics   a range of teaching approaches that involve teaching phonemes and their representations by letters in a systematic way.

Systematic synthetic phonics   the term used by the Department for Education in England to describe their approach to synthetic phonics. The term is tautologous because synthetic phonics is by definition systematic. There are other phonics approaches that are systematic and effective.

Trigraph   a group of three letters representing a single speech sound.

Voice   with regard to writing, refers to tone of writing, word choices, and points of view, supported by syntax, punctuation, and rhythm.[2]

Vowel   a speech sound produced when the breath flows out through the mouth without being blocked by the teeth, tongue, or lips. There are short vowels in words like 'cup' or 'dog' and long vowels in words like 'rain' and 'light'. Also means a letter that represents a vowel sound.

Whole-Language Teaching   an approach to teaching reading that emphasises the use of engaging whole texts first and foremost to teach children how to read. Smaller units such as phonemes, letters, and words are taught non-systematically.

Working memory   the information that is used in support of cognitive tasks. For writing, working memory includes phonological, visuospatial, and semantic components. Working memory is different from long-term memory.

Notes

1 International Literacy Association. (2023). *Research Advisory: Dyslexia*. International Literacy Association. Retrieved October 30, 2023, from https://www.literacyworldwide.org/docs/default-source/where-we-stand/research-advisory-dyslexia.pdf

2 The 'Ear of the Writer' was the related concept developed in the book *How Writing Works: From the Invention of the Alphabet to the Rise of Social Media* by Dominic Wyse (Cambridge University Press).

References

Academic

Adams, M. J. (2000). *The three-cueing system*. Retrieved July 30, 2023, from http://www.ednews.org/articles/6017/1/The-Three-Cueing-System/Page1.html

Adesope, O., Lavin, T., Thompson, T., & Ungerleider, C. (2010). Pedagogical strategies for teaching literacy to ESL immigrant students: a meta-analysis. *British Journal of Educational Psychology*, *81*, 629–653.

Amass, H. (2022, 22nd April). How phonics became an education culture war. *Tes Magazine*. Retrieved December 1, 2023, from https://www.tes.com/magazine/teaching-learning/primary/how-phonics-became-education-culture-war

Anders, J., Shure, N., Wyse, D., Barnard, M., Abdi, F., & Frerichs, J. (2021a). *Power of pictures: evaluation report*. Retrieved December 1, 2023, from https://educationendowmentfoundation.org.uk/projects-and-evaluation/projects/power-of-pictures

Anders, J., Shure, N., Wyse, D., Sutherland, A., Barnard, M., & Frerichs, J. (2021b). *Learning about culture overarching evaluators' report*. Education Endowment Foundation (EEF).

Andrews, R., Torgerson, C., Beverton, S., Freeman, A., Locke, T., Low, G., Robinson, A., & Zhu, D. (2004). *The effect of grammar teaching (sentence combining) in English on 5 to 16 year olds' accuracy and quality in written composition*. Retrieved December 1, 2023, from http://eppi.ioe.ac.uk/cms/

Arizpe, E., Noble, K., & Styles, M. (2023). *Children reading pictures: new contexts and approaches to picturebooks* (3rd ed.). Routledge.

Aukerman, M. (2023). *The Science of Reading and the Media: Is Reporting Biased?* Retrieved November 25, 2023, from https://literacyresearchassociation.org/stories/the-science-of-reading-and-the-media-is-reporting-biased/?s=09

Barras, C. (2023). As tricky as ABC. *The New Scientist*, 42–45. Retrieved December 1, 2023, from https://www.newscientist.com/article/mg25834350-200-we-know-how-kids-learn-to-read-so-why-are-we-failing-to-teach-them/

Barrs, M., & Cork, V. (2001). *The reader in the writer*. Centre for Language in Primary Education (CLPE).

Berninger, V. W., Vaughan, K., Abbott, R., Begay, K., Coleman, K., Curtin, G., Hawkins, J., & Graham, S. (2002). Teaching spelling and composition alone and together: implications for the simple view of writing. *Journal of Educational Psychology*, *94*(2), 291–304.

Bishop, R. S. (1990). *Multicultural literacy: mirrors, windows, and sliding doors*. Retrieved October 19, 2023, from https://scenicregional.org/wp-content/uploads/2017/08/Mirrors-Windows-and-Sliding-Glass-Doors.pdf

Bowers, J. (2020). Reconsidering the evidence that systematic phonics is more effective than alternative methods of reading instruction. *Educational Psychology Review*. Retrieved December 1, 2023, from https://doi.org/10.1007/s10648-019-09515-y

Bradbury, A. (2018). The Impact of the Phonics Screening Check on Grouping by Ability: A 'Necessary Evil' amid the policy storm. *British Educational Research Journal*, *44*(4), 539–556.

Bradford, H., & Wyse, D. (2020). Two-year-old and three-year-old children's writing: the contradictions of children's and adults' conceptualisations. *Early Years*, *42*(3), 293–309.

Bryant, P., & Bradley, L. (1985). *Children's reading problems: psychology & education*. Basil Blackwell.

Bryant, P., Bradley, L., Maclean, M., & Crossland, J. (1988). Nursery rhymes, phonological skills and reading. *Journal of Child Language*, *16*, 407–428.

Buzzeo, J., Muir, D., & Patel, R. (2023). *Closing the vocabulary gap: project evaluation report.* Retrieved December 1, 2023, from https://www.employment-studies.co.uk/system/files/resources/files/CVG%20evaluation_final%20report%20%28003%29.pdf

Calkins, L. M. (1986). *The art of teaching writing.* Heinemann.

Castles, A., Rastle, K., & Nation, K. (2018). Ending the reading wars: reading acquisition from novice to expert. *Psychological Science in the Public Interest, 19,* 5–51. Retrieved December 1, 2023, from https://doi.org/10.1177/1529100618772271

The Centre for Education and Youth. *Bridging the word gap at transition: the Oxford language report 2020.* Oxford University Press. Retrieved December 1, 2023, from https://fdslive.oup.com/www.oup.com/oxed/wordgap/Bridging_the_Word_Gap_at_Transition_2020.pdf?region=uk

Centre for Language in Primary Education (CLPE). (1988). *The primary language record: handbook for teachers.* Centre for Language in Primary Education.

Centre for Language in Primary Education (CLPE). (1991). *The reading book.* CLPE.

Centre for Literacy in Primary Education (CLPE). (2023a). *The corebooks collections.* Centre for Literacy in Primary Education (CLPE). Retrieved October 23, 2023, from https://clpe.org.uk/books/corebooks/corebooks-collections

Centre for Literacy in Primary Education (CLPE). (2023b). *Reflecting realities research.* CLPE. Retrieved October 19, 2023, from https://clpe.org.uk/research/reflecting-realities

Centre for Literacy in Primary Education (CLPE). *The Power of Pictures Book Selections.* Retrieved October 25, 2023, from https://clpe.org.uk/books/power-of-pictures

Centre for Literacy in Primary Education (CLPE). *Poetry Video Archive.* Retrieved October 25, 2023, from https://clpe.org.uk/poetry/videos

CLPE Corebooks Database. Retrieved October 26, 2023, from https://clpe.org.uk/books/corebooks

Centre for Literacy in Primary Education (CLPE), & Hacking, C. (2020). *The power of a rich reading classroom.* SAGE.

Chall, J. (1983). *Learning to read: the great debate (updated edition).* McGraw Hill.

Chambers, A. (1993). *Tell Me: children, reading and talk.* Thimble Press.

Chambers, A. (2011). *Tell me: children, reading and talk with the reading environment.* Thimble Press.

Chiaet, J. (2013). *Novel finding: reading literary fiction improves empathy.* Retrieved November 13, 2023, from https://www.scientificamerican.com/article/novel-finding-reading-literary-fiction-improves-empathy/

Clarke, M. M. (1976). *Young fluent readers: what can they teach us?* Heinemann Educational.

Clarke, P., Snowling, M., Truelove, E., & Hulme, C. (2010). Ameliorating children's reading-comprehension difficulties: a randomized controlled trial. *Psychological Science, 21*(8), 1106–1116.

Clay, M. (1979). *The early detection of reading difficulties* (3rd ed.). Heinemann Education.

Clay, M. (2016). *Literacy lessons designed for individuals.* The Marie Clay Trust.

CLPE. (2018). *The Power of Poetry Research Summary.* Retrieved December 1, 2023, from https://clpe.org.uk/system/files/The%20Power%20of%20Poetry%20Research%20Summary%202017.pdf

Compton-Lilly, C. (2023). Into the fray: Black English, reading politics, and the legacy of Dr. Ken Goodman. *Journal of Adolescent Adult Literacy, 67,* 111–121.

Connolly, P. (2018). The trials of evidence-based practice in education: a systematic review of randomised controlled trials in education research 1980–2016. *Educational Research, 60,* 276–291.

Cousins, L. (2014). *Peck Peck Peck.* Walker Books Limited.

Cremin, T. (2022). *Reading teachers: nurturing reading for pleasure.* Routledge.

Cripps, C., & Cox, R. (1996). *Joining the ABC: teaching handwriting and spelling together.* LDA.

Crystal, D. (2010a). The Cambridge encyclopedia of language (3rd ed.). Cambridge University Press.

Crystal, D. (2010b). Evolving English: one language, many voices. The British Library.

Clayton, E. (Ed.). (2019). *Writing: Making Your Mark.* The British Library.

Cummins, J. (1984). *Bilingualism and special education: issues in assessment and pedagogy.* Pro Ed.

Cunningham, A. (1990). Explicit versus implicit instruction in phonemic awareness. *Journal of Experimental Child Psychology, 50,* 429–444.

Cushing, I., & Snell, J. (2022). The (white) ears of Ofsted: A raciolinguistic perspective on the listening practices of the schools inspectorate. *Language in Society, 52,* 363–386.

Davis, A. (2017). *A critique of pure teaching methods and the case of synthetic phonics*. Bloomsbury.

Degé, F., Kubicek, C., & Schwarzer, G. (2015). Associations between musical abilities and precursors of reading in preschool aged children. *Frontiers in Psychology*, *6*(1220). Retrieved December 1, 2023, from https://doi.org/10.3389/fpsyg.2015.01220

Department for Education (DfE). (2019). *The ITT core content framework*. Department for Education.

Department for Education (DfE). (2022). *Validation of systematic synthetic phonics programmes: supporting documentation*. Updated 18th January 2022. Retrieved March 2, 2022, from https://www.gov.uk/government/publications/phonics-teaching-materials-core-criteria-and-self-assessment/validation-of-systematic-synthetic-phonics-programmes-supporting-documentation#essential-core-criteria

Department for Education (DfE). (2023). *The reading framework*. Department for Education.

Doherty, J. (2019). *Strategic school improvement fund (SSIF): round 2 diminishing the gap for disadvantaged pupils in key stage 2 reading*. Centre for Literacy in Primary Education (CLPE).

Dombey, H. (2013). What we know about teaching writing. *Preschool & Primary Education*, *1*(1), 22–40. Retrieved December 1, 2023, from https://doi.org/10.12681/PPEJ.40

Dombey, H., & United Kingdom Literacy Association (UKLA). (2010). *Teaching reading: what the evidence says*. Retrieved December 1, 2023, from https://ukla.org/product/teaching-reading-what-the-evidence-says-2/

Doonan, J. (1993). *Looking at pictures in picture books*. The Thimble Press.

Dunsmuir, S., & Blatchford, P. (2004). Predictors of writing competence in 4- to 7-year-old children. *British Journal of Educational Psychology*, *74*(3), 461–483. Retrieved December 1, 2023, from https://doi.org/10.1348/0007099041552323

Durkin, D. (1974). A six year study of children who learned to read in school at the age of four. *Reading Research Quarterly*, *10*(1), 9–61.

Education Endowment Foundation (EEF). (No date). *Improving literacy in key stage 1: guidance report* (p. 16). Education Endowment Foundation (EEF). Retrieved November 23, 2023, from https://d2tic4wvo1iusb.cloudfront.net/production/eef-guidance-reports/literacy-ks-1/Literacy_KS1_Guidance_Report_2020.pdf?v=1700712326

EdWeek Research Centre. (2020). *Early reading instruction: results of a national survey*. Retrieved December 1, 2023, from https://epe.brightspotcdn.com/1b/80/706eba6246599174b0199ac1f3b5/ed-week-reading-instruction-survey-report-final-1.24.20.pdf

Ehri, L. (2009). Grapho-phonemic enrichment strengthens keyword analogy instruction for struggling young readers. *Reading and Writing Quarterly*, *25*(2–3), 162–191.

Ehri, L. (2014). Orthographic mapping in the acquisition of sight word reading, spelling memory, and vocabulary learning. *Scientific Studies of Reading*, *18*(1), 5–21.

Ellis, V. (2023). *England's ITE crisis is a wake-up call on academic autonomy*. Times Higher Education. Retrieved November 22, 2023, from https://www.timeshighereducation.com/opinion/englands-ite-crisis-wake-call-academic-autonomy

Fazackerley, A. (2023). *'Shocking' Scale of UK Government's Secret Files on Critics Revealed*. Retrieved November 18, 2023, from https://www.theguardian.com/politics/2023/nov/18/shocking-scale-of-uk-governments-secret-files-on-critics-revealed

Fleming, M. (2017). *Starting drama teaching*. Routledge.

French, V., & Ahlberg, J. (2012). *Yucky Worms*. Walker Books.

Fuller, K., & Stevenson, H. (2019). Global education reform: understanding the movement. *Educational Review*, *71*(1), 1–4.

Gaiman, N. (2013). *The reading agency annual lecture: why our future depends on libraries, reading and daydreaming*. Retrieved October 12, 2023, from https://www.theguardian.com/books/2013/oct/15/neil-gaiman-future-libraries-reading-daydreaming

Galuschka, K., Ise, E., Krick, K., & Schulte-Korne, G. (2014). Effectiveness of treatment approaches for children and adolescents with reading disabilities: a meta-analysis of randomized controlled trials. *PLoS One*, *9*, 1–12. Retrieved December 1, 2023, from https://doi.org/doi:10.1371/journal.pone.0089900

Gersten, R., & Baker, S. (2001). Teaching expressive writing to students with learning disabilities: A meta-analysis. The Elementary School Journal, 101, 251–272.

Gersten, R., Darch, C., & Gleason, M. (1988). Effectiveness of a direct instruction academic kindergarten for low-income students. *The Elementary School Journal*, *89*, 227–240.

Gersten, R., Haymond, K., Newman-Gonchar, R., Dimino, J., & Jayanthi, M. (2020). Meta-analysis of the impact of reading interventions for students in the primary grades. *Journal of Research on Educational Effectiveness*, *13*(2), 401–427.

Gibb, N. (2021). *My advice to my successors at the department for education*. Retrieved September 29, 2023, from https://www.nickgibb.org.uk/news/my-advice-my-successors-department-education

Gibb, N. (2023). *Nick Gibb MP to step down at next general election*. Retrieved November 18, 2023, from https://www.nickgibb.org.uk/news/nick-gibb-mp-step-down-next-general-election

Goodman, K. (1967). Reading: a psycholinguistic guessing game. *Literacy Research and Instruction*, *6*(4), 126–135. Retrieved December 1, 2023, from https://doi.org/10.1080/19388076709556976

Goouch, K., & Lambirth, A. (2016). *Teaching early reading and phonics: creative approaches to early literacy*. SAGE.

Goswami, U. (1990). A special link between rhyming skill and the use of orthographic analogies by beginning readers. *Journal of Child Psychology*, *31*(2), 301–311.

Goswami, U. (1995). Phonological development and reading by analogy: what is analogy, and what is it not? *Journal of Research in Reading*, *18*(2), 139–145.

Goswami, U. (1999). Causal connections in beginning reading: the importance of rhyme. *Journal of Research in Reading*, *22*(3), 217–240.

Goswami, U., & Bryant, P. (1991). *Phonological skills and learning to read*. Lawrence Erlbaum Associates.

Goswami, U., & Bryant, P. (2016). *Phonological Skills and Learning to Read: Classic Edition*. Routledge.

Gough, P. B., & Tunmer, W. E. (1986). Decoding, reading and reading disability. *Remedial and Special Education*, *7*(1), 6–10. Retrieved December 1, 2023, from https://doi.org/10.1177/074193258600700104

GOV.UK. (2023a). *Academic year 2022/23. Key stage 1 and phonics screening check attainment*. Retrieved November 24, 2023, from https://explore-education-statistics.service.gov.uk/find-statistics/key-stage-1-and-phonics-screening-check-attainment#

GOV.UK. (2023b). *Academic year 2022/23. Key stage 2 attainment: national headlines*. Retrieved November 24, 2023, from https://explore-education-statistics.service.gov.uk/find-statistics/key-stage-2-attainment-national-headlines/2022-23

GOV.UK. (2023c). *Academic year 2022/23: schools, pupils and their characteristics*. Retrieved October 26, 2023, from https://explore-education-statistics.service.gov.uk/find-statistics/school-pupils-and-their-characteristics

Government of Ontario. (2023). *Curriculum and Resources: B2. Language Foundations for Reading and Writing*. Retrieved November 27, 2023, from https://www.dcp.edu.gov.on.ca/en/curriculum/elementary-language/grades/grade-1/b/b2

The Government Office for Science. (2008). *Foresight mental capital and wellbeing project (2008). Final project report*. The Government Office for Science.

Graham, J., & Mills, C. (2022). Margaret Meek Spencer: taking her work on. *English in Education*, *56*(3), 205–208.

Graham, S., Harris, K., & Chambers, A. (2016). Evidence-based practice and writing instruction: a review of reviews. In C. MacArthur, S. Graham, & J. Fitzgerald (Eds.), *Handbook of writing research* (2nd ed., pp. 211–227). The Guilford Press.

Graham, S., & Herbert, M. (2011). Writing to read: a meta-analysis of the impact of writing and writing instruction on reading. *Harvard Educational Review*, *81*, 710–745.

Graham, S., McKeown, D., Kiuhara, S., & Harris, K. (2012). A meta-analysis of writing instruction for students in the elementary grades. *Journal of Educational Psychology*, *104*(4), 879–896.

Graham, S., & Perin, D. (2007a). A meta-analysis of writing instruction for adolescent students. *Journal of Educational Psychology*, *99*(3), 445–476.

Graham, S., & Perin, D. (2007b). What we know, what we still need to know: teaching adolescents to write. *Scientific Studies of Reading*, *11*, 313–335. Retrieved December 1, 2023, from https://doi.org/10.1080/10888430701530664

Graham, S., & Sandmel, K. (2011). The process writing approach: a meta-analysis. *The Journal of Educational Research*, *104*, 396–407.

Graham, S., Xinghua, L., Bartlett, B., Ng, C., Harris, K., Aitken, A., Barkel, A., & Kavanaugh, C. (2018). Reading for writing: a meta-analysis of the impact of reading interventions on writing. *Review of Educational Research*, *88*, 243–284.

Gregg, L., & Steinberg, E. (2018). *Cognitive processes in writing*. Routledge.

Griffiths, Y., & Stuart, M. (2013). Reviewing evidence-based practice for pupils with dyslexia and literacy difficulties. *Journal of Research in Reading*, 36(1), 96–116.

Gunn, B., Smolkowski, K., & Vadasy, P. (2011). Evaluating the effectiveness of read well kindergarten. *Journal of Research on Educational Effectiveness*, 4(1), 53–86.

Hall, C., Dahl-Leonard, K., Cho, E., Solari, E., Capin, P., Conner, C., Henry, A., Cook, L., Hayes, L., Vargas, I., Richmond, C., & Kehoe, K. (2022). Forty Years of Reading Intervention Research for Elementary Students with or at Risk for Dyslexia: A Systematic Review and Meta-Analysis. *Reading Research Quarterly*, 1–28. Retrieved December 1, 2023, from https://doi.org/10.1002/rrq.477

Hammond, C. (2019). *Reading fiction has been said to increase people's empathy and compassion. But does the research really bear that out?* Retrieved November 13, 2023, from https://www.bbc.com/future/article/20190523-does-reading-fiction-make-us-better-people

Hanford, E. (2022). *Sold a story*. Retrieved December 1, 2023, from https://features.apmreports.org/sold-a-story/

Harmey, S., & Kabuto, B. (2018). Metatheoretical differences between running records and miscue analysis: implications for analysis of oral reading behaviors. *Research in the Teaching of English*, 53(1), 11–33.

Harste, J. C., Woodward, V. A., & Burke, C. L. (1984). *Language stories & literacy lessons*. Heinemann Educational Books.

Hatcher, P., Hulme, C., & Ellis, A. (1994). Ameliorating early reading failure by integrating the teaching of reading and phonological skills: the phonological linkage hypothesis. *Child Development*, 60, 41–57.

Hayes, J. R. (2006). New directions in writing theory. In C. MacArthur, S. Graham, & J. Fitzgerald (Eds.), *Handbook of writing research* (pp. 28–40). The Guilford Press.

Henderson, E., & Templeton, S. (1986). A developmental perspective of formal spelling instruction through alphabet, pattern, and meaning. *The Elementary School Journal*, 86(3), 304–316.

Hennessey, B. (2010). Intrinsic motivation and creativity in the classroom: have we come full circle? In R. Beghetto & J. Kaufman (Eds.), *Nurturing creativity in the classroom* (pp. 342–365). Cambridge University Press.

Higgins, S., Kokotsaki, D., & Coe, R. (2012). *The teaching and learning toolkit: technical appendices*. Education Endowment Foundation & The Sutton Trust.

Higgins, S., Martell, T., Waugh, D., Henderson, P., & Sharples, J. (n/d published 2021). *Improving literacy in key stage 2: guidance report*. Education Endowment Foundation (EEF).

Hogan, T., Bridges, M. S., Justice, L., & Cain, K. (2011). Increasing higher level language skills to improve reading comprehension. *University of Nebraska – Lincoln Special Education and Communication Disorders Faculty Publications*, 79, 1–20.

Holdaway, D. (1979). *The foundations of literacy*. Ashton Scholastic.

Horner, S. (2010). *Magic dust that lasts. Writers in schools – sustaining the momentum*. Arts Council England. Retrieved December 1, 2023, from https://www.suehorner.com/resources/ACE_published_version_of_Magic_Dust.pdf

International Literacy Association. (2023). *Research advisory: dyslexia*. International Literacy Association. Retrieved October 30, 2023, from https://www.literacyworldwide.org/docs/default-source/where-we-stand/research-advisory-dyslexia.pdf

James, M. (2012). *Background to Michael Gove's Response to the Report of the Expert Panel for the National Curriculum Review in England*. Retrieved March 30, 2022, from https://www.bera.ac.uk/bera-in-the-news/background-to-michael-goves-response-to-the-report-of-the-expert-panel-for-the-national-curriculum-review-in-england

Jones, G. (2019, 12th November). *Early reading and the education inspection framework*. Retrieved December 1, 2023, from https://educationinspection.blog.gov.uk/2019/11/04/early-reading-and-the-education-inspection-framework/

Juel, C., Griffith, P., & Gough, P. (1986). Acquisition of literacy: a longitudinal study of children in first and second grade. *Journal of Educational Psychology*, 78(4), 243–255.

Kerswill, P. (2007). Standard and non-standard English. In D. Britain (Ed.), *Language in the British Isles*. Cambridge University Press.

Kim, Y.-S. G. (2023). Simplicity meets complexity: expanding the simple view of reading with the direct and indirect effects model of reading (DIER). In S. Cabell, S. Neuman, & N. Patton-Terry (Eds.), *Handbook on the science of early literacy* (pp. 9–22). Guilford Press.

Kraft, M. (2020). Interpreting effect sizes of education interventions. *Educational Researcher, 49*(4), 241–253.
Kress, G. (1982). *Learning to write.* Routledge & Kegan Paul.
Labov, W. (1972). The logic of nonstandard English. In A. Cashdan & E. Grugeon (Eds.), *Language in education: a source book.* Routledge and Kegan Paul.
Layton, N. (2011). *Stanley's Stick.* Written by John Hegley and Illustrated by Neal Layton. Hachette Children's UK.
Lyster, S.-A. (2002). The effects of morphological versus phonological awareness training in kindergarten on reading development. Reading and Writing: An Interdisciplinary Journal, 15, 261–294.
Mackinlay, M., & Coles, R. (2023). *Farshore storytime trial research report.* Retrieved December 1, 2023, from https://www.farshore.co.uk/wp-content/uploads/sites/46/2023/09/Farshore_Storytime-in-Schools_Whitepaper_FINAL.pdf
Madhaus, G., & Russell, M. (2009/2010). Paradoxes of high-stakes testing. *The Journal of Education, 190,* 21–30.
Maine, F. (2015). *Dialogic readers: children talking and thinking together about visual texts.* Routledge.
Manguel, A. (1996). *A history of reading.* Flamingo.
Marrin, M. (2007, 21st October). Read my lips, I can fix our schools. Interview with Ruth Miskin. *The Sunday Times.*
McArthur, G., Sheehan, Y., Badcock, N. A., Francis, D. A., Wang, H. C., Kohhen, S., Banales, E., Anandakumar, T., Marinus, E., & Castles, A. (2018). *Phonics training for English-speaking poor readers.* Cochrane database of systematic reviews 2018, issue 11. Art. No.: CD009115. John Wiley and Sons.
Meek, M. (1988). *How texts teach what readers learn.* Thimble Press.
Michaels, W., & Walsh, M. (1990). *Up and away: using picture books.* Oxford University Press.
Ministry of Education. (2007). *The New Zealand curriculum for English-medium teaching and learning in years 1–13.* Learning Media Limited.
Miskin, R. (2021). *Read write Inc. Phonics handbook 1.* Oxford University Press. Retrieved December 1, 2023, from https://global.oup.com/education/content/primary/series/rwi/phonics/?region=uk
Molotsky, A., Dias, P., & Nakamura, P. (2022). *Read write Inc. Phonics and fresh start: evaluation report.* Retrieved December 1, 2023, from https://educationendowmentfoundation.org.uk/projects-and-evaluation/projects/read-write-inc-and-fresh-start
Morris, R., Lovett, M., Wolf, M., Sevcik, R., Steinbach, K., Frijters, J. C., & Shapiro, M. (2012). Multiple-component remediation for developmental reading disabilities: IQ, socioeconomic status, and race as factors in remedial outcome. *Journal of Learning Disabilities, 45*(2), 99–127.
Nation, K., Dawson, N., & Hsiao, Y. (2022). Book language and its implications for children's language, literacy, and development. *Current Directions in Psychological Science, 31*(4), 375–380.
National Education Union. (2023, 13th November). *Nick Gibb departure. All the problems facing the educational system have deepened during the period in which Gibb has presided over schools.* Retrieved November 23, 2023, from https://neu.org.uk/latest/press-releases/nick-gibb-departure
National Handwriting Association. (2023). *Homepage.* Retrieved November 13, 2023, from https://nha-handwriting.org.uk
National Reading Panel. (2000). *National reading panel. Teaching children to read. An evidence-based assessment of the scientific research literature on reading and its implications for reading instruction. Reports of the subgroups.*
Neitzel, A., Lake, C., Pellegrini, M., & Slavin, R. (2021). A synthesis of quantitative research on programs for struggling readers in elementary schools. *Reading Research Quarterly, 57*(1), 149–179.
Ontario Human Rights Commission. (2022). *Right to read. Public inquiry into human rights issues affecting students with reading disabilities, Executive Summary.* Government of Ontario. Retrieved December 1, 2023, from www.ohrc.on.ca
Oreskes, N., & Conway, E. (2011). *The merchants of doubt.* Bloomsbury.
O'Sullivan, O., & McGonigle, S. (2010). Transforming readers: Teachers and children in the centre for literacy in primary education power of reading project. *Literacy, 44*(2), 51–59.
O'Sullivan, O., & Thomas, A. (2007). *Understanding spelling.* Routledge.
Otaiba, S., McMaster, K., Wanzek, J., & Zaru, M. (2022). What we know and need to know about literacy interventions for elementary students with reading difficulties and disabilities, including dyslexia. *Reading Research Quarterly, 58*(2), 313–332.
Pearson, D. (1976). A psycholinguistic model of reading. *Language Arts, 53*(3), 309–314.
Perfetti, C. (1995). Cognitive research can inform reading education. *Journal of Research in Reading, 18*(2), 106–115.

Perfetti, C., & Stafura, J. (2014). Word knowledge in a theory of reading comprehension. *Scientific Studies of Reading*, *18*(1), 22–37.

Perryman, J., Bradbury, A., Calvert, G., & Kilian, K. (2023). *BEYOND OFSTED an inquiry into the future of school inspection. Final report of the inquiry*.

Phillips, L., Norris, S., & Mason, M. (1996). Longitudinal effects of early literacy concepts on reading achievement: a kindergarten intervention and five-year follow-up. *Journal of Literacy Research*, *28*, 173–195.

Pugh, A., & Kearns, D. (2023). Text types and their relation to efficacy in beginning reading interventions. *Reading Research Quarterly*, 1–23. Retrieved December 1, 2023, from https://doi.org/10.1002/rrq.513

The Reading Agency. (2015). *Literature review: the impact of reading for pleasure and empowerment*. Retrieved December 1, 2023, from https://tra-resources.s3.amazonaws.com/uploads/entries/document/2277/The_Impact_of_Reading_for_Pleasure_and_Empowerment.pdf

Reinking, D., Hruby, G., & Risko, V. (2023). Legislating phonics: settled science or political polemics? *Teachers College Record*, *125*(1), 104–131.

Richmond, J. (2015). *English, language and literacy 3 to 19: Writing 7 to 16*. Owen Education and UKLA.

Ryder, J., Tunmer, W., & Greaney, K. (2008). Explicit instruction in phonemic awareness and phonemically based decoding skills as an intervention strategy for struggling readers in whole language classrooms. *Reading and Writing: An Interdisciplinary Journal*, *21*, 349–369.

Robinson, N. (2019). Reading Wars Rage Again as Australian Government Pushes to Introduce Phonics Test. *ABC News*. Retrieved December 1, 2023, from https://www.abc.net.au/news/2019-06-30/australian-phonics-war-on-how-to-teach-kids-to-read-rages-on/11258944

Robinson, N., & Armitage, R. (2017). *Australia urged to use phonics in reading strategy as British schools minister tours country*. Retrieved September 29, 2023, from https://www.abc.net.au/news/2017-04-11/could-introducing-phonics-help-children-learn-to-read/8435562

Roche, M. (2014). *Developing children's critical thinking through picturebooks*. Routledge.

Rogers, L. A., & Graham, S. (2008). A meta-analysis of single subject design writing intervention research. *Journal of Educational Psychology*, *100*, 879–906.

Rose, J. (2006). *Independent review of the teaching of early reading: final report*. DfES Publications.

Rosenblatt, L. (1978). The reader, the text, the *poem: the transactional theory of the literary work*. Southern Illinois University Press.

Santangelo, T., & Graham, S. (2015). A comprehensive meta-analysis of handwriting instruction. *Educational Psychology Review*, *28*, 225–265.

Sassoon, R. (2003). *Handwriting: the way to teach it* (2nd ed.). Paul Chapman Publishing.

Savage, R., Burgos, G., Wood, E., & Piquette, N. (2015). The simple view of reading as a framework for national literacy initiatives: a hierarchical model of pupil-level and classroom-level factors. *British Educational Research Journal*, *41*(5), 820–844.

Scarborough, H. (2001). Connecting early language and literacy to later reading (dis)abilities: evidence, theory, and practice. In S. Neuman & D. Dickinson (Eds.), *Handbook for research in early literacy*. Guilford Press.

Seidenberg, M. (2017). *Language at the speed of sight: how we read, why so many can't, and what can be done about it*. Basic Books.

Seidenberg, M., & McClelland, J. (1989). A distributed, developmental model of word recognition and naming. *Psychological Review*, *96*(4), 523–568.

Share, D. (1995). Phonological recoding and self-teaching: sine qua non of reading acquisition. *Cognition*, *55*(2), 151–218.

Shireen, N. (2020). *Barbara throws a wobbler*. Penguin Random House.

Shukla, N. (Ed.). (2017). *The good immigrant* (p. 96). Unbound.

Siraj-Blatchford, I. (2009). Learning in the home and at school: how working class children 'succeed against the odds'. *British Educational Research Journal*, *36*(3), 463–482.

Slavin, R., Lake, C., Davis, S., & Madden, N. (2011). Effective programs for struggling readers: A best-evidence synthesis. *Educational Research Review*, *6*, 1–26.

Smith, F. (1995). *Writing and the writer* (2nd ed.). Routledge.

Solari, E., Terry, N., Gaab, N., Hogan, T., Nelson, N., Pentimonti, J., Petscher, Y., & Sayko, S. (2020). Translational Science: A Road Map for the Science of Reading. *Reading Research Quarterly*, *55*(S1), 347–360.

Stainthorp, R., & Hughes, D. (1999). *Learning from children who read at an early age*. Routledge.
Strauss, V. (2023). *ANSWER SHEET: on the latest obsession with phonics*. Retrieved November 25, 2023, form https://www.washingtonpost.com/education/2023/05/23/phonics-reading-analysis/
Styles, M., & Drummond, M. J. (1993). Editorial: the politics of reading. *Cambridge Journal of Education, 23*(1), 3–13.
Suggate, S. (2010). Why what we teach depends on when: grade and reading intervention modality moderate effect size. *Developmental Psychology, 46,* 1556–1579.
Suggate, S. (2016). A meta-analysis of the long-term effects of phonemic awareness, phonics, fluency, and reading comprehension interventions. *Journal of Learning Disabilities, 49,* 77–96.
Sullivan, A., & Brown, M. (2015). Reading for pleasure and progress in vocabulary and mathematics. *British Educational Research Journal, 41*(6), 971–991. Retrieved December 1, 2023, from https://doi.org/10.1002/berj.3180
Tennent, W., & Reedy, D. (2016). *Guiding readers – layers of meaning: a handbook for teaching reading comprehension to 7–11-year-olds*. UCL IOE Press.
Torgerson, C. J., Brooks, G., Gascoine, G., & Higgins, S. (2018). Phonics: reading policy and the evidence of effectiveness from a systematic 'tertiary' review. *Research Papers in Education*. Retrieved December 1, 2023, from https://doi.org/10.1080/02671522.2017.1420816
Torgerson, C. J., Brooks, G., & Hall, J. (2006). *A systematic review of the research literature on the use of phonics in the teaching of reading and spelling*. Department for Education and Skills (DfES).
Torgerson, C. J., & Torgerson, D. (2017). 'True' experimental designs. In D. Wyse, N. Selwyn, E. Smith, & L. Suter (Eds.), The BERA/SAGE *handbook of educational research* (pp. 416–435). SAGE.
Torgerson, D., Torgerson, C. J., Ainsworth, H., Buckley, H., Heaps, C., Hewitt, C., & Mitchell, N. (2014). *Improving writing quality: evaluation report and executive summary*. Education Endowment Foundation.
Treiman, R., Mullennix, J., Bijeljac-Babic, R., & Richmond-Welty, E. D. (1995). The special role of rimes in the description, use, and acquisition of English orthography. *Journal of Experimental Psychology: General, 124*(2), 107–136.
Trelease, J. (2013). *The read aloud handbook*. The Penguin Group.
Tufte, E. R. (1983). *The visual display of quantitative information*. Graphics Press USA.
US Department of Education. (2011). *Reading first implementation study 2008–09: final report*. Abt Associates Inc.
Vadasy, P., & Sanders, E. (2012). Two-year follow-up of a kindergarten phonics intervention for English learners and native English speakers: contextualizing treatment impacts by classroom literacy instruction. *Journal of Educational Psychology, 104,* 987–1005.
Waterland, L. (1985). *Read with me. an apprenticeship approach to reading*. Thimble Press.
Weale, S. (2022). *Focus on phonics to teach reading is 'failing children', says landmark study*. Retrieved January 19, 2022, from https://www.theguardian.com/education/2022/jan/19/focus-on-phonics-to-teach-reading-is-failing-children-says-landmark-study
What Works Clearinghouse. (2013). *Beginning reading: reading recovery*. US Department of Education. Institute of Education Sciences. Retrieved December 1, 2023, from https://ies.ed.gov/ncee/wwc/InterventionReport/420#:~:text=Reading%20Recovery®%20was%20found,1%20with%20low%20literacy%20achievement
Whitehead, M. (2010). *Language and literacy in the early years 0–7*. SAGE.
Willmore, A. (2022). *The Great Paint*. Written and illustrated by Alex Willmore. Tate.
Wydell, T. (2023). Are phonological skills as crucial for literacy acquisition in Japanese as in English as well as in accounting for developmental dyslexia in English and in Japanese? *Journal of Cultural Cognition Science, 7,* 175–196.
Wynder, E. (1988). Tobacco and health: a review of the history and suggestions for public health policy. *Public Health Reports, 103*(1), 8–18.
Wyse, D. (2007). *How to Help Your Child Read and Write*. Pearson Education Limited.
Wyse, D. (2017). *How writing works: from the invention of the alphabet to the rise of social media*. Cambridge University Press.
Wyse, D. (2020). Presidential address: the academic discipline of education. Reciprocal relationships between practical knowledge and academic knowledge. *British Educational Research Journal, 46*(1), 6–25. Retrieved December 1, 2023, from https://doi.org/10.1002/berj.3597
Wyse, D. (2023a, 9th October). *Teaching phonics and reading: PIRLS of wisdom?* Retrieved December 1, 2023, from https://neu.org.uk/latest/blogs/teaching-phonics-and-reading-pirls-wisdom

Wyse, D. (2023b, 20th October). *Teaching synthetic phonics and reading: PIRLS of wisdom?* Retrieved December 1, 2023, from https://blogs.ucl.ac.uk/ioe/2023/10/10/teaching-synthetic-phonics-and-reading-pirls-of-wisdom/

Wyse, D., Aarts, B., Anders, J., de Gennaro, A., Dockrell, J., Manyukhina, Y., Sing, S., & Torgerson, C. (2022a). *Grammar and writing in England's national curriculum. A randomised controlled trial and implementation and process evaluation of Englicious.* Retrieved December 1, 2023, from https://discovery.ucl.ac.uk/id/eprint/10144257/

Wyse, D., & Bradbury, A. (2022a). The passion, pedagogy and politics of reading. *English in Education.* Retrieved December 1, 2023, from https://doi.org/10.1080/04250494.2022.2091987

Wyse, D., & Bradbury, A. (2022b). Reading wars or reading reconciliation? A critical examination of robust research evidence, curriculum policy, and teachers' practices for teaching phonics and reading. *Review of Education.* Retrieved December 1, 2023, from https://doi.org/10.1002/rev3.3314

Wyse, D., & Bradbury, A. (2023). *The politics of 'scientifically-based' teaching: phonics for reading and grammar for writing.* Retrieved November 25, 2023, from https://www.bera.ac.uk/blog/the-politics-of-scientifically-based-teaching-phonics-for-reading-and-grammar-for-writing

Wyse, D., Bradbury, A., & Trollope, R. (2022). *The independent commission on assessment in primary education. Final report.* Retrieved December 1, 2023, from https://www.icape.org.uk

Wyse, D., Bradford, H., & Winstanley, J.-M. (2023). *Teaching English, language and literacy.* (5th ed.). Routledge.

Wyse, D., & Goswami, U. (2008). Synthetic phonics and the teaching of reading. *British Educational Research Journal, 34*(6), 691–710.

Wyse, D., & Torgerson, C. (2017). Experimental trials and 'what works?' in education: the case of grammar for writing. *British Educational Research Journal, 43*(6), 1019–1047. Retrieved December 1, 2023, from https://doi.org/10.1002/berj.3315(30)

Ziegler, J., & Goswami, U. (2005). Reading acquisition, developmental dyslexia and skilled reading across languages; a psycholinguistic grain size theory. *Psychological Bulletin, 131*(1), 3–29.

Books for children and young people

Ahlberg, A., & Ahlberg, J. (1984). *Please Mrs Butler.* Puffin.
Alizadeh, K. (2017). *Quiet!* Child's Play International Limited.
Atinuke. (2007). *Anna Hibiscus.* Walker Books Limited.
Atinuke. (2020). *Too Small Tola.* Walker Books Limited.
Bently, P. (2020). *Octopus Shocktopus!* Nosy Crow.
Bloom, V. (1997). *Fruits: a Caribbean counting poem.* Macmillan Children's Books.
Brady, J., & Ashwin, K. (2019). *Claire, Justice Ninja.* David Fickling Books.
Bright, R. (2018). *The way home for wolf.* Hachette Children's Group.
Burningham, J. (2001). *Mr Gumpy's outing.* Red Fox.
Cameron, A. (2013). *The Julian stories.* Tamarind.
Cameron, N. (2018). *Mega Robo Bros.* David Fickling Books.
Carter, J. (2023). *A ticket to Kalamazoo! Zippy poems to read out loud.* Otter-Barry Books.
Coelho, J. (2022). *Blow a kiss, catch a kiss.* Andersen Press Limited.
Cousins, L. (2013). *Peck Peck Peck.* Walker.
Davies, B. (2015). *Grandad's island.* Simon & Schuster UK.
Davies, N. (2015). *White owl, barn owl.* Walker Books Limited.
Davies, N. (2021). *Grow: secrets of our DNA.* Walker Books Limited.
Donaldson, J. (2013). *Poems to perform.* Macmillan Children's Books.
Durant, A., & Rickerty, S. (2011). *Unfortunately.* Orchard.
French, V. (2015a). *Growing frogs.* Walker Books Limited.
French, V. (2015b). *Yucky worms.* Walker Books.
Goodfellow, M. (2021). *Caterpillar cake: read-aloud poems to brighten your day.* Otter-Barry Books.
Gough, J. (2016). *Rabbit's bad habits: book 1.* Hachette Children's Group.
Gray, K., & Parsons, G. (2004). *Billy's bucket.* Red Fox.
Hegley, J., & Layton, N. (2012). *Stanley's stick.* Hachette Children's Group.
Hepworth, A. (2021). *How it works: the body.* Little Tiger Press.

Hoffman, M. (2015). *The great big book of families.* Frances Lincoln Children's Books.
Hopgood, T. (2022). *My big book of outdoors.* Walker Books Limited.
Hughes, S. (1990). *The big Alfie and Annie Rose storybook.* Red Fox.
Hutchins, P. (1968). *Rosie's walk.* Macmillan.
Jarvis. (2023). *Bear and bird: the picnic and other stories.* Walker Books Limited.
Kooser, T., & Wanek, C. (2022). *Marshmallow clouds: poems inspired by nature.* Walker Books Limited.
Layton, N. (2019). *A planet full of plastic: and how you can help.* Hachette Children's Group.
Lewis, G. (2013). *Moon bear.* OUP Oxford.
Lobel, A. (2017). *Frog and toad are friends.* HarperCollins.
Lucas, D. (2008). *The robot and the bluebird.* Andersen Press.
McCardie, A. (2017). *Our very own dog.* Walker Books Limited.
Meek, M., & Spencer, M. M. (1988). *How texts teach what readers learn.* Thimble Press.
Mole, S. (2023). *A first book of dinosaurs.* Walker Books Limited.
Mucha, L. (2021). *Rita's rabbit.* Faber & Faber.
Newberry, J. (2020). *Big green crocodile: rhymes to say and play.* Otter-Barry Books.
Percival, T. (2020). *Ravi's roar: a big bright feelings book.* Bloomsbury Publishing.
Portis, A. (2021). *Hey, water!* Scallywag Press.
Powell, S., Goouch, K., & Werth, L. (2015). *Seeking Froebel's 'Mother Songs' in Daycare for Babies.* Retrieved October 19, 2023, from https://tactyc.org.uk/pdfs/Sacha%20Powell.pdf
Rayner, C. (2022). *My pet goldfish.* Walker Books Limited.
Reeve, P., & McIntyre, S. (2013). *Oliver and the Seawigs.* Oxford University Press.
Rosen, M. (2015). *A great big cuddle: poems for the very young.* Walker Books Limited.
Rubbino, S. (2011). *A walk in London.* Walker Books.
Scheffler, A., & Green, A. (2022a). *Goldilocks and the three bears.* Scholastic.
Scheffler, A., & Green, A. (2022b). *The three little pigs.* Scholastic.
Scheffler, A., & Green, A. (2023a). *The hare and the hedgehog.* Alison Green Books.
Scheffler, A., & Green, A. (2023b). *Puss in boots.* Alison Green Books.
Schwarz, V. (2008). *There are cats in this book.* Walker Books.
Sharratt, N., & Tucker, S. (2009). *The three little pigs.* Pan Macmillan.
Sharratt, N., & Tucker, S. (2010). *Goldilocks.* Macmillan Children's.
Sharratt, N., & Tucker, S. (2017a). *Little red riding hood.* Pan Macmillan.
Sharratt, N., & Tucker, S. (2017b). *The three Billy goats gruff.* Pan Macmillan.
Sharratt, N., & Tucker, S. (2021). *Cinderella.* Pan Macmillan.
Shireen, N. (2021). *Barbara throws a wobbler.* Penguin Random House Children's UK.
Smart, J. (2016). *Bunny vs monkey.* David Fickling Books.
Smith, A. T. (2013). *Claude in the city.* Hachette Children's Group.
Smith, A. T. (2015). *Little red and the very hungry lion.* Scholastic.
Song, M. (2023). *Donut feed the squirrels: book one of the Norma and Belly series.* Pushkin Children's Books.
Souhami, J. (2012). *No dinner! The story of the old woman and the pumpkin.* Frances Lincoln Children's Books.
Souhami, J. (2022). *Please, Mr magic fish!* Otter-Barry Books.
Soundar, C. (2016). *Pattan's pumpkin: an Indian flood story.* Otter-Barry Books.
Soundar, C. (2021). *Nikhil and Jay save the day.* Otter-Barry Books.
Taylor, S., & Morss, A. (2021). *Busy spring: nature wakes up.* Happy Yak.
Taylor, S., & Morss, A. (2022). *Wild summer: life in the heat.* Happy Yak.
Taylor, S., Morss, A., & Chiu, C. (2019). *Winter sleep: a hibernation story.* Quarto Publishing Group UK.
Todd-Stanton, J. (2016). *Arthur and the golden rope.* Flying Eye Books.
Tolstoy, A. N. (2006). *The gigantic turnip.* Barefoot Books.
Vere, E. (2018). *How to be a lion.* Penguin Random House Children's UK.
Wakeling, K. (2023). *A dinosaur at the bus stop: poems to have fun with!* Otter-Barry Books.
Walsh, M. (2008). *10 things I can do to help my world.* Walker Books Limited.
Waring, R. (2019). *Hungry hen.* Oxford University Press.
Webb, S. (2004). *Tanka Tanka skunk.* Red Fox.
Weil, Z. (2023). *Cherry moon: little poems big ideas mindful of nature.* Welbeck Publishing.
Welsh, C. H., & Seal, J. (2021). *Sit in!* HarperCollins.
Wildsmith, B. (1986). *Cat on the mat.* Harper Collins.

Willems, M. (2018). *Don't let the pigeon drive the bus!* Walker Books Limited.
Willems, M. (2023). *We are in a book!* Walker Books Limited.
Willmore, A. (2021). *The great paint*. Tate Publishing.
Wilson-Max, K. (2018). *The drum*. Tiny Owl Publishing Limited.
Wilson-Max, K. (2019). *Astro girl*. Otter-Barry Books.
Wilson-Max, K. (2023). *Lenny has lunch*. Alanna-Max Books.
Woollvin, B. (2017a). *Little red*. Pan Macmillan.
Woollvin, B. (2017b). *Rapunzel*. Two Hoots.
Woollvin, B. (2018). *Hansel and Gretel*. Two Hoots.

Index

Note: Page numbers in *italics* indicate a figure and page numbers in **bold** indicate a table on the corresponding page. Page numbers followed by 'n' indicate a note on the corresponding page.

Adams, Marilyn Jager 31
Adeola, Bryon and Dapo 57, 106
Adesope, Olusola **68**
affixes 93, *97*, **188**, 252
agency 9, 220, 221, 226, 244–246, 249, 252
Ahlberg, Alan 31
Ahlberg, Jessica 221, *222*
Alfie Out of Doors Storybook (Hughes) 58
Alizadeh, Kip 110
alliteration 112, 123, 210
alphabet books 56
alphabetic code 7, 9, 20, *37*, 48n41, **68**, **69**, **100**, 118–141; as affixes on words 93, *97*, **188**, 252; in balance with other linguistic features 87; capital letters *99*, 139, 141n3, 144–145, 191; contextualising the basic code 76–77, 80, 120–122; knowledge of morphemes and other word structures 93; letter formation **101**, 125–126, 129, 159, 224–225, 226; phonological awareness and 93; teaching children to 'crack the code' through *Stanley's Stick* 123–141; use of letter-cards 125, *125*, 129, 136, 138, 150, *150*; using real books to teach phonics 118–119; *see also* phonemes; words; vowels
Alphabetics systematic review 67
American Psychological Association (APA) 66
American Reading Company 53
analogies 19, *99*, **101**, 252; when learning to read 111, 112, 115, 123, 162–163, 175, 176, 178, 182, 228
Andrews, Richard 70
Anna Hibiscus books (Atinuke/Tobia) 58
APA PsychInfo 66
Art of Teaching Writing, The (Calkins) 17
Asquith, Ros 59
Astrogirl (Wilson-Max) 193, *194*
Atinuke 57, 58
audiobooks 56, 57, 204, 221

Australia 7, 11, 59, 247, 253; Cunningham Library 66; the reading wars in 8–9; screening phonics in 14–15
Australian Council for Education 66
Australian Education Index 66

babies *see* early development
Baby Room Project (Froebel Trust) 113
Baker, Scott **71**
balanced approach to teaching 1–3, 87–102, 247–251; *see also* Double Helix of Reading and Writing; reading *and* writing
Barbara Throws a Wobbler (Shireen) 205, 206, *207*
Barras, Colin 21, 78
Barrs, Myra 232–233
Bartlett, Alison 234, *235*
basic interpersonal communicative skills (BICS) 218
Beardshaw, Rosalind 57, *108*
Bently, Peter 112
Big Alfie books (Hughes) 58
Big Green Crocodile: Rhymes to Say and Play (Newberry) 56, 113, *114*
Bishop, Sims 106
blending 54, 55, 77, 90, 95, **100**, 110, 126, 146
Bloom, Valerie 198, *199*, 231
Blow a Kiss, Catch a Kiss (Coelho/Killen) 56, 113
book gifting programmes 59
books: age appropriate 13, 197; alphabet books 56; audiobooks 56, 57, 204, 221; comics/graphic novels 56, 58, *97*, 109; picture books 2, 56–58, *96–97*, 133, 212–213, 221, 237–238, 241–244, *244*; scheme books and real books 51–55, 87, 143; trade press 49, 51, 60, 66, **88**; *see also* reading; texts

'book talk' 138, 208–209
Bowers, Geoffrey **68**
Bradbury, Alice **68**, 78
Bradford, Helen 180
Bradley, Lynette 111
Brady, Joe 58
Bright, Rachel 183, *184*, *185*
British Educational Research Index 66
Brown, Matt 105
Brownstone Series (Todd-Stanton) 58
Bryant, Peter 111
Bryon, Nathan 57, 106
Bunny vs Monkey (Smart) 58
Burningham, John 115
'business as usual' (BAU) 64, 74
Busy Spring (Morss/Chiu) 59

Calkins, Lucy 10, 15–17, 39, 72
Cameron, Ann 58
Cameron, Neil 58
Canada 59, 76, 79–80; children's rights to read in 21–23, 28n69; the reading wars in 10–11, 247
capital letters *99*, 139, 141n3, 144–145, 191
Caribbean dialect 198
Carter, James 56
Caterpillar Cake (Goodfellow/Patel-Sage) 56, *211*, 212
Cat on the Mat (Wildsmith) 51–54
Centre for Independent Studies 14
Centre for Literacy in Primary Education (CLPE) 1; CLPE Poetry Award (CLiPPA) 204; Corebooks4 database of books 144, 214; with the Dolly Parton Imagination Library UK 59; Learning to Read collection 144, 214, 219; Power of Pictures programme 204, 237, 241, 242, *243*,; Power of Poetry programme 231; Power of Reading Programme 209, 233, 237; Primary Language Record (PLR) 95; Reading and Writing Scales 95, *96–99*; *Reflecting Realities* survey 106
Chall, Jean 15
Chambers, Aidan 55, 138, 209
Chambers, Amber 72
Cherry Moon (Weil/J. Song) 56
Chetty, Darren 231
children's development: awareness of sound 43, 93; basic interpersonal communicative skills (BICS) 218; child and their environment, including texts 90–92; children and their language(s) 89–90; encountering objects 43, 45, 110–111; fine motor control 109, 125, 153–154, 155, 159, **220**, 224, 226, 232; gross motor control 159, 224, 232; language mistakes/errors as 'miscues' 29–30, 50–51, 197; phonological development **100**, 103, 110–111, 178, 253; poetry and emotional literacy 210; role of parents 14, 51, 59, 76, 89, 90, 112–113, 133, 204, 208, 214, 218–219, 230; search for meaning and communication 103; 'typically' developing readers 17, 34, 37, 42–43, 67, **68**–69, 73, 75–79; 'typically' developing writers 42, **70**–71, 161; *see also* pupils
Chiu, Cinyee 59
Church, Caroline Jayne 57
Claire: Justice Ninja (Brady) 58
Clarke, Paula 79
Claude series (A. Smith) 58
Clay, Marie 10, 16–19, 24, 32–33
CLPE Poetry Award (CLiPPA) 204
Coelho, Joseph 56, 113
cognitive academic language proficiency (CALP) 218
cognitive process of writing 39–42, *41*
comics/graphic novels 56, 58, *97*, 109
communications technology 15, 34, 89
composition 38–39, **39**, 73, 231–232, 237, 245; and the complexities of writing 231; comprehension and 224; the Double Helix Model of Reading and Writing 43, 45–46, 80; early development of 89, 90, 92–93, *98*, *99*,; oral composition 232; spelling and 180; teacher modelling tasks 109, 139
comprehension 12, 19, 20–22, 25; composition and 224; contextualisation in 36–37, 42–43, 46; developing fluency and 201–216; in the Double Helix of Reading and Writing 42, 45, 46, **88**, 91; extending comprehension through whole books 138–139; fluency and 201–216; fostering discussion to support 53–54; phonics interventions and reading 67, **68**–69; in the 'Simple View of Reading' (SVR) 33–36; in the Reading Rope model 36–38, *37*; writing instruction and **70**, 71–73, 77, 79–80
Compton-Lilly, Catherine 50
consonant clusters 12, 55, **100**, 120, 139, 146–148, **146**, 155, 157, 166, 168–169
contextualisation: in a balanced approach to reading and writing 103–104; in phonics teaching 67, 76–79, 118–120, 123, 129, 138, 141, 142, 165; in reading comprehension 36–37, 42–43, 46; supporting learning through 230, 232–234; variety and 178; whole-language approach 9, 11, 15–24, 49–52, **68**, 77, 87, 253; *see also* real books
conventional spelling system (orthography) *see* spelling
Cork, Valerie 232–233
Cornwall, Gaia 57

Cousins, Lucy 54–55, 148, *149*, 151, *152*, 153.156
Covid-19, 11
creation 238–239, 241, 249
Crystal, David 181
Cumbria, England 79
Cunningham, Anne 43, 77–78
Cunningham Library (Australia) 66
Cushing, Ian 51

Davies, Benji 57, 213
Davies, Nicola 59
Davis, Andrew 63
'deep orthography' 180
Department for Education (DfE) 11–13, 53–54, 73–75, 247, 253
development, children's: awareness of sound 43, 93; basic interpersonal communicative skills (BICS) 218; child and their environment, including texts 90–92; children and their language(s) 89–90; encountering objects 43, 45, 110–111; fine motor control 109, 125, 153–154, 155, 159, **220**, 224, 226, 232; gross motor control 159, 224, 232; language mistakes/errors as 'miscues' 29–30, 50–51, 197; phonological development **100**, 103, 110–111, 178, 253; poetry and emotional literacy 210; role of parents 14, 51, 59, 76, 89, 90, 112–113, 133, 204, 208, 214, 218–219, 230; search for meaning and communication 103; 'typically' developing readers 17, 34, 37, 42–43, 67, **68–69**, 73, 75–79; 'typically' developing writers 42, **70–71**, 161
dialects/accents 50, 90, 147, 198, 233
dictionaries 48n36, 177, 197, 224, 245
digraphs 55, **100**, 145–146, **146**, 252; consonant clusters 12, 55, **100**, 120, 139, 146–148, **146**, 155, 157, 166, 168–169; developing blending and segmenting through 148–151, *151*, 153–154, 157; split vowel digraphs 163, **163–164**, 253
Dinosaur at the Bus Stop, A (Wakeling/Muldoon) 56
Direct and Indirect Effects Model of Reading (DIER) 38
discrete (isolated) phonics approach 20, 24, 67, 79, 80
disyllabic words 142, 147, **148**, 151, 252
Dolly Parton's Imagination Library 59
Dombey, Henrietta 231
Donaldson, Julia 56
Donut Feed the Squirrels (M. Song) 58
Double Helix of Reading and Writing 2–3, 11, 42–46, *44*, 71, 63, 65, 77, 80–81, 88, 109, 119, 237, 260

drama/performance 11, *99*, 168, 172, 187, 189, 192, 208, 223, 228; dramatising reading 209–210; performing poetry 56–57, 113, 210, 212
Drum, The (Wilson-Max) 111
Durant, Alan 187–192, *188*, *191*
dyslexia 21, 34, **69**, 216, 217, 220, 252

Early Detection of Reading Difficulties, The (Clay) 16
early development *see* children's development
'Ear of the Writer' 92, 253n2
Ebsco 66
Education Endowment Foundation (EEF) 13, 19, 27n56, 38, 74–75, 81n10, 242, 246n21
education policy: 'high-stakes' testing 1, 13, 14, 250; importance of 24–25; the reading wars 7–28
effect sizes 66, **69**, 72, 74, 81n10
Elephant and Piggie books (Willems) 58
ellipses 192, 252
Ellis, Andrew 43, 79
emotional literacy 210
England 7, 8; centralising synthetic phonics in 11–14; children eligible for free school meals (FSMs) 242; concerns over its approach to synthetic phonics 104; Cumbria 79; Department for Education (DfE) 11–13, 53–54, 73–75, 247, 253; Education Endowment Foundation (EEF) 13, 19, 27n56, 38, 74–75, 81n10, 242, 246n21; Fresh Start (FS) 74–75; House of Commons 11; Oak National Academy 12; Office for Standards in Education, Children's Services and Skills (Ofsted) 12–14, 26n22, 51; Phonics Screening Check (PSC) 7, 12–14, 21, 253; positive benefits of progressive education in Britain 27; private/independent schools (UK) 26n26; the reading wars in 8; reception class in 25; Rose Report 23, 28n76, 35–36, 37, 67; Scotland 36, 67; 'Standard English' 51, 63, 231
English and Media Centre (EMC) 95
English in Education journal 49
English language: complexities of the 161–180; dialects/accents 50, 90, 147, 198, 233; as the most-used language 7; orthography 147, 161–162, 178, 193, 197; schwa sound in the **145**, 175, 176, 253; 'Standard English' 51, 63, 231
expanded noun phrases 99, 151, 169, 252
extent of difference 66
"Eye Caterpillars" (Coelho) 113

Fairy Tales series (Scheffler) 57
Farshore children's book publisher 59
Field, Jim 58, 183, *184*, *185*

fine motor control 109, 125, 153–154, 155, 159, **220**, 224, 226, 232
First Book of Dinosaurs, A (Mole/Hunt) 56
fluency 201–216, 252; in blending 54, 55, 77, 90, 95, **100**, 110, 126, 146; dramatising reading 209–210; opportunities for children to read independently 214–216; in oral language 252; presenting informational writing 213; providing opportunities to discuss texts 208–209; in reading 252; reading aloud 204–208; reading and performing poetry 210–212; in segmenting 55, 95, **100**, 110, 120, 136, 138, 141, 142, 146, 148, 153–154, 159, 182–183, 201, 226–227, 234; using picture books with children of all ages 212–213
Foreman, Michael 59
forward slashes (/) 25n10, 141n3
Fountas, Irene 15
free school meals (FSMs) 242
French language 163, 181
French, Vivian 221, *222*, 234, *235*
Fresh Start (FS) 74–75
Froebel Trust's Baby Room Project 113
Frog and Toad Are Friends (Lobel) 58
Fruits (Bloom) 198, *199*

Gaiman, Neil 58
Galuschka, Katharina **68**, 78
genres: knowledge of 37, *41*, 42, 43, 48n36, 56; variety among reading texts 56, 106, 178, 221; writing in different genres 71, *99*, 178, 242; *see also* books; drama/performance; poetry; texts
Gersten, Russell **69**, 71
Gibb, Nick 11–12, 14, 74
Gigantic Turnip, The (Tolstoy/Sharkey) 57
Goodfellow, Matt 56, *211*, 210
Good Immigrant, The (Shukla, ed.) 231
Goodman, Ken 16, 29–32, 50–51
Goodman, Yetta 50–51
Goouch, K. 105
Goswami, Usha 19, 67, 111
Gough, Julian 58
Gough, Philip 33–36
Graham, Evarts 65
Graham, Judith 49
Graham, Steve 39, **70**, **71**, 71–72
Grandad's Island (B. Davies) 213
grapheme phoneme correlation 23, 95, *98*, 123, 143–144
graphophonic cues 30–31
'grapho-phonic information' 23–24, *32*
Graves, Donald 39, 72
Greaney, Keith 80
Great Big Book of Families, The (Hoffmann/Asquith) 59

Great Big Cuddle, A (Rosen/Riddell) 56
Great Paint, The (Willmore) 165, *167*, *171*, *173*
Griffiths, Yvonne 36
gross motor control 159, 224, 232
Grow: Secrets of Our DNA (N. Davies/Sutton) 59
Growing Frogs (French/Bartlett) 234, *235*

Hacking, Charlotte 1, 246n21
Hall, Colby **69**
handwriting 39, 42, **70**, *98–99*, *131*, 134, 150, 177; fine motor control 109, 125, 153–154, 155, 159, **220**, 224, 226, 232; letter formation **101**, 125–126, 129, 159, 224–225, 226; *see also* writing
Hanford, Emily 10, 15–22, 71–72
Hansel and Gretel (Woolvin) 57
Harmey, Sinead 32–33
Harris, Karen 72
Harste, Jerome 31
Hatcher, Peter 36, 43, 79
Haughton, Chris 57, 241
Hayes, J. R. 39–42, *41*
Hearson, Ruth 57
Hebert, Michael **70**, 71
Hegley, John 123–141
Hey, Water! (Portis) 59
'high-stakes' testing 1, 13, 14, 250
Hirst, Daisy 57
Hoffmann, Mary 59
home corner 225, 252
home learning environment (HLE) 218
homographs 193–194
homonyms 193–194, 197
homophones 163, 193–194, 197, 252
Hopgood, Tim 59
Horáček, Petr 57
How It Works series 59
How Texts Teach What Readers Learn (Meek) 49
How to Be a Lion (Vere) 238, *240*
How Writing Works (Wyse) 253n2
Hughes, Shirley 58
Hulme, Charles 43, 79
Hungry Hen (Waring/Church) 57
Hunt, Matt 56
Hutchins, Pat 49
'hyperlexia' 34

ideation 223, 238, 241, 242
Independent Review of the Teaching of Early Reading, The (Rose Report) 23, 28n76, 35–36, 37, 67
Information and Book Learning (Meek) 58
Institute for Employment Studies (IES) 59
Ireland 7, 9, 12, 25n13, 59, 65, 247, 248

isolated (discrete) phonics approach 20, 24, 67, 79, 80
ITT Core Content Framework of Initial Teacher Training 13
Iwu, Onyinye 58

Jones, Richard 56
Journal of the Reading Specialist, The 29
Journey Game, The (Coelho) 113, 115
Julian books (A. Cameron) 58

Kabuto, Bobbie 32–33
Kebede, Daniel 12
Killen, Nicola 56, 113
Kim, Young-Suk Grace 38
Kooser, Ted 56
Kress, Gunther 31

Labov, William 51
Lambirth, A. 105
language: non-English languages 163, 180–181; psycholinguistic aspects of 19, 253; *see also* alphabetic code; English language; oral language
language development *see* early development
Language Development Reading Series 77
Language for Life, A 231
Layton, Neal 56, 59, 123–141
learning (to read and write) *see* early development; teaching; pupils
Learning to Read collection 144, 214, 219
Lenny series (Wilson-Max) 106, *107*, 112
Lenton, Steven 112
Lessac, Frané 57
'letter fans' 226
letters *see* alphabetic code; digraphs; words
Lewis, Gill 238, *239*
Lift the Flap Fairy Tales series (Sharratt/Tucker) 57
linguistic knowledge *41*, 42
Literacy Research and Instruction 29
literacy *see* comprehension; fluency; reading; writing
Litte Red (Woolvin) 57
Little Tiger children's book publisher 59
Little Wandle synthetic phonics scheme 51–53
Lobel, Arnold 58
long-term memory 40, *41*
Lucas, David 57
Lulu and Zeki series (Lola and Leo in the US) 106, *108*
Lyon, Reid 17
Lyster, Solveig-Alma 76

Manguel, Alberto 63
Marshmallow Clouds (Kooser and Wanek/Jones) 56

Mason, Jana 76
McArthur, Genevieve **68**
McCandliss, Bruce 17–18
McCardie, Amanda 59
McClelland, James 37
McIntyre, Sarah 58
McQuinn, Anna 57, 106, *108*
medial position (of a word) 112, 138, 252
Meek Spencer, Margaret 49, 58, 233
Mega Robo Bros (N. Cameron) 58
memory 29, *40*, *41*, 40–42
meta-analysis 66–67, 69, 71, 78
Mills, Colin 49
'miscue analysis' 50–51
'miscues' in language 29–30, 197
Miskin, Ruth 74–76
Mole, Simon 56
Moon Bear (Lewis) 238, *239*
morphemes 43, 93, 94, 187, 252
morphology **101**, 157, 161–162, 166, 172, 174, 182–183, 186–187, **188**, 192, 198, **220**, 228, 252
Morris, Robin 79–80
Morss, Alex 59
Mr Gumpy's Outing (Burningham) 115
Mucha, Laura 112
Muldoon, Eilidh 56
multilingual education resources 219
'multilingual pupils' 90
My Big Book of Outdoors (Hopgood) 59
My Pet Goldfish (Rayner) 59
"My Shell" (Goodfellow) 210

National Association for Advisors in English (NAAE) 95
National Association for the Teaching of English (NATE) 49, 95
National Council for Curriculum and Assessment 248
National Education Union (NEU) 12
National Handwriting Association 225
National Institute of Child Health and Human Development 17
National Reading Panel (NRP) 15, 22–23, 67, 71, 78
Neitzel, Amanda **69**
Newberry, Jane 56, 113, *114*
New Zealand 80, 247, 248; isolated phonics approach 80; Reading Recovery remedial programme 10, 16, 18, 23, 32–33; the reading wars in 7, 8–9, 10; whole language in 23–23
Nikhil and Jay series (Soundar/Soofiya) 58
No Child Left Behind 71
No Dinner! (Souhami) 57
Norma and Belly series (M. Song) 58
Norris, Stephen 76–77

Northern Ireland 19
Norway 76
nursery rhymes 19, 93, *96*

Oak National Academy 12
Octopus Shocktopus (Bently/Lenton) 112
Office for Standards in Education, Children's Services and Skills (Ofsted) 12–14, 26n22, 51
onomatopoeia 110, 112, 170
onset 12, 162, 252, 253
oral language 89–90, 95, *98*, 103, 124, 144–146, 149, 166, 208, 224; fluency in 252; oral composition 232
orthographic mapping 182
orthography *see* spelling
O'Sullivan, Olivia 162
Otaiba, Stephanie **69**
Our Very Own Dog (McCardie/Rubbino) 59

parents 14, 51, 59, 76, 89, 90, 112–113, 133, 204, 208, 214, 218–219, 230
Parliament (UK) 8, 9, 11, 247
Patel-Sage, Krina 56, *211*, 212
Pattan's Pumpkin (Soundar/Lessac) 57
Pearson, David 31, *32*
Peck, Hannah 112
Peck Peck Peck (Cousins) 54–55, 148, *149*, 151, *152*, 153, 156
Percival, Tom 54, 112
Perrin, Delores **70**, 72
Phillips, Linda 76
Phoenix Has Taken Off, The 58
phonemes: digraphs 142–160; English language complexities 161–180; forward slashes (/) and representing 25n10, 141n3; onomatopoeia 110, 112, 170; represented by more than one letter 145–147; rimes 12, 112, 115, 153, 162–163, 212, 228, 252, 253; schwa sound in the English language **145**, 175, 176, 253; spelling 180–200; tuning into sounds in words 112; *see also* alphabetic code; digraphs; spelling
phonemic awareness 22–23, **69**, 78, 80, 110, 253
phonics 1–3; 'business as usual' (BAU) 64, 74; discrete (isolated) phonics approach 20, 24, 67, 79, 80; prosody 51, 115, 154, 169, 201, 202, 204, 215, **220**, 253; science of teaching phonics and reading 67–69; single-letter representation 142; systematic phonics 10, 15, 17, 20, 22, 50, 54, **68**, 76, 77, 81, 93, 161, 253; systematic synthetic phonics (SSP) 8, 253; *see also* synthetic phonics
Phonics Screening Check (PSC) 7, 12–14, 21, 253
phonological awareness 37, 43, 46, 72, 93, 94, *96*, 110, 162, 169

phonological development **100**, 103, 110–111, 178, 253
phonological linkage hypothesis 43, 79
phonological memory 40, *41*
picture books 2, 56–58, *96–97*, 133, 212–213, 221, 237–238, 241–244, *244*
ping-pong balls 226, *227*
Pinnell, Gay Su 15
PIRLS (Programme in International Reading Literacy Study) 9, 10, 11, 25n12, 26n17
PISA (Program for International Student Assessment) testing 9, 10, 11 14–15, 23, 25, 25n12, 26n17
play 19, 91, *96*, *98*–99, 104, 111, 153; 'letter fans' 226; letter-cards 125, *125*, 129, 136, 138, 150, *150*; ping-pong balls in 226, *227*; rhyme cards 109, 225; 'small world play' 187, 209, 253; word-cards 123, 126, *131*, 131; wordplay 113–114, 139
Please Mr Magic Fish (Souhami) 57
Poems to Perform (Donaldson) 56
poetry 31, 211; CLPE Poetry Award (CLiPPA) 204; performing 56–57, 113, 210, 212; Power of Poetry programme in England 231; reading and performing 210–212; vital role of rhyme and poetry 112–115
politics *see* education policy
Portis, Antoinette 59
Power of Pictures programme 204, 237, 241, 242, *243*,
Power of Poetry programme 231
Power of Reading programme 209, 233, 237
Primary Language Record (PLR) 95
private/independent schools (UK) 26n26
Programme in International Reading Literacy Study (PIRLS) 9, 10, 11, 25n12, 26n17
prosody 51, 115, 154, 169, 201, 202, 204, 215, **220**, 253
psycholinguistic aspects of language 253
psycholinguistic grain size theory 19
publication (of student work) 72, 87, 223, 238, 241–242, 245
public libraries 59
publishers 51–52, 58–59, 66, 143
pupils: ability to blend and segment 226–227; children who can already read 228–229; children's agency 9, 220, 221, 226, 244–246, 249, 252; decomposing writing 221–223; developing automaticity 227–228; developing comprehension 224; developing fluency 223; ensuring access to texts 219; knowledge of letter-phoneme correspondences 226; lack of motivation as a reader and/or writer 220–221; learning language through children's own names 126, 135–136; letter formation and handwriting 224–225; meeting the needs of all 217–229;

multilingual pupils 90; one-to-one correspondence 225–226; recognising and responding to children's needs 219–220; struggling readers and writers 10, 18, 67, **68**, **69**, **71**, 72–73, 78; for whom English is an additional language 218–219; *see also* early development; testing/evaluation

Quality First Teaching (QFT) 94–95, **101**, 233
Quiet! (Alizadeh) 110

Rabbit and Bear books (Gough/Field) 58
Rabei, Carolina 56, 113
race and racial stereotypes 50, 231
randomised controlled trials (RCTs) 16, 19, 22, 27n56, 64, 72–75, 79, 233, 242
Rapunzel (Woolvin) 57
Ravi's Roar (Percival) 112
Rayner, Catherine 59
Read and Wonder series 58
reader in the writer 230–246; *see also* reading; reading *and* writing; writing
Reader in the Writer, The (Barrs/Cork) 232–233
reading: alphabetic code 118–141; analogies and 111, 112, 115, 123, 162–163, 175, 176, 178, 182, 228; classroom practices for teaching 73–81; developing reader identity 105–109; developing understanding the purpose of writing 109–110; developing word reading 22, 50, 69, 71–72, 143, 147, 162, 166, 181, 216; dramatising reading 209–210; dyslexia 21, 34, **69**, 216, 217, 220, 252; fluency and reading aloud 204–208; importance of reading for pleasure 104–105; importance of re-reading 208; multi-modal reading experiences 58; Power of Reading Programme 209, 233, 237; the reader in the writer 230–246; reading as a model for writing 232–233; the reading wars 7–28; reflection and 40, *41*, 132, 154–155, 208, 241; the 'science of reading' 3, 15, 20–22, 50, 64–65, 80, 247–249; science of teaching 67–69; 'Simple View of Reading' (SVR) 22, 33–39, 50; struggling readers 10, 18, 67, **68**, **69**, **71**, 72–73, 78; syntactic cues 29–31; three cues of 29–31, *32*; time to read 59–61; 'typically' developing readers 17, 34, 37, 42–43, 67, **68–69**, 73, 75–79; *see also* texts
"Reading: A Psycholinguistic Guessing Game" (K. Goodman) 29
Reading Agency 58, 105
reading *and* writing 1–3, 29–48; Double Helix of Reading and Writing 2–3, 11, 42–46, *44*, 71, 63, 65, 77, 80–81, 88, 109, 119, 237, 260; fluency and comprehension 201–216; lessons in authentic purposes for 92; politics of 7–28; Reading and Writing Scales 95, *96–99*; science of teaching 63–85; *see also* phonics; reading; writing
reading buddies 214, 219, 253
Reading Environment, The (Chambers) 55–56, 60
Reading First (RF) initiative 20, 71
Reading (F. Smith) 38
Reading Recovery programme 10, 16, 18, 23, 32–33
Reading Rope 2–3, 22, 36–38, *37*
Read With Me (Waterland) 49–50
Read Write Inc synthetic phonics scheme 54, 73–74
real books: approach to teaching phonics 49–55, 87, 118–119, 143; role of publishers 51–52, 58–59, 66, 143; scheme books and real books 51–55; whole-language approach 49–55, **68**, 77
Reeve, Philip 58
Reflecting Realities survey 106
reflection 40, *41*, 132, 154–155, 208, 241
reliability 64, 253
Remedial and Special Education (journal) 33
research *see* science of teaching
rhyme 53–56, 91, 93, 123; nursery rhymes 19, 93, *96*; poetry and 112–115, 210, 212; rhythm and **100**, 111–113, 144; use of rhyme cards 109, 225
rhythm 56; prosody 51, 115, 154, 169, 201, 202, 204, 215, **220**, 253; rhyme and **100**, 111–112, 144; syllabic 136–137
Rickerty, Simon 187–192, *188*, *180*, *191*
Riddell, Chris 56
rimes 12, 112, 115, 153, 162–163, 212, 228, 252, 253
Rita's Rabbit (Mucha/Peck) 112
Robot and the Bluebird, The (Lucas) 57
Rogers, Leslie Ann **70**
Rosen, Michael 56
Rose Report 23, 28n76, 35–36, 37, 67
Rose, Sir Jim 22
Rosie's Walk (Hutchins) 49
Royal Society of Arts (RSA) 242
Rubbino, Salvatore 59
Ryder, Janice 80

Said, S.F., 241
Sandmel. Karin **71**, 72
Santangelo, Tanya **70**
Savage, Robert 34–35
Scarborough, Hollis 37
Scheffler, Axel 57
schools: free school meals (FSMs) 242; home corner 225, 252; 'literacy-rich' curricula 118; multilingual education resources 219;

private/independent schools (UK) 26n26; senior leadership team (SLT) at 242; *see also* education policy; pupils; teaching
schwa **145**, 175, 176, 253
Schwarz, Viviane 57, 58
'science of reading' 3, 15, 20–22, 50, 64–65, 80, 247–249
science of teaching: classroom practices for teaching reading 73–81; effect sizes in research 66, **69**, 72, 74, 81n10; evidence from systematic reviews and longitudinal research studies 80–81; extent of difference in research 66; general findings from systematic and tertiary reviews 67–73; how texts teach what children learn 49–62; meta-analysis 66–67, **69**, 71, 78; neuroscience and education research 17–20; a note about 'science' 64–65; randomised controlled trials (RCTs) 16, 19, 22, 27n56, 64, 72–75, 79, 233, 242; reliability in research 64, 253; selecting research studies 65–67; studies of struggling readers 78–80; studies of typically developing readers 75–78; systematic qualitative meta-synthesis (SQMS) 67, 68, 75; teaching phonics and reading 67–69; teaching reading for writing and writing for reading 71–73; teaching writing 69–71; tertiary reviews in the 66–69, **68**; which research and why? 63–67
Scotland 36, 67
screening phonics in Australia 14–15
Seal, Julia 51–53
segmenting 55, 95, **100**, 110, 120, 136, 138, 141, 142, 146, 148, 153–154, 159, 182–183, 201, 226–227, 234
Seidenberg, Mark 17–19, 37
self-efficacy and independence 9, 145, 220, 221, 226, 242, 244–246, 249
self-teaching 142
self-teaching hypothesis 76
semantic cues 29–30
senior leadership team (SLT) at schools 242
sentences 174–176; expanded noun phrases 99, 151, 169, 252; syntax 29–31, *37*, **70**, **88**, 144, 253; *see also* comprehension
Sharkey, Niamh 57
Sharratt, Nick 57
Shireen, Nadia 58, *205*, 206, *207*
'Simple View of Reading' (SVR) 22, 33–39, 50
Sit In! (Welsh/Seal) 51–53
Slavin, Robert **68**
'small world play' 187, 209, 253
Smart, Jamie 58
Smith, Alex T. 57, 58
Smith, Frank 38–39
smoking and lung cancer 65
Snowling, Margaret 78–79

social media 2, 34, 57
Sold a Story podcast 10, 15–22, 71–72
Song, Junli 56
Song, Mika 58
Soofiya (illustrator) 58
Souhami, Jessica 57
Soundar, Chitra 57
sound, early awareness of 43, 93; *see also* phonemes
Spanish language 180
spelling 180–200; 'deep orthography' 180; emphasising investigation 197–199; English language orthography 147, 161–162, 178, 193, 197; exploring etymology 193–197; exploring homophones, homographs, and homonyms 193–197; exploring morphology 187; introducing children to visual patterns in words 182–187; introducing compound words 182; notions of conventional spelling systems (orthography) 93–94, 180, 197–198, 234, 252; orthographic mapping 182; orthography 12, 18, 38, 93, **101**, 112, 135, 161, 162, 178, 179, 180, 181, 252; recognising word families 182; segmenting 182–183; as socio-linguistic phenomenon 198; 'typical' development in 161
split vowel digraphs 163, **163–164**, 253
Stainthorp, Rhona 35
'Standard English' 51, 63, 231
Stanley's Stick (Hegley/Layton) 123–141
strategy instruction **70**, 72
Stuart, Morag 35–36
Styles, Morag 63
Suggate, Sebastian **68**, **69**, 69, 73, 78
Sullivan, Alice 105
summarisation **70**, 72
Sustainable Development Goal (SDG) 7
Sutton, Emily 59
syllabification 111, 147
syllables: disyllabic words 142, 147, **148**, 151, 252; syllabic rhythm 136–137; *see also* phonemes
syntax 29–31, *37*, **70**, **88**, 144, 253
synthetic phonics 1–2, 7–24, 31, 36, 87, **88**, 253; critique of 63–64, **68**, 72–75, 104, 249–250; in England 11–14, 72–77, 79, 104; lack of children's agency in 249; Little Wandle scheme 51–53; Read Write Inc synthetic phonics scheme 54, 73–74; scheme books and 49, 51–54; teaching spelling through 180; in the USA 15–17
systematic phonics 10, 15, 17, 20, 22, 50, 54, **68**, 76, 77, 81, 93, 161, 253
systematic qualitative meta-synthesis (SQMS) 67, 68, 75
systematic synthetic phonics (SSP) 8, 253

Tanka, Tanka Skunk (Webb) 111–112
task schemas *41*, 42
Taylor, Sean 59
teacher educators 14, 18, 20–21, 248
teachers: autonomy of 9, 24; criticism in the USA 20–21; teacher education/professional development 1–2, 10, 11–12, 14, 22, 74, 237; *see also* science of teaching
teaching: building the foundations for learning 103–117; fostering self-efficacy and independence 9, 145, 220, 221, 226, 242, 244–246, 249; planning teaching based on children's development 95–102; a programme of lessons 94–95; strategy instruction 70, 72; teaching writing to improve reading 71; top-down vs. bottom-up approaches to 15, 87; *see also* science of teaching
technology: communications technology 15, 34, 89; social media 2, 34, 57
10 Things I Can Do to Help My World (Walsh) 59
tertiary reviews 66–69, **68**
testing/evaluation: 'high-stakes' testing 1, 13, 14, 250; PIRLS (Programme in International Reading Literacy Study) 9, 10, 11, 25n12, 26n17; PISA (Program for International Student Assessment) testing 9, 10, 11 14–15, 23, 25, 25n12, 26n17; Reading and Writing Scales 95, *96–99*
text interpretation 40, *41*
texts: environment including texts 43; how texts teach what children learn 49–62; importance of variety 56, 106, 178, 221; real books and whole language 49–51; scheme books and real books 51–55; selecting texts for three- to eight-year-olds 55–59; structure in 42, 43; time to read 59–61; *see also* books; poetry; real books; genres; whole texts
Thatcher, Margaret 231
thesauruses 197, 245
Thomas, Anne 162
Ticket to Kalamazoo, A (Carter/Layton) 56
Tobia, Lauren 57, 58
Todd-Stanton, Joe 57, 58
Tola series (Atinuke/Iwu) 58
Tolstoy, Aleksei 57
topic knowledge *41*, 42
Torgerson, Carole 67, **68**, 233
trade press 49, 51, 60, 66, **88**
"Translational Science" 249
Trelease, Jim 204
Truelove, Emma 79
Tucker, Steven 57
Tunmer, William 33–36, 80
Turkish language 180

UCL Institute of Education blogposts 11
Unfortunately (Durant/Rickerty) 187–192, *188*, *191*
United Kingdom: Northern Ireland 19; Parliament 8, 9, 11, 247; Scotland 36, 67; *see also* England
United Kingdom Literacy Association (UKLA) 95
United Nations 7
United States: advocacy of synthetic phonics in 15–17; criticising teachers and teacher educators 20–21; National Reading Panel (NRP) 15, 22–23, 67, 71, 78; neuroscience and education research 17–20; No Child Left Behind 71; Reading First (RF) initiative 20, 71; the reading wars in 9–10
University of Wisconsin–Madison 106

Vadasy, Patricia 77, 83n54
Vere, Ed 57, 238, *240*
visuospatial sketchpad 40, *41*
voice, in writing 92, 98–99, 157, 198, 204–205, 208, 210, 220–221, 231, 236–237, 244–245, 253
voice, when making sound 110–112, 129, 213
vowels 93, 112, 129–130, 138; consonant vowel consonant words 52; digraphs **145**, 157, 234; long vs. short 183, 186; pronunciation of 162–163, **164**; split vowel digraphs 163, **163–164**, 253

Wakeling, Kate 56
Walker Books publisher 58
Walk in London, A (Rubbino) 59
Walsh, Melanie 59
Wanek, Connie 56
Waring, Richard 57
Waterland, Liz 49–50
Way Home For Wolf (Bright/Field) 183, *184*, *185*
Webb, Steve 111–112
Weil, Zaro 56
Welsh, Clare Helen 51–53
White Owl, Barn Owl (N. Davies/Foreman) 59
whole-language approach 9, 11, 15–24, 49–52, **68**, 77, 87, 253
whole texts 9, 15, 46–55, 75, 77, 80, **203**, 253; in the classroom 87, **88**, 90–93, 103, 110, 111, 118, 138, 144, 165–166
"Wibble Wobble Clown" 113, *114*
Wildsmith, Brian 51–54
Wild Summer (Morss/Chiu) 59
Willems, Mo 58
Willmore, Alex 165, *167*, *171*, *173*
Wilson-Max, Ken 57, 106, *107*, 111, 193, *194*
Winstanley, John-Mark 180
Winter Sleep (Morss/Chiu) 59

Woolvin, Bethan 57
wordplay 113–114, 139
words: affixes and 93, *97*, **188**, 252; alliteration among 112, 123, 210; compound words 181, 182, 186–187, *186*; disyllabic words 142, 147, **148**, 151, 252; high-frequency 12, 120, 123, 129, *131*, 139, 141, 148, 151, 154–155, 165, 176, 186, **220**, 227–228; homographs 193–194; homonyms 193–194, 197; homophones 163, 193–194, 197, 252; linking the spoken word with the written 115–116; medial position of a word 112, 138, 252; morphemes 43, 93, 94, 187, 252; morphology **101**, 157, 161–162, 166, 172, 174, 182–183, 186–187, **188**, 192, 198, **220**, 228, 252; onomatopoeia 110, 112, 170; word reading 50, 69, 71–72, 143, 147, 162, 166, 181, 216; word-cards 123, 126, *131*, 131
working memory *40*, 40, *41*
writing: cognitive model of 39–42, *41*; complexities of writing 231–232; creation 238–239, 241, 249; developing writer identity 230–231; 'Ear of the Writer' 92, 253n2; example writing lesson 234–236; following an authentic writing process 236–242; Hayes' cognitive perspective on 39–42, *41*; ideation 223, 238, 241, 242; importance of summarisation **70**, 72; in different genres 71, *99*, 178, 242; letter formation **101**, 125–126, 129, 159, 224–225, 226; modelling writing 109, 139; models of 38–42; presenting informational writing 213; publication (of student work) 72, 87, 223, 238, 241–242, 245; the reader in the writer 230–246; reading as a model for writing 232–233; science of teaching 69–71; 'typically' developing writers 42, **70–71**, 161; voice, choice, and agency 244–246; *see also* composition; handwriting
Writing and the Writer (F. Smith) 38–39
Wynder, Ernest 65
Wyse, Dominic 25n13, 67, **68**, 78, 92, 109, 180, 233, 246n21, 253n2

Yucky Worms (French/Ahlberg) 221, *222*

Zeigler, Jo 19

For Product Safety Concerns and Information please contact our EU representative GPSR@taylorandfrancis.com
Taylor & Francis Verlag GmbH, Kaufingerstraße 24, 80331 München, Germany

www.ingramcontent.com/pod-product-compliance
Lightning Source LLC
Chambersburg PA
CBHW082059230426
43670CB00017B/2890